Business Writing

Process and Forms

Richard P. Batteiger
Oklahoma State University

Business Writing

Process and Forms

Wadsworth Publishing Company
Belmont, California
A Division of Wadsworth, Inc.

English Editor: Cedric Crocker
Production Editor: Harold Humphrey
Managing Designer: MaryEllen Podgorski
Designer: Design Office / Peter Martin
Copy Editor: Susan Thornton
Print Buyer: Karen Hunt
Signing Representative: Thomas P. Nerney

Printed in the United States of America

4 5 6 7 8 9 10—89 88 87

ISBN 0-534-04620-7

Library of Congress Cataloging in Publication Data

Batteiger, Richard P.
Business writing.

Includes index.
1. English language—Rhetoric. 2. English language—Business English. I. Title.
PE1479.B87B38 1985 808′.066651 84-20879
ISBN 0-534-04620-7

Preface

This text presents skills, working methods, and knowledge that will help everyone who writes on the job produce effective letters, memos, proposals, reports, visual aids, and oral presentations. The fundamental premise of the book's content and organization is that effective business writing, like other kinds of writing, is the result of—

1. Adoption and use of a productive, efficient writing process that includes the important prewriting steps of setting goals, analyzing readers, gathering information, and organizing before attempting a finished draft
2. Careful and thorough revision
3. Ability to use language effectively in sentences and paragraphs
4. Knowledge and problem-solving ability that enable a person to analyze and respond to a variety of business situations that require writing
5. Practice in applying process, language, and knowledge to writing situations typical of those found in business and industry

Process

Part I, Chapters 1 through 5, presents an overview of the writing process and attempts to relate this process to business situations. This section begins with setting goals and analyzing readers and then proceeds through the steps of gathering (or remembering) information, organizing, writing, revising, editing, and proofreading. Each chapter explains what writers must do as they work through a stage of the writing process and provides instructions in specific skills and working methods. For example, Chapter 2, "Finding Something to Say," presents various methods of invention, including brainstorming, freewriting, using information trees, and a questioning heuristic based on the journalistic questions Who? What? Where? When? Why? and How? Students are free to use and adapt any or all of these to their own needs as they complete their writing assignments. Exercises at the end of each chapter in Part I are designed to teach and reinforce the skills and methods presented in the chapter and the various strategies associated with the writing process.

Of course, there is no such thing as a single correct writing process that everyone should use. People are different, and they do not all write in the same way, any more than they learn in the same way. But the research of the past twenty years indicates that experienced, successful writers use what is now called "the writing process" when they work. That is, they plan, organize, write, and, above all, revise. Research also shows that writing processes are not linear; that is, writers do not work in a step-by-step, fixed sequence, doing first one step and then the next. Instead, studies of experienced writers show that several stages of the writing process can occur simultaneously. Writers may organize or search for new information as they revise, or they may not be able to establish a goal until they begin writing. In short, writing is really too complex and creative an activity to be done only one step at a time.

However, Part I of this text presents a generalized writing process as though it did occur in a linear, step-by-step sequence. The primary reason for this is my belief that such a sequence allows the text, the student, and the teacher to focus clearly on each stage and the skills and working methods it requires, without being distracted by the hundreds of other things that are happening simultaneously when a person writes. I am convinced that students, who are usually not experienced writers, will be able to put the process together and make it work for them only if they have learned the individual stages well.

Forms

Parts II and III, Chapters 6 through 15, present typical business writing situations and the written forms that businesses customarily use to respond to them. The chapters in this section introduce letters, memos, proposals, reports, visual aids, and oral presentations. Part IV, Chapters 16 through 18, presents the process of seeking employment and includes chapters about conducting an employment search and writing the various kinds of resumes and letters that are necessary in such a campaign.

Throughout Parts II, III, and IV the emphasis in each chapter is on learning how to do the planning, writing, revising, and final text preparation that are required for every business document. Many chapters contain extended examples not only of finished writing, but of writing that is in progress, since part of the learning process consists of watching a letter, memo, or report evolve from idea to first draft, to revised draft, to final copy. This progression allows students to see the choices and decisions that a writer makes in the process of composing a letter, memo, or report. Throughout these chapters, prewriting and revision receive special attention.

Applications: Learning By Doing

But no one learns to write merely by watching writing in progress or reading about how to write. It is also necessary to write. Thus, each chapter concludes with exercises designed to teach, reinforce, and test the concepts and skills that it has presented. The exercises have been designed to present realistic business situations, but they are also meant to teach the business writing, research, and problem-solving skills that have been introduced in each chapter.

At the end of the text are cases that present longer and more complex business writing and problem-solving situations than do the end-of-chapter exercises. Each case provides opportunities to draw on several different parts of the text, and each holds the potential for a number of writing assignments. Although end-of-chapter exercises may require only a certain kind of letter, memo, or report, a single case may require several letters and memos, a proposal, a report, visual aids, and an oral presentation. Each case can be adapted to specific classroom situations and can be modified so that students do as much or little of the work as their instructor wishes.

Appendices

At the end of the text are five Appendices, which present important supplementary information that instructors may wish to use, as well as additional resource tools for students. The Appendices include—

A. A Guide to Careful Editing

B. Formats for Letters and Reports

C. Business Writing and the Law

D. Some Additional Resources

E. Business Writing and Word Processing

Using the Text in Class

This text is organized so that students can begin by acquainting or reacquainting themselves with the writing process and the strategies that are available to them for inventing, organizing, writing, and revising. However, some students who use this book will already be familiar with process methods, and some instructors may wish to begin their courses with another section of the book.

The text can be adapted quite easily to the needs of specific classes. A course can follow the sequence set out in the text, or it can begin with Part II, III, or IV, should an instructor wish to do so. For example, it is possible to introduce reports and cases at the beginning of a course and let students begin working early on long-term projects, so there will be time to do the necessary planning, research, and writing. Then, as students encounter specific situations and writing strategies in the other chapters of the text, their work in these chapters can be related to the cases or reports that they are working on. In this way, it is possible for all of the work that students do in one semester to relate to a single project. The Instructor's Manual suggests other course organizations and methods of adapting the text to a syllabus.

Acknowledgments

When I began this book, without a co-author, I mistakenly believed that I would be working alone. Instead, I have had the assistance of a number of people, and without them I would never have begun, let alone finished.

At Wadsworth, Tom Nerney first encouraged me to begin, and Kevin Howat, then the English Editor, saw me through numerous revisions with infinite patience. Hal Humphrey has brought the manuscript through production with care and thoroughness.

A number of fellow teachers have read all or part of the manuscript. These include Kathleen L. Bell, University of Miami; Kenneth Dowst, University of Iowa; Eileen B. Evans, Western Michigan University; David P. Ewing; Kelsie B. Harder, State University College, Potsdam, New York; Phillip A. Holcomb, Angelo State University; Barbara Loush, Oakland Community College; George Miller, University of Delaware; Michael G. Moran, Clemson University; Jerome Rosenberg, Miami University, Ohio; Jack Selzer, Pennsylvania State University; Ellen L. Tripp, Forsyth Technical Institute; and Thomas Willard, University of Arizona. John C. Thoms of New York Institute of Technology deserves special mention for the two careful, thorough reviews he did of the entire manuscript.

At York College of Pennsylvania our department secretary, Mrs. Mildred Curry, has assisted with typing and other tasks. My colleagues Edward Jones, Florence Ames, Thomas V. Hall, and David Lawrence gave generously of their time to read and criticize various chapters. In addition, many students have, over the years, shown me what can and cannot be accomplished with a book of this sort. York College generously provided a sabbatical leave during which I was able to do the first draft. Our Academic Dean, Dr. William A. DeMeester, has provided tangible and intangible support, including reductions in my teaching load while the book was in progress.

I also wish to thank members of our local business community for providing access to their files and some of the examples of letters and memos that appear in the book. Especially helpful were Mr. Charles S. Wolf, President, York Container Company; Mr. John C. Schmidt, President, The York Bank and Trust Company; Mr. Frederick B. Shearer, President, York Machinery & Supply Company; Mr. Ralph Meisenhelder, Vice President, Borg–Warner Air Conditioning, Inc.; and Mr. Jerry M. Dyer, York.

Finally, three people deserve more than mere acknowledgment. My wife, Claudia, typed portions of the manuscript—several times—and provided important moral support throughout the process of writing the book. She has also been one of my best readers and critics. Our children, Paul and Adrienne, have done their best to provide me a quiet place to work and have been remarkably patient when they thought we should all have been doing something else.

Contents

Appendices 397

Business Writing

Process and Forms

Part 1

Business Writing Processes and Skills

1

Getting Words on Paper: Where to Begin

You probably do not think of yourself as a writer. You have chosen a career in management, marketing, accounting, finance, or some other related business subject because you want to work with objects, numbers, or people, not words. But working with any of these will also require you to use words. Perhaps you have already discovered that writing is an important, daily part of almost every management or technical job in business and industry. In fact, many people in business may write the equivalent of a medium-length book each year, even though they do not consider themselves to be writers. Writing is a tool that you use to do your job. And employers will expect you to write as effectively as you do the rest of your job. Your company's success, and your own, may depend on how well you can present your ideas on paper.

What Does It Mean to Write Effectively?

Too many people find writing frustrating, difficult, and even terrifying. After all, writing *looks* easy. It appears to be simply a matter of picking up a pen and putting words on paper, one after another. Begin at the beginning and keep going until you reach the end. What could be simpler?

The notion that writing is easy, or that it ought to be easy, comes in part from our reading. When we read a book, a magazine article, a business report, or even a brief memo, we see only the finished text. We have no way of knowing whether it was easy or difficult to write. We can't see the false starts, the rough drafts, or the hours of work that went into it. We read from beginning to end, and the finished, polished text seems to say that it came from someone's pen just the way we see it. Certainly our own writing ought to go as smoothly, and as well.

People find writing difficult and frustrating for a variety of reasons. Perhaps someone has told them that their writing is no good, that they make too many mistakes, or that their writing too often doesn't make sense. Perhaps their writing does not accomplish the goals they had in mind for it (whatever those goals might be). Perhaps they have received low grades on their writing assignments in school. Or the writing itself may be difficult to do. It becomes an ordeal, something to be faced, rather than something to do. They spend too much time staring at a blank page or waiting for inspiration and end up rushing through a draft at the last minute. For these reasons and others, many people find writing difficult to do. They avoid writing, or they are constantly unhappy with their own writing.

To say that you should write effectively is to identify two separate but related goals. The first is to learn how to write a finished draft that says what you want it to say and accomplishes its goal. The second is to learn how to use working methods that will actually help you produce a finished draft efficiently, with a minimum of frustration. Most inexperienced writers concentrate on the first of these goals, without realizing that their ability to produce a well-written final draft depends, to a larger extent than they are aware, on the working methods they use. That is, writing is difficult or ineffective for them because their working methods get in the way.

Writing is not a gift, but a skill you can learn. The goal of this book is to help you learn that skill by focusing not only on what to say and how to say it, but also on the working methods that are most likely to help you write successfully.

Taking Tips from Experienced Writers

One way to learn any skill is to seek advice from experienced, successful practitioners. If you want to improve your golf or tennis game, you will probably take lessons from a local pro and read articles and books that explain how championship players play the game. You can learn to make a long, difficult putt or to improve your serve by taking tips from the experts. What works for golf or tennis can work for writing. We can learn a great deal about how to write by looking at what experienced, successful writers do when they write.

Who are the experts? Some of them are professional writers, people who write for a living. Others are not professional writers. That is, writing is not their livelihood, but something they must do as part of their jobs. They are engineers, managers, executives, teachers, and students just like you who use writing as a tool. In recent years a number of researchers have observed these experienced writers, as well as inexperienced writers, to discover what they do when they write. As a result of this research, we can distinguish experienced writers from inexperienced ones in a number of ways, not only by the quality of their final drafts, but also, and especially, in the working methods they use. As you read the following list of comparisons, think about your own working methods and decide whether you are closer to the experienced or inexperienced group. How could you change your own methods to bring you closer to those used by experienced writers?

1. *Experienced* writers spend from 50 to 80 percent of their time planning, thinking about what they will write, before they attempt to write a draft.
   Inexperienced writers often spend less than 30 percent of their time planning.
2. *Experienced* writers delay attempting to produce a draft until they believe they have a workable plan.
   Inexperienced writers often begin to write immediately.
3. *Experienced* writers take time to identify the goals they want their writing to accomplish.
   Inexperienced writers seldom think about goals.
4. *Experienced* writers spend a considerable amount of their planning time thinking about their readers. They try to see their subjects and their goals from a reader's point of view and to find ways to adapt their writing to their audience.
   Inexperienced writers spend comparatively little time thinking about readers, if they think about them at all.
5. *Experienced* writers take time to explore and thoroughly understand their subjects. They often gather more infor-

mation than they will need, but they focus their search on information that will help them achieve their goals.
Inexperienced writers tend to extremes when they explore their subjects. On the one hand, they may gather only the absolute minimum that they think they will need. Or they may attempt to gather all information that is available about their subjects.

6. *Experienced* writers use a variety of methods to organize their information before they write.
Inexperienced writers frequently use only a conventional outline to help them organize.
7. *Experienced* writers often consider their first draft to be a "discovery draft" in which they try to find out what they know and how well their plan will work. As they write this draft they pay little attention to such details as spelling, punctuation, and other editorial details.
Inexperienced writers often write their first drafts with considerable attention to editorial details. They may work to get everything "right" the first time; they often believe they should be able to write from beginning to end and that the writing should flow smoothly and easily.
8. *Experienced* writers expect to revise their drafts, perhaps several times. And revision often involves a complete rethinking and restructuring of the draft. They may add or delete large sections. They may abandon their original draft and start over.
Inexperienced writers do not often thoroughly revise their drafts. When they do, their revisions often focus on the editorial details of spelling, word choice, and punctuation.
9. *Experienced* writers edit and proofread carefully, perhaps several times.
Inexperienced writers seldom pay close attention to editing and proofreading.

Of course, not all writers work in exactly the same way, and one writer may use different methods at different times. But these distinctions between experienced and inexperienced show that, in general, experienced writers have learned or discovered a reasonably well-defined working method that seems to help them get their writing done.

1. They plan.
2. They consider their readers.
3. They investigate their subject.
4. They organize.

5. They write.
6. They revise.
7. They edit and proofread.

It makes sense to give this method a try, to see if it makes writing both easier to do and more effective. It is not necessary to go through these stages in the sequence in which they are listed here. In fact, it is unlikely that you will do so. When you write, many things happen at once. As you plan you may discover that you are thinking of facts and ideas that you want to include in your draft, or that you know something important about your reader. As you organize you may find that you are once again investigating your subject. The steps listed here are guidelines, not rigid rules. You are free to change and adapt them so that they fit your own situation.

Effective Writing Begins with Effective Planning

A thorough, carefully constructed plan is the basis of any success you have with your writing. A complete plan will show you where you are going and how you will get there. Plans allow you to solve problems, test solutions, and make decisions about your writing on a scale that is smaller and less time-consuming than completing an entire writing project. Thus, effective planning allows you to reduce the risk that you will fail and have to do the entire project over again.

Some people avoid planning because they believe it takes much more time than they would otherwise spend on a project. But, as R. Alec McKenzie points out in his book *The Time Trap* (New York: American Management Association, 1972), taking time to plan actually saves time in the long run. Insufficient or inadequate planning often produces mistakes, and the time you spend correcting these mistakes may far exceed the time you would have invested in careful planning.

A well-constructed plan is like a miniature model of your completed project. It will tell you not only what you want to achieve, but also what you need to do. One of the chief advantages of planning is that you can test your plan or model to see if it will actually lead you to the goal you are trying to achieve.

An architect who designs a building relies on plans and models to reveal problems and flaws in the design. Once the project is under way, changes become considerably more difficult and expensive. But problems discovered in the process of planning are relatively easy and inexpensive to solve, because changes are confined to the plan. You will find that the same is true when you write. A plan for a letter, memo, or report will give you a preview of what the finished product will be like. Changing the plan will be far easier than throwing your work away and starting over. In fact, once you have learned to plan efficiently and quickly—and you will learn that with experience—you will find that you can design and test several ways of doing a writing project. Then you can choose the one that is most likely to achieve your goal.

Effective planning consists of:

1. Identifying your subject
2. Understanding your purpose
3. Establishing and stating your goal(s)
4. Knowing your reader
5. Searching for the information you need
6. Organizing for your reader

The remainder of this chapter and the two that follow it will cover these six planning steps. Throughout all of the steps it is important that you do your planning on paper. Few of us can effectively keep track of ideas and information by relying on memory alone. If you write as you plan, you will have a permanent record of what you have discovered and what you want to do with it. Writing as you think will help you discover what you know and how well you know it. It is easy to believe that you know a subject well so long as you are just "thinking" about it. Writing forces you to probe your memory and knowledge and state what you actually know, rather than what you think you know. And writing is also a way to help unlock your mental processes and become accustomed to the flow of language. Many of your best insights and some of your most effective writing will come to you as you write, even if you are writing only notes for your plan. Later, when you return to your notes, you are likely to find useful ideas, sentences, and perhaps entire paragraphs that you will be able to develop further as you write a draft.

Identifying Your Subject

Many of the subjects you write about on the job will be assigned to you. Someone, usually a supervisor, will give you a writing project. But too often the people who hand out these assignments assume that their job is finished once they have told someone to write a memo or report about "our new sales campaign" or "the problems we have been having in the shipping department." Occasionally, the person who assigns a writing project will say something helpful, like "You know what I want," or "I'm sure you'll come up with something interesting." Roughly translated, both of these mean "I'm not sure what I want. You find it and tell me about it."

The trouble with subjects is that they seldom come with directions telling you what to do with them. Subjects can be rather large, uncharted areas, but they are rarely barren. Rather, they are like interesting landscapes that tempt you to move off in all directions at once. And that is precisely what you want to avoid. You need to focus on that part of the landscape that is most relevant to your situation. Unless you do, you will be like those tourists who give blow-by-blow accounts of their travels, including every boring detail, because they have not taken the time to decide what is important and what will interest their listeners. If their listeners recognize the points of interest, it will be purely by accident. Or they will decide for themselves what is interesting and important, and the trip they hear about will have little to do with the one the speaker is describing.

Identifying your subject carefully, for yourself and for your readers, is like using a telescope to isolate part of a landscape and bring it into sharp focus. When you do this, you are in charge. You are identifying what is important and pointing it out to your readers, with some assurance that they will see what you want them to see.

Suppose you have been assigned to write a report about using personal computers in the office. That's a big subject, and you will need to focus on part of it if you are to satisfy your readers and avoid spending the next three years doing the research and writing. Which part of this large subject will you write about? What will be your focus? Will you concentrate on the uses of computers to streamline office procedures, to reduce personnel costs, to increase productivity, or any of the dozens of other services they can perform for a modern business? You will need to answer this question before you can do anything with the assignment.

One way of focusing on your subject is to ask the person who gave you the assignment. In the process you will probably discover why you are writing about this particular subject. That is, you can identify your subject, in part, by discovering your purpose.

Identifying Your Purpose

It is important to know *why* you are writing about a subject. Why is this subject important to you, to your supervisor, to your company, or to all three? Knowing why you are writing will help you isolate that part of a large subject that you should concentrate on. And it will help you formulate a goal, do your research, and organize.

For example, if you have been assigned to write a report about using microcomputers in the office, knowing your purpose will help you plan, organize, and write so that your report satisfies your readers' needs. Unless you know your purpose, the best report you can write may make no sense at all to your readers. If you explain all of the uses of microcomputers in the office, readers may respond that they already know what you have told them. If you assemble statistics to show the costs and savings that other businesses have experienced with a conversion to computers, your readers might have no idea why you are giving them this information. If you recommend the purchase of a specific machine, your readers might respond that you have not addressed the proper issue. None of these embarrassing results would have occurred if you had taken the time to establish that your purpose was to evaluate computers that could be used in the department that processes and keeps track of orders.

You need to identify and state your purpose so that:

1. Your various audiences will understand what you are writing about and why it is important to you and to them.
2. You will understand why you, your supervisor, and your company need to know about a subject.
3. You will be able to identify and gather the information that is most relevant to your readers and your goal.
4. You will be able to establish specific goals for your writing.

Establishing and Stating Your Goals

What do you hope to accomplish with a particular writing project? Having a clearly stated goal is like having a destination when you take a trip. Once you have identified a destination, you can establish how you will reach it. Without a destination, your trip is likely to become a random tour of points of interest, with no focus. Without a goal, your writing project is likely to become a collection of miscellaneous information, with no focus or point. An explicit goal statement will help you:

1. Identify the steps you must take to reach your goal.
2. Concentrate your search for information on that which is related to your goal. Otherwise, you are likely to collect any information that is available.
3. Test whether you actually accomplish your goal. That is, you will be able to measure what you do against what you set out to do.

Suppose you have been assigned to find space in your company's building for a new department and then to write a report that presents your recommendation. This assignment, like most of the ones you will receive, involves two tasks. The first is to solve the problem of finding space for a new department. The second is to write the report. A carefully constructed goal statement will help you do both of these.

First you need information. You need to know about:

The new department

The building

The limitations within which you are working

You can get this information by asking the person who assigned the report (who may or may not be your reader), by surveying the building, and by studying the new department. Preliminary research of this sort should tell you what, if anything, your reader/supervisor has in mind. Thus, you will know if there are any hidden agendas or preferred solutions. You will also know something about the department's function in the company. This might give you some idea of where it should be located to best do its job. And you will also know something about the department's requirements for physical space. For example, you will probably not recommend locating a shipping and receiving department on the eighth floor, nor would you assign a department of twenty people to a space built for ten.

Finally, you will have information about limitations on what you can recommend. For example, can other departments be moved to accommodate the new one? If so, which ones? Will there be money for remodeling and redecorating? How much? Will the new department's equipment fit through the door? When must the decision be made? When will the move take place? All of these questions require answers if your report is to do its job.

You will also want to learn something about the decision-making process that will take place after you submit your report. Are you expected to recommend a single course of action and then support it as the best solution? Or should you present several possible solutions so that decision makers can choose the one they believe will best meet the company's needs?

Answers to these and similar questions will enable you to conduct your project and write your report. They tell you the kinds of information you will need to gather, the people you will need to talk to, and the kinds of solutions that decision makers are likely to find attractive. At this point you should be able to write a reasonably precise goal statement. It might be something like this one:

> To identify and recommend a location, within the home office, which will accommodate the Central Billing Department. This space should provide approximately 1000 square feet of working area and include two private offices and sufficient room for twenty-five individual desks with computer terminals. The area should require no more than $5000 in remodeling, and it should be near the Accounting Department.

Stating your goal in this way will help you solve the problem you have been given and write your report. You know what you are looking for and what you will do with it because you have taken the time to find out where to begin and where you want to go.

Knowing Your Readers

If you have done most of your writing in school, for teachers, then you have usually had a rather thorough knowledge of your readers. You saw them in class several times each week, talked with them privately, and used your observations of them to figure out "what they wanted" when you wrote papers for them.

Outside the classroom, in the so-called real world, this frequent and informative give-and-take between you and your readers will exist far less often, if at all. Many of your readers will be members of your organization, but you will not always know all of them. When you write for your supervisor or a member of your own department, you will be able to take advantage of your personal knowledge of these people. But you will often write for people who are much further away from you in the organization: members of other departments and executives who are further up the hierarchy. You may have little contact with these readers and little opportunity to observe them and figure out how to write for them. In fact, it may not be obvious that you are writing for them. A memo or report that you prepare for your supervisor may find its way to several other departments and to a number of executives when your supervisor passes it along to provide information about what your department is working on. These readers can play a role in your life that is disproportionate to their day-to-day knowledge of you and your work. They are often the people who must approve promotions, raises, and transfers, yet they may know you only by what you write. Thus, for both business and personal reasons it is important that you be aware of these readers.

You will also write to people who are not members of your company. They may be clients, suppliers, customers, or potential customers. Their reactions to what you write will affect not only the success of a particular project, but also the general impression that they form of you and your company. Their only knowledge of you will come from what you write to them. If they find that you are wrong, are unable to understand you, or discover that you have been less than truthful or tactful, the consequences for your relationship with them can be far-reaching and even disastrous.

You need to know as much as you can about your readers so that you can provide them with what they want and need to know. This will not always be what you want to tell them, because you and your readers will often be significantly different from each other. These differences can include:

1. Differences in experience, education, and ability
2. Differences in management and technical knowledge
3. Differences in familiarity with a specific project, subject, or situation, in spite of apparent similarities in education and experience
4. Differences in perspective on a subject or situation because you occupy different positions within your organization
5. Differences in the amounts of time and effort you are willing or able to invest in a subject or project
6. Differences in what you need to know

For example, an engineer who develops a new product and manufacturing process must sell an idea within the company before it can be marketed. A report that does this selling job will have as its readers not just other engineers, but those whose positions in the company dictate that they pay attention to costs, profits, marketability, safety, and a host of other issues. While the engineer may want to describe the technical elegance of the discovery and the cleverness of the process, readers will be interested in manufacturing costs, profit margins, and markets. One design engineer has reported being told to make a computerized control look "rugged," even though its appearance had nothing to do with its function. Writers who consider their readers carefully will be able to write to the demands of these differences in knowledge, interest, and perspective.

Learning about Your Reader

You should spend some of your planning time investigating all of your readers, even if you think you know them well. There is always the chance that you will discover or rediscover something that you were unaware of or thought unimportant.

One of the easiest ways to learn about your readers is to ask and answer a series of systematic questions that attempt to explore readers' ideas, attitudes, and knowledge. The results will not be exact, because you will not be doing a formal marketing or scientific survey. But the results will be more than adequate to your task. You will emerge with a profile of your readers and a sense of what you have in common with them. You can use the same questions that journalists often use to be sure they have gathered all of the necessary information about an event: Who? What? Where? When? Why? and How?

Even though you may think of your reader as a "Who," that is not the only question that applies. Use all of the questions and try to apply them in as many ways as you can think of. Ask and answer them conscientiously. Figure 1-1 provides examples of the kinds of questions you can ask, but the list is certainly not exhaustive. You can make up more questions to fit your situation.

It is important to take these questions seriously enough that you will give answers that will help you. For example, if you answer "Who is my reader?" with "Jane Smith," you have not really said very much. The purpose of the question is to get you to deal seriously with what Jane Smith is like. What does she do? What are her professional interests? Will she support your project or recommendations? What kinds of evidence will appeal to her? In a sense, all of the other questions in the list are aids to help you answer this one: "Who is my reader?"

On the other hand, if you allow the questions and answers to become too

Figure 1–1 Questions for Writers

WHO?
Who is my reader?
Who is my reader similar to?
Who does my reader believe?
Who are my reader's associates and peers?
Who does my reader think I am?

WHAT?
What does my reader know about this subject?
What does my reader need to know about this subject?
What does my reader want to know about this subject?
What is my reader's stake in this issue?
What will interest my reader in this subject?
What will help my reader understand this subject?
What do I want my reader to do?
What is my reader likely to do?
What does my reader expect of me?
What is my reader like?
What is my reader's socioeconomic background?
What is my reader's educational background?
What is my reader's position in (or in relation to) the company?
What do my reader and I have in common?

WHERE?
Where do my reader's attitudes and opinions come from?
Where can my reader confirm what I say?
Where can I get the information my reader needs/wants?

WHEN?
When does my reader need this information?
When does my reader expect a reply?
When do I want a reply from my reader?
When will these events take place?
When did my reader last encounter this situation?

WHY?
Why have I chosen this reader?
Why is this person my reader?
Why is this reader important to me and my goal?
Why is this subject important?
Why should this reader pay attention to me?
Why should this reader ignore me?
Why does my reader need this information?
Why is my reader interested in this subject?
Why is my reader *not* interested in this subject?

HOW?
How much information does my reader need?
How much time and effort am I asking for?
How much time and effort will my reader give me?
How much will my goal cost my reader?
How will my reader do what I ask?
How can I help my reader understand this subject?
How can I show my reader what we have in common?
How does my reader feel about this subject?

complicated, then you will have turned this planning step into an end in itself. There is little point in learning more about your reader than you need to know to write your draft and accomplish your goal. Some writing jobs are more complex than others, and some readers and groups of readers are more difficult to analyze than others. There is no need to do a complicated, extensive audience analysis every time you write. Try to keep the time and effort you spend on audience analysis in proportion to the complexity and importance of the writing job you are doing.

An Example

For an example of how you might use these questions, let's continue with the problem of recommending where a new Central Billing Department might be located within an existing company building. The job is to recommend a location to your supervisor, who will forward it to the Vice President for Administration, who will approve or disapprove the recommendation. Because we seldom see the Vice President, we will base this analysis mostly on what we can infer about him from his position in the company. We will not be answering all of the questions in Figure 1-1, but only those that seem related to the problem at hand.

Who is my reader?

John J. Phillips, Vice President for Administration. He joined the company ten years ago after a stint as president of a smaller company in the same business. He has a law degree, which helps him deal with federal and state regulatory agencies. This suggests an eye for detail and careful use of evidence. Office allocations are probably of minor interest to him so long as they create no problems and come in well under budget.

What does my reader know about the subject?

He really knows very little about what Central Billing does or how it functions. He does know that space allocation is a delicate political subject in the company. All department heads believe they have too little space and that everyone else has too much. He will be concerned to see that the plan will not arouse jealousies or interdepartmental rivalries.

What does my reader need to know about the subject?

He needs to know the criteria that have been established and that the recommended plan will satisfy them. He will probably also want to know that all affected department heads have been consulted and agreed to the recommendation.

What does my reader expect of me?

He expects me to state the criteria and then present a plan that meets them. He will expect all details to be included in the report so that he will be able to make a decision without further study or delay.

What do I want my reader to do?

He should approve my recommendation without substantial changes.

When does my reader need this information?

I have been given a two-week deadline, so there will be time to plan the move and do the remodeling before the new department is scheduled to begin working.

How much information does my reader need?

He needs to see that I have considered several alternatives and that I have evidence to support the one I recommend. In addition, he will probably expect a precise breakdown of required changes and costs.

This brief example is far from exhaustive, but it illustrates how asking questions about your reader can assist your planning by giving you valuable information about the people who will read your report. Once you have gone through the questions you will have a clear idea of how much information you will need to gather, how much detail you will need to include, and how you can present it for maximum effect. In short, by investigating your reader you will make your goal more specific, and the report itself will begin to take shape as you discover what specific readers will want you to include. In this sense, analyzing your reader is an extension of stating your subject, purpose, and goal, and it prepares you for investigating your subject more thoroughly.

Summary

Writing effectively is a matter of knowing both what makes a draft appeal to a reader and accomplish its goal and how to use working methods that will help you get your writing jobs done. These methods are best learned from experienced, successful writers, most of whom use a process that involves the following steps:

Planning

Considering readers

Investigating the subject

Organizing

Writing

Revising

Editing and proofreading

■

Exercises: Chapter One

1. For each of the following subjects write at least three goal or problem statements.

Computers	Profit(s)
Word processing	Money
Accounting	Corporate responsibility
Management	Consumerism
Technology	Age discrimination

2. Think of a problem you are experiencing right now or a goal that you want to achieve. Develop a complete statement of this problem or goal, so that you specify what a solution will consist of and what steps you must take to solve the problem or achieve the goal.

3. In courses such as the one in which you are using this text, the goal is often stated as "learning to write" or "improving your writing." Can you develop a more complete and descriptive goal statement for yourself, or for the course? What results do you want to achieve, what means will you use to achieve them, and how will you know when you have achieved them?

4. Do a brief demographic survey of your class or some other group you are involved with. Collect information about age, marital status, sex, hobbies and interests, favorite sports, academic majors and minors, and any other data you believe will help you understand the group as a whole.

   Once you have conducted the survey and compiled the results, write a brief profile of the group. Then compare your profile with the ones that your classmates or other members of the group have written. Were all profiles the same, or do different people see the group in different ways? If there are differences, how would you explain them?

5. Choose a popular magazine, preferably one that you are familiar with or read frequently. Read two or more issues carefully and then make a list of the characteristics of the magazine's readers. Using your list, write a brief profile of the magazine's typical reader.

6. Use the questions Who? What? Where? When? Why? and How? to help you develop a profile of your instructor or of someone else you know. Try to apply each question as many times and in as many different ways as you can, and then write a brief profile or description that introduces this person to someone else.

7. Do exercise 6 as a group project in which several people apply the questions to the same person. Work independently to apply the questions and then write individual descriptions. Then compare your description with those of the other members of the group. What similarities and differences exist in these descriptions?

8. Find a magazine or journal article (or a portion of a book) that is about a subject in your major field of study (or about a subject you know very well). Choose a passage that you believe most persons will not understand because they do not know either the concepts or the vocabulary. Then rewrite the article or passage so that someone who does not have your specialized knowledge will be able to understand it.

■

2

Finding Something to Say

Many people report that the most difficult part of writing is finding something to say, in spite of their preparation and their knowledge of the subject they are writing about. The words and ideas simply will not come as quickly and fluently as these writers think they should. The problem is likely to be one of the following:

1. They do not know their subject as well as they think they do and need to investigate it more thoroughly.
2. They are attempting to write too soon, before they have taken the time to review what they know and make it explicit to themselves.
3. They need a method or procedure for discovering what they know and getting it on paper.

In this chapter you will learn several methods for exploring your subject and generating ideas and information quickly and efficiently. The focus will be on learning methods that will help you discover and use what you already know.

You Know More Than You Think You Know

Most of us carry around a great deal of information that we use in our jobs. Some of this information is immediately available to us because we use it all the time. But much of it is stored deep in long-term memory, at a subconscious level. We know it, but we are not always aware that we know it. This information is often the raw material for writing, but we can use it only if we can retrieve it.

The working methods you will find in this chapter are designed to help you tap this rich source of information within yourself. Some people can do this rather easily. They can juggle a great deal of data without overloading, and they seem to speak and write without obvious preparation. All of us can do that on occasion. But there are times when we need ways of bringing the information to the surface and placing it under conscious control.

All of these methods will generate more information than you will be able to use. They are supposed to. It is important to begin writing with more information than you think you will need. The greater your choice, the more likely it is that you will be able to select the ideas, facts, and opinions that will best help you accomplish your goal. If you begin with only five or ten facts or examples to support your main concepts, you are likely to have to use all of them, regardless of their quality. But, if you gather forty or fifty facts and examples, you will be able to use the ten that do the job best. As a result, there will be fewer gaps in your presentation, and your reader will be less likely to raise questions and objections.

Some people try to take shortcuts as they search for something to say. In the name of efficiency they decide that it is useless to gather more information than they will use. So they do the minimum and then attempt to stretch it to cover the ground. The result is that these writers often tell their readers less than they want or need to know. The time saved earlier must eventually be spent clarifying or expanding the original presentation.

At the other extreme are writers who take their research and information gathering so seriously that they invest too much time and effort in it. Then, when it is time to write, they feel compelled to use everything they know because they have invested so much time and effort in every piece of information. These writers often present their readers with a grab bag of miscellaneous facts, opinions, and information and leave the readers to sort out what is useful.

There is an advantage to being between these two extremes. You want to be able to generate or retrieve a great deal of information quickly and inexpensively, so that you will not feel compelled to use everything you know. The working methods that follow are designed to help you generate more information than you need, and to do that at the lowest possible cost in time and effort per unit.

Using the Tools

As you practice the procedures that follow, keep these guidelines in mind:

Work on paper. Make notes as you go. Note-keeping is not really very difficult, and the payoff is that you will take the burden off your short-term memory and get the information on paper, where you can keep track of and manipulate it. Keeping notes will also force you to be specific, because it is more difficult to write something down than simply to pretend that you know it. As you work, you will be getting important practice in putting your ideas into words and phrases.

Withhold evaluation. Concentrate on gathering information. Wait until later to decide whether that information is valuable or important. Try to treat each fact or idea that you discover as though it were as good as any other fact or idea. There will be time later to see if some are better than others. We all have a mental editor or censor who is constantly telling us "Don't say that," or "That doesn't make sense," or "That's no good." For the time being it is important to tell that editor to be quiet. Criticizing yourself can only hamper your efforts to find out what you know.

Be flexible. You will need to practice using the methods that follow if you are to use them successfully. But you will probably discover that they will not all work equally well all the time. Be prepared to shift from one method to another, or even to combine them, if that seems likely to be productive. There is no point in persisting with a method that is getting you nowhere. And remember that these are not mathematical formulas that always work in the same way and yield the same result. All of these methods will stretch you, because they all require that you exercise a bit of creativity, imagination, and ingenuity.

Brainstorming

Brainstorming is a well-known and very productive method of generating a great many ideas, facts, and opinions very quickly. Not all of them will be of equal quality or usefulness, but you can evaluate them later. The purpose of brainstorming is to allow you to cover a great deal of territory to be sure you do not miss something that seems, at first glance, unimportant or irrelevant.

The goal of brainstorming is to think of and record as many ideas, facts, opinions, or other kinds of information as you can in the time available. You can work in a group or by yourself. Brainstorming has few rules, but they make the process easier and more productive.

Brainstorming in Groups

Encourage openness. Brainstorming works best if everyone involved feels free to contribute ideas and information. This freedom is important, because it tends to open the way to ideas and approaches to problems that might not surface under more rigidly structured conditions. The best way to ensure this openness is to make it clear at the beginning that everything anyone says is worth listening to, pursuing, clarifying, and understanding. In groups, especially, this often means that participants must leave their concern with status outside. Everyone in the group is equal to everyone else. All ideas and observations are equally valid and valuable until later evaluation proves them otherwise.

The easiest way to stifle a group's productivity is to begin evaluating or rejecting ideas as they come up. When you ask questions, try to phrase them so that they will keep the ideas and words flowing. Instead of saying "That won't work" or "I don't agree," ask questions such as "What does that mean?" or "How would we do that?" Always make it clear that you are pursuing an idea to see where it will lead, not challenging or rejecting it. When group members stop trusting one another, productive brainstorming will stop.

Keep records. The information you develop in a brainstorming session will do you no good unless you keep track of it. Decide in advance how you or your group will keep records, and be sure you are properly equipped. Groups often appoint one member to act as recorder. But custom removes that person from active participation. The recorder will need to pay more attention to taking notes than to contributing to the group. It is probably more effective to bring in a recorder who is not needed as an active group member. Or you can use a tape recorder. It will take time to go back and listen to the tape, but you have the advantage of hearing not only the ideas, but also the context in which they occurred. If you do use a tape, assure group members that their remarks will not be reported outside the group. Some people simply will not participate if they believe their statements might be played later for supervisors or others.

Encourage writing. Be sure that all members of the group have plenty of pens and paper. It is often productive to use large sheets of paper, posted on the walls or on an easel. Provide large markers in various colors and encourage all members of the group to write their concepts on the sheets. As each sheet fills up, post it on the wall where it will remain visible to everyone. This will help group members deal actively with a large number of ideas at the same time.

Set and observe time limits. It is important to keep the time you spend on a problem in proportion to its importance. And it is easy to spend more time on a project than it is worth. You can prevent this by setting time limits. Decide ahead of time when you will begin, how long you will work, and what you want to accomplish. If you are working with a group, it will help to provide every member with a written agenda that shows the topics the meeting will cover and the goal it is meant to accomplish.

Brainstorming by Yourself

Working by yourself is a little different from brainstorming in a group. To begin with, you will need to motivate yourself to generate the intensity that usually accompanies a group activity. You can do this best by conducting a thorough review of your notes and materials before you begin brainstorming. You can also prepare an agenda and set time limits, just as you would if you were working in a group. Doing these things will help keep you on track, so that your brainstorming will be directed toward your goal. Ideas and words will flow more easily if you have primed yourself with adequate preparation. Before you begin a brainstorming session, try to find a quiet location where you can work undisturbed. Interruptions will slow you down and distract you from your subject. Keep track of the ideas and information you generate by making a list or speaking into a tape recorder or dictating machine. There is no need to write or speak in complete or connected sentences. Your goal is to generate as much information as you can through rapid thinking and free association. You can evaluate the information later.

Results of Brainstorming

When you finish a group or individual brainstorming session you will have a great deal of information on paper and/or tape. Your records may consist of words, sentences, paragraphs, and diagrams. Tapes may be easiest to deal with if you have them transcribed, but transcription is practical only if the importance of the project will justify the time and expense. None of this material will be organized, since it will occur in your notes in the order in which you or the group thought of it. You will need to spend some time sifting through and evaluating this information. You may eventually discard much of what is in your notes. Remember, that was the idea to begin with: Generate a great deal of information and use only the best.

Brainstorming: A Summary

Brainstorming has few rules. Observing them will help you stay on the right track and make your sessions productive.

1. Concentrate on generating information rather than on evaluating it.
2. Keep track of everything.
3. Ask questions that encourage and clarify.
4. Keep your thinking, or the discussion, focused on the problem at hand.
5. Observe time limits.
6. Prepare. Review your notes before you begin. Provide group members with a written agenda.
7. Stop when you have accomplished your goal or the session becomes unproductive.

Freewriting

Freewriting is another method of covering a great deal of territory to find out what you know and whether any of it is useful in helping you accomplish your goal. Freewriting will also help you produce words and ideas quickly and fluently, even when you think you have nothing to say. The objective of freewriting is to get you to recall and write about whatever is on your mind (or buried in your subconscious memory) without editing, evaluating, or rejecting it before you have had a chance to see whether it will be useful.

Freewriting works this way: Begin by setting a time limit. At first you may want to work with blocks of five or ten minutes, until your hand gets used to writing steadily for longer periods. Try to arrange your schedule so that you will not be interrupted during this time. This is especially important in the office, and you may want to ask that your calls and visitors be held. Or perhaps you can find a table or desk that is out of the main traffic pattern. You can even hang a "Do Not Disturb" sign on your door or on the corner of your desk and let it be known that you are serious about it.

When you begin a five- or ten-minute session, start writing. Keep writing, no matter what happens. Keep your pen moving across the page. There is no need to edit, cross out, or stop to think of a word. No other people are going to see your writing unless you show it to them. Keep the words flowing, and keep your mind and imagination moving. Some useful things will begin to happen once the words begin to flow. Write whatever comes to you. You will discover, with some practice, that you are writing about subjects you did not realize you were thinking about. Solutions and new ideas are lurking in your subconscious, and you will soon be surprised at your ability to get them on paper.

Whatever you do, don't stop until your time is up. Stopping usually involves an attempt to edit or censor something, and there will be time for that later. If you get stuck for a word, make a dash on the page and move on, or write "stuck, stuck, stuck" until something else happens. You will eventually break through the block. You can even write "I can't think of anything to say" several times or several dozen times or describe the awful morning you have had. Any subject will do, so long as it gets the words flowing.

When your time is up, stop. You can, of course, keep going if you are into something really good. That often happens after you have had some experience with freewriting. But at first your hand will probably beg for some relief. Also, if you make the exercise too long or difficult you may be reluctant to try it again. Freewriting is a technique that improves with practice and experience, so success depends on your willingness to go back to it again and again.

Your first few attempts at freewriting may not seem very productive. But, as you get used to it and become less self-conscious about the act of writing itself, you will be more able to concentrate on the subject you need to write about or the problem you want to solve. In time your freewriting will help you produce highly relevant, useful ideas and information. One of the advantages of freewriting is that it can help you become less preoccupied with your anxieties about writing correctly and thus allow you to become more fluent with words.

Timed freewriting exercises usually will not give you a finished draft, especially at the beginning. Instead, you are more likely to find that you have produced ideas, facts, phrases, and sentences that you can use as building blocks for a plan or draft, or as the subject of further brainstorming or freewriting sessions. Once you have finished a freewriting session, read through what you have written and mark those passages that seem valuable. You can then expand and organize these ideas in future sessions in which your focus on your goal will be more precise. Sometimes freewriting *can* lead to a finished draft. If you would like to know how, or simply know more about freewriting itself, you can consult Peter Elbow's book *Writing Without Teachers* (Oxford University Press, 1973).

Issue Trees

A third technique you can use to help you recall concepts and information is to build an issue tree. Brainstorming and freewriting are primarily verbal techniques that require you to record your ideas in words. Issue trees, however, are primarily visual. That is, as you think of concepts and information you construct a visual display or diagram that arranges your information in a hierarchical structure that allows you to see each concept's relative importance and relationship to other concepts. Figure 2-1 shows a typical issue tree.

Issue trees are organized in the same way as the typical organization chart for a company. At the top of the chart you will find the most important or inclusive positions or divisions of an organization. Since a president's responsibilities include the whole company, that position will usually be at the top. At the next level the responsibilities are divided into smaller spans, and there you will find vice presidents for various functions. The tasks and divisions that pertain to each of these areas will be grouped under the vice president who is responsible for them.

The ideas and concepts that you place in an issue tree will have the same relationships to each other as the positions and departments listed on an organization chart. Some will be subordinate to others; others will be parallel or equal, either within one branch of the tree or on separate branches. Each time you add a concept or piece of information to an issue tree you will need to decide where it belongs in relation to the other items you have included.

Issue trees are an effective tool for both generating and organizing concepts and information. Thus, you can use them to help you organize the results of a brainstorming or freewriting session. We will explore their uses as an organizing tool in Chapter 3. For now, we want to take advantage of their ability to generate information and arrange it in a hierarchy.

Begin by placing your subject or goal, your most inclusive concept, at the top of the tree. As you devise the next level you need only subdivide the top level into its component parts of equal importance or inclusiveness. To create the third level of the tree simply subdivide each concept on the second level into its component parts. At each level your job is to generate subconcepts

Figure 2–1 A Typical Issue Tree

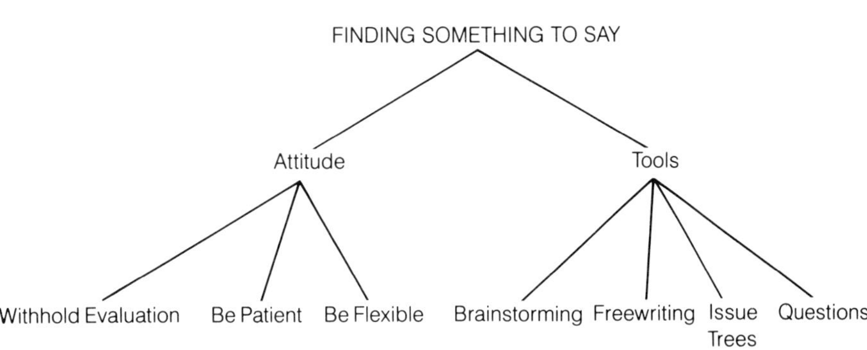

that are related to the main concept and to each other. As you work, it will help to be sure that you are developing the tree's branches more or less equally and that the items on each level are in fact parallel to each other.

Gaps in your knowledge will appear as empty or short branches on the issue tree or as concepts without subconcepts under them. If you find that you cannot subdivide a concept any further, check to see if it is as small as you can make it, or if it perhaps belongs elsewhere in the tree. Once you have finished the tree you will have a visual, hierarchical structure that allows you to see your entire project in a glance. You should be able to see at once whether you have placed examples or facts in the wrong branch, under the wrong concept, or at an inappropriate level of the tree. You should also be able to see very quickly just how much you know and how much you must yet learn.

How to Make an Issue Tree

Suppose you have been assigned to make arrangements for your company's annual awards dinner and then to write a brief announcement that will invite employees to attend. How would an issue tree help you do these jobs?

Begin by writing your goal at the top of a sheet of paper: "to plan and announce the annual awards dinner." On the next line you could list the major components of your task, the jobs that will result in achieving your goal. The result might look like the issue tree in Figure 2-2.

The issue tree in Figure 2-2 is a plan for doing the job you have been assigned. It will see you through from the first phone call to the evening of the dinner itself. You can expand this tree, of course, by including the details

Figure 2–2 Issue Tree

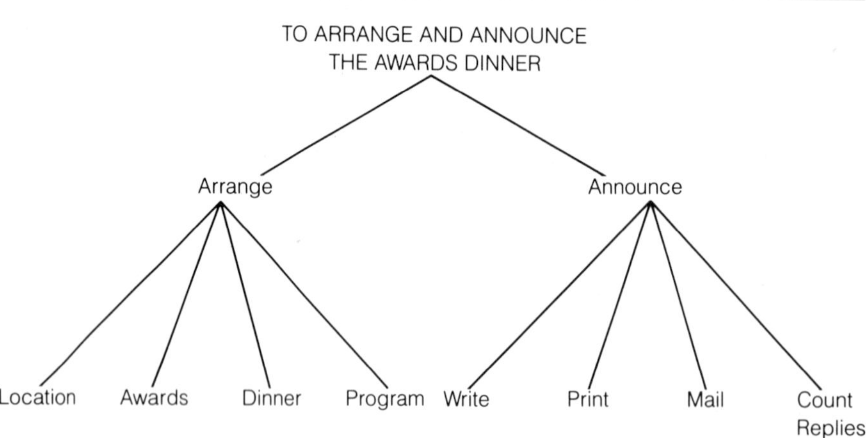

of each subcategory. For example, what would be an appropriate location? How many people must it accommodate? You can get both these details and further suggestions for the categories and concepts to include by talking with those who have the authority to make final decisions about the dinner. Common sense will usually tell you the rest. For example, you will need a menu. What you serve may be dictated by the number of people who attend, because you will probably be expected to stay within a fixed budget.

When you expand the left branch of the tree in Figure 2-2, which deals with the arrangements themselves, the result might look like the tree in Figure 2-3.

The expanded issue tree begins to display the details that follow from your major subcategories. It does this because the tree itself encourages you to think about your goal in an organized way. Asking where the dinner will be should naturally lead you to ask when it will take place, including the date and the time of day. You know there will be a program because the purpose of the dinner is to present awards. By checking the files or talking with the person in charge, you can learn that the program may include entertainment and speeches by certain executives.

At this point these details are probably questions for which you need answers and decisions. A later version of the tree, which you will make to help you plan the announcement itself, will reflect the decisions that have been made about these questions. That later tree should also reflect the information that your readers will need. Figure 2-4 shows what that tree might look like. Because this final tree contains all of the information your readers will need, it will serve you as a plan for writing the announcement or invitation.

Figure 2–3 Detailed Issue Tree

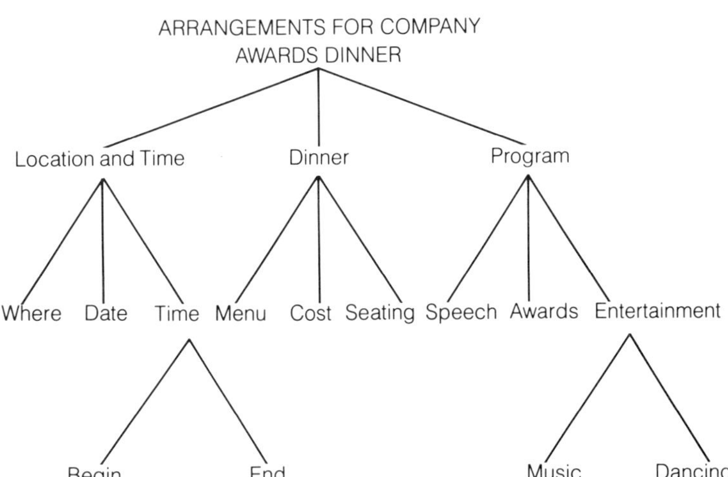

Figure 2–4 Completed Issue Tree

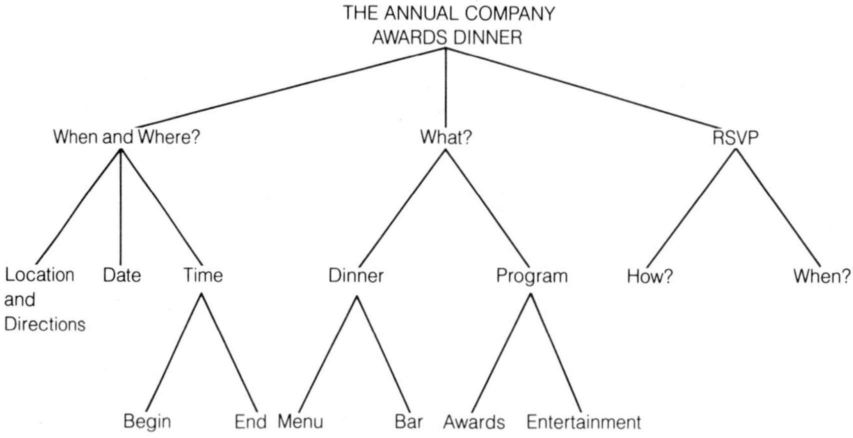

You may be wondering where all of this information has come from. It is important to realize that issue trees do not come to you already filled with information. Rather, like brainstorming and freewriting, they are tools for helping you recall what you already know. They accomplish this by giving you an organized, structured way of approaching your subject. In order to make issue trees work, you must bring your own intelligence and memory to bear on the problem you are trying to solve. If you would like to know more about issue trees and how they work, read the relevant chapters of *Problem-Solving Strategies for Writers,* by Linda Flower (Harcourt Brace Jovanovich, 1981).

Questions

The questions Who? What? Where? When? Why? and How?, which you used in Chapter 1 to learn about your reader, will also help you find out what you know and what you need to know about your subject. They are:

Familiar

Easy to use

Open-ended

Efficient

A small or uncomplicated project may require that you ask each of these questions only once. Used this way, to help you plan a memo announcing a meeting, the questions will tell you, for example:

Who should attend (and thus who should receive a copy of the memo).

What the meeting is about.

Where the meeting will take place.

When the meeting will begin and end.

Why a meeting is necessary (its purpose).

How the results will be used.

The questions will help you recall the information your readers will need, and they will also give you a plan for writing the memo itself. It is easy to record your response to each question and then work your answers into sentences and paragraphs. Answering the above questions about a meeting might result in a memo somewhat like this one:

TO: Product Marketing Group
FROM: A. Schwartz
SUBJECT: Meeting of Product Marketing Group

The Product Marketing Group will meet on August 1 at 3:00 p.m. in the Sales Conference Room to consider Welltech Corporation's new pump mechanism and its impact on our plans to release the new P-20 pump in September.

The new Welltech pump could significantly affect our sales during the next fiscal year, especially since they will have six weeks lead-time before we can begin to market the P-20. Be prepared to suggest changes to our sales strategy, pricing, and timing.

Longer or more complex projects may require that you use the questions somewhat differently, to generate both more information and more complex information. You can do this in two different ways. The first is to ask each question more than once, until you have exhausted its possibilities. For example, there will often be more than one person or group involved in a situation. Simply ask, "Who?" until you have figured out who they all are. Like this:

Who was involved?

Who is my reader?

Who needs to know about this?

Who will make the final decision?

Whom will the decision affect?

Who will agree or disagree with this?

Who has the information I need?

Using the questions productively is really quite easy so long as you become actively involved and use your imagination and creativity to find different ways of asking them. No one can possibly tell you ahead of time *all* of the ways that you can ask a given question. You will have to think of them yourself.

A second way of making the questions more powerful and productive is to remember that they are related to each other. That is, when you ask one of the questions, use the others to help you answer it. This way, each single question becomes six questions. Each time you ask "Who?" for example, you are also asking "What?" "Where?" "When?" "Why?" and "How?" In fact, you can ask each of the subsidiary questions as many times as you need to. Your results might look something like this:

Who will make this decision?

To whom does he report?

Whom will he consult?

What does he need to know?

What does he want to know?

On what will he base his decision?

What kind of evidence will be most effective?

What is this person's position in the company?

What will motivate him to say yes?

What other factors will he consider?

What does my recommendation commit him to?

What do I want him to do?

Where will he confirm what I say?

When does he need this information?

When must the decision be made?

Why am I asking for this decision?

Why will this person make the decision?

How will he communicate his approval?

How will the decision be implemented?

Of course, there are more questions that you could ask. This brief example is meant simply to give you an idea of how they can all be used together. Using them this way will probably result in a certain amount of duplication, but that is not really wasted effort. Rather, it assures that you are viewing your subject from a variety of perspectives. You should emerge with information about your readers, your subject, and your approach to both.

Patience

Patience is a vastly underrated working method. Answers, insights, and solutions will not always come to you on demand. Sometimes you will have to wait for them as they form slowly in your subconscious. And they will often present themselves to you when you least expect them, as you are doing something completely unrelated to the project they pertain to. So, if you sense that you are not making progress, it will sometimes help to put a project away for a while, even an hour, and do something else. Even such a short time away from a project can be quite productive.

Summary

Finding something to say about your subject is an active and often demanding part of writing. Rather than procrastinate or wait for inspiration, it is often more productive to use methods such as brainstorming, freewriting, issue trees, and questions. Using these methods separately or together will usually provide you with more information than you need. Thus, when you are ready to organize and produce a draft, you will be able to choose the best concepts and illustrations that are available to you.

■

Exercises: Chapter Two

1. Select one of the following topics (or one of your own choice) and brainstorm a list of forty to fifty facts or observations about it. Remember, you do not need to write sentences or paragraphs. You are simply making a list. (Keep your list; you will use it for exercises in later chapters.)

   Effective communication on the job
   The effective supervisor
   Developing effective study or work habits
   The social responsibilities of business
   What is a "good" job?

2. In ten minutes you will have to stand up in front of a group and speak about one of the following subjects. Choose one and brainstorm a list

of what you might say about it. (Save your list so you can use it later.)

> ____________ as a career
> I returned to school (or am attending school) because . . .
> The most important skill you can have in business is . . .
> I enjoy/hate writing because . . .

3. You have been appointed to a group that has been asked to suggest improvements in the function and appearance of your campus. Working in small groups of five or six people, do the following:

- **a.** Agree on a problem or goal statement that includes the results you want to achieve, the constraints on what you may do, and how you will achieve the results.
- **b.** In a group brainstorming session, develop a list of at least 100 improvements you want to make.
- **c.** As a group, agree on no more than ten of these improvements for your final recommendation.
- **d.** For each item on your final list write a brief description of the condition that exists now, the ways it could be improved, and the effects that such an improvement will have.
- **e.** Arrange your list in order of importance, from the most important to the least important. Then consult the group so that you all agree on the order of importance.

4. Use the questions Who? What? Where? When? Why? and How? to explore one of the following subjects.

- **a.** Industrial theft (by employees)
- **b.** Motivating employees
- **c.** Establishing nonsmoking areas at work
- **d.** How computers make life easier or more difficult

5. You have been assigned to help design a sales campaign for one of the following products. Use a combination of brainstorming, freewriting, and questions to help you decide what you might say about the product you choose.

- **a.** A pen that writes when held upside down
- **b.** A voice-controlled light switch
- **c.** A radio-controlled suitcase/briefcase lock
- **d.** A flashlight that works for ten years

6. Identify a problem you have been experiencing at school, home, or work. Use a combination of brainstorming, freewriting, and questions to explore the problem. Then write a comprehensive goal or problem statement.

3

Organizing

Almost anything is easier to do or understand if it is organized, that is, if it is set up in a recognizable pattern or arrangement that allows us to make sense of it. The specific arrangement or the way you achieve it is not really important, so long as it works by allowing you to accomplish your goals, whatever they might be. When we encounter a task or a body of information for which no pattern is obvious, we often make one up because we know that doing so will make our job easier.

Consider the familiar task of assembling a jigsaw puzzle with 500 or 1000 pieces. We know that we will increase our chances of assembling the puzzle in a reasonable period of time if we go about it in an organized way. So we are likely to dump all of the pieces on a table and begin sorting. Many people begin by trying to separate all of the edges from the rest, for these can be assembled and will serve as a frame for the puzzle. The frame places *limits* on the puzzle and separates it from the rest of the world. But, even before the frame is together, another kind of sorting begins, this time based on color. This allows us to determine where within the frame a particular group of pieces belongs. Finally, we begin paying attention to the details printed on each piece and the individual shapes. These allow us to decide exactly where one piece will fit in relation to others.

This kind of sorting is merely one way of devising a system for solving a jigsaw puzzle. Certainly there are others that are equally useful. No matter which system we choose, we are constructing a *plan* for completing it, and the plan *organizes* our activities into a series of systematic steps. The alternative is a lengthy trial-and-error procedure of comparing each piece with each other piece until we find two that will fit together. The number of steps involved in such a trial-and-error procedure is staggering. Even a simple ten-piece puzzle presents an unimaginably large number of possible combinations. (You have probably figured out that trial-and-error is also a structured plan, an organized way of doing the puzzle. That's true. But it would require almost limitless amounts of time and patience. Both of these are in short supply in real life.)

Organizing also helps us understand. We will have an easier time understanding and using information if it is organized than if it is not. If someone gives me instructions for tuning an engine or doing an accounting procedure, I will find them easier to follow if they are organized in the sequence in which I must do them, rather than in the sequence in which my instructor thought of them, or in no particular sequence at all.

Organizing for Writing

What does all of this have to do with writing? Organizing makes the writing itself easier to do, so to begin with you are helping yourself. And, from your reader's perspective, writing that is organized is easier to read, understand, and remember than writing that is not organized.

From a writer's point of view, organizing involves having a way of approaching your information systematically, just as you might approach a jigsaw puzzle, so you can develop a finished product in which each piece of information fits. The difference between writing and assembling a puzzle—and it is an important difference—is that the pieces of the puzzle will fit together in only one way. You are searching for a single correct solution that is predetermined by the shapes of the pieces. But when you write there is no single correct solution to the shape or organization of your final product. Instead, you are searching for a pattern or sequence that is appropriate to your information, your goals, your reader's needs, and the letter, memo, or report format that you must use. Your reader expects that you will create a pattern that will make what you say easy to read, understand, remember, and use.

In short, readers expect that you will organize your writing and save them the time, effort, and aggravation of doing it themselves. They do not want to solve puzzles; they want them already solved, made sense of, and ready to use. This means that they expect you to:

Focus on the problem or situation at hand

Identify important data and concepts

Point out conclusions and solutions

Support conclusions with evidence and examples

Separate the essential from the important from the merely interesting

To do any less than this is simply to dump the puzzle in front of your readers and assume (or demand) that they will gladly do the rest. Worse, it assumes that all of your readers will be capable of solving the puzzle and making sense of what you say. Too often they are not, or they will solve it in a way that does not suit you.

Begin organizing by trying to construct or discover a systematic way of managing the information you have gathered. The ideal procedure will work in as many different situations as possible, and it will allow you to do a great deal in the fewest possible steps.

Simplify Your Data

The first step in controlling your information, rather than having it control you, is to simplify it. One way to simplify any body of information is to get rid of some of it. But we do not yet have any way of knowing what to keep and what to throw away. One alternative is to try to arrange the data into groups, just as we did with the pieces of the puzzle. By doing this you reduce the number of possible combinations to something the human mind can at least comprehend. For example, if you have only ten pieces of data you are facing more than three million possible combinations. By grouping those ten into five or six groups, you reduce the mathematically possible combinations to 120 or 720.

Group Data into Categories

It helps to group your data into categories, but where do the categories come from?

You begin by remembering your goals. Organizing always occurs within a conceptual framework, and this framework is most often furnished by your goal. Just what is it that you want to accomplish with this information, and this reader, in this situation?

Perhaps your job is to write a report about your company's employees. There may be several hundred or thousand of them. Unless your job is to write a profile or employment history of each one, you will want to simplify by categorizing them in some way. The categories you use will depend on your reasons for writing the report and your goals. Some categories, such as classifying employees into management and labor or according to the department each one is assigned to, will suggest themselves almost automatically. But those will be large categories, and they may neither simplify your job nor help you accomplish your goals.

But suppose your subject has been defined a bit more carefully: to determine and report the effects on the company of various retirement ages. In this case you might begin by establishing categories based on employees' ages. That will allow you to determine how many will retire in a given year, depending on the retirement age you assume. Figure 3-1 projects the number of employees who will retire during the next five years if the company uses retirement ages of 62, 65, or 70.

At this point, then, we have classified employees not by age, but by the year in which they will retire. But this system leaves a number of questions unanswered. Remember, the goal or assignment was to examine the *effects* of various retirement ages, not simply the number of people who will retire in a given year. So there are conclusions that our present categories will not allow us to reach. For example, we cannot tell whether those retirements will involve people who have essential skills or occupy key positions.

Retirement, by itself, is not sufficient as a conceptual framework for organizing the data. We need a way of constructing categories that are more informative. To learn how retirements might be distributed throughout the company, we would need to add another concept, such as "department," and allow it to intersect with the first two: age and year. The question has become "How many workers in each department will reach a particular retirement age in a given year?" Because there are three concepts, one of them will have to control the other two, as in Figure 3-2. When one concept controls, the others fall into a two-dimensional table under it, as in Figures 3-3 and 3-4.

Once you have constructed the tables or other displays of your data, you can extract information from each one for a summary, which can be set up by department, year, or retirement age. The process simply uses different concepts to:

1. Simplify data by putting it into categories
2. Explore what different arrangements and conceptual frameworks *tell* you about the data
3. Refine your goals, which change and become more precise as you work

So, in the beginning, organizing is a way of helping you get control over your data. It is also an extension of the processes of inquiry and planning that began in Chapter 1.

Figure 3–1 Projected Retirements During the Next Five Years

Employees Retiring at Age	1986	1987	1988	1989	1990
62	15	1	3	7	2
65	2	1	6	15	1
70	0	0	0	2	5

The different contexts and concepts that you use to categorize and arrange data in various ways are helping you learn how to focus the data on your goals effectively. Eventually, as you play with the data and categories, moving them around to see what you can learn, you will see that some of the information you have does not contribute to reaching your goals. When that happens, eliminate it, at least for the time being. You will also see that you are missing some information that you need. So you will have to find it and see where it fits.

Figure 3–2 Projected Retirements in Each Department

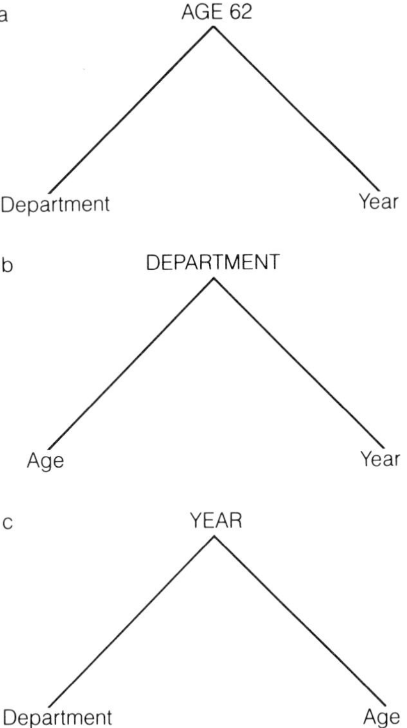

Figure 3–3 Impact on Selected Departments of Retirement at Age 62

Department	1986	1987	1988	1989	1990
A	1	3	6	0	1
B	2	1	0	6	5
C	0	0	33	1	1
D	12	—	—	—	—
E	0	—	—	—	—

(The controlling concept here is age 62; see Figure 3-2a.)

Figure 3–4 Retirements in Department A are Scheduled as Follows, Depending on the Retirement Age Selected

Age	1986	1987	1988	1989	1990
62	1	3	2	6	0
65	0	2	1	1	3
70	0	0	2	0	1

(The controlling concept here is a specific department; see Figure 3-2b.)

Identify Major Concerns

Organizing can also help you refine and sharpen your goals to help you decide exactly what you want to show or why you are writing. For example, the purpose of writing about the effects of retirement has to be more than simply finding out who will retire when. Any personnel office can provide that information in about ten minutes. The assignment is to find out how those retirements will *affect* the company and whether the effects will vary with different retirement ages. So we need to ask what those effects might be, regardless of the established retirement age. Among those effects might be that—

1. Retirements could wipe out a whole department at once.
2. Retiring workers may not need to be replaced.
3. Later retirements may cost the company more money.

These are general effects that we will need to express as concepts. Note that they did not materialize out of thin air, but grew out of the activities of placing data into categories, looking for contexts and frameworks, and asking questions. It is in this way that organizing helps you explore your subject and generate new concepts and information. You can express the general effects of retirement in the following categories or concepts:

1. *Financial.* The longer people work, the longer the company will have to pay them. Since salaries usually increase with seniority, employees near retirement will probably earn more than new employees. So, raising the retirement age from 65 to 70 will cost more, in the long run, to do the same work. How much more? Can the company afford it?
2. *Experience and ability.* We often assume that the longer people work, the better they get at their jobs. Whenever employees retire, the company loses their expertise. Are there benefits in having employees stay with the company longer? Do these benefits outweigh the added costs?

3. *Hiring.* If the retirement age is revised, and people work longer, the company will not be hiring replacements as often, unless it expands. This will affect training and apprenticeship programs and possibly the company's social atmosphere.
4. *Morale.* Because people work longer, promotions of younger employees may be delayed. Could this cause them to move to other companies where they can expect more rapid advancement and the money, authority, and responsibility that accompany it?
5. *Productivity.* Just because we assume greater expertise with an older workforce, does that mean the company will be able to maintain existing productivity rates? Will workers slow down as they get older? Will this offset their increased knowledge and ability? Will the company need to hire more workers to compensate for decreased productivity?

We have now identified five ways in which an extended working life might affect the company. These five concepts can be arranged into 120 different combinations. The questions in each category, and their answers, have enough potential combinations to stagger the imagination. And there are no rules that say that one sequence is better than another.

Simplify, Again

Can these five categories or concepts be reduced to four, three, or even two? The next step is to test the concepts to see if they are related to each other closely enough that they can be combined as subconcepts within a larger category. In this case, "Financial" and "Productivity" seem to fit together, because they have to do with costs and income. "Hiring" and "Morale" seem to belong together because they both concern the effects of later retirement on other employees, even potential employees, and the policies that will affect them. "Experience and Ability" seem related to "Productivity," but not to "Financial." Figure 3-5 shows some preliminary issue trees that display these relationships.

But notice that although these issue trees group subcategories, they provide no major concepts that will unite all of the subconcepts under one all-inclusive concept or goal. Each group is tied together by a concept that is more inclusive than either member of the group, but one category is still by itself. The next step is to try another issue tree, which attempts to find out where "Experience and Ability" will fit. The result is Figure 3-6.

"Experience and Ability" seems to belong with "Productivity," but not

Figure 3–5 Relating Concepts to Form Subcategories

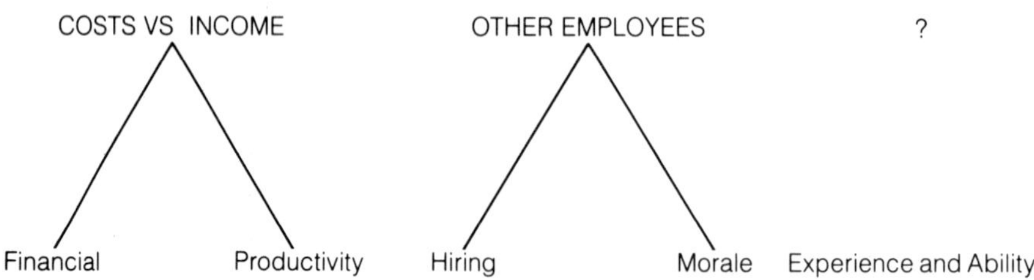

Figure 3–6 The Role of Experience and Ability

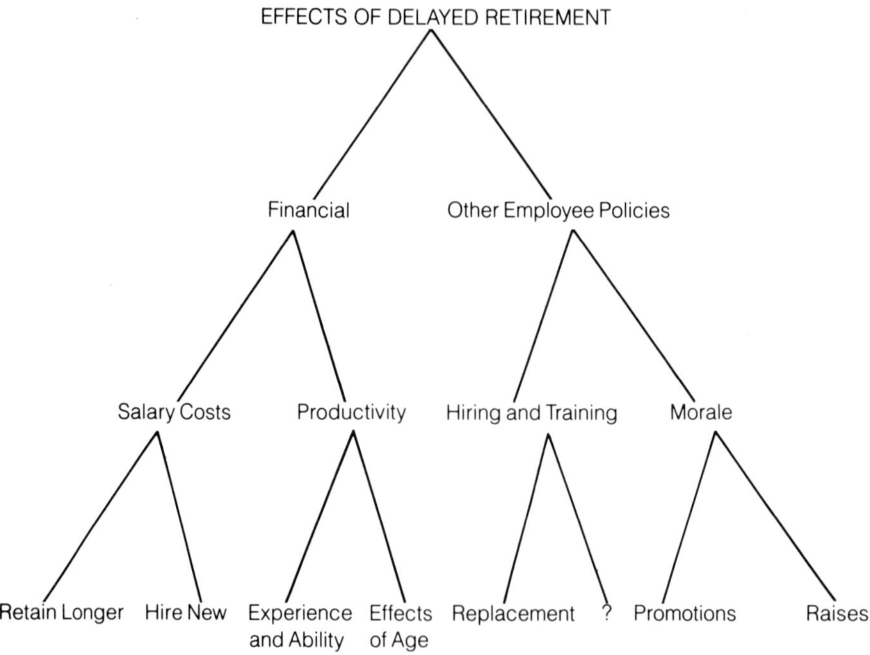

completely with "Financial." In Figure 3-6 "Financial" has become an organizing or controlling concept with "Salary Costs," a new concept, under it, along with "Productivity." Once that was done it seemed obvious, as it had not before, that "Experience and Ability" is a factor that influences "Productivity." Remember that the question about productivity concerned whether it would increase because of greater experience, decrease because the work force was getting older, or remain the same.

What is beginning to emerge here is a pattern of relationships among the concepts. We have come a long way from "who retires when?" though that information can now be used to show the effects of different retirement ages.

For example, you may have discovered that almost all of the workers in one department will retire in a two-year period. Does that fit anywhere on the issue tree? Where could it be used to point to a difficult problem or propose a solution that your reader can use? It will certainly fit with "Salary Costs," because you will probably replace retiring workers with new ones at lower salaries. Depending on your conclusions about productivity, you could predict an increase or decrease during those two years and plan your production schedule accordingly.

But to put this information in either of these places would serve to make a point about only a particular year. A more effective use of these kinds of data is as an example or illustration to make a general point, something that can apply to more than a single event. To accomplish that, you might put this observation under "Hiring and Training" in the other branch of the tree. Why? Because it suggests that retirement schedules need to be plotted carefully and planned for. You may want to recommend that the company begin training new members of the department while the older employees, with their experience and expertise, are still available to do it.

Of course, there are other ways of arranging these categories. You might, for example, decide to concentrate on the financial effects of delayed retirements. If that were the case, then "Financial Considerations" would become the controlling concept for your entire report. The point is not that there is only one way of organizing major and minor concepts or even that there are many ways. Rather, as you search for a structure you are also thinking through the problem itself and looking for ways in which you can accomplish your goals.

Once you have established the major categories and subcategories you will use, the rest of your organizing will consist of sorting specific data, observations, and examples into the places where they fit. Because you have taken the time to set up the categories carefully, this part of the job should go rather smoothly as you expand and refine your issue tree.

Issue trees are often an adequate basis for writing. Each major branch of the tree can be a main section of your letter report, and each subbranch will be a subsection. You can follow the issue tree in this way, as you do a first draft, producing sentences and paragraphs that reflect the structure of the tree. The tree will show you what comes next and where to put the major divisions and subdivisions.

Using Typical Organizing Patterns

Once you have determined the relationships that exist among the concepts and data you have gathered, you must still decide how you will present your subject to your readers. It is possible, of course, to follow the issue tree or other scheme you have constructed and create your first draft by following the plan you have developed there. Or you may wish to consider using some of the more common organizing schemes that people have found useful in their writing. There are three basic sequences that you can use as they are or adapt to your own needs. At times you will find that you need to use all three in a single letter, memo, or report.

Space/Time Sequence

The space/time sequence pattern does exactly what its name implies: It arranges information according to the sequence in which you or your readers might encounter it in the real world. For example, you might use time sequence to report a series of events or to give instructions for a series of steps that must be performed in a precise sequence. Similarly, space sequence presents a series of objects in the same spatial sequence or relationship that they have in the world. For example, when you introduce people in the order in which they are seated around a table, you are using space sequence. When you give directions to someone, you will probably list the landmarks in the same order in which your listener or reader will encounter them.

Deductive Sequence

When you use the deductive pattern, you begin with your most general or inclusive concepts (just as you did when you constructed issue trees) and then proceed to subconcepts, examples, and specific details. This pattern is similar to the inverted triangle of journalists, who begin their news stories with an overview that, in effect, tells the whole story. Then they provide details. You might visualize this pattern as it is shown in Figure 3-7.

The deductive pattern is especially useful when you want to announce conclusions or recommendations quickly, at the beginning of a letter or re-

Figure 3–7 The Deductive Sequence

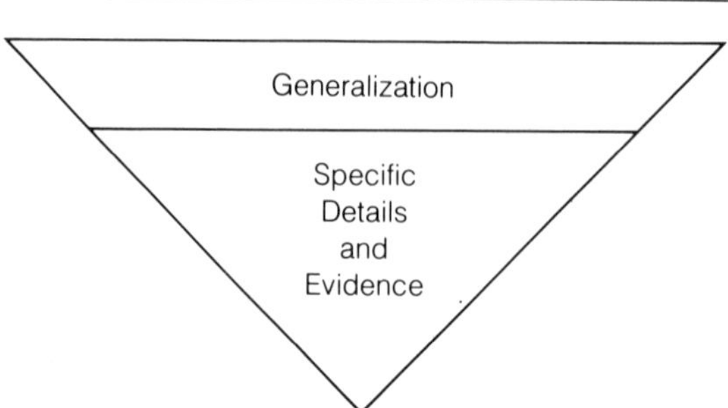

port. This method will orient your reader to your subject. Then you can go on to provide necessary details and explanations. Doing this calls immediate attention to your most important point or concept and then follows that central concept with support, illustrations, or proof.

Inductive Sequence

The inductive sequence is the opposite of the deductive. It begins with specific details and uses them to build up to a general conclusion or recommendation. When you use this pattern you are taking your readers step-by-step through a carefully designed sequence of facts or ideas, or a reasoning process, so you can bring them to a conclusion that you have already reached. The inductive pattern says, in effect, that if *a, b,* and *c* are true, then *d* must also be true. You can visualize this sequence as a triangle, this time sitting on its base, as in Figure 3-8.

The inductive pattern is useful when you want to delay stating your recommendation or conclusion until you are certain your readers understand your evidence and reasoning. Or perhaps you suspect that your readers may be uncomfortable with, or even hostile toward, your recommendation. The same readers may willingly accept your evidence and reasoning so long as they do not, at the same time, have to commit themselves to a particular conclusion. However, once they have accepted the evidence, you can hope that they will find the conclusion inescapable.

Combinations

It is rare that you will use one of these organizing patterns to the exclusion of the others. Rather, you will often combine them in one letter, memo, or report. Thus, if you are writing to provide details about an upcoming meeting, you might organize it this way:

Figure 3–8 The Inductive Sequence

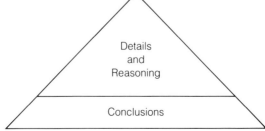

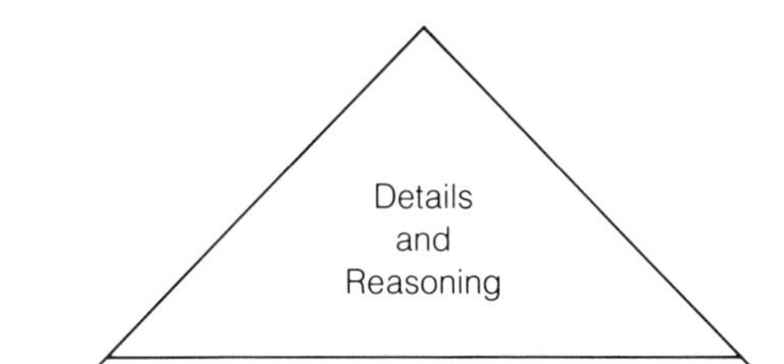

1. The overall scheme might be deductive, because you want to announce the meeting at once, as the subject of your memo.
2. Within the overall deductive organization you might use space/time sequence to provide an agenda.
3. Later in the same memo you might use an inductive pattern to explain why the meeting is necessary or why it will address a specific issue.
4. At the end, no matter which overall pattern you use, you will want to make a brief statement that reminds your readers of some important fact or reemphasizes an important point you have made (such as the date and time of the meeting).

Summary

Organizing for writing involves more than making an outline or finding a sequence in which to present your information and conclusions. Rather, organizing is an important tool in the writing process that allows you to—

1. Get control of your subject by simplifying and categorizing it
2. Find and use relationships between and within categories
3. Discover information that is missing from your plan
4. Explore your subject further and generate new information and concepts
5. Evaluate and refine your goals
6. Devise a plan that you can use as you write

■

Exercises: Chapter Three

1. Use issue trees to organize the following information in at least three different ways.

Sales: $16 million	Current debt: $2 million
Profits: $3 million	Credit rating: excellent
Employees: 285	Inventory: $4 million
Number of factories: 2	Quarterly dividend: $0.89
Market area: East Coast	Headquarters: Boston
President: Randolph Stone	Market share: 6 percent
Product: novelty papers	
Share price: $2.50	

2. Use the questions Who? What? Where? When? Why? and How? to help you generate information about a person or place you know well. Then select the information you would choose to tell someone else about this person or place. You will, of course, need to establish your purpose. Then organize the details, using (a) a direct approach, (b) an indirect approach, and (c) space/time sequence.

3. Select a brief article from a business publication or journal. Read it carefully, take notes, and then answer the following questions about it:
   a. What evidence can you find that the writer organized the subject for you?
   b. Construct an issue tree that shows the main concepts and supporting details that are present in the article.
   c. Outline the article, using a traditional outline.
   d. Suggest an organization that would be more appropriate, if you can.

4. As part of a class project you have been assigned to give a five-minute report about a company or industry from the following list. Select one and find as much information about it as you can. Then use the methods explained in this chapter to explore your subject and organize the information you will present.

A company of your choice
The nuclear power industry
The lumber industry
The housing industry
The paper industry
The transportation industry

5. Choose one of the following subjects and find out as much about it as you can. Then organize and write a brief explanation that someone who knows nothing about the subject will understand.

Microchips	Monetary policy	Inflation
Profit	Fiscal policy	Bankruptcy

■

4

Writing and Revising

Ideally, we would like our notes, issue trees, and other planning papers to evolve smoothly into finished drafts. But we all know that seldom happens. Instead, writing a draft is too often a frustrating experience that can intimidate us into inaction. Fortunately, there are a number of ways to take the sting out of writing and revising. These include:

1. Using a hierarchy of editorial concerns
2. Mastering efficient writing and revising strategies
3. Making writing and revising part of your day at school or work, instead of an overtime marathon at the last minute

The Intimidating First Draft

Of course, you have been writing all through the planning process: making notes, lists, and issue trees and perhaps even writing paragraphs or entire sections as you developed some of your ideas. But sitting down to write a first draft may seem more formal and imposing than the writing you did while you were planning. Drafts require that you write in sentences and paragraphs, and that you pay some attention to the format and organization you want the finished product to have. No matter how much planning you have done, you are suddenly coping with questions of length, shape, word choice, coherence, sentence structure, paragraphing, and format, among many others. These decisions can be a major source of the difficulty and frustration of writing, especially if you attempt to deal with all of them at the same time.

Too many writers, especially inexperienced ones, attempt to deal with all of these decisions at once. And, to complicate matters further, they try to make decisions at the same time that they execute them. Trying to do everything at once usually results in doing nothing well. We overload our short-term memories, become frustrated with not being able to keep track of everything, and are haunted by the knowledge that we are not doing our best job. The result is often a severe case of writer's block or, worse, a finished letter or report that is less than our best work. You can avoid these problems, and most of their consequences, by using what Donald Murray has called "the natural hierarchy of editorial concerns."*

The Hierarchy of Editorial Concerns

The *hierarchy of editorial concerns* is a way of helping you focus on a limited number of decisions and writing tasks at one time. It does this by arranging those decisions and tasks in a relative order of importance that corresponds to the relative order in which you need to be concerned about them when you write or revise. Of course, there are no set rules about when you should do anything when you write or revise. The hierarchy is a set of general guidelines for helping you put "first things first" and thus save time and effort as you work. Figure 4-1 provides an overview of the hierarchy and shows the order in which you will approach the tasks involved in writing and revising.

According to the hierarchy, you begin writing or revising by paying attention to the larger, more important decisions that will affect your entire draft. These include decisions about meaning, content, and organization. Once you have made these decisions and are satisfied with what you have done,

*I have borrowed this phrase, and the concept behind it, from Donald Murray's essay "Teaching the Other Self: The Writer's First Reader," *College Composition and Communication* (May, 1982), 140–147. The details of the hierarchy, as they are presented here, are my own.

Figure 4–1 A Hierarchy of Editorial Concerns

I. Writing a First Draft
Your first draft is an experiment, a test, to find out what you have to say. It is an attempt to build a rough framework of content, meaning, and form, which you will fill in later.

II. Revising
Revising begins with a careful review of your first draft to find out if you have actually done what you set out to do. As you review, check to see how close you have come to achieving your original intention and where and how far you have fallen short. At this point you are concerned with—

What you have left out
What you have included that you do not need
Whether you can make this draft achieve your goals

Now is the time to work on major revisions, deletions, and reorganizations. Rereading will stimulate your thinking and help you generate new ideas.

III. Refining
Once you have settled on the major concepts you will include in your draft and the way you will organize them, you can shift your attention to the next level. Look at your secondary concepts, examples, illustrations, and evidence. Do they support the major ideas? Do the subsections follow each other logically? Do your illustrations really illustrate? Do your examples really exemplify and explain?

This is also a good time to look for gaps in your presentation. Is anything missing? There is still time to add explanations and details without having to rewrite the whole draft so they will fit.

---

you can turn your attention to the finer points, which will affect only a single paragraph or sentence. These include such issues as word choice, paragraph and sentence structure, spelling, and punctuation, among others.

Many writers, especially inexperienced ones, work in the opposite sequence: that is, they spend a great deal of time making decisions about spelling, punctuation, and word choice first. Too often these writers discover that they have invested time and effort in parts of their draft that they must ultimately throw away. Thus, their time and effort have been wasted on producing correct writing that they do not use. The whole point of the hierarchy is to help you avoid this waste. It assures that you will concentrate on details such as word choice, spelling, and sentence structure only after you are sure you will use the parts of your draft you are working on. In this way, the hierarchy helps you produce the best draft you are capable of, in the shortest possible time, with the least amount of effort. The hierarchy has other advantages, too.

Advantages of Using the Hierarchy

1. The hierarchy of editorial concerns encourages *provisional* writing. That is, it encourages you to write quickly at the

IV. Review Paragraphs and Sentences

Are your paragraph divisions both logically and visually appropriate? Try to achieve a balance of long and short paragraphs. But try also to keep related sentences within the same paragraph.

Within each paragraph review the sentences carefully. Are they all related to each other? Does each one make a statement about the paragraph's main idea? Are sentences arranged in a sequence that gives each paragraph a beginning, middle, and end?

By this time you have probably tried to stop adding new material. You have been working to weave your writing tighter and tighter, sentence by sentence. It is becoming increasingly difficult to add anything without making major adjustments in everything else.

V. Words

Focus closely on the words you have used. Are you using words that mean what you want them to mean? Will they have the same meanings for your readers? If your vocabulary is a specialized one, you may need to define some of your terms. Is each word appropriate to your overall tone?

VI. Editing

Editing is a matter of picking up loose ends: checking details of word choice, grammar, punctuation, and spelling. You are preparing your final draft for a typist, and this is your last chance to make changes. It will be embarrassing to ask a typist to do work over again because of your mistake.

VII. Proofreading

Once you are satisfied that your draft is the best you can make it, the last step is to proofread for mistakes. Proofread twice: once before you send a draft to be typed and once again when it is returned to you. Only then are you ready to sign a letter or report and send it to your readers.

beginning, in an attempt to stake out the general meaning, content, and organization of your draft. When you finish you will not have spent so much time and effort that you will be unwilling to change or discard part or all of what you have written.

2. It encourages *revision.* Because your draft is provisional, you will write with the knowledge that you will revise it, perhaps several times, before you are satisfied with it. Because the first draft was inexpensive in time and effort, you will be more willing to revise.

3. It encourages *selective attention.* Even though the hierarchy separates writing and revising into tasks of manageable size, you will still be trying to pay attention to more detail than most of us can cope with at one time. As much as we might try, it is difficult to put all of these details out of sight and mind and concentrate on only a few of them at one time. The hierarchy can help by teaching us about central and peripheral focus. As you move

one issue into central focus, you will continue to be aware of other matters at the edge of consciousness. Thus, as you work at the top of the hierarchy you will probably also change words, rewrite sentences, and make other decisions about matters that should come later. That will present no problem unless you allow these smaller details to take over the field.

4. It encourages us to separate *creating* from *evaluating.* Writing is a creative activity. It is difficult to create something, and maintain your confidence in it, if you are attempting to evaluate it at the same time. Evaluation, if it is to be effective, requires that you look at your creative effort with an objective, critical eye. It is difficult to be objective about something you are still producing because you are investing time, effort, and ego in it. Evaluation is important. So save it for when you can devote your full attention to it.

Writing a First Draft

When you write your first draft you are working at the top of the hierarchy of editorial concerns. Your first concerns are the overall content, meaning, and organization of the draft. In a sense, you are staking out a territory that you will later develop. At this stage you can afford to ignore questions of precise word choice, correct sentence structure, paragraphing, and even examples. Your job is to attempt to execute your plan to see whether it will work. The following writing strategies will help you produce your draft.

1. **Plan ahead.** Obviously, you should try to plan *before* you begin to write a draft. It is difficult to think of and execute a plan at the same time. Planning gives you a chance to make many decisions ahead of time and provides you with a general structure or organization for your draft. Organizing will help you divide your subject into segments that you can work on one at a time. Each segment will be controlled by its major concept. If you try to rely on your memory, rather than a written plan, you will probably write whatever you can think of in whatever sequence it occurs to you. The result will probably be a mess that will take even more time to straighten out.

2. **Have realistic goals.** If you expect perfection on your first draft, you are putting yourself under a great deal of pressure. And you may be building failure into the process. On the other hand, if you don't expect much,

you will almost always come up with a draft that is better than you thought it would be. When that happens, the feeling of success will help motivate you to keep working. So, it may pay you to write a quick draft that you expect to revise, rather than to labor over a draft that you expect to be perfect.

3. **F**ollow your plan. Since you took the time to make a plan, try to follow it. It represents your best judgment about the subjects to include and the way to organize them. But try to be flexible, too. That is, as you write you may find that you think of new information you want to include or of new ways to organize your information. Take advantage of the insights that come to you as you work. Incorporate them into your first draft and see whether they work.

4. **U**se freewriting. In Chapter 2 you used freewriting as a tool for discovering what you know about your subject. You can use it now as a means of producing a draft. The main difference is that this time your freewriting will be focused on the goal of completing a text, rather than on uncovering information and ideas. Using freewriting in this way is an excellent means of getting yourself to work at the top of the hierarchy, rather than becoming bogged down in decisions (or indecisions) about details. It is also an excellent way to get yourself to write when you would much rather do something else. If you need to, go back to Chapter 2 and review the rules for freewriting.

5. **W**rite your draft in parts. Readers will usually begin reading at the beginning of your letter or report and read through to the end. But you need not write your draft in that sequence. You can begin wherever you are most comfortable and write the parts of your draft that you know most about. For example, introductions, such as the one in this book, usually appear at the beginning. But they are often written last, after writers have had a chance to get the whole project in focus. Once you have finished writing all the parts, you can fit them together, even move them around, and write the transitions that will get your reader from one part to the next.

6. **T**alk about your subject. You may feel more relaxed and confident talking than you do writing. Or you may feel that writing is too slow, that your hand cannot keep up with your thoughts. Perhaps you think more clearly when you talk. If so, recruit someone to listen to you as you talk about the draft you want to write. Having someone listen to you may help you focus your thoughts and concentrate on the job of making your ideas clear to a reader. But do make arrangements to keep track of what you say, so that your ideas will not disappear into the air. Ask your listener to take

notes, or use a tape recorder. It will help to keep your plan in front of you as you talk and refer to it often.

Your talking session may result in enough material for a first draft. If possible, have the tape transcribed into a triple-spaced, typed draft. Or listen to it and take notes.

7. **Change your tools.** Sometimes a simple change of tools or place (which also changes your pace, posture, and muscle use) will help you write. If you usually write with a pen and white paper, try a different kind of pen or paper. Or try a pencil. Try dictating. Change the size of the paper you use. Try composing on the typewriter. Change your chair or use a lapboard instead of a desk. Find an empty table down the hall. Just remember that the point of doing all this is to get something written.

8. **Change strategies.** Give each of these working methods a chance to work for you but try not to trap yourself by working in the same way all the time. If you have been using freewriting or dictating, and it dries up, try something else. You can use several or all of these methods and still emerge with a respectable first draft. Yes, it will need to be revised. But then almost everything needs to be revised.

9. **Wait.** Waiting can be one of the most valuable strategies of all. Once you have written something, get away from it for a while. You may be able to take only fifteen minutes to do something else, but that may be enough. If possible, let your writing sit overnight or longer. You will return to the job with new insights that have been developing since your last session, and your break may have helped you see your work more objectively.

Revising Your Draft

Most of us balk when we are told that we must redo something, especially if that something is writing. Doing it once is usually quite enough. We would like to finish and move on to something else. We too often think of rewriting or revising as a punishment for not doing something right the first time. But revising is not a punishment. Rather, it is an integral part of the writing process. You should expect to revise. So try to think of revising as finishing the job you have started, rather than as doing it over.

When you revise, just as when you write, you will work in the sequence outlined in the hierarchy of editorial concerns in Figure 4-1. That is, you will begin with the larger issues of content, meaning, and organization, which affect your entire draft. Then you will move to smaller and smaller details and finish your job with editing and proofreading.

The First Step: Review Your Draft

Revising begins with a thorough review of your first draft. You want to know whether the draft says what you think it says. And you must try to read your draft through your readers' eyes. But what exactly are you looking for?

1. **Does it make sense?** Of course, what we write almost always makes sense to us. But will it make sense to someone else? Review your draft carefully and ask the following questions.

Does your draft begin with a recognizable introduction that states your subject or the problem you are working on? Can you identify the subject in the first paragraph, or do you have to search for it? And does your introduction place your subject into a context for your readers, so they will know what they are reading, why they are reading it, and where it fits into their other business concerns? Your introduction, no matter how long or short it is, needs to announce your subject and provide recognizable reference points for it.

Try to answer the following questions about the middle sections of your draft:

a. Does each major section have some relationship to the subject or problem that you announced in the introduction?

b. Is each part related to the paragraphs or sections that precede and follow it?

c. Does each section contain data or examples that help your reader progress toward your conclusion?

d. Does any section repeat what you say in another section? If so, is that repetition useful? That is, will it help your reader by reinforcing an important point? Or are you simply writing several versions of the same section, trying to get it right?

e. Does each paragraph contain a main point that you explain?

f. Are your examples clearly related to the points you are using them to illustrate?

Have you provided a series of clues to help your reader follow your organization? It is true that you oriented your readers to your subject in the introduction. But you need to do this more than once. Readers always need to know where they have been and where they are going. You can help by providing summaries; transitional paragraphs; and brief, clear introductions and conclusions in each section. Be sure you do everything possible to make your organization explicit, and then do everything you can to follow the organization you have told your readers you are using.

Do you end with a well-supported conclusion? This might consist of a summary of your main points, a recommendation, or a solution. All of these, of course, must be based on the concepts and examples that you have provided throughout the draft. Read your conclusion carefully, and then review your draft to see that everything you mention in the conclusion has been mentioned somewhere earlier. Read your introduction and then your conclusion. Are they related to each other? If your introduction states a problem, does the conclusion offer a solution that is related to that problem?

2. **C**ompare your draft and your plan. As you wrote your first draft you used an issue tree, an outline, note cards, or perhaps simply a list of the major concepts that you wanted to include. Now is the time to compare that plan with what you have written.

Does your draft contain all of the major concepts, illustrations, and examples that you included in your plan? If it does, then you have executed your plan. If your draft does not reflect your plan, you need to find out why. Did you deliberately remove what is missing? Did you add something that is not in your plan? In each case, can you justify your decision? Is there a gap in your draft where you have removed something? Is the addition really important, or does it seem to be a digression?

You can check the structure and organization of your draft by making an outline or issue tree of it, without looking at your original plan. This will show you what you have actually achieved, rather than what you think you have achieved. Compare your new issue tree with the plan you used when you wrote; try to combine the two if they are significantly different.

3. **A**sk questions you think your reader will ask. You need to try to read your draft from your readers' point of view. Remember, they are trying to understand what you already know. Be tough on yourself. Whenever you make a statement or assertion, ask yourself, "How do you know?" When you use an example, a visual aid, or a list of data, ask, "How does this help make the point?" When you give statistics or other evidence, ask, "Where does this come from? Who says?"

Be sure you ask questions about the subject itself and the way you present it. Try to find those places in your draft where your reader will ask, "What does this mean?" And then try to answer that question honestly and thoroughly. Try to resist the temptation to assume that your readers will not notice when you have tried to evade contradictory evidence or gloss over missing facts. Assume that your reader will read your draft carefully and scrutinize every statement you make. Of course, not all readers will do that. But, if you have prepared for careful readers, you will also be prepared for busy readers who look only at the high points.

Once you have completed a review of your draft, you may be ready to write a second draft. If so, then go ahead and write it. If not, you may want to see how someone else reacts to your draft.

Getting Feedback from Test Readers

Ask someone to read your draft as soon as it is in good enough shape to be understood. It is not always easy to ask for help, because you are inviting criticism. Most of us don't like criticism, even when it is supportive and constructive. We have invested time and effort in our writing, and we want others to like it as it is. So the temptation is often to wait until the project is finished before we let anyone else see it. But by then we have so much invested in it that we are less willing than ever to listen to and benefit from their comments and reactions.

Try to collect comments and criticism as early as possible in the process, so you will have time to evaluate them, understand them, and incorporate the best into your revisions.

Select your test reader carefully. Look for someone whose opinions you respect and whose honest comments will not threaten you. Honesty is especially valuable in a test reader. The person who always praises your work is not giving it the thoughtful, probing review that you need.

It may help to select a reader who is like your intended reader. If you are trying to explain a complicated subject to a reader who knows very little about it, then select a test reader who knows little about your subject. If your intended reader is an expert in your subject, then only an expert will be able to help you strengthen your draft.

Encourage your test reader to ask difficult questions; encourage specific, detailed comments. Don't be satisfied with "That's fine" or "I like it." You can encourage your test reader to be thorough by asking specific questions about your introduction, transitions, examples, evidence, and conclusions. Make a special point of asking about those portions of your draft that you have doubts about. It may help to tell your test reader why you are writing, what you want to accomplish, and who your intended reader is. This will provide some context for your draft, and it may also give your test reader a standard for judging your success.

Ask your test reader some substantive questions about your subject. Assume that an attentive reader will have learned something from what you have written. So it is fair to ask a reader to identify your main point and to cite some of the supporting evidence. Ask test readers to summarize your draft in their own words. You may be surprised at some of the things they think you have said.

It is often useful to show your draft, clearly marked as such, to your supervisor or to the person who assigned the writing project to you. This will allow you to incorporate suggested changes without having to redo a final draft. Most supervisors will respect you for seeking assistance so long as you do not expect them to do your job for you.

Once you have had time to think about your test reader's suggestions, you can begin to work them into your plan, or to develop a new plan, and then write another draft. If you need to, you can take this draft through the same review process that the first draft has gone through.

Revising: An Example

The best way to learn to revise is to do it, lots of it. Proficiency will come with practice and with the repeated testing of your writing against others' reactions to it. It also helps to watch someone else revise. But, just as we seldom see working drafts, we seldom get to watch other people as they write and revise. In this section you will be able to watch the process that transforms a draft into a finished memo that is ready for its readers.

We will work with a memo (Figure 4-2) that a sales manager sent to his company's sales force, with copies to the President, Executive Vice President, and Advertising Manager. He considered the memo finished, but you will see that there is plenty of room for revision. Read it carefully and refer to it as you read the discussion that follows it. The paragraphs are numbered for easy reference.

Because you know the subject of this discussion is revision, you have probably already noticed a number of things in this memo that you think should be changed. List them now and then check your list against the comments and suggestions that follow.

Figure 4–2 Memo, Before Revision

INTERNAL CORRESPONDENCE

TO: All Sales Personnel
FROM: Cliff Morgan DATE: 3/9/81
SUBJECT: Fiscal 1981 Planning

(1) As everyone realizes very vividly, we have been an extremely successful company. Much of this success stems from the sales force we have, the sales clientele the force deals with, and, of course, the combination of these outer forces with the plant, drawing upon talent, capabilities, qualities, and existing and innovative technology.

(2) However, we have also been a very opportunistic organization. That, in itself, is not negative action but exploitation of presented situations. Where we have fallen is not building upon that opportunity across the board using all of our strengths and capitalizing on the full potential of the situation.

(3) We have also been an organization wherein our marketing planning leaves much to be desired. Our advertising and promotion efforts have not always supported the direction in which we want to proceed.

(4) These are only a few points but, yet again, reemphasization must be made that we have been successful! The question is, how successful can we really be?

(5) We do not want to disrupt the flow of individual activity. <u>But</u>, we must be certain that this flow of individual activity flows into a mainstream; that this mainstream has an organized beginning and that all of us together have a common direction of course, thereby increasing many fold over, the true strength of our force--our combined strength.

(6) With this thought in mind, we want <u>you</u> to be a vital part of this planning process. We need <u>your</u> input. By the end of March, we would like to have your thoughts as to where our direction of marketing activity should go; speak in both general and specific areas.

CM/dt

Getting Started: Overall Review

One of the first things you might have noticed while you read this draft is how easy and tempting it is to focus immediately on small, obvious problems and mistakes. It is difficult to ignore a word such as *reemphasization* in paragraph (4) or the repetition of *flow* in paragraph (5). But remember the hierarchy of editorial concerns. If you settle the larger issues of content, meaning, and organization first, many of the smaller problems will disappear before you have to deal with them. So begin with an overall review that focuses on subject, content, and goals.

1. **S**ubject, content, and goals. The subject line announces that the memo is about "Fiscal 1981 Planning," but it does not specify what kind of planning: budget planning, fiscal planning, or promotion and sales planning? In fact, the subject, which is marketing planning, is not clearly identified until paragraph (3). In paragraphs (1) and (2) the comments about success and opportunism may be an attempt to provide some background and prepare the way for a discussion of planning. Or they could be an attempt to soften the implied criticism in the memo that the company does not plan very well or very much. Paragraph (4) returns to the concept of "success," and readers are left to ponder the connections between marketing planning and potential success: "The question is, how successful can we be."

The subject of planning comes up again in paragraph (6), as the writer encourages everyone to participate and respond to the memo. Paragraph (5) is apparently meant to prepare the way for this. Its stress on the "flow of individual activity" and the need for a "common direction of course" seems meant to allay fears that centralized planning will somehow stifle individual initiative.

The memo's main goal seems to be to announce a process of marketing planning for the coming fiscal year, and to ask for ideas and comments from executives and sales personnel. There also seems to be a major subgoal of not appearing to criticize the company's past efforts (or lack of effort) at planning. Other subgoals seem to include:

Showing the potential value of planning

Showing that planning has not been done before

The writer has created problems for his readers because he has devoted most of his attention to his subgoals. He barely mentions his main goal or subject. Because of this, most readers are likely to react to this memo just as the company's President did: "What does he want?" Revision should focus on that question. In addition, we will need to decide whether the memo can bear the weight of the major goals and the subgoals together.

2. **O**rganization. Many of the problems in this memo can be corrected through careful organizing. We do not know what the writer's original organizing plan looked like, but we can work backward and infer it. One

way of doing this is to make an issue tree of the memo as we have it (see Figure 4-3).

We notice immediately that the issue tree in Figure 4-3 is "flat." That is, its ideas and subjects are not arranged in a hierarchy, but are all of relatively equal value. This impression is confirmed in the memo itself, where we find that about the same amount of space is devoted to each of the topics listed on the issue tree. It seems apparent that some thought has gone into this arrangement. The writer seems to want to focus on planning but also wants to avoid offending anyone by suggesting that past efforts at planning have been less than adequate. In the process, he has buried his main point where readers will almost certainly miss it.

We will need to reorganize the memo so that the main point, which is the plan to begin a marketing planning process, receives the attention it deserves. At the same time we will try to pay attention to the major subgoal of not criticizing past performance.

3. **Questions a reader might ask.** The third part of our review is trying to see the memo as a reader would and trying to ask questions a reader might ask. These would certainly include:

What is the main point here?

What do you mean by *opportunistic?*

How have past marketing plans fallen short?

How can we build on opportunities?

How successful *can* we be? Will you speculate?

What kinds of individual activity?

What do you want me to do?

Note that, at this point, the questions focus on major issues rather than minor ones. We are trying to settle on the memo's overall subject, content, and goals, not to argue about fine points. There are certainly other questions a reader might ask, and perhaps you can think of some of them. Do that, and incorporate your own questions into a plan for revising the memo.

Figure 4–3 Issue Tree for the Memo

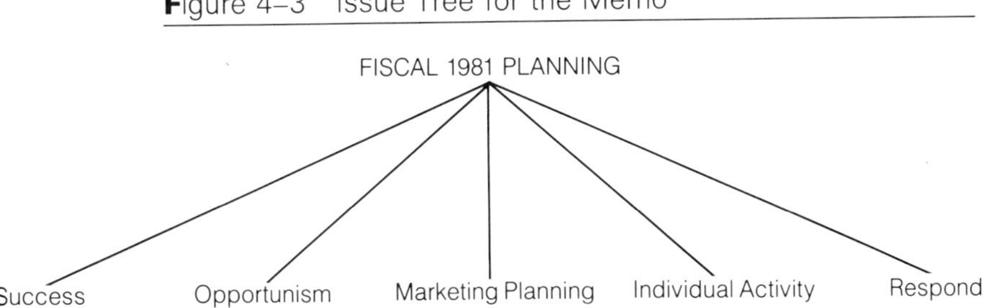

Suggested Changes: A Plan for Revising

This brief review has given us plenty to work with; yet we have barely touched on matters of grammar, punctuation, sentence and paragraph structure, or style. (These will receive more attention in Chapter 5.) But, if we revise carefully for goals, content, and organization, many of the smaller problems are likely to disappear before we have to do anything about them. At this point a plan for revising might include:

1. **A** new subject line. We want readers to know right away the kind of planning the memo is about. The subject line is the place to let them know that. It might read "Marketing Planning for Fiscal 1981." That immediately eliminates any other kinds of planning that readers might be involved in.

2. **F**ocus on major goals. The reorganized memo should make the main point, and the actions readers are to take, obvious. One way to do this is to begin with an issue tree that places the main topics and subtopics in a hierarchical order consistent with the writer's goals. Remember, the issue tree in Figure 4-3 needs depth. The new issue tree, in Figure 4-4, groups the memo's original six concepts into three main categories, and places them in a different sequence. The revised memo will:

   a. Announce that a planning process is under way and explain its purpose

   b. Explain why such a process is necessary and what it can accomplish for the company

   c. Request specific responses and tell readers when their suggestions are due

Figure 4–4 In-Depth Issue Tree

This plan should result in a memo that is more effective than the original. Here is a suggested second draft.

> During the next two months we will be planning our marketing campaign for the 1981 fiscal year. Our goal is to produce a comprehensive marketing plan for all of our divisions.
>
> We are a very successful company, but much of our success has come from taking advantage of opportunities that are presented to us. We do most of this through individual initiative and creativity, without much central coordination.
>
> We can be even more successful, and make the company even more profitable, if we can learn to direct individual efforts toward a common goal. Individual and unexpected opportunities will still be important, but we will be able to build on them for long-term growth and profits.
>
> It is important for everyone to take part in this planning. You each have an extensive knowledge of your departments, customers, and products. Put that knowledge to work. What should be our sales and marketing priorities for next year? For the next five years?
>
> I know that you all have ideas about what we should be doing in marketing. Give this some thought and let me hear from you by the end of March so we can discuss your ideas during our sales meeting.

Keep in mind that this is a second draft. Parts of it need more work. Particularly, since this is a new experience for the company, the Sales Manager might give more details to indicate the kinds of ideas he is looking for. That is, he can give his readers some guidance so they can productively answer the question "What does he want?"

Once you have taken revision this far, you have settled most of the major issues of content, organization, and goals. You may need to add illustrations and examples. You will certainly want to edit carefully for sentence structure, style, and correctness. The next chapter will consider those issues in some detail. In addition, you can consult Appendix A for questions of grammar and usage.

Making Writing and Revising Part of Your Day

How are you going to get the space, time, and quiet you need to write? Offices, dormitories, apartments, and lounges are busy places, and something is always happening to distract you from whatever you are doing. Phones ring, people need to see you, or they stop simply to take a break and talk. Sometimes, when the space around us is quiet, we create our own distractions. Some of us can work easily in the midst of confusion and clatter. Others need quiet and privacy.

You need to take positive steps to help you get your work done in noisy, confusing surroundings. Some of the following suggestions may help. Remember, if you wait for the quiet or the time you need, you will never get anything written.

Schedule Writing Time

Check your schedule carefully to find a time each day when you are most likely to be uninterrupted. Your goal is to find time to do your writing, to make it part of your day rather than something extra that you do when you have the time. When you have identified a time for writing, treat it as you would any other appointment or scheduled activity. Put it on your calendar. Tell secretaries and receptionists to hold your calls and divert casual visitors. If there are no people who can help you defend your time, then do it yourself by closing your door or posting a sign. Above all, avoid the temptation to schedule appointments for your writing time. That time is already committed.

If you take your own calls, learn to tell callers that you are busy and will call them back. You need not tell them what you are doing. They probably will not take you seriously if you tell them you are writing, since few people regard it as work. But you know that it is. Get off the phone as quickly as you can and get back to work. If visitors get through your defenses, look up at once and ask what they want. If you let them sit down, all is lost. One rather effective tactic is to stand up when people enter your office. They will be reluctant to sit unless you do, and they will soon leave.

Schedule Time for the Mail

The daily mail delivery is one of the reasons you write. You will need to answer much of what you receive. Get in the habit of handling the mail all at once, at a time convenient to you. There is no reason to deal with the mail at 10:00 A.M. just because that is when it is delivered. Keep pens, pads, and dictaphones handy as you read the mail and try to answer as much of it as you can in one sitting. Otherwise, if you read it once and then wait until later to do something about it, you will have wasted the time it took to read it the first time. Dictate replies right away or write your answers on the backs of incoming letters and memos. Ideally, you want to handle each piece of incoming, routine correspondence only once. Anything more is a waste of time.

Plan a Writing Schedule

When you receive a writing assignment that you cannot complete right away, assign a due date and put it on your calendar. Be sure you schedule adequate time to complete it. Try to estimate how much time it will take, how many work sessions you will need, and how soon you will be ready to start a first draft. Then set realistic goals for the amount of progress you want to make in each session. At worst, you will always know how far behind you are. At best, you will have divided the project into manageable chunks and set workable deadlines.

One common mistake is to underestimate the time it will take to write, revise, edit, and distribute a final draft. Thus, many people leave themselves inadequate time for these stages of the job. In most cases you should allow at least one-quarter of your time for writing. Thus, if you estimate that a project will take a month, allow at least one week for writing the draft and seeing it through to finished copy.

Organize Your Writing Jobs

Try to keep your writing tools and the projects you are working on organized and together so you can find them when you need them. If you have only half an hour to work, there is no point in spending it looking for pencils or the file you need.

A well-organized filing system will help you keep track of the ideas and information you gather. You may work on projects for several weeks, and you will have ideas about one while you are working on another. When this happens, you will need a place to file your notes so you can find them later. Keep a folder or card file for each major project you work on and identify a safe place in your office or desk so you can put your notes where you will be able to find them later. When it is time to go to work, you can simply pick up the file you need and begin.

Writing at School

Writing at school is not much different from writing at work, but the differences that do exist may require special steps. To begin with, your schedule at school is much less tightly structured than your schedule at work. To handle that freedom from supervision you will need effective study habits on which to build effective writing habits. School may present you with more of a problem in finding a quiet place to work, so you may have to look harder for a place where you can write. School also offers more distractions than an office. Something is always going on. Someone is always tempting you to leave your desk and do something else. You will need to resist these attractive nuisances and stick to your writing schedule.

Summary

Writing and revising are work. No one will deny that. They will, at times, be difficult, aggravating, and frustrating. But you can remove some of the frustration if you approach them systematically as a job to be done and as a job you can do. The major barriers to your success are procrastination and the belief that writing ought to be easier and faster than it usually is.

As you approach your writing tasks:

1. Remember the hierarchy of editorial concerns.
2. Develop and use effective writing and revising strategies.
3. Make writing part of your schedule at work or school, just as you would any other job you must do.

■

Exercises: Chapter Four

1. When you are assigned a writing project, how do you get it done? What methods do you use? Describe your own writing process or method in one or two pages.
2. Think about the place and time that you use when you write (at home, school, or work). Is it really equipped and organized for writing? How would you rearrange the place or reschedule the time? What methods can you use to defend this place and time?
3. For one week do an audit of how you spend your time. Divide each working day into half-hour or fifteen-minute segments and keep track of what you do during each segment. Then try to reorganize the way you spend your time so that you will be able to do everything that you are expected to do. Write a description of how you use your time and how you can use it more effectively in the future.
4. Choose one of the following topics and freewrite about it for five minutes.

Writing	Consumerism
Speaking	Listening
Advertising	Spelling
Success	Work

5. In exercise 1, Chapter 2, you were to brainstorm a list of facts or observations about one of the following topics. Return now to that list, organize the information, and write a brief presentation about the topic.

   Effective communiction on the job
   The effective supervisor
   Developing good study and work habits
   The social responsibilities of business
   What is a "good" job?

6. Exercise 1 in Chapter 3 asked you to organize a list of information about a fictitious company. Using the organizing plans you developed there, write three descriptions of the company. Each one, you will recall, should have a different goal or purpose.

7. Choose a subject from your major field of study, something you are interested in. Brainstorm, or use some other method, to generate information about this subject and then use an issue tree to help you organize this information. Rather than write, *talk* your explanation to someone else or to a tape recorder. While the talk is still fresh, freewrite to capture as much of it as you can recall.

8. Locate passages that need to be revised in magazines, government documents, or textbooks. Then use the hierarchy of editorial concerns to review these passages carefully and make whatever revisions you believe are necessary.

9. Use the hierarchy to revise the following letter. At each stage try to explain the changes that you make and why you think they are necessary.

   Ms. Brenda Smith, President
   Smith Corporation
   1138 Belleview Way
   Industrial City, GA 25000

   Dear Ms. Smith:

   I have lived now in Industrial City for over two years and I must say that I have never lived in a finer place. And I have lived in a good many of them both here and in other countrys.

   I am writing you becuase I have an idea and I think you might be able and willing to help me with it. I am a retired military man and I know that many of our retired servicemen need help with their problems with alcohol. They get thrown out of the service after 20 years and cant really get the help they need in the veteran's hospitals. I am sure that with just a little help they could dry themselves out and continue with a productive life.

I know that your company gives grants every year to charitable groups, and this group would be charitable, since we would not charge for our services. I would like to set up a halfway house for veterans and retired military to help them kick the bottle habit and get back on their feet. It would only take about $10,000 to rent an office in the Taylor Building on Fourth Street and advertise for those who need help. We would provide counseling, job help, and friendship to these people, who need it so much.

I would appreciate your assistance. Please let me know if you or your company can do this for us. We served our country well.

Sincerely,

Arnold J. Billingsley, Ret.

10. Find a set of instructions for assembling or using a product and review them carefully. Use the hierarchy to revise them so that they will be easier to follow. (User manuals for computers, software, calculators, and electronic components will often provide instructions in need of revision.) Include a copy of the original with your revision.

5

Revising for Style

Once you are satisfied that your draft contains all of the information your reader needs, and that you have organized it as well as you can, you need to turn your attention to questions of style. Style concerns *how* you say something, rather than *what* you say. It is important because readers will often pay as much attention to style as they do to content.

A clumsy sentence or an inappropriate word may be enough to distract your readers from your message. The result is that they pay more attention to your mistakes than they do to your successes. And they will judge you by your mistakes. That is the same as judging a product by its packaging rather than by its quality. It may seem silly, but it happens. This means that you must see that your packaging is of the same quality as your information and ideas.

Losing Your Reader: Seven Easy Lessons

Ideally, we would like our readers to stay with us through an entire letter, memo, or report. It may be too much to ask them to read every word, but we would at least like them to stay around long enough to get the gist of what we are saying. However, readers are notoriously easy to lose. Give them the slightest excuse and they go sliding off the page into something more interesting. Readers do have some responsibility to pay attention, but we need to help them. If you *want* to lose your readers, try these easy methods.

1. **U**se too many words. Whenever you can, make twelve words do the work of two. Instead of saying, "Please join us on Friday," say "We would be delighted, if you have the time, if you would give us the pleasure of your attendance at our meeting on this coming Friday in the morning." Instead of explaining that "there was a mistake on the shop drawings," tell your readers that "the situation is the result of an unavoidable oversight in the engineering drawing department that provided incorrect information to the machine operator." Do this consistently in every sentence and you will send your reader to the water cooler faster than the hottest August day.

Many people write this way deliberately. They believe, or someone has told them, that they sound more important and impressive if they use as many words as they can. Long, wordy sentences also seem to make everyday, uncomplicated ideas seem more profound than they really are, and no one wants to seem common or unprofound.

But, if you want your reader to stay around, you will need to simplify your draft and use fewer words. You can do that the same way you made it longer: sentence by sentence and word by word. It won't do to simply cut whole paragraphs or sections. You might throw away something important. Instead, you will need to look carefully at each sentence and try to find a shorter, more straightforward way of saying it. It may take time to do this, but it is time well spent, as this example shows:

> It has come to our attention through many years of experience that when customers become aware of malfunctions they invariably place a service call instead of referring to the instruction manual provided and attempting to see whether they can make the necessary repairs themselves at considerably less expense.

A shorter version of this sentence will accomplish the same goal. Try this:

> You can often correct malfunctions on the spot by reading the instruction manual and making needed adjustments.

2. **R**epeat yourself. Always assume that your readers need two or three passes through a phrase or idea before they finally get the point. Like this:

> On Wednesday January 15 at 3:00 P.M. there will be a meeting of Ms. Baker, Mr. Helm, and Mr. Throckmorton in the small conference room. These representatives of their departments,

> Finance, Accounting, and Data Processing, will meet at that time to discuss ways in which their respective departments can cooperate in processing and making available the weekly cash-flow and investment reports so that they will be available as early as possible each week for review by the Vice-President for Finance.

Are you still there? Possibly your readers will be, because they need the information. But why should they have to wade through that to find out what they need to know? Eliminate the repetitions, consolidate what is left, and you might get something like this:

> TO: Mr. Helm(Accounting)
> Ms. Baker (Finance)
> Mr. Throckmorton (Data Procesing)
> FROM: J. Henley, VP, Finance
> SUBJECT: Meeting
> We will meet at 3:00, Friday, January 15 in the small conference room to find a way of making the weekly cash-flow and investment reports available earlier in the week than they are at present.

Note how the use of a heading and subject line allowed this writer to simplify the body of the memo. With the incidental information out of the way, the writer was able to focus on the location, time, and purpose of the meeting. Everyone who receives a copy will know exactly what is required.

3. **U**se big words. Big words and unusual words will probably make you sound important. They will certainly give your readers some much-needed practice with the dictionary. Never take something apart; *disassemble* it. Never put something together; *integrate* it. Refer to the snack bar as a *refreshment stand.* Never simply talk with people; always *conference* or *interface* with them. Files are more impressive if you call them *repositories,* and cardboard boxes can be *containers.* Jobs become *positions,* people become *personnel,* and offices and factories become *facilities.*

The secret to writing this way is to replace as many one-syllable words as possible with multisyllable words. Never change a product; *reconfigure* it.

Of course, such an inflated vocabulary can make you seem pompous rather than important. And it often provides your readers with comic relief rather than dictionary practice. You can prevent this by reviewing your drafts very carefully for multisyllable and unusual words that seem to be doing the work of perfectly adequate shorter words. In most cases you can safely choose the shorter, simpler, clearer word.

4. **U**se oblique references. Never use *I* or *you* or refer to anything by its name or title. Instead, call yourself *the writer* or *the undersigned,* and

always call your reader *the reader.* Always refer to *the above-mentioned subject* or *the above-captioned document,* rather than calling anything by its name. And remember that people don't have names. Refer instead to *the parties in question* or *said customer.* These kinds of references sound vaguely legal and official, so they will probably make your reader think you are writing about something that is really important. They will certainly keep your reader digging around on the page, looking backward and forward, trying to find out exactly what you mean.

5. **B**e obvious. Readers are not very smart anyway, so they won't mind if you tell them what they already know. Always begin by saying something like: "I have received your request for information about the WIT-50 timekeeper punch clock." Maybe your reader will not notice that you could not answer the request unless you had received it. Sometimes it helps to label your statements as obvious, in case your readers are too slow to notice that they already know what you are telling them. When you want to do this, you can use phrases such as "As you know," or "As Ms. Smith told us last week."

Astute readers will ask why you are taking their time to tell them something they already know. And they may take that as an insult to their intelligence. After all, if Ms. Smith told both of you, what makes you think that your reader is the one who forgot it? Phrases such as these are often mere crutches for people who have not taken the time to think about what they are writing. Their pens are moving, but their minds are not in gear. If your reader already knows something, then use that knowledge as the starting point for what you write.

6. **U**se clichés. Whenever you have trouble thinking of a word that expresses your meaning, use one that everyone else has used at least 50,000 times.The boss's new son-in-law is probably a chip off the old block, especially if his ideas hold water. You might run a new product up the flagpole to see if anyone salutes it. If not, you could suffer a fate worse than death. But, if it works, you will be the apple of the boss's eye, a budding genius who has invented the greatest thing since sliced bread.

See? Clichés can give your writing the sparkle and vitality that will make you the envy of everyone in the office. With very little effort you can write an entire letter or report without saying anything original. And that is just the problem. Clichés mean whatever people want them to mean, rather than what you want them to mean. They give your readers the feeling that they are hearing reruns of old comedy shows, and thus they rob your writing of the seriousness and precision that you want it to have. There are other ways of achieving sparkle and originality.

7. **U**se plenty of nouns. Unlike verbs, which suggest movement, nouns just sit there. Never decide; always make a decision. Never simply answer a question; construct a reply. Remember that nothing ever smells or stinks; it has an odor or stench. Never do something quickly; always act in an expeditious manner.

You can sometimes turn your use of nouns into a high art. Instead of taking charge of a situation, you can practice a management intervention technique. Never simply take something apart; use integrated disassembly techniques. Rather than test a market, you can do a product feasibility study. The beauty of these noun phrases is that they are easy to make up. In a few minutes of doodling you can think of enough of them to last you all week. Think of it as a coordinated communications strategy.

Here is an example:

> It is of the utmost importance that management personnel whose positions require involvement in on-site discussions of manufacturing process disputes use established conflict resolution techniques that have the approval of Corporate Headquarters and the Grievance Officer of the union local.

This may get the job done, but it seems a roundabout approach to say:

> Managers who resolve grievances should use procedures that Corporate Headquarters and the union local have approved.

Your readers will probably love your noun phrases, because they will know that there is no point in trying to figure out what you are saying. And you will be providing material for the next time they have to confuse their readers.

These seven strategies are not the only ways to lose, confuse, and mystify your readers, but they are among the most effective. If you use them all in the same letter or report, it will be months before anyone figures out that you have nothing to say. That will give you plenty of time to look for a new job.

Building Relationships with Readers

Of course, it is possible that you don't want to lose or confuse your reader. You might even be interested in building a positive relationship by portraying yourself and your reader as intelligent, capable, sensitive people. Style plays a role in that too, because your style is responsible for the *tone* of what you write. Tone is easy to create and detect when you are speaking or listening, because much more information is available in those situations. Tone of voice and nonverbal messages will give us clues about how we are to take what is being said. We know, for example, that it is easy to say "hello" in either a welcoming or nasty way, and that both meanings are easy for us to give and detect.

But when you write you have only the words on the page to carry the meanings that you usually convey through your tone of voice and nonverbal messages. That means you must be sensitive to the connotations or implied meanings of the words and phrases you use. When you discover that you have used a word or phrase that has a negative, accusing, or unflattering connotation or implication, replace it with another word that does not carry that meaning. Here are some of the typical connotations and implications you will need to watch for.

"I Don't Believe You"

Disbelief is often implied through words such as *claim, trust,* and *alleged.* For example, if you say, "You claim that you have followed instructions," you are suggesting that you really believe otherwise. If you say, "I trust you will find these arrangements satisfactory," you may be suggesting that you know they are anything but satisfactory, but that you want your readers to accept them because, in fact, they have no choice.

"You're Stupid, and I'll Prove It"

If you have stepped into the trap of trying to prove your reader's stupidity, you will find yourself using phrases such as "Only a few, select customers are receiving this offer." Such offers, of course, usually arrive third class, bulk rate mail, complete with preprinted signature. Or you may say, "This exciting discovery will change your life." Most of your readers know that there are few "exciting new discoveries" in this world, and that even fewer of them will change anyone's life. Sometimes you will find that you have used a phrase like this one: "If you will merely look at the instructions. . . ." This suggests that your reader was too dense to have read the instructions in the first place (she probably *has* read them), but it is the *merely* that does the real damage because of its impatient, condescending tone.

"You Must Be Wrong (Because I'm Not)"

Some writers will come right out and say that their readers cannot possibly be correct, but most of us are more subtle. We write sentences like this one: "I was surprised to hear that the product did not work." Products, for this person, are infallible, and customers not to be trusted. Sometimes this attitude is not the result of a single word or phrase, but pervades an entire passage, like this:

> The product has been thoroughly tested in our laboratories and has been test-marketed in several geographical regions. Most of our customers reported that they liked the new version much better than the old one.

This writer is really saying, "So what's wrong with you? If everyone else likes it, you must be weird." It might be better to give the real reasons for the change (perhaps the old product was not profitable), rather than trying to justify it at the expense of offending a customer.

"If You Insist"

Consider this phrase: "Although the error did not originate in our accounting department, we will reprocess the statement in order to preserve our long-standing relationship." That writer is really saying, "I'll do it, but under protest. It's really your fault." Surely there are better ways to preserve relationships.

Someone else might say, "We are under no obligation to honor contracts made by the former owner. However, in your case we have reluctantly decided to do so." My, my, aren't we being magnanimous today. Even if the decision is "reluctant," why advertise it that way once you have made it? On the one hand, writers like this want us to appreciate their generosity, but then they tell us that they are not being generous at all. Your readers and your relationships with them would be better served by a simple explanation of what you are going to do.

"We Really Want Your Business"

In fact, we are absolutely desperate for it. These writers say things like "Thank you in advance for your order" and sprinkle the page with phrases like "we would be very pleased," "our pleasure," "if you wish," "if it is convenient," and others that suggest they are bowing, scraping, and practically drooling for your business. Their letters and memos drip with sincerity, and it is the excess that causes the problem. No one is *that* sincere.

Editing

After you have revised your draft to eliminate the stylistic excesses that might confuse or offend your readers, it is time to edit. Editing is a last, careful pass though the draft to ensure that everything is the way you want it and that there are no mistakes to embarrass you. Remember, you have already settled the major issues of content and organization, and you have made most of the necessary major changes in your draft. When you edit, you are working at the lower end of the hierarchy of editorial concerns, so your attention will be on details.

Editing will be easier if you know how to go about it and what to look for. You can follow the general outline of the hierarchy, just as you did for revising. That is, begin with those details that affect your entire draft and then move to those that affect only a single sentence or word. Thus, you will begin with a review of your entire draft and then move to smaller and smaller sections. When you have questions you can consult any standard grammar reference or handbook, your company's style manual (if there is one), or Appendices A and B of this book. For now, we will concentrate on what you should look for.

Format

1. Headings and subheadings. Levels of headings should be consistent throughout the draft. That is, all main headings should have the same typography, spacing, and placement. All subheadings should also be alike.

This is a good time to check once again to see that all main headings introduce major concepts that are of equal importance. Subheadings should indicate the major subdivisions of each main concept.

2. Indentation. Indentations from the left margin, for whatever purpose, should be consistent throughout your draft. All paragraphs should begin at the same number of spaces from the left margin. Quotations and other materials you wish to separate visually from the rest of your text should also be consistently indented. If you have used indentation and numbering to indicate subsections of your draft, review these to be sure you have used a consistent system throughout.

3. Page numbering. Numbering is a small detail, but one that is easily overlooked. Be sure all of your pages are numbered and that you have arranged them in the proper sequence. Make it easy for a typist to follow your draft.

Visual Aids

Take a minute to look at all of your visual aids, including graphs, charts, tables, drawings, and any other supplementary materials you want to include. The first step, of course, is to be sure that they are all there. It is easy to misplace or forget to make a visual aid. If anything is missing, get it now and include it in the draft. This is also a good time to be sure that you have all of the enclosures you want to include with letters or memos. Once you are sure all of your supplementary material is present, check it for:

1. **N**umbering. Visual aids should be numbered sequentially throughout your draft, and they should be referred to by their numbers. So make sure the numbers are correct and that references in your draft direct readers to the proper visual aid.

2. **L**egends and labels. Be sure each visual aid has a title or legend that explains what it is. While you are checking this, you can also look at each visual aid to be sure all labels and legends are legible. Readers should not have to wonder what any part of a graph, chart, or drawing means.

3. **P**lacement. Have you indicated where the visual aids should be placed in your draft? If they are to be interspersed in the text, you should indicate where they belong. If they are to be on separate sheets but following the discussion that refers to them, they should be interleaved in the draft in their proper places. If they are to be gathered at the end of your draft, they should all be there in the proper sequence.

Paragraphs

You have already reviewed each paragraph for content and organization. You have also checked format, so you know each paragraph begins with the proper indentation and spacing. Take a minute now to review the length of your paragraphs. There are no rules for paragraph length. But remember that long, dense blocks of writing increase the possibility that you will lose or confuse your reader. Most of your writing will come back from the typist single-spaced, and this will increase the appearance of density. It is important to give your readers a visual break rather often. Check your draft to see if you can achieve an *average* paragraph length of between eight and twelve lines. Of course, some will be longer, and some shorter. But, as an average, a length of eight to twelve lines will make life much easier for your readers. If you need to make adjustments, look for places where you can break long paragraphs into two or three shorter ones. Try to follow the logic of your content, rather than making the breaks arbitrary. In the same way, you can combine extremely short paragraphs, especially if there are several of them in a row. You may, of course, need to write brief transitions to put them together smoothly.

Sentences

Now is the time to look closely at each sentence. Read each one carefully, one by one. What are you looking for?

1. **C**omplete sentences. Look for comma splices, fragments, and run-on sentences. Appendix A will help you identify these problems if you have questions. As you edit, you might look in the places that these seem most likely to occur: first and last paragraphs. Many writers begin letters and memos with phrases such as "Referring to your letter of June 14." (Letters and memos should not begin with such stock phrases, but many do.) This one is not a sentence, but a fragment. Similarly, many writers end their letters and memos with fragments such as "Hoping to hear from you." Review your sentences carefully for completeness.

2. **P**arallel structure. Whenever you use a series, either in a sentence or in a list, try to give the parts of the series in parallel grammatical structure. That is, call attention to the similarities of the items in the series or list by using the same grammatical structure to introduce or name each one. If one is, for example, expressed as a verb phrase, then make all of them verb phrases. If one is a noun phrase or infinitive, make all of them noun phrases or infinitives. A sentence like this one, "The meeting will deal with manufacturing, distributing, and how we market our products," should be rewritten this way (changes are in italic): "The meeting will deal with manufacturing, distributing, and *marketing* our products."

Parallel structure can also be important in signaling transitions or continuity in or between paragraphs. For example, you can emphasize similarity and continuity by using the same phrase to introduce a series of sentences. "Our new five-year plan *should* help us accomplish three goals. *It should* allow us to predict fluctuations in our market. *It should* allow us to allocate limited financial resources to products with the greatest profitability. *It should* allow us to develop products for new and expanding markets."

If you need help with parallel structure, consult Appendix A.

3. **P**ronoun reference. Pronouns (*I, you, he, she, it, we, you, they, them, their, me, mine, my, our, ours, who, whom, some, any, few,* and so on) should clearly refer to the nouns they stand for. For example, "Managers like engineers because they are pragmatic and logical" is ambiguous because

it does not tell clearly whether the managers or the engineers are "pragmatic and logical." You might revise the sentence this way: "Managers like the logical, pragmatic approach that engineers take to problems." In this sentence, "John called the Quality Assurance manager, but he was busy and didn't follow through," who was busy, John or the manager? Try it this way: "After he called the Quality Assurance manager, John got busy and didn't follow through."

If you need help with pronoun reference, consult Appendix A for assistance.

4. **M**isplaced modifiers. Always place modifiers so that they point clearly to a word or phrase they modify. If you get them out of place, they will refer to the wrong part of your sentence. To illustrate this, let's look at the word *only,* which often causes problems. In the sentence "He only arrived this morning," you would be saying that he arrived this morning and did nothing else. What you would mean, though, is that "He arrived only this morning." In the revised sentence, *only* modifies when he arrived, rather than his arrival itself. Similarly, *only* is misplaced in this sentence: "He only said that to make you feel good." Instead, you should write, "He said that only to make you feel good."

5. **D**angling modifiers. Dangling modifiers point to something that is not part of the sentence. That is, in the process of writing the sentence, a writer leaves out the word or phrase that the modifier points to. For example, "Knowing that you are a careful worker, the finished product will be excellent," says that the finished product knows you are a careful worker. Revise the sentence to show who knows, like this: "Knowing that you are a careful worker, we are sure the finished product will be excellent."

While misplaced and dangling modifiers will sometimes obscure your meaning, more often they will suggest that you are a careless writer who does not know or care enough to construct sentences carefully. Some readers will not understand sentences with misplaced or dangling modifiers, and other readers will simply refuse to take you seriously because of your error.

6. **A**ctive or passive voice. English sentences can use either the active or the passive voice. The distinction is really quite simple. In the active voice the subject comes first, then the verb, then the predicate. Someone (the subject) is doing something (the verb) to, with, or for someone or something else. For example, "Ms. Barnes told me to see if the Jones order is ready yet," is in the active voice. So is this sentence: "George is going to bring the auditor's report over this afternoon."

The passive voice reverses the order of the sentence parts. The following sentences are in the passive voice. "I was told by Ms. Barnes to see if the Jones order is ready yet" and "The auditor's report will be brought over this afternoon by George."

Many people will advise you to avoid the passive voice, and in general that is not bad advice. Passive constructions usually take more words than active constructions that say the same thing. And passives can often seem tortuous and difficult to read. For the most part, you will want to write in the active voice.

But there are uses for the passive voice. Primarily, it allows you to achieve obscurity when you need to, and you *will* need to on occasion. Try this: "Because of rising costs and decreasing sales, I have decided to reduce the number of people in each department by 20 percent." This sentence, in the active voice, clearly identifies the *I* who is making the decision and puts that person on the spot. The passive, on the other hand, often allows the writer to disappear entirely: "Because of rising costs and decreasing sales, it has been decided to reduce the number of people in each department by 20 percent."

6. **P**unctuation. As you read each sentence, check for punctuation. The most common problems you will encounter will probably be with internal punctuation, so check that carefully.

a. Be sure that all items in series are separated by commas. "We traveled to Milwaukee to see how the home office wants us to deal with accounting, data processing, and financial reporting."

b. Be sure you separate independent clauses with a comma and a coordinating conjunction. If you do it this way—"We went to Chicago, we saw the World Trade Center"—you have written a comma splice. Insert *and* after the comma.

c. If you use a semicolon, remember that it usually has the same function as a period, so it belongs at the end of clauses that could stand by themselves as sentences, like this one: "We'll call John; he has the new marketing plan." You can also use semicolons to separate items in a series when commas alone would be confusing, or when phrases in the series already contain commas. If you want to refer to "Tom, the Vice President, Ann, the Marketing Director, and Toby, the Advertising Manager," you may need to clarify that you are referring to only three people. You can do that with semicolons: "Tom, the Vice President; Ann, the Marketing Director; and Toby, the Advertising Manager."

7. **W**ords. At this stage you need to be sure you have used words correctly and consistently. Later, when you proofread, you can check spelling and other potential problems with words.

Read your draft to be sure that you have not written *affect* when you meant *effect,* or *then* when you meant *than.* It is also easy to confuse *accept* and *except,* and other words that sound alike. You will find a list of such confusing words in Appendix A. Consult it as you edit.

In addition to using words correctly, you will need to be sure you use words consistently. That is, does a word mean the same thing to you every time you use it? Or are there slight variations in meaning that you will be aware of but your reader will not. Do you give people the same, correct titles each time you mention them? Have you defined technical terms and used them with the same meaning each time? Are objects, concepts, procedures, and locations given the same name or title each time you mention them? Consistency will help your reader make sense of what you write.

Proofreading

When you have finished editing your draft, you should be ready to send it to a typist. Before you do that, you need to proofread it carefully. Proofreading is more than rereading. It is a careful, word-by-word or line-by-line review of your draft to be sure that everything is as it should be. You need to proofread your draft both before and after it is typed.

Most of us do not like to proofread, so we need some way of forcing ourselves to do it carefully. Otherwise, we will start to skim over the text very quickly, and we are sure to miss something.

Step One

Use a card, ruler, or sheet of paper to cover the lines that you are not reading. Place a full sheet of blank paper on your draft so that it covers everything except the bottom line. That's right, the bottom line. The blank paper will keep your eyes focused on that line until you are finished with it.

Now read the bottom line *backward,* from right to left. This will force you to focus on one word at a time. The text will not make sense, but it does not need to. You are looking for misspelled words and typographical errors, such as *thier* and *nto.* You will find them only if you look carefully, word by word. When you finish one line, move the blank page up and go on to the line above the bottom line. In this way, work your way up the page. Read everything, including the subject line, inside address, even the date.

Step Two

Once you have finished reading word by word from bottom to top, right to left, you will read it again. This time use the card or blank sheet of paper to mask off everything but the *top* line, and read the draft through in normal sequence. This will give you different kinds of information than you got from reading backward. Now you will be able to tell whether all of the words in the draft are the right words, the ones you want. Earlier you might have passed by *our* because it is spelled correctly. This time you will notice that it should be *are* or *hour* and that *their* should be *there.*

You will also be able to see whether any extra words have slipped in or if you have left anything out. If you leave *not* or *never* out of a sentence, you reverse the meaning you intend.

As you read forward, you will also be able to check once again for punctuation and sentence structure. The blank sheet of paper will continue to help you focus on one line at a time, so you will be able to resist the natural tendency to skip ahead.

When the typist returns your draft to you, proofread it again, using the same method, and compare it with your original. Good typists always return your original to you. If you dictated the draft, you can get the tape or belt and listen to what you said. Typists are human, and they make mistakes. They will not resent your asking them to correct an error. In fact, those who take pride in their work will insist on it. Only when you are satisfied that the final version is exactly as you want it should you sign it and send it to your reader.

Summary

Revising for style, editing, and proofreading are the last steps of preparing your manuscript for your reader. If you have followed the hierarchy of editorial concerns you have established the content and organization of your letter or report. Now look closely at each sentence and word. Try to avoid confusing, losing, or offending your reader.

■

Exercises: Chapter Five

1. Almost every day most of us receive letters that attempt to sell us something or ask us to donate money to worthy causes. Collect a few

of these letters and review them carefully to see if they violate or observe the guidelines presented in this chapter. When they depart from these guidelines, revise them so that they are more effective.

2. Locate a magazine or journal article that is about some subject in your major field of study. As you read it, watch for repetition, wordiness, and words that are too obscure or complicated for the message they convey. Revise several paragraphs of the article to eliminate these (and any other) problems.

3. In a local or campus newspaper find an editorial, a column or feature, or a letter to the editor. Use the hierarchy of editorial concerns to revise it so that it accomplishes its goal more effectively. Include a copy of the original with your revision.

4. Your great-aunt, Miss Alma Bartlett, has received the following letter. Revise it and then write a letter to the person who wrote it. Explain your revisions and recommend a change in style for future letters.

> Dear Miss Bartlett:
>
> We have your letter of January 14 about the Model 14 food blender that you claim does not work as our advertisements say it should.
>
> We have researched this blender thoroughly and subjected prototype and production models to extensive tests. Frankly, we are surprised that you say you are experiencing difficulty with it. Our tests indicate that this model will work under almost all conditions. It should, as you point out, shred carrots, turnips, and radishes without difficulty.
>
> We believe the blender operates as advertised. However, because we do not want to offend you or any of our customers in any way, we will replace yours if you wish. After all, we have found that the best advertisement is a satisfied customer.
>
> When you return your blender to us, we will ship you a new one. Before you use it, please read the instructions carefully. After all, a stitch in time saves nine, and it's better to be safe than sorry.
>
> Very truly yours,
>
> R. W. Calendar

5. Edit and proofread the following letter.

> Dear Ms. Dent:
>
> Thank you for your recant purchase of the XL-100 television from our local distributor, Bud's, at 443 Market Way in Baltimore.
>
> We are sure that you will find, over a period of time and with conscientious use, that the XL-100 is among the finest, most exciting, highest quality televisions you could own. It was developed over a period of years, six to be exact, during which extensive time we attempted to combine all of the best, most popular, high-quality features of the most popular television sets on the market and available to the public.
>
> The XL-100 is the result of these years of research and development.

> It is truly a fine piece of electronic equipment. We hope it will serve you for many years to come, many trouble-free, enjoyable viewing years.
>
> Be sure to stop by Buds whenever it is convient and look at the other lines of electronic equipment and appliances that are available there. We'd like to keep you using our products for years and years.

6. Rewrite the following sentences so that they avoid the stylistic faults pointed out in this chapter. Keep in mind that there is more than one way to revise each sentence.

- **a.** A count will be made tomorrow morning to determine how many tools owned by the company are missing from the shop area.
- **b.** The new union contract should do three things. Reduce the number of grievances. We should be able to go three years without a strike. And it should also enable us to increase our production.
- **c.** He can only speak for himself, not for the company.
- **d.** Looking at next year's production, custom-built products should be up about 50 percent.
- **e.** We will need to have all field reports as soon as possible. Certainly by the end of March.
- **f.** When the auditors have finished their report, send it to myself for approval.
- **g.** When somebody sees this report they will think we had a terrible sales record this year.
- **h.** We received the latest shipment of new parts yesterday, it will take us a week to be sure we have received everything we ordered.
- **i.** There are several reasons for our decision to close the plant. It is an old building. We have found it difficult to heat and maintain. Population shifts have left a smaller, older work force in the area.
- **j.** It has been decided that all new employees will serve a six-month probationary period.
- **k.** Yesterday, while we were looking for the latest shipment on the loading dock, we decided the company needs a new invoice control system.
- **l.** The Anderson contract was finally completed yesterday at five o'clock, after we located the missing copies of the specifications.
- **m.** By rearranging the typing pool, productivity increased by 15 percent.
- **n.** We recovered a copy of the report from the Midwest office that we thought had been lost in the fire.
- **o.** We established the Sales and Marketing Group so that it could monitor sales. We also want it to establish quotas for sales territories, and we won't object if it does some redrawing of territorial boundaries.

- **p.** Tom Grimes said that he saw Mr. Anderson last week but he was unable to convince him of the need for a new production schedule.
- **q.** The Production Control Department has designed a new inventory form. Which they say will help them keep track of raw material more closely.
- **r.** As was said by the Vice President last week, the decision to eliminate the product was the result of a careful study conducted by the Marketing and Accounting Departments.
- **s.** Management Information Systems has devised a computer program that will allow everyone in the Accounting Department to know about transactions as soon as they occur, this should keep our cash flow at a maximum. Especially on weekends.
- **t.** The company has devised a new retirement plan. They hope it will encourage a number of people to retire early.
- **u.** Before we approve the new product we need to know if it will be profitable, whether it will attract new customers, and how durable it is.
- **v.** The St. Louis office sent in this request for a price quotation, they want us to try to come in at least 10 percent under our most recent quotation, or the competition may get the contract.
- **w.** We finally gave up all hope of finishing on Thursday. The meeting having lasted well past five o'clock.
- **x.** The campaign having lasted for six weeks, the product was approved for nationwide distribution.
- **y.** The personnel department has notified us that we should invite no more candidates for interviews without their approval.

■

Part 2

Writing Business Correspondence

6

Writing Letters: An Overview

Much of your writing at work will consist of letters. You will write to clients, customers, suppliers, consumers, government agencies, and many others. Some of your letters will provide information that your readers need. Others will ask for information that you need. Still others will attempt to persuade your readers to do something you want them to do. Every letter you write will be unique in some way, because each one will respond to its own, specific situation and reader. But, in spite of their individual differences, all letters have a great deal in common. These common features will make your job easier because they will allow you to plan, organize, and write more efficiently than if you had to approach each letter as a unique task. The purpose of this chapter is to introduce and explain those matters of planning, organizing, and style that all letters have in common.

At the end of this chapter you should have a set of guidelines and planning strategies that you can apply to any letter you write, in any situation, regardless of its subject, goal, or reader. These guidelines will include:

1. Planning for your subject, goal, and reader
2. Deciding whether writing is appropriate
3. Using three basic organizing patterns
4. Observing some basic rules of style

Subject, Audience, and Purpose

Subject

Each letter you write will have its own subject, and you will need to know that subject thoroughly if you are to write about it intelligently and informatively. But we can generalize about subjects that are appropriate to letters: They are limited, often to one or two main points. There are good reasons for this. First, business letters are not usually long. Most do not exceed one single-spaced page, and very few are longer than two single-spaced pages. To write more than this is to ask your readers to invest more time and energy in your subject than they might think it is worth. Topics that are too complex to be treated within the space of the usual business letter are best made the subject of reports. Then, if the situation still requires a letter, you can include a cover letter that introduces your report and explains its highlights and conclusions.

A second reason that letters treat limited subjects is that they often deal with very specific questions or requests. Perhaps someone has written to ask about a particular product or service your company provides or to ask you to do a specific job. Your reply will provide information related to the request or question. There is no need to explain bulldozers if you have been asked about lawnmowers. If you have a question about a product or service, your letter will explain why you are interested and what you want the product to do for you. That is, you will confine yourself to information that will help your reader answer your question.

Audience

Almost every letter you write will have a specific reader. (You will, of course, find a use for form letters, but even in this case you are writing to a group of readers who are quite similar in specific ways.) It is unlikely that you will know most of your readers, and your exchange of letters may be the only time that the two of you interact with each other. So what can we say that is almost always true of almost all readers?

Perhaps the most important fact you can remember about those who read your letters is that most of them will not belong to your organization. They are "outsiders"; they do not know you or your company. Nor do they know what you are like, how you operate, the kinds of problems you face, or the kinds of people your company employs. They may also lack your technical expertise.

Writing to an outsider is not the same as writing to someone who understands you, your company, your products, and your job as thoroughly as you and your coworkers do. You need to learn to think like an outsider and ask "What does my reader need to know in order to understand what I'm saying?"

Try to remember that your reader lacks information, not the ability to understand it. We are all outsiders somewhere, no matter how intelligent or informed we may be about our own jobs. When you are on the inside, your job is to be aware of the need to *explain* corporate policies, technical concepts, and your specialized vocabulary. That is, you must make the outsiders into insiders to the extent that is necessary for them to understand what you are saying.

For example, perhaps a supplier has sent you a product that does not quite match your specifications. When you return it you need to explain. But explain what? That it does not meet your specifications? That may be a good place to start. But it will be helpful to do more. Are there reasons for your specifications, or are you simply being inflexible? Explain those reasons. Perhaps your product will not work properly unless each part is within certain tolerances.

Always remember that your readers are people, outsiders who are asking to become insiders, if only for the moment.

Purpose

Every letter you write will have its own purpose, and to this extent each one will be unique. But all of your letters will have the common purpose of presenting a positive image of you and your company to your readers.

Most of your readers will not have much direct experience of you or your company. Their impressions of what your organization is like will be based on advertising and public relations campaigns and on their perceptions of the quality of your products. Your letter may be the *only* direct contact that your readers have with you or your company. The letter makes the relationship personal, no longer a matter of a television commercial or a product sitting on a shelf. Remember that we all tend to attach more importance to the way people and companies treat *us* than we attach to what they say about themselves. You can advertise that "People are Important," but all of your efforts (and money) will be wasted if you treat them like last year's disease when you write to them.

Of course, that does not mean that "the customer is always right." Your readers can be wrong, and they often will be. But even when they are wrong it is important that you treat them tactfully and courteously. Remember, you will be wrong sometime, too.

Should You Write at All?

Writing a letter should not be an automatic response but the result of a carefully made decision. There are other ways of communicating. A phone call, a carefully planned meeting, a visit, or a lunch meeting might be more effective in helping you accomplish your goals. How can you make this decision?

Cost

Is the cost of writing a letter consistent with the importance of achieving your goal? By the time you write a letter, have it typed, and mail it, it may cost you more than the situation is worth. A call or visit may be both cheaper and more effective. Cost should be a factor in your decision to write but not the only factor. That is, you may choose to write or not to write for other reasons, such as one or more of the following.

Timing

Letters take time to write and send, and then they take time to get to your reader. If speed is a factor, you may want to call, or call *first* and then follow up with a letter. If you call, and the person you need to talk to is available, then you will finish your business today rather than next week.

Although the telephone may be faster and less expensive most of the time, it also has disadvantages. If the person you want to talk with is not available, you can both spend a lot of time calling each other back. And conversations are ephemeral; it is difficult to put them in the files for future reference. There are times when it is important to know what you said.

Permanence

One of the advantages of writing is that it gives you a permanent record. You can file it, copy it, and look at it whenever you need to. When someone sends you 50,000 parts instead of 5000, it is useful to have a copy of your order so you can see what you ordered before you scream. It may be that you should scream at yourself for not proofreading carefully. As permanent records, letters have a number of legal uses, as well. They can be contracts, they can make implied or explicit warranties, and they can serve as evidence in lawsuits. Some people consider these good reasons not to write letters, at least not all the time.

Complexity

The complexity of your subject or situation can be a reason for writing. On the one hand, some subjects are simply too complicated to trust to conversation. You may need a carefully written document that covers all necessary information as clearly as possible. That is the only way you can have some assurance that you won't forget or garble something important. Of course, you can forget and garble when you write, too. But you have opportunities to remember and clarify before you send your writing to anyone.

On the other hand, the information itself may be fairly simple but part of a complex situation that requires the give-and-take of negotiation, explanation, discussion, questioning, and clarification. When that is the case, it is probably best not to write, at least not right away. Negotiate first, then try to write a letter that all can agree to. That way you get the advantages of discussion *and* permanence.

In the end, your decision to write a letter should be a conscious one based on how well a letter will help you to accomplish your goals within the constraints of time, cost, complexity, and permanence. Always consider other ways of getting your message across and whether they might be more effective than writing.

Three Basic Organizing Patterns

You can further simplify your job by taking advantage of the traditional classification of letters into three broad categories. These are based on the goal you want to achieve and your reader's likely reaction to that goal and to what you say. Each category provides you with a way of organizing the letter you are writing. By doing that, it gives immediate shape to both the letter itself and the process of organizing and writing it. Thus, the number of choices you must make is much more restricted than it would be if you had no such guidelines.

The purpose of categorizing letters in this way is to give you a means of making your point in a way that is consistent with your goal. Each type of letter will receive detailed treatment in the remaining chapters in this section. What follows here is a brief preview. As you read, remember that the categories are somewhat arbitrary and that you are reading *guidelines,* not rigid rules. The guidelines will provide you with a general scheme or structure for a letter but will not make decisions for you about every question of organizing and phrasing. It is more important that a letter respond to its situation than that it fit neatly into an abstract category.

Direct or Good News Messages

If you believe that your reader will react positively or at least feel neutral about what you have to say, you can use a direct or deductive approach. Keep in mind that neutrality is not the same as indifference. It simply means that your reader will consider your message as neither "good news" nor "bad news." If you predict indifference, which means that your reader will not *care* about your subject, then the direct approach is not appropriate. Of course, to predict how your reader will react you will need to put yourself into your reader's place and look at the situation from there. What seems like good news to you will not always be good news to someone else. Different readers will have different reactions to the same information. The key to making your decision is to know your readers as well as possible.

When you use a direct approach, you state your main point first; follow it with whatever explanation or information is necessary; and close with a strong, positive point. This is sometimes called a *deductive* approach, since it begins with a general principle and follows up with details. The diagram in Figure 6-1 will help you visualize this structure.

The Indirect Approach

Not all news is good news. You will often have to make a decision that you know your readers will not like. But you have to tell them, and you know what you say may make them angry (at you or at themselves), sad, frustrated, or disappointed. Perhaps you have decided not to hire someone or not to use a particular product, or you simply cannot fill an order.

Your reader may or may not have pinned high hopes on receiving favorable

Figure 6-1 The Direct, or Deductive, Approach

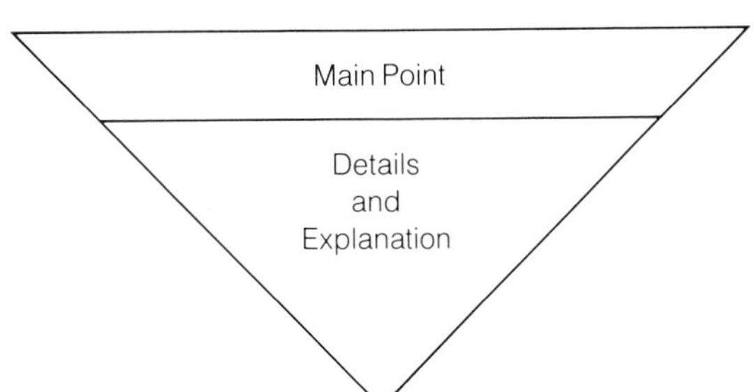

information from you. But you can't be sure about that and you want to minimize the potentially negative effects of what you say.

Remember, one of the purposes of any letter is to present a positive, favorable image of you and your company to your reader. In this situation, that may be difficult, since you have already predicted that your reader will *not* react favorably.

This situation usually calls for something a bit more subtle than the direct approach. Usually, if we *begin* by telling people something they don't want to hear, they tune us out. When that happens, your readers are no longer paying attention to you. So you need a plan that allows you to keep your readers' attention when you need it most: while you are explaining *why* you are doing or saying something that will make them unhappy.

In this case, it is usually easier to keep your readers' attention by using an indirect, or *inductive,* approach to your subject. That is, instead of putting your main point first, put it in the middle. Then surround it with a carefully reasoned explanation. The diagram in Figure 6-2 illustrates this structure.

Persuasion

There are times when you will ask your readers to do something, buy something, or believe something, and they will resist. This situation is different from the one in which you would use an indirect approach, because you are not necessarily telling your readers what they consider "bad news." Rather, their resistance has a variety of sources. Perhaps they are happy with things the way they are and have no desire to change, no matter what the advantages. Perhaps they have a well-developed resistance to sales efforts, or are simply indifferent to your product or service. Perhaps they have deeply entrenched attitudes and beliefs that are contrary to the ones you are offering.

People even resist requests that are clearly for their own good. Have you noticed that people still smoke, drink alcohol, drive too fast, and take other risks, in spite of widespread, expensive advertising campaigns that advise against these activities?

Figure 6-2 The Indirect, or Inductive, Approach

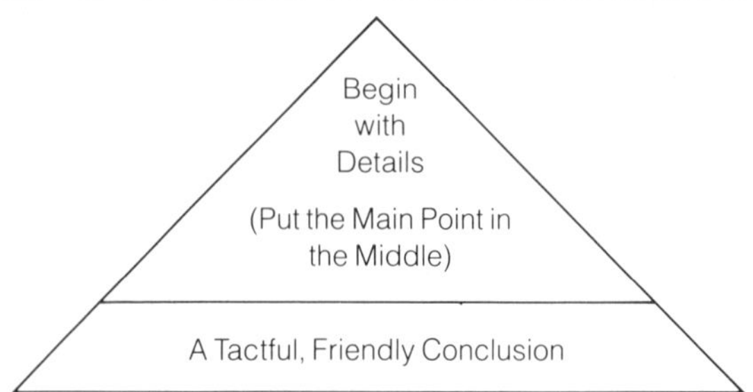

Persuasion requires something more powerful and convincing than the direct approach, and it needs to be directly addressed to your readers' points of resistance and agreement to your point of view or request. Ideally, you need to be able to identify those points of resistance and agreement. Once you have done that you will be able to develop arguments and appeals that will help you overcome resistance and reinforce agreement. And you will need to assemble evidence that supports your own point of view.

There are a number of ways to organize your writing for persuasion. We will consider some of them in Chapter 9.

Using Natural Points of Emphasis

We can predict with some certainty when readers are likely to be paying attention and when their minds are likely to wander.

Readers are most likely to be paying attention to you as they read the first and last paragraphs of your letter. They are least likely to be paying complete attention to you in the middle of your letter. This is also true of paragraphs and sentences: Readers are more likely to be paying attention to beginnings and endings than to middles.

These beginning and ending positions provide you with a way of emphasizing what you believe is important and de-emphasizing information that you must include but that you consider to be less important or even to work against you. The three types of letters that have been discussed here (direct, indirect, and persuasive) all depend on your ability to make use of these positions of emphasis.

In each the first paragraph is a place for establishing common ground with your reader and announcing your subject. Indirect letters, which tell your readers something they don't want to hear, require special attention. When you are writing about matters that may bring an unfavorable reaction from your reader, you will want to avoid placing bad news at these points of emphasis. That information goes in the middle, where it is less likely to call attention to itself and cause your reader to argue with you rather than pay attention.

The last paragraph of a letter is almost as important as the first. It is your last chance to say something important, something you want your reader to remember. It is an ideal place to tell your reader what to do and how to do it. Have you noticed how many letters tell you, in the last paragraph, exactly how to order a product or the deadline for taking advantage of a "once-in-a-lifetime offer"? You need to work actively to use this last paragraph, rather than simply allowing your letter to trail off into insignificant details.

Limits on Reader Attention

Thinking about how to emphasize important information should also help you remain aware of the limits on reader attention. Too often we assume that people will read a letter simply because it is in front of them. But your readers have many other things to do in a day. They must read *many* letters and reports. Your letter must compete for attention not only with those, but also with the telephone and with people walking in and out of the office.

You can improve your chance of winning a few minutes of your reader's day by making your letter *look* inviting and easy to read. One way to do this is to be aware of the length of your sentences and paragraphs. A whole page of solid, single-spaced typing just looks as if it doesn't want anyone to read it. So try not to scare your reader with the weight of the ink on the page (which too often has little to do with the weight of the thought behind the ink). Instead, *invite* your readers by giving them frequent breaks. Try to write sentences that average fifteen to twenty-five words. Of course, some sentences will be much shorter, perhaps only five or six words. Others may be much longer. You can do the same with paragraphs, ending them after eight or ten lines.

By providing frequent breaks you increase the odds that you will keep your readers with you, rather than lose them in the middle because the phone just rang or someone asked about the meeting at ten o'clock. The spaces in the text, where new paragraphs begin, make the page easy to cope with visually. Readers are more likely to find their place or be willing to reread short passages if they don't have to search through paragraphs of fifteen or twenty lines. There is also a bonus for you when you write a number of short paragraphs rather than a few long ones. You create more places where you can place important ideas or information for emphasis.

Style: Your Relationship with Your Readers

Do business letters have a special style of their own, something that sets them apart from other kinds of writing? Some writers seem to think so. They apparently believe that letters should be stiff, formal, and filled with words and phrases that no one would ever use in other situations. It seems odd, but it is true. Tell someone to write a business letter and the result is likely to sound as if it came directly from the nineteenth century. (Perhaps that tells us something about where we get much of what we know about writing letters.) Try this as a composite example:

> Dear Mr. Smith:
>
> We have received your gracious letter of the thirteenth in which you request information about the Gimcrack Model 4.

> Pursuant to your inquiry we are most highly pleased to be able to inform you that the Gimcrack is once again available after a long absence.
>
> Please be advised that we have every assurance that the newly designed Model 4 will serve you for many years, as did its justly famous predecessor.
>
> The undersigned has personally tested the Model 4 herself and can vouch for its outstanding quality and performance. Enclosed herewith is an order blank that you may use should you wish to become a proud owner of a Gimcrack Model 4. Will you be so kind as to send your remittance with your order?
>
> Thanking you in advance for your kind attention, I am,
>
> Most sincerely yours,
>
> J. Rachel Thomas

OK, I confess that you will probably never see a letter quite like this one. It is an exaggeration, but it is also an honest attempt to suggest some of the traps we can fall into when we set out to write a letter. We often complain that letters sound as though they were written by computers. That is certainly not the problem here, since computers are rarely so unintentionally humorous. In fact, a letter like this might be an attempt to counteract the effects of computerized impersonality. But in the attempt to be polite and personal it succeeds mostly in being trite, mushy, and finally false.

What is the alternative? How do you write a letter that projects a positive image of you, your company, and your relationship with your reader? The question is an important one, because you and your readers are often doing more than simply trying to communicate with each other. There is a business relationship between you (which may be your only reason for writing), and one of you almost invariably wants something from the other. That fact stands behind and influences everything you say and do.

Much of the image that you project of yourself and your company depends on style: the way you use words and phrases. Each letter, of course, will have its individual circumstances and requirements. But it is possible to identify matters of style that are common to all letters.

Understand Your Reader's Point of View

It is essential that you understand your reader's situation and that you demonstrate this understanding in your writing. This is the foundation of being able to communicate with anyone.

One way to show your understanding is to restate your reader's position in your own words. In even the simplest of situations it is possible to do this in such a way that you are not simply telling your readers something they already know. Rather, you are showing your understanding of what has been said or asked. You might write:

> Your order for 5000 pressure-sensitive labels (#Z-4692-1) can easily be shipped in time to reach your Boston plant by March 31.

This is a simple restatement of a customer's order; but don't make the mistake of thinking it simpleminded. It accomplishes many important goals that are not immediately obvious. Upon reading this sentence your customer will learn:

> That you received the order
>
> That you are sending the correct number of parts
>
> That you are shipping the correct part (Z-4692-1)
>
> When the order will arrive

If you had said, "We have received your order," your customer would have only one-quarter of the information in the first paragraph above. There would be no way of knowing whether you got the order right. And, since you probably wouldn't write at all unless you *had* received the order, you would have told the reader nothing new.

But understanding your reader's needs is more than simply restating a position or request. It involves being able to think as your readers think and to see the world from their point of view. What does this mean, and how do we do it?

Everyone who is involved in a given situation will have a different point of view and will often consider that point of view to be the most important one. Because of our responsibilities or our personalities, we often focus on what *we* want or need from a situation, to the exclusion of everything else. This is true of intimate groups, such as families, and of companies, as well as of people who have never met. Your job as a writer is to discover the other points of view that are involved in a situation and to respond to them. This often means that you must adopt these other points of view, at least temporarily, so that you will understand them.

Consider the different points of view that can exist within a single company about the apparently simple matter of developing a new product. The person who had the idea to begin with is most likely interested in seeing the product manufactured and out the door. He no doubt thinks it is a good idea that will contribute to the company's well-being. This person may see the project as easy and even simple. Design the product, manufacture it, and sell it.

But when the rest of the company gets involved the situation becomes complicated. Manufacturing engineers want to know if they will have the technology and money to develop and make a good product. The Marketing Division will want to know if the product will sell: Is anyone interested in it, and can it be introduced and advertised effectively?

Executives will want to know how the product fits into the company's budget and existing facilities. How much will it cost to make this product, and how much must be invested in new equipment and facilities? Will it fit into existing product lines? Is it consistent with the direction in which the company is going, or will it require a revision of long-range plans? Finally, some spoilsport will no doubt ask whether it will make any money.

Obviously, developing and selling a new product is not simply a matter of forging ahead. Everyone involved must be convinced that the product is indeed a "good idea." And they must be convinced of this on their own terms.

Finding Out What Readers Think

Sometimes you can simply ask your readers what they think. Talk with the manufacturing engineers or the accountants and ask them what they need to know before they can support a proposal. Sometimes, of course, you can't ask. Distance, or time, or politics gets in the way. Then you have to *discover* the various points of view on your own. One way to do this is to ask yourself questions and then try to gather enough information to answer them. You can use the questions who, what, where, when, why, and how as the framework for your inquiry.

Who? Who is involved in making this decision? If I were the Marketing Director, what would be my perspective here? What am I interested in? What do I want to know about this product? What do I already know about the company and the products it sells? Where does this product fit? Where will we get the money to promote it? To whom will it appeal? Why should we make it at all? What will it do that similar products don't do? What is the competition?

See how quickly and easily the questions follow one another? Put yourself in your readers' place and begin asking the questions they would ask. Then try to answer those questions honestly and fully. Tackle the hard ones as well as the easy ones. Remember that your readers will not avoid the difficult questions. Once you have finished this process you should have a rather detailed picture of how your reader views a particular situation. When you write you will be able to show that you can understand the situation in the same way, that you and your reader have something in common. And you do. You have the ability to understand and approach a situation from a common point of view, even though your goals or needs may be quite different.

Choose Your Words Carefully

Each job, profession, and industry has its own vocabulary that allows insiders to communicate with each other easily, in a kind of shorthand. People who work with computers talk about bytes, hardware, boards, discs, and other things that seem strange to outsiders. Accountants talk about balance sheets, profitability, and profit and loss statements. Just as these words help to identify insiders to each other, they also exclude the rest of us.

Specialized technical and jargon terms are part of your working vocabulary. But your words are not always part of your reader's working vocabulary. When you use these words with people who do not understand them, they get in the way. When you catch yourself using one of these words, find another or translate, so that your reader will understand what you mean. You can do this without insulting your reader. Simply ask yourself which words your reader will probably know already.

Your reader also has a special vocabulary. You may not be familiar with all of it, just as your reader will not know all of yours. But you will know *some* of your reader's technical language and jargon. If you can use your reader's own words—accurately—then try to work them in. We are all more comfortable when we are in familiar surroundings, and those words are part of your reader's everyday world. Using them will help your reader view your writing as a familiar, comfortable place. You will also gain for yourself something of the status of an insider.

Understanding your readers does not mean that you disappear or that you are giving up on your own goals. It is merely another way of communicating to your readers that you have given their situation and point of view some attention and thought.

Write with a "You" Attitude

If you have succeeded in really understanding your reader's situation and point of view, then you will have no trouble writing with a "you" attitude. In fact, you will probably fall into it naturally. You will know that has happened when you discover that you are writing *you* and *your* more often than *I, me,* and *my.* It is practically that simple. If you really understand your readers, you will write more about what interests them than you do about what interests you. The following sentences fall short of that goal.

1. We are presently processing your order and should ship it by April 9.
2. Our accounting department has reviewed your accounts very thoroughly and has determined that we have not charged you improperly.

These sentences clearly state what the writer is doing, what the writer has found out, and that the writer, not the reader, is right. If you write sentences like this your reader will certainly understand you, and you will have communicated. But you may be communicating information that you would be better off keeping to yourself. You are telling your reader that you and your view of the situation are most important here. Your reader's concerns are subsidiary, unimportant, and even bothersome.

The "you" attitude places your readers and their concerns at the point of focus, like this:

1. Your order is being prepared and will be shipped before April 9. ("Preparing" an order sounds a bit better than "processing" it, which is something we do to meat and cheese.)
2. Your account has been carefully reviewed in our accounting department. This review shows that you have been charged only for the orders you have placed and the shipping and finance charges that are associated with them. Complete copies of your records are enclosed so that you may review them.

In these sentences the writers have attempted to focus on and write about you, the readers, rather than on themselves. Your readers will appreciate this effort, because it allows them to view the world from their favorite and most familiar point of view: themselves. To achieve this, you must give up, temporarily, your own favorite perspective on the world.

For example, many writers like to begin letters with an apparently harmless phrase such as this one: "I was pleased to receive your request for information about the new PRZ-10 high-pressure valve." "What's wrong with that?" they ask. "My reader should be pleased that I am pleased." Think about it. Your readers *expect* you to be pleased, because you sell these valves and their letters are sales possibilities. The issue is not what pleases you, but what would please your reader; this opener says nothing about that. Besides, the sentence tells readers only what they already know: That they wrote a letter to you, that you received it (otherwise you would not be answering it), and that the subject is their need for information about the PRZ-10 valve.

How can you revise a sentence like this to put your readers and their interests at its center? You could be direct and get right to the point: "Here is the information you requested about the PRZ-10 high-pressure valve." A sentence like that tells your readers right away that you are doing what they asked. Or you could take advantage of the potential sale that the request represents: "You will find that the PRZ-10 high-pressure valve is ideally suited for use in FLOW pumping systems." This shows that you have taken the time to learn something about your readers' products and the uses they might have for yours. Both revisions improve on the original because they put the reader at the center of the sentence.

Write Positively

Do you remember the old definition of an optimist and a pessimist? Each one received half a glass of water. The pessimist complained because his was half-empty; the optimist was delighted because his was half-full. Both glasses were the same, but one saw what was there and the other saw what wasn't there. Writing positively is writing as though your glass were half-full.

Of course, we all know that sometimes our glass is not half-full. Sometimes it is empty. There are days when nothing goes right and the world appears to be coming apart at the seams. We miss deadlines and send orders to the wrong place. But what do we tell the customer? It's tempting to say that "Some stupid jerk in the shipping department put your order on the wrong truck. Right now it's in Fargo, North Dakota, and you probably won't get it for another week, if then." While that may be the truth, it also inflicts your own anger and disappointment on your readers. In doing that, it could make them wonder if their confidence in you is misplaced. "Why," they might ask, "do you employ 'stupid jerks' and not check up on them?" The net effect of concentrating on the negative is that it invites your reader to be negative, too. That serves no purpose. Instead, try to focus your reader's attention on what is positive in a situation and thus invite a positive response. So you might try that sentence this way:

> Your recent order was mistakenly shipped to another of our customers. Fortunately, the error has been discovered, and the shipment is being returned to us. You should receive it no later than August 4, as it will be shipped to you by the fastest means available.

While this version does not deny that there has been a mistake, it focuses on the positive by telling what has been done to correct it. It shows that you are in charge of events, rather than allowing the events to be in charge of you.

Writing positively is a result of looking at a situation to find what you can do, have done, or will do, rather than what you can't do, won't do, or haven't done. It is a matter of reorienting yourself, and thus your reader, to what is, rather than to what isn't. If you can do that, you are well on your way to succeeding with the fourth stylistic guideline.

Be Confident

Confidence, the feeling that you can succeed in accomplishing your goals, is contagious. If you feel it yourself, you are likely to communicate that feeling to your readers. Believing you will succeed, and having someone else believe it, increases the odds that you will succeed. When you write, you are in charge, and most people like to believe that those in charge know what they are doing.

Confidence is usually easy to convey when we are face-to-face with someone. We communicate confidence through our posture, facial expressions, and clothes. Others feel it in our direct eye contact with them and our firm handshake. We don't have to say, "I'm confident," and people probably would not believe us if we did. Rather, they watch us for behavior that indicates we are confident. But how do we convey confidence when we write, when we have only words?

Use positive words. Avoid words that can undermine your feeling of confidence, words such as *perhaps, maybe, hopefully* and *I hope, possibly,* and *might.* There are others, but you get the idea. These words suggest that you are not really sure about what you are saying. They are like the fine print in a TV commercial. By qualifying your main point they call it into question.

Watch out for the sneaky "if." *If* is such a small word, and so easy to use. But it is powerful out of all proportion to its size. We may use it to suggest that we are humble or at least not arrogant. And we know our readers don't like arrogance. So we say, "If you would like to take advantage of . . ." or "If you agree with this . . ." or "If you would like to know more about. . . ." Readers *do* have choices. No one knows that better than they do. The *if* in these phrases undermines the confidence you're projecting. It does that in two ways.

First, it openly suggests that your readers might *not* want to take advantage of your offer or might not agree or want to know more. To suggest this option is to invite them to take it. The second problem is more serious than the first. *If* and words like it suggest that you are not entirely convinced yourself, that there may be good reasons why your readers might not agree or want to know more.

Avoid questions that invite your reader to say no. My all-time favorite question that encourages a negative answer is "Wouldn't you really rather drive a Buick?" I say no every time I hear this one. But this type of question has many versions, and it is an easy trap to fall into: "Wouldn't it be easier to . . . ?" or "Why not . . . ?" Remember, you want to make it easy for your reader to say yes. So, when you catch yourself asking this kind of question, look for another, more confident way of saying it. You might try one of these:

"To take advantage of this offer . . ."

or

"Call me today to let me know your reaction."

or

"To learn more about the IVR investment program, write . . ."

These revisions give your readers specific instructions and at the same time show you are confident your readers will comply. Will they always? Not likely, but more will if you are confident.

Writing and Revising

No matter how thoroughly and carefully you plan a letter, you will probably need to write it more than once. There is a great deal to think about as you write, and it is difficult for any of us to remember everything all of the time. Planning can help you make choices about audience, subject, goals, and organization. But as soon as you begin to write you face a constant stream of decisions about style as you attempt to write from your reader's point of view, write with a "you" attitude, and be positive and confident. It is difficult to keep the engine running on all cylinders at the same time. The solution is to revise, to take advantage of a second and even third chance to address these matters of style.

Editing

Once you have finished a draft that satisfies you, edit it carefully. This is your final opportunity to be sure everything is the way you want it. Now, before you send your letter to the typist, is the time to make changes.

Work carefully. Examine each sentence and make the minor corrections and changes you think are necessary. Many of us are fortunate in having secretaries or typists who can "clean up" our writing as they type. But that is no reason to do less than your best. You may misspell a word or put a comma in the wrong place. And your typist may catch that. But do the best you can.

You can contribute to harmony in the office if you give typists clean, legible drafts of your letters. You will also help to reduce the number of times a letter must be retyped. It is embarrassing to ask a typist to retype a letter when the mistake was in your original draft. It is also a waste of time and money. If you can, have your final draft typed, double-spaced, so you can make final corrections on it. It will be easier for you and the typist to work with it that way.

When you send a letter to be typed, always indicate the number of copies you will need and who is to receive them. The typist also needs to know how many items are to be enclosed with the letter and what they are, because this information is included on the letter. All enclosures should accompany the draft so they can be photocopied and attached to all of the copies.

When the finished letter comes back to you it should be ready for the mail. All it needs is your signature. But wait! Don't sign it yet.

Proofreading

Who is responsible for the accuracy, neatness, and appearance of your letter? Right: You are. Your signature indicates that you have read the letter and approve of what it says. If anything goes wrong, the boss will come looking for you, not the typist. (If a typist is having difficulty doing high-quality work, it is your job to correct that situation. When you sign letters that are inaccurate or of low quality, you accept responsibility for them.)

So proofread carefully. Check the letter for:

Overall appearance

Correct format

Accurate date and addresses

Compare it with your final draft, rather than relying on your memory. Then use the methods explained in Chapter 5 and proofread the letter line by line. When you are satisfied, sign the letter and move on.

Examples

Figures 6-3 through 6-7 are examples of letters typical of those produced by both large and small corporations. They are here for your review and study, but their presence is no indication of their quality. You can acquire valuable experience by revising these examples so that they observe the principles explained in this chapter.

■

Figure 6-3 Company Letter to Employees

TO: A L L O U R E M P L O Y E E S

SUBJECT: YORK DIVISION, BORG-WARNER
EMPLOYEE CHRISTMAS SAVINGS FUND

Membership application cards for the EMPLOYEE CHRISTMAS SAVINGS FUND for 1982 will be distributed to Supervisors on Thursday, October 1, 1981. If you desire to join -- all you have to do is indicate the amount to be deducted each pay period, sign your name, return the card to your Supervisor. These application cards must be returned to the PAYROLL DEPARTMENT no later than Thursday, October 15, 1981. If you do NOT wish to participate in the Christmas Savings Fund, DO NOT RETURN THE CARD.

Again, this year, interest at the rate of five and one-quarter per cent (5¼%) per annum will be paid This will be added to the checks when they are issued, approximately October 19, 1981. It is to be understood that the Company acts only as the service agent in making your deposits.

Your signed application will authorize the Company to deduct the amount you indicate from your pay check for a period of fifty (50) weeks, (24 pay periods for salaried employees) and deposit the amount in an Employee Christmas Savings Account with the York Bank & Trust Company in your name.

Deductions for the Employee Christmas Savings Fund will be made each pay period -- weekly for hourly paid employees -- semi-monthly for salaried employees.

Request for withdrawal of the Savings Fund prior to final distribution by the bank must be received IN THE PAYROLL DEPARTMENT ten (10) days prior to actual issuance of Letter of Withdrawal.

The first deduction for the 1982 Fund will be made from wage pay checks of October 30, 1981, and from Salary checks for the pay period ending October 30, 1981.

The final deduction for this year's Club (1981) will be made from the wage pay checks of October 9, and from the salary checks of October 15.

This year's Employee Christmas Savings checks will be mailed on or about October 19, 1981. NOTE -- Your check for the 1981 Fund will be mailed to the address shown on your pay check. If this is incorrect - notify the Human Resources Department immediately.

If you do not receive an application card and wish to participate, contact your Supervisor.

HUMAN RESOURCES DEPARTMENT

INDUSTRIAL RELATIONS—YORK DIVISION—BORG WARNER

Figure 6-4 Company Letter to Potential Customers

717/843-8651

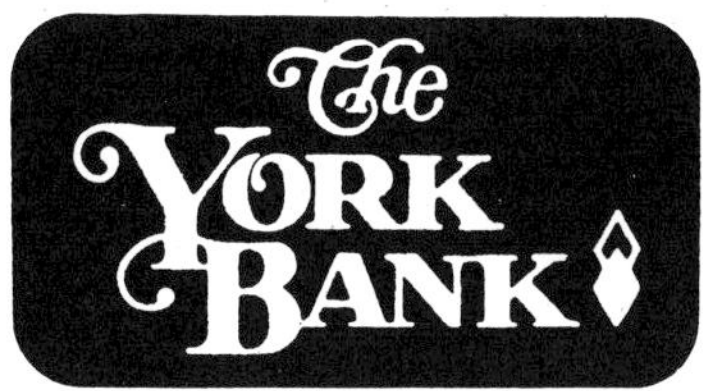

(Date)

(Name)
(School)
(Address)
(City, State, Zip Code)

Dear (Title and Last Name):

The materials we provide for you to teach the program "Banking is . . ." have been ordered and will be delivered to you at your school in September, 1981.

These study guides and practice checkbooks are intended for use during the 1981-82 school year. They will be delivered in time to be included in the curriculum plans of your teachers for that school term.

We hope these materials will again prove valuable to you and your students. If you are interested, an officer of the bank will visit your classroom to answer any questions and provide first-hand information on the services of the banking industry.

Please contact me if you have any questions.

Sincerely,

(Author)
Assistant Treasurer

wp

THE YORK BANK & TRUST COMPANY • P.O. BOX 869 • YORK, PENNSYLVANIA 17405

Figure 6-5 Company Letter to Another Company

August 8, 1983

Tom Poulson
Manager
Poulson's Supply
2309 Riverside
Greenville, SC 27000

Dear Mr. Poulson:

Just a note of appreciation for your thoughtfulness in introducing Dan Swartz of Swartz Machinery to us.

It makes us very happy to know that your regard prompts such an evidence of your good will, and you may be sure that we will try to justify it by making Mr. Swartz's association with Mid-Town Supply as pleasant as possible.

Sincerely,

Randall Smith
President
Mid-Town Supply

Figure 6-6 Company Letter to a Customer

717/843-8651

(Date)

(Name)
(Address)
(City, State, Zip Code)

Dear (Title and Last Name):

Our signature card file is incomplete on your (Type) account, number (Number), in the name of (Names on the Account). Please sign the enclosed signature card and furnish us with the Social Security Number of (First Named Person on the Account). This Social Security Number will be used in reporting interest income to the Internal Revenue Service.

Please return the signature card to us as soon as possible in the enclosed envelope.

Thank you for banking with The York Bank.

Sincerely,

(Author)
(Title)
(Branch Location)

wp

Enclosure

THE YORK BANK & TRUST COMPANY • P.O. BOX 869 • YORK, PENNSYLVANIA 17405

Figure 6-7 Company Letter to a Potential Customer

June 5, 1983

Andrew K. Williams
331 Strathclyde Dr.
Belmont, California 94002

Dear Mr. Williams:

The Belmont Travel Agency announces...

"I N F O A N D I D E A S"

...a newsletter designed with the businessman in mind.

"Info and Ideas" is a bi-monthly publication of the Belmont Travel Agency which contains information for you, the traveler, as well as for you, the businessman.

We are pleased to include you, Mr. Williams, as a recipient of this "first edition" and hope it will provide interesting and informative reading.

"Info and Ideas" ...ENJOY!!!

Sincerely,

Paul Richards
Manager

Exercises: Chapter Six

1. Rewrite the following statements so that they reflect a "you" attitude, a positive approach to your subject, and confidence in yourself and your company.
   a. We'll ship your order for 5000 brass candlesticks on August 15, if we get them finished.
   b. I can't approve your request for a June vacation until I find out what everyone else wants to do.
   c. It's not possible to give your department any more computer time this month.
   d. No employees may leave their work stations until the end-of-shift whistle sounds.
   e. I'm not sure we can provide the information you have asked for.
   f. This request is highly unusual.
   g. I can't possibly get to this until Friday.
   h. I hope you realize how much trouble this is causing everyone.

2. For each of the following situations, decide whether you would use a direct, indirect, or persuasive approach.
   a. Someone has written to ask for information about one of your company's products.
   b. You are writing to encourage your company's sales force to exceed fixed quotas for the fiscal year.
   c. You are announcing a one-week layoff/plant shutdown as a cost-cutting measure.
   d. You are requesting a transfer to your company's Boston office to a job identical with the one you now have.
   e. You are writing to Joan Fries to announce that she will receive the scholarship that your organization sponsors each year.
   f. You are writing to John Smith to tell him that he will not receive a scholarship.
   g. You are writing a letter of reference for a former employee whose performance was barely adequate in your company.
   h. You are writing a policy statement that will inform all employees age 59 and over that they will be retired early.

3. Look through the materials that arrive each month with your bills. Many companies include brief explanations of their charges, cost-cutting tips, or promotional materials. Review one of these notices and, if necessary, revise it so that it observes the principles explained in this chapter.

4. Review the direct mail materials that you receive from businesses, fund-raising organizations, and politicians. Do they observe the principles outlined in this chapter? If so, how? Identify and explain exam-

ples. If not, identify examples of this, as well, and then revise them so that they are more suitable.

5. Review the examples included in this chapter to see whether, after reading the chapter, you think they need to be improved. Make whatever revisions you think are necessary.

■

7

Inquiries, Replies, and Goodwill Letters

This chapter will present three of the most commonly used business letters. All of them use the direct, or deductive, organizing plan that you encountered in Chapter 3 and Chapter 6. They are:

The inquiry or request, which asks your reader to provide you with information or to take a specific action

The reply, which answers an inquiry or request by doing what its writer has asked you to do

The goodwill letter, which says "thank you" or "congratulations," or expresses sympathy in an effort to create or maintain a positive relationship between you and your readers

These are often called "good news" letters because you will use them when you believe your readers will agree with or react favorably to what you say.

Inquiries: The Art of Asking Good Questions

To illustrate writing inquiries we will use a situation much like the ones you are likely to encounter at work and go through it step-by-step, from setting goals to writing. Although it may differ in its details from other letters, the planning, thinking, and organizing follow the same methods that you will use for any inquiry.

Identify and State Your Goals

In our example, you have been assigned to find a place to hold your company's annual sales meeting. How will you do this? You could pin a map on the wall and throw darts at it. That would accomplish your goal because, as it stands, your goal simply specifies that you should find "a place." Buckingham Palace and the Mojave Desert will do equally well. Your goal needs a bit of work.

A well-stated goal gives you two kinds of information. It tells you what to do to achieve the goal and how you will know that you have achieved it. So expand your goal by trying to add that kind of information to it. What will you *do* to find a place for the annual sales meeting? You will probably write to a number of resorts, hotels, and conventions centers to see what they have to offer. In fact, that is an easy letter to write. You can simply say, "We'd like to hold our annual sales meeting at your hotel. What do you have to offer?" There. Now you can sit back and wait for the replies to roll in.

Problems? Just a few small ones. Of course, everyone who replies will offer you the best deal since the Model T. Who would write you and say "Sorry. We're the worst excuse for a resort you've ever seen, and we probably can't help you at all"? When you get the answers, how will you evaluate them? How will you know who is offering you the best place for your meeting? You won't, because right now you don't know what the best place should have that the others don't have. That is, you have no way of knowing when you have achieved your goal. And you won't know until you learn, or decide, what criteria the "best" location must satisfy.

If you were to actually *state* your goal at this point (and it is a good idea to do that), it might look like this:

> I want to decide on (or recommend) a location for the annual sales meeting by writing to at least ______ hotels, resorts, and

convention centers. I will state our criteria for a meeting place and see which one can come closest to them.

Note that goal statements need not include specific details (though they can). It is enough that they show you what specific details you need to include.

Consider Your Reader

Inquiries often have a single reader. In our example we'll be writing a letter that can be sent to many readers, who all have one thing in common: They occupy similar positions in similar businesses, and we want the same information from all of them. So, for our purposes, they are all the same reader.

We select readers according to whether they can help us achieve our goals. If we need information, we write to the person who can provide it. If we need a policy decision, we write to the person who can make that decision. In the present case we will select a reader for one reason: He or she works at a hotel or convention center that is likely to meet our needs. You know that *all* such facilities won't do, so it will save time and money to do some homework first. Using whatever criteria seem useful, you will select a reasonable number of places to write. Perhaps your company is interested in a warm climate and exotic surroundings. If so, you will avoid writing to resorts in Minneapolis for a February meeting or to the Down Home Motel.

In order to get what you want you must explain your needs clearly and thoroughly enough that your reader can understand and reply to them. In a sense, the information you supply in an inquiry contains the directions that will help your reader prepare a reply. A vague, all-purpose question will probably get you a vague, all-purpose answer. If you are specific about what you need, you encourage your reader to be specific, too. To some extent you are doing your reader's job. But remember, you *need* your reader to do a good job. Your own success depends on it.

Information is not the only thing that will pass between you and your reader. This exchange will take place within a relationship. Since you will often write to people you do not know, and who do not know you, where does this relationship come from? You construct it out of the information you present, the statements you make about yourself, the assumptions you make about your reader, and the words you use. It does not exist before you write the letter, but it forms the basis of all of your future interaction with that reader.

Readers can do more than just answer your questions, and they will, if you allow them to. They can be valuable to you as consultants, because they often know your needs better than you do. If you allow them to, they can help you evaluate your goals and the means you have chosen to achieve them.

In our letter about the annual sales meeting the ideal reader is someone who is experienced at making arrangements for groups. It may help to write to a specific person, by name; but even if you can't do that your letter will probably make its way to the person who has the information you need. In this case readers who are experienced with group meetings will be able to do more than simply answer your questions. They will know something about what groups need and how things can go wrong. They will also be able to compare your requirements with their past experience and decide whether they can provide what you are looking for. Most importantly, they can evaluate your needs and tell you whether you have made the right assumptions.

So it might help to take your readers into your confidence and allow them the role of expert. But you will still need to know enough to evaluate the reply and decide whether the experts actually know anything.

Finding Something to Say

Ultimately, the success of your inquiry will depend on knowing enough about your subject to ask the right questions. It is your knowledge of your subject (in this case, what it takes to conduct an annual sales meeting) that allows you to identify what you need and ask for it. Knowing your subject can help you in these ways:

It allows you to ask specific rather than general questions. These, in turn, encourage your readers to be specific in their replies.

By encouraging your reader to be specific, you reduce the amount of irrelevant information that is likely to appear in the reply. At some point in the process you need to separate the useful information from everything else. You can do that as you write or as you read the reply. But the earlier you do it, the more likely it is that you will achieve your goal.

Good questions, based on solid knowledge, can encourage your readers to focus on *your* needs (a place to have a meeting) rather than their own (selling you a convention spot).

The more you know, the better you will be able to evaluate the reply you receive and to be sure it is accurate and complete.

Of course, you already know a great deal about your subject: it's part of your job. Converting your knowledge into what you will say in a letter is a matter of selecting what you need to say out of what you know. You have already begun that process by stating your goal. You will continue it by examining your subject thoroughly and making your goals and your reader's needs explicit.

Your goal of finding a location for the annual sales meeting specified that you must tell your reader your criteria for adequate accommodations:

> One hundred twenty people will attend.
>
> They will meet in ten groups of twelve and four groups of thirty.
>
> They will meet as one group at least once a day.
>
> You will need at least sixty double rooms.
>
> The restaurant must accommodate everyone, especially for breakfast.
>
> On the last night of the meeting, everyone will attend a banquet.
>
> You will need at least ten overhead projectors, four slide projectors, and two 16mm film projectors. Each meeting room should have a screen.
>
> You will want some recreational facilities, such as a swimming pool and tennis courts.
>
> It should be located in an interesting tourist area.
>
> It should have a pleasant climate for the time of year (June, in this case).
>
> It must be available June 14, 15, and 16.
>
> People will check in on June 13 and out on June 17.
>
> It must fit within the company's budget for the meeting.

Once these criteria are established, you can use them to determine what you will actually say in the letter. To do that, you will need to ask:

1. What your readers need to know
2. What your readers do not need to know
3. What your readers need to know that is not on your list yet

1. **W**hat does your reader need to know? Obviously, your readers need to know what you expect to find when you get to the meeting. They need enough information to compare your requirements with their facilities and tell you whether they match. This will include the number of people who will attend and the arrangements you want to make for meetings, meals, and sleeping. Readers also need to know about the special equipment you will need and the kinds of recreational opportunities you expect. So the bulk of your letter will state the criteria that a meeting site will have to meet.

But sometimes simply stating what you want will not get you the information you need. You want to have the meeting in what everyone will consider a "nice place." It need not be elegant, but no one wants to spend three days in a dump with bad mattresses and paper-thin walls. If you simply *ask* whether the resort or hotel is "pleasant," what are you likely to get? That's right. "Of course it is." And it is, because "pleasant" means anything anyone wants it to mean. So how do you find the truth, or get the information you need?

You obviously need a good question, something that goes beyond simply stating your desire for "pleasant" surroundings. While there is no substitute for a personal inspection, you might ask for photographs (most resorts and convention centers can provide illustrated brochures). Or you could ask for the names and addresses of other companies that have used this establishment for a similar purpose. Since they will have nothing to sell you, they will be inclined to give you their honest opinion. And remember, it will be their *opinion,* because their idea of pleasant may not be the same as yours.

2. **W**hat your reader doesn't need to know. If you have done your homework you won't need to tell your readers that you want a location with a pleasant climate or nearby tourist attractions. You have already selected the places you will write on the basis of these criteria.

You do need to know how much all of this will cost. After all, that will be important in selecting a site. But your readers do not need to know how much money you have to spend. Telling them that is a good way to spend your whole budget. You need to ask about the cost of the arrangements, but do it without saying how much you are prepared to spend.

3. **W**hat *else* does your reader need to know? Now examine your lists to see what your reader needs to know that you haven't thought of yet. It might help at this point to run through the questions *who, what, where, when, why,* and *how* just to see what additional information you can pick up from your memory or your knowledge of the situation. Or you might discover something that you need to learn. What you have done so far pretty much covers the ground here. You've told your reader who will attend the meeting, what you need, why you need it, and when the meeting will take place. So try to get beyond this first level of knowledge that the questions can provide.

For example, if you ask *why* you are writing, the obvious answer is that you are writing to find a place for your meeting. Your readers know that, but is there a *Why?* that they don't know? Why, for instance, are you writing to him or her? Because she can give you the information you need. Yes, but can't other people do that? Yes. And there it is: You're not writing just *one* reader, but several. You are shopping around. If you let your readers know that, tactfully, you are also telling them that you will compare their answers very carefully. If your readers know there is competition, they might see the need to give you convincing reasons for doing business with their firm rather than with another.

We can do the same thing with *when*. Of course, you have already said when the meeting will take place. But are there other important *when* questions? One of them might be "When do I need an answer?" If the meeting is to take place on schedule, you will need time to plan it. Give your readers a deadline. Their ability to meet it is another indication of their competence and good faith.

Once you are sure you have control of your subject and know what you need to say, you can move on to organizing and writing the letter.

Organize and Write

Remember, you are using a direct pattern. Your first job is to select an opening that will announce your subject and carry your main point. Then you need to present your explanations and questions in a sequence that your reader can make sense of. Finally, be sure that you end with a positive note that takes advantage of the emphasis your last paragraph will receive.

Writing beginnings. Sometimes it works to begin with a direct question, like this:

> Can Greenwoods Resort accommodate our sales force of 120 salespersons and executives for their annual sales meeting on June 14, 15, and 16?

Or you could explain what you are doing:

> Planning is now underway for our annual sales meeting, which will be held on June 14, 15, and 16 of this year. We would like you to provide some information about Greenwoods so that we may decide whether it is a suitable location for our needs.

Or you could include more details at the beginning:

> We are looking for an attractive location that can accommodate 120 salespersons and executives for our annual sales meeting on June 14, 15, and 16.

All of these satisfy the requirement for the beginning of a direct letter because they come right to the point. Best of all, they avoid the temptation to do this:

> Last week, as we started to plan our annual sales meeting, I was assigned to write to several resorts and hotels to find out which ones might be good locations for our meeting. One of our ex-

> ecutives has stayed at your hotel before, so I decided to write to you, and to several other places, to see what I could find out.

That's not quite a classic example of beating around the bush, but it comes close.

Writing the middle. Once you have your reader's attention, you need to move immediately to the detailed questions and explanations that will tell your reader what you want. It's a two-stage process of grouping information so that it makes sense and then writing questions or explanations or making lists. Whatever you do, make it easy for your reader to understand.

You might organize it this way:

> **General**
> Attractive setting
> Recreation and meetings
>
> **Meetings**
> Rooms needed
> Supporting equipment
>
> **Details**
> Banquet
> Other meals
> Sleeping arrangements
> Arrival and departure times

Let's give this a try and see what happens:

> The annual sales meeting tries to mix business with pleasure. We like our people to work, but it is also a chance to relax together. So we want a place that provides attractive surroundings and opportunities for recreation and sightseeing. The swimming pool and tennis courts are usually the most popular. It would help us if we could have color photographs to see what Greenwoods looks like.
>
> Various groups will meet during each day and evening. We need ten small conference rooms for twelve people each, four meeting rooms that will hold thirty, and a room large enough for all of us to meet together. Speakers will also need some audiovisual support:
>
> Ten overhead projectors
> Four slide projectors
> Two 16mm film projectors
> A public address system (portable)
> A projection screen for each room
>
> Can you let us know whether you can provide this equipment or if it can be rented locally?

> On the evening of June 16 the entire group will meet for a banquet. For other meals everyone will make individual arrangements. They will certainly want to sample the excellent restaurants in your area. But since meetings begin promptly at 9:00 A.M., everyone will probably eat breakfast in your dining room. Would that create problems? Will you have sufficient staff and kitchen facilities to handle a group of that size?
>
> Our group will arrive during the evening of June 13 and check out on the morning of June 17. Two people will share each room, and if you can provide us with a block of rooms, we will make the assignments.

This gives the necessary information and asks the essential questions. If your readers do their job, you should be able to decide where to have the meeting. (Of course, this is not to say the middle couldn't stand some revision.) All that remains now is to write the ending.

Writing endings. Remember, at the end of your letter your reader will be paying attention, so make the last paragraph count.

As you planned this letter, you decided that your reader should have a deadline and should know that you are looking at other possibilities. So why not use that at the end? It can provide both a reminder and motivation to do the job well.

> So that everything can be ready for June 14, please let me know by February 1 whether you can provide what we need. We'll appreciate an itemized estimate of the costs, so we can compare them with those of the other convention centers we are contacting.

Or you could say it this way:

> We'll need to decide soon where to have the meeting, so please let me have your answer, with an itemized estimate of costs, no later than February 1. I'm looking forward to hearing from you.

Replies: Giving Good Answers

A "good news" or favorable reply is one that answers a reader's question or approves a request. In short, it says yes. Because you are responding, rather than initiating the exchange, you have some assurance that your readers will pay attention to what you write because they have a vested interest in it. But this does not relieve you of the responsibility to be interesting and informative.

Favorable replies may or may not be opportunities to sell your company's products or services. But they are always opportunities to present a positive image of you and your company, so that you can establish or maintain feelings of goodwill and mutual respect between you and your reader.

A well-done reply is one that:

1. Presents the information or decision your reader has requested
2. Explains what your reader needs to know
3. Concentrates on information that your reader needs, rather than giving all that is available
4. Provides additional information that your reader may not have known enough to ask for
5. Works to establish a relationship of goodwill and mutual respect
6. Convinces your reader that it is complete and correct and that you are a reliable source

Let's look at a situation similar to those you might encounter at work and use it to learn how to write replies. We will begin with the request and follow it through to the final letter. If you worked for a company that makes computerized manufacturing controls (the kind used in automating manufacturing processes) you might find a letter like this one in the day's mail.

> Gentlemen:
>
> For some time I have been reading about the use of computers to automate manufacturing processes. I believe it is time I learned more about this to see if it is possible to automate part of my own operation.
>
> Barrington-Black manufactures specialty metal products on a special-order or contract basis. Most of our products are used as components in pumps, heat exchangers, and air conditioners. We work to exacting specifications and often to extremely close tolerances.
>
> We are obviously not ready to install computers, because we don't know if they will help us. We would like to know how much money would be involved, how many new people we would need to hire, and the length of time it would take to automate our operation. It would also help if we could talk with other companies that have installed your controls.
>
> I know that you can't answer these questions with the information I have given you. You'll need to look us over first. But

it might save both of us some time and money if we can get some information first. I will appreciate anything you can tell me.

Sincerely,

J. Reed Barrington
President
Barrington-Black

Setting Goals

Of course, your goal is to answer this letter. But you will help yourself and your reader by deciding what your answer must do.

Begin with the goal that your reader states: to learn more about the use of computers to control manufacturing processes. That establishes your subject, but it does little more. You will find that readers display varying degrees of skill in writing inquiries. Some will give you detailed directions about what they want and thus tell you how to construct your reply. Others are more like Mr. Barrington. Their requests will be sufficiently vague that you will have to do most of the work of deciding what they need to know and how to give it to them.

Mr. Barrington does make it clear that he is looking for information rather than a sales pitch. At this point he does not even know what he needs to know, let alone how to put that knowledge to work. He has probably written to other companies like yours, and he will compare the answers closely. The more help you give him now, the more likely it is that he will come back to you for more information. Eventually, he may even buy your product. This request contains the potential for a sale, but that is some distance in the future. You have an opportunity to begin building a business relationship. The quality of the information and service that you provide now can be the basis of that relationship. Thus, it can put you in a position to make a sale later on.

Set your goal carefully. A goal that is too narrow, such as "answer the letter," might tempt you to send a few glossy brochures from the marketing department. A goal that is too broad might lead you to tell your reader everything you know about computerized industrial controls. That would clearly be more than he needs to know right now. In fact, if you overwhelm your reader with technical information you may drive him away. He will decide, quite rightly, that you don't understand his needs.

What goal is appropriate for your letter to Mr. Barrington? It might be one of the following:

To explain what would be involved in converting to a computerized operation

To give names of some of your customers

To explain what an on-site visit would involve

To tell him how or where he can learn more

This much will satisfy Mr. Barrington's needs, but what about your own? Try to give him what he wants in such a way that you can also show:

Your company's range of experience in this field

Your willingness to help, even without a sales commitment

That you realize he is setting out on a complicated and expensive project

That you will not sell him something that is inappropriate to his needs

Your goal is to provide Mr. Barrington with the information he has requested (names of customers), along with some information that he needs (answering his implied questions) in a way that establishes a goodwill relationship between you.

Your Reader

Mr. Barrington may not know much about computerized controls for manufacturing, but that does not mean he is completely ignorant. He has to know something to have become president of the company. It's a safe bet that he understands manufacturing and corporate financing. He is probably keenly interested in the cost of such a conversion and the money he may lose while the conversion is underway. In fact, he has asked you specifically about costs for equipment and new employees. Because he is president, he will be closely involved in any decision to buy your product or a competitor's. He may be wary of high technology or may know more about it than you do. You have no way of knowing that. If he installs controls and makes them a permanent part of his operation, he will be interested in service. What happens after you install the controls and he writes a check? Will he ever see you again?

You know all of this about Mr. Barrington, even though you have never met him. If you think about it, you can extend this list of observations and picture him even more completely. This knowledge will help you decide that Mr. Barrington must be approached as an intelligent, successful manufacturer, a decision maker who needs an overview, with a minimum of technical detail. He is not asking to be "sold," but informed.

What Will You Say?

If there is a problem with writing replies, it is not that you know too little, but that you know too much. Your job is not to find *enough* to say, but to select information that is to the point. When people ask accountants whether a particular business expense is deductible, they want an answer to their question, not a discussion of corporate tax law.

Telling Mr. Barrington what he needs to know will include answering his implied questions as well as the ones he asked. A good brainstorming session might come up with the following:

> While computerized installations can cost a lot of money, they can pay for themselves in savings in a short time (five years?).
>
> Actual costs are given in a detailed proposal that you will write after an on-site visit.
>
> You can provide the names of four or five customers who use your equipment and are within driving distance of Mr. Barrington's factory.
>
> You can enclose several brochures that explain exactly what your equipment does.
>
> You provide service on an annual contract basis.
>
> He can learn more by visiting computerized factories and by reading. Give him a short reading list.
>
> You will be pleased to send a technical representative to talk with him.
>
> You have been providing computerized controls to manufacturers for fifteen years.
>
> You want him to take the time to make an informed decision (because you want him to be pleased with the results).

This is probably not a complete list of what you will say in your letter. You will no doubt think of more as you organize and write. But there is enough here to get you started.

Organizing and Writing

Now we need to organize this information, or some of it, into a direct approach. Mr. Barrington will want your main point first, so begin there. If you look at your brainstorming list, you might find a main point there. It could be that automated controls can pay for themselves, or that your company has fifteen years of experience in installing them. But reread his letter. One thing that Mr. Barrington seems to want is reassurance that he's doing the right thing by raising the question of computerizing his manufacturing process. Maybe *that* could be your main point. This could include the opinion that computerizing is an economically smart move (or that it can be). It might help to do an issue tree at this point, just to see how the information you have might fit together. Figure 7-1 shows such an issue tree.

The issue tree gives a main point at the top and groups the rest of the brainstorming list into three categories of information: (1) making an informed decision, (2) analyzing his needs, and (3) analyzing what you have to offer. If we write the letter using this sequence, it might look like the following, at least as a first draft. Remember, we want to keep the reader, not ourselves, at center.

> Dear Mr. Barrington:
>
> You are right. Many companies are modernizing their manufacturing facilities by installing computerized controls. And the business press has been full of success stories that tell of reduced costs and short cost-recovery periods. Computerized controls can provide savings and have allowed many companies to stay competitive in demanding markets.
>
> But few of the success stories tell of the need to make informed decisions when you install computerized controls. You really need to know what you're doing when you select a system or even when you decide that you want one. The initial cost of installing a system can make mistakes quite expensive. We know that's not good for you, and it doesn't help us any either.
>
> You can get the information you need in several ways. You might begin by talking with presidents of other companies that have installed BRX systems, and then visit their facilities

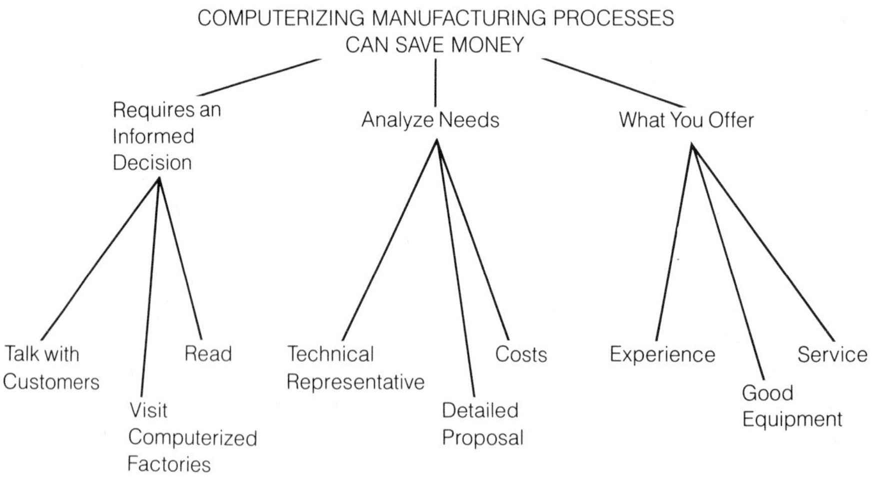

Figure 7-1 Issue Tree Illustrating Money-Saving Features of Computerizing the Manufacturing Process

to see the systems in operation. The enclosed list will give you the names and addresses of companies that are now using BRX systems. They have all agreed to meet with representatives of companies that are considering conversion to computerized controls. They are a very candid group, and I'm sure they will tell you about the problems they have encountered, as well as the benefits.

You can also learn by reading. I've enclosed copies of several articles that will give you a good idea of what is involved in converting to a computerized system. They are written for the executive rather than the specialist. Many of the companies on the enclosed list assigned a task force to study the conversion, and they have found this method helpful. I have also enclosed some materials about BRX systems, so you can see what we have to offer.

Before you make a decision, and before we can give you detailed information about costs, equipment, and personnel, we would have to make a detailed study of your needs. That would begin by sending a Technical Representative to visit with you and study your operation. Then a team would visit you to prepare a detailed study and proposal.

BRX has been providing high-quality controls to manufacturers for fifteen years. The companies on the enclosed list will all tell you that they enjoy doing business with us. Our reputation is based on selling an up-to-date product that we service as long as you own it, or even if you sell it to someone else.

I will look forward to hearing from you again when you have had a chance to learn more about computerized controls and BRX.

Sincerely,

David R. Masten
Customer Service Engineer

Revision of this letter should probably concentrate on making it more positive and motivating Mr. Barrington to call or write for more information or assistance.

Writing Goodwill Letters

Every letter you write is a goodwill letter, because creating goodwill is always one of your goals. But many letters have goodwill as their main purpose. They offer congratulations, condolences, welcome, apology, and thanks, or they respond to special occasions or events. In your private life you would send a greeting card or perhaps a brief note in these situations. In business you write personal letters. They make your readers feel good about themselves and, not incidentally, about you. Your readers benefit from the compliment or emotional support you are providing. You benefit because you were thoughtful enough to write, and you hope to be remembered for your thoughtfulness.

Sometimes you will write goodwill letters simply because you want to: because it makes you feel good to make others feel good. Or you may be obligated to write. When someone does you a favor, or has you to dinner, or sends you a gift, there is an unspoken obligation to show your appreciation. This is true even though that person clearly expects nothing in return. Or you may write goodwill letters because it's good business. They help you maintain a friendly relationship with your customers and members of the public. And they do this even though no overt business transaction takes place in the letter.

The business motive for goodwill letters presents a challenge. If you state it too overtly your reader may question your sincerity. And the result of that will not be goodwill. Most people who have been promoted to an important position have received this kind of goodwill letter. It congratulates them for their good fortune (forgetting to mention the hard work and ability that were required) and suggests that new-found status requires a new car, house, or insurance policy to match.

Goodwill letters usually respond to a special occasion or event. You may wish to congratulate someone for a promotion or appointment, welcome a new employee to your company, or wish someone well in a new business venture. The occasion might be a business anniversary (yours or your reader's), a death, or a salesperson's excellent sales record for the past year. Or you might feel the need to apologize for an inconvenience you have caused or are about to cause. A number of companies have attracted favorable attention with letters and advertisements that say, in effect, "We goofed."

Whatever the occasion, you will need to plan so that you will know what you want to say, why you are saying it, and what you hope to accomplish by writing.

Setting Your Goal

Your goal is to create or maintain a relationship of goodwill between you and your reader. To do that you will need to incorporate the specific details of the situation. Perhaps you want to congratulate a salesperson who has had a particularly successful year. Why do you want to do that? If you are the Sales Manager, you will do it because you understand that people need to know that you think they have done a good job. We all like appreciation, and we don't always get that from a paycheck, no matter how big it is. We want more.

Some people don't realize just how special their achievements are. Since you are the boss, you can put that record in the perspective of the entire sales force. In the long run you might even have something to gain. If employees are well-paid and know that you appreciate their work, they might stay with the company, in spite of many opportunities to move on. Your goal is to congratulate a salesperson for outstanding achievements during the past year and show that you are aware of an excellent job.

If you own a small business you may write people whose appointments and promotions are announced in the local paper. You want to congratulate them or welcome them to town. But you also want to let them know that you are aware of their needs and have experience serving a clientele that is much like them. Your goal is to create goodwill by welcoming your readers to the area and to let them know that you are available. You will do this, of course, in a low-key way that stops well short of actually trying to sell them something.

Your Reader

You will think about your readers in all the usual ways, considering their position, their knowledge, their needs, and their specific relationship to you. But some details are specific to the situation. To begin with, readers will almost always know more about the situation than you do. People usually know they have been promoted, or done you a favor, or had a good year. And they know how hard they have had to work to accomplish their goals or how much trouble it was to do the favor. So even though the event or occasion is what prompts you to write, you reader does not need information. The event, the reason you are writing, becomes the background, not the main focus of your letter.

The goodwill letter's main business is attitudes, feelings, and emotions. A psychologist would say that their job is affective rather than cognitive. Greeting cards provide a good analogy here. When you send birthday cards your purpose is not to tell people how old they are or that it is their birthday. You are expressing an attitude of friendship or approval and using the birthday as an occasion for doing so. It is this expression of approval, or gratitude, or sympathy that is important.

Sometimes who you are is as important as what you say. We all like to receive compliments, approval, friendship, sympathy, and even apologies from people who are important to us. We take their comments more seriously than we would those of someone we don't know. A Sales Manager's acknowledgment of an excellent record is likely to have considerable impact. Local businesspersons who welcome a new executive to town or congratulate someone for a recent promotion will have less impact because they are less significant in that person's life. In practice this means that the more remote you are from your reader, the more you will have to work to show why it is appropriate for you to write a goodwill letter.

It is important that the relationship you attempt to establish in your letter be consistent with the relationship that actually exists between you and your reader. If you are close, if your opinions matter to each other, then you can adopt a familiar tone. If you are not close or do not know each other at all, then a more formal, businesslike tone is better suited to the situation.

Consider this:

> Dear Ms. Smith:
>
> During the five years you have been with Smallco you have established a commendable sales record. Last year you were our top sales representative.
>
> I want to take this opportunity to thank you for your efforts on behalf of the company and to express my personal congratulations.
>
> Best wishes.
>
> Andrew T. Dempster
> Sales Manager

If you have worked for Mr. Dempster for five years, you might wonder what's going on here. The tone seems much too formal and even curt for someone you have worked closely with for five years. Does he mean this, or is he just going through the motions?

Or what about this one, from someone you have never met?

> Dear George,
>
> Congratulations on that big promotion. You worked hard for it, you got it, and now you should enjoy it.
>
> Eastwind Motors has the finest selection of prestige and executive autos in town. You and Jean will really knock their socks off when you drive up to the Country Club in a car that shows them who you are.
>
> Stop in anytime. We're eager to help. Just ask for
>
> "Bud" Robertson

This writer has adopted a personal tone and used personal details that may be inappropriate. He has no idea how hard his reader worked for the promotion or whether he belongs to the country club. The use of the wife's name is apparently based on picking it out of the newspaper. And the phrase "knock their socks off" seems risky. This reader may not be someone who *wants* to knock socks off, and he may find the phrase itself offensive.

Finding Something to Say

So how *do* you find something appropriate to say in a goodwill letter? Begin by asking yourself how well you know your reader. The better you know someone, the more you will be able to draw on your experiences with each other. You will be able to use specific details that actually apply to the situation, and you will know the degree of familiarity and informality you can assume. The more remote you are from your readers, the more you will need to rely on general information about their socio-economic or professional group. Specific, personal information may be either unavailable or inappropriate.

The Sales Manager who writes to congratulate a successful salesperson may want to write a letter that:

> Puts that record into the context of what the other salespersons have done
>
> Uses specific details about what the salesperson has done
>
> Shows appreciation for the contribution this salesperson has made to the company's success

The letter will use a direct pattern of organization. It may be similar to the next example.

> Dear ______,
>
> By now you know that you are QWIKMATIC'S top salesperson for 198_. Congratulations.
>
> I know you appreciate how much work went into achieving this outstanding year, and I want you to know that I appreciate it, too. You should feel especially good about the job you have done this past year. The annual sales report shows that every member of the sales force exceeded his or her quota by at least 15%.
>
> But you led the way by being 35% over your quota. That's outstanding in any year, but it's especially impressive to be the best in a highly successful group.
>
> And I want you to know that you accomplished all of this in unusual circumstances. You turned in the greatest number of small accounts (under $50,000) and new customers. That's a direct result of your hard work in finding new prospects and your superior knowledge of your products and the market.
>
> I have a copy of Dave Smith's letter announcing the healthy increase in your base salary for next year and the nice bonus you will receive. But I know that sometimes money alone isn't enough to express our appreciation. I want you to know that I noticed the excellent job you are doing.
>
> Say hello to your family for me. I plan to be in San Francisco in March and I look forward to seeing you then.
>
> Best wishes,
>
> John R. Dresden
> Sales Manager

Because John Dresden and his reader share common experiences and interests, this letter uses personal details and an informal, familiar tone. The praise is obviously sincere, and because it comes from a person who is important to the reader it will be valued.

When reader and writer do not know each other well, or at all, and the writer obviously has something to gain from the letter, the approach will be somewhat different. Suppose that you own a small, exclusive clothing store that caters to executives, both men and women. Much of your reputation is by word-of-mouth among your customers, but you like to be sure that people know you exist. So you regularly write "welcome" letters to executives who have been transferred to your city, and you send "congratulations" to those who have been promoted to executive levels.

In this situation you will not be able to draw on personal experiences or direct knowledge of your readers. Instead, you will need to focus on the attitudes and needs of these executives *as a group.* That is, you may know nothing about your readers as individuals, but you do know their needs for clothing and accessories that suit their business and leisure activities.

Today's letter is to Ms. Joan Randall, who has just been appointed Executive Vice President of a local company. She comes from Chicago, where she was an account executive with a major public relations firm.

> Dear Ms. Randall:
>
> Congratulations on your appointment as Executive Vice President of Wall and Williams. And welcome to Beaver Valley.
>
> I hope you are settling comfortably into your new home and office, and that you have begun to enjoy the relaxed lifestyle of our small but pleasant city. It's a far cry from the fast-paced, busy life of a city like Chicago. But I wanted you to know that you didn't leave all of the advantages of the big city behind you.
>
> Bernard's has been providing apparel and accessories to Beaver Valley executives for twenty years. You will find that we carry sensible, up-to-date apparel that is appropriate to any executive suite. And we also provide a full range of leisure and sports wear. You can shop in Chicago without leaving Beaver Valley.
>
> Again, welcome to Beaver Valley. I hope you will enjoy it here as much as I do.
>
> Sincerely,
>
> Roberta Saxon
> Manager

This letter uses no personal details about the reader beyond those announced in the newspaper. It is more formal in tone than the letter to the salesperson, yet it is still friendly.

Chapter Checklist

When you need to write a good news or goodwill letter, remember:

1. Set your goals carefully. Give yourself something to do.
2. Think about your reader.
3. Know your subject thoroughly. Your job is to ask specific questions and give complete answers.
4. Use a direct pattern of organization that begins and ends positively.
5. Review what you have written. Be sure you have asked or answered the important questions.
6. Revise your letter to:
    a. Adapt the subject and style to your reader
    b. Show a "you" attitude
    c. Write positively
    d. Be confident

Examples

Figures 7-2 through 7-8 are examples of how business writers in various corporations have presented good news and goodwill messages. You can use them for independent review or as the basis of in-class discussions. Any of these letters may be in need of revision, and you can gain valuable experience by revising them so that they observe the principles outlined in this chapter.

■

Figure 7-2 Letter Acknowledging Good Service

YORK CONTAINER COMPANY

YORK, PENNSYLVANIA 17402

CHARLES S. WOLF
President

June 2, 1982

Mr. John R. Clugston
Metropolitan Edison Co.
Parkway Boulevard
York, PA 17404

Dear John:

Tuesday evening, June 1, was a busy one for many people in your company.

The unbelievably hard rains and winds knocked our power out at our home at 189 South Eighth Street in Mt. Wolf. Your people came promptly, and Phyllis had a chance to chat with your men who climbed a pole and found out, of all things, that the transformer that serves our home had been invaded by a squirrel. Maybe you're used to unusual happenings, but this is the first I've ever heard of that. At any rate, our power was restored by about 8:05 p.m., and we truly appreciate it.

I don't know the names of the two men who worked on our project, but if it is possible, Phyllis and I would appreciate your thanking them for us. We appreciated their skilland courage in a most dramatic night and their courtesy to us.

Warmest regards,

Charles S. Wolf

CSW:mrg

Figure 7-3 Letter Confirming a Meeting

March 27, 1980

Chandler & Farquhar Co., Inc.
900 Commonwealth Avenue
Boston, Massachusetts 02215

Attention: Mr. J. M. Edinburg, President

Dear Joe:

This will confirm our telephone conversation of Thursday, the 27th, concerning our visit to your company to learn more about your computer programs. Monday, May 5, will suit us and we hope that it will be convenient for you. As it stands now, three of our people will be coming - Ed Nitchman, Dick Marquette and Clyde Snyder. I will not be able to accompany them on this trip.

I, indeed, appreciate your offer and your hospitality. Someone will call you closer to the time and advise of the time that they will be visiting you on May 5.

Thanks again for giving us this opportunity to visit with you.

Very truly yours,

YORK MACHINERY & SUPPLY CO.

F. B. Shearer
President

FBS:ns

Figure 7-4 Letter to a Client

April 22, 1982

Carboloy Systems Dept.
General Electric Co.
10 Great Valley Parkway
Suite 120
Malvern, Pennsylvania 19355

Attention: Mr. Jack Curtis

Dear Jack:

I am enclosing a copy of our monthly mailer that we mail to selected purchasing agents. You can see that this particular month we highlighted Carboloy.

This is just another way in which we try to promote your products.

Very truly yours,

YORK MACHINERY & SUPPLY CO.

F. B. Shearer
President

FBS:ns

Figure 7-5 Letter Giving Information to a Prospective Client

November 5, 1982

Mr. Phil Jones
Design Engineer
Foreman Laboratories
Industrial Avenue
Baltimore, MD 00000

Dear Mr. Jones:

I'm delighted to hear from our New England Sales Manager, Ralph Barber, that you and Foreman Labs have expressed an interest in Holotech's capabilities in the keyboard/membrane switch field.

Here is some literature dealing not only with our touch switch activities but with our operations in general. As you will see, we may be ideally positioned to be of immediate creative service to you.

Mr. Barber will shortly be in touch to discuss specifics, but after reviewing this material, please don't hesitate to call him or me for further information.

Sincerely,

J. M. Danner

cc: Al Fruth
Tom Snyder, R&D Purchasing Dept, Foreman Labs

Figure 7-6 Letter Requesting Information

(Date)

(Name)
(Title)
(Company)
(Address)
(City, State, Zip Code)

Dear (Name)

Now you can relax! You've finally gotten caught up on all the work that piled up while you were in Boulder. You've finished and mailed your final assignment for BMA. So sit back, prop your feet up, and take it easy.

Sounds good, doesn't it? Well, here I go, I'm going to ruin it all. I need your help! I'd like to pick your brain for some information.

We (my boss and I) would like to know how the Marketing Division of your bank is structured. A little background information on The York Bank might help to clarify why we'd like the information:

> The York Bank is a $580,000,000 Bank in Southeastern Pennsylvania. We are situated entirely in York County and have twenty (20) branches in a 914 square mile area.
>
> Recently (January 1982), a bank holding company, York Bancorp, was formed to allow us to expand on the number of services we offer and to provide for possible physical expansion into other areas of Pennsylvania.
>
> Presently, our Marketing Division consists of two (2) people, my boss and myself. We perform all the traditional marketing functions, advertising, research, product development, public relations, etc. In addition, we administer the MasterCard and Visa Merchant Program, develop and present training programs, and coordinate the Office Call program. We are closely involved in the day-to-day operation of the Bank, as well as in the planning for the position of The York Bank in the future.
>
> The formation of the Bank holding company has led us to the opinion that, perhaps, a restructuring of the Marketing Division is necessary to facilitate the accomplishment of the corporate goals.

That is where we need you. We ask that you complete the enclosed survey with information concerning the structure of your Marketing Division. If you would like the results of the survey, include your calling card when you return the survey to me.

Thank you for your attention. Now, you can sit back, relax, and recall all your fond memories of Boulder: the Rockies, the raft trip, the skiing . . .

Sincerely,

Cheryl L. Keener
Assistant Treasurer

wp
Enclosure

Figure 7-7 Letter Explaining a Service

January 15, 1983

Mr. John Quigley
Manager
Accounts Department
Mid-Atlantic Gas Co.
4322 Expressway Dr.
Baltimore, MD 21333

Dear Mr. Quigley:

We are presently serving as a collecting agent for your utility payments. On occasion a customer requests to make a payment and does not have a bill. For this purpose we have constructed a universal receipt which, hopefully, could be used for the various utility companies we service.

Enclosed is a copy of the receipt. The receipt would be completed in duplicate. The original copy would be your record of payment received, and the duplicate would provide a receipt for the customer. Would you please review the receipt and let me know if your company would have any objections to this method of payment. Of course, we prefer to process the original bill and will do so whenever possible.

Your prompt reply with your comments would be appreciated.

Very truly yours,

Angela Hartley
Operations Manager

Figure 7-8 Letter to Company Employees

May 5, 1982

SUBJECT: EMPLOYEE PURCHASE PLAN FOR WHOLE-HOUSE
AIR CONDITIONING HEAT PUMPS AND FURNACES
FOR BORG-WARNER EMPLOYEES

As you are aware with the acquisition of Westinghouse Heating and Air Conditioning facilities, York Division Unitary Products became a subsidiary of BORG-WARNER CORPORATION with the new name of BORG-WARNER CENTRAL ENVIRONMENTAL SYSTEMS INC. Under the new subsidiary, in addition to the York heating and air conditioning line, three additional brands will be manufactured and distributed throughout the U.S.A. They are FRASER-JOHNSTON, LUXAIRE and MONCRIEF.

BORG-WARNER EMPLOYEE REBATE PROGRAM
IS EXPANDED TO ALL BRANDS

Through December 31, 1982, all BORG-WARNER EMPLOYEES are eligible for the following rebates on the purchase of any BORG-WARNER Furnaces, York Air Conditioning and Heat Pumps, along with Fraser-Johnston, Luxaire or Moncreif Furnaces, Air Conditioning and Heat Pumps.

For any of the above BWCES Central Home Systems, Borg-Warner employee rebates are as follows:

AIR CONDITIONING & HEAT PUMPS

SYSTEM SIZE	AMOUNT OF REBATE AIR CONDITIONING	HEAT PUMPS
2 Tons	$ 50.00	$ 75.00
2½ Tons	75.00	100.00
3 Tons	100.00	125.00
3½, 4 & 5 Tons	125.00	150.00

HEATING UNITS

GAS	REBATE	OIL	REBATE	ELECTRIC	REBATE
65 - 80,000 BTU	$20.00	85 BTU	$20.00	5-15 KW	$20.00
105 - 120,000 BTU	25.00	125 BTU	30.00	20-35 KW	30.00
140 - 200,000 BTU	30.00	150 BTU	40.00		

Here's how it works. The Borg-Warner employee negotiates the best possible price on any of the BWCES Heating and Air Conditioning Central Home Conditioning System with the local Air Conditioning and Heating dealer of his choice. The installed (or total) price will, of course, be dependent upon each home's specific installation requirements.

After the unit is installed and working to the employee's satisfaction, he submits a BWCES Personal Use Rebate Form (Form No. Y80-4967A) to his Human Resources Department who simply authenticates that he is a Borg-Warner employee in good standing and forwards the material to the BWCES. A copy of the dealer's invoice (marked "paid") should also be attached. We will then issue the rebate check directly to the employee.

The Personal Use Rebate forms may be obtained from the Personnel Department by calling extension 2555.

HUMAN RESOURCES DEPARTMENT

Exercises: Chapter Seven

1. Your company has recently established a "friendly coworker" program in which employees are assigned to orient new employees to the company and, if necessary, to the area. Present employees volunteer for this program so that only those who are interested are involved, and all volunteers are screened carefully.

   You have just been assigned your first new employee in this program. She is Ms. Sarah Barnes, who will join the company next month as Assistant Advertising Manager. Write her a letter in which you introduce yourself and describe the area in which the company is located. (For this, you will probably want to use a city or town with which you are familiar.) All you know about Ms. Barnes is that she is single, twenty-four years old, and has worked in Chicago for four years as an advertising copywriter.

2. Select a nationally advertised product or service that you want to know more about and write a letter that requests the information you would need if you were to purchase this product or service. You may write on behalf of yourself or your company.

3. Your company has decided that rather than purchase cars and trucks for its fleet, it will rent or lease them if that course is more economical. At the moment it uses four prestige cars, fifteen economy cars, and twenty compact pick-up trucks. You have been receiving a 20 percent discount on the sticker price for purchasing all of these vehicles at once. Your job is to write a letter that you can send to a number of dealers and leasing companies to inquire about the types of vehicles you could rent or lease, the terms of the transaction, the services that would be available during the term of the lease, and the cost.

4. In this morning's mail you received a request for a letter of reference for Paul Randolph. He worked for your company for eight months last year (March 15 to November 15) as a machinist's assistant. Now he is applying for a job as an auto mechanic at a large new car dealership across town. You saw little of Paul while he worked for you but remember that he seemed to be a pleasant person. His former supervisor reports that he was always on time for work, cooperative, and seemed to know his job. He can operate a turret lathe and a milling machine and can produce machined parts to precision tolerances. His records show that he missed only one day of work and gave two weeks' notice before leaving his job. Write the reference to Mr. Arlen James, A-J Cars, Inc., 1225 Winthrop St., Homeville, KY 00000.

5. Your boss, Theresa Anderson of Anderson Products, 3248 Industrial Highway, Flagstaff, AZ 00000, has decided that she would like to ex-

plore the concept of shared jobs. She thinks a number of good workers, many of them women, would like to split a full-time job into two part-time jobs. She wants you to write to other companies to find out whether they have tried this and, if so, whether it has worked. She is also interested in how these companies have handled the question of fringe benefits (Anderson does not pay benefits to part-time employees at present), vacations, time off, and pay increases. Write a letter, for Ms. Anderson's signature, that will get her the information she wants.

6. You work in the Employee Relations Department of GRV Corporation, a multinational defense contractor. You have been assigned to write a series of form letters that management in the home office can send to employees who have been promoted, married, or had a baby. The president of the U.S. division of the company will sign these and send them to employees in the United States.

7. Mr. Samuel Sands, owner of Sam's Appliances, 509 Severn Street, Bartlett, IN 00000, has been a customer of yours for twelve years. Each year he orders about $250,000 worth of refrigerators, air conditioners, and dishwashers. Next week he will celebrate the twenty-fifth anniversary of his business. Write him a letter that congratulates him for this achievement. (You might begin by finding some statistics about how long the average small business survives.)

8. Your aunt, Mildred Sams, owns a small clothing store in the city where you live. She has decided to retire, and she will either go out of business or turn it over to you if you are interested in it. Once you decide what you will do, she wants you to write a letter to the customers listed in her credit file. This letter should either announce the going-out-of-business sale or the change in management. If there is to be a sale, discounts will range from 50 percent to 70 percent, and credit customers will be invited to shop for one day before the general public is admitted. The shop carries all of the usual items of men's clothing. Decide which you will do, and then write the letter to the customers.

9. Your company is considering converting its typing pool and individual secretaries from typewriters to word processing equipment. Before you begin calling sales representatives and inviting them to demonstrate their machines, you would like to hear from other companies that have made this conversion. You want to know which machines they think are best (why they bought the ones they now use); whether they are rented, leased, or purchased; and whether service has been adequate. You might also ask about the training period that is required. You can, of course, ask any other questions that you think are important.

10. Your company has recently experienced numerous time losses and missed deadlines because of employee accidents, both on and off the job.

a. Write a letter of inquiry in which you ask other companies about their safety policies and the steps they have taken to reduce lost time due to accidents.

b. Write a notice to employees in which you stress the need for safety in all things that they do, both on and off the job. (You may need to do a bit of research to find out what the main safety hazards are.)

11. You have decided to start a part-time sales business, either to help you pay your way through school or to help provide extra income.

a. Write letters to local and state agencies to inquire about applicable regulations and licensing requirements.

b. Choose three companies that use part-time sales representatives and write them to inquire about their products, procedures, and other information you might need to get started in business for yourself. Be sure that you think through this carefully so that you ask all of the questions that are applicable.

■

8

Writing Letters That Say No

In this chapter you will learn how to tell your readers what they would really rather not know and to do so in a way that:

1. Makes it clear that you understand and respect your reader's position and the reasoning behind it
2. States your own position and decision in a way that encourages your reader to understand and respect you and your reasoning
3. Encourages your reader to see that the two of you have enough in common to reach a mutually satisfactory resolution of your differences*

---

*For some of the ideas in this chapter I am indebted to Richard Young, Kenneth Pike, and Alton Becker, *Rhetoric: Discovery and Change* (New York: Harcourt Brace Jovanovich, 1970).

It's OK to Say No

It is inevitable that you will make decisions that will disappoint those who are affected by them. This occurs at all levels of the working world. Supervisors turn down workers' requests. Customer Relations departments refuse to make adjustments. Personnel managers must tell people they will not be hired. Salespersons must tell customers that orders cannot be produced in the short lead times requested.

There are powerful motivations for all of us to avoid disappointing others. Perhaps the most common is that none of us wants to be the bad guy, the person who keeps others from being what they want to be or achieving their goals. We value the goodwill and respect of others, and we sometimes believe we can get or keep these by always saying yes. Perhaps that will make it easier to get along with others and keep our relationships working smoothly.

But saying yes to everything amounts to not making decisions at all. Eventually, it will undermine your position as a decision maker, and it may actually harm your organization.

Your responsibility to yourself, your company, and those who depend on you for leadership requires that you always try to make the best possible decision in the situation at hand. Sometimes that means you must say no, and that is OK. It doesn't make you a louse, a rat, or less of a human being. In fact, it may be the best thing you can do.

Planning Letters That Say No

Defining Your Goals

Before we consider specific goals and ways of achieving them, let's look at some very general results that you *might* achieve:

1. You could get readers to change their minds completely, realize their requests were foolish, and adopt your position and reasoning as their own.
2. You could get your readers to modify their positions, adopting *some* of your reasons and at least understanding, if not accepting, your decision.
3. You might accomplish nothing at all. The impasse between you and your reader might remain, each of you continuing to hold your own positions.

Of these three possible results, the second and third are more likely to occur than the first. The second, a partial change in your reader's position, is perhaps the most realistic goal to work toward. There is no need to try to achieve the third. It will happen all by itself, sometimes in spite of your best efforts.

So, in setting goals the question becomes "What can I do to achieve a partial change in my reader's position?" But this is a large, abstract goal. It tells you where you want to go but gives you nothing to do to get there. The first step is to break the large goal into subgoals, which are specific enough that you can work with them and are stated such a way that they suggest what you can do to achieve them. A typical list of subgoals might look like this:

1. Stating your decision so your readers know what it means.
2. Getting your readers to read and pay attention to all that you have to say. That is, you want your readers to consider your position, so you must state it completely.
3. Getting your readers to understand your position (which is different from simply reading it) and, if possible, to accept it. As part of this goal, you will also want to:
   a. Show your readers that you understand their positions.
   b. Show that you recognize those parts of your readers' positions that are valid.
4. If you can accomplish the first three of these goals, then you are well on your way to achieving the final one of attempting to resolve the conflict that your decision has brought to light and thus retaining goodwill. To accomplish this you will need to show your readers that you have enough in common to be able to reach a mutually satisfactory resolution.

Each of these subgoals is specific enough that you can actually do something to achieve it. Later, when we discuss ways of organizing and writing this kind of letter, we'll identify what you can do to achieve each of these goals and use the result to construct your letter. For now, there is one remaining step in the planning stage, and it's an important one.

Thinking about Your Reader

It is time to focus rather intensely on your reader. If you want your readers to understand your decision, you are going to have to make an even greater effort to understand theirs. What are they thinking about? What are the possible emotional and intellectual responses to what you will say? How do people react when they make what they think is a reasonable request, only to have it turned down?

Begin by remembering those times that you have been refused. Think about how it felt. What did you want to do when you heard the answer? Were you happy? Relieved? Angry? Disappointed? Did you play "sour grapes" and say you didn't want that anyway? Did the refusal seem natural, expected, and thus help to confirm an already weak self-concept? All of these responses are possible.

Begin by assuming that readers are, or see themselves as, rational, mature people making what they believe are reasonable requests that have a better-than-average chance of success. Very few people really *like* to be refused, so most of us begin by doing a quick cost/benefit analysis before we ask for something. If it looks like we will gain more than we might lose, then we go ahead.

Once people decide to go ahead, they usually develop a rather thorough, carefully constructed rationale for their own position. This serves a dual purpose. First, it is a means of convincing themselves that their request is valid and worth pursuing. Later, this rationale becomes the evidence to convince a decision maker that they are right, that there is no reason to say "no." This rationale is usually based on a well-developed body of attitudes and beliefs that provide your readers with a mental image of what the world is like, how it works, and where they fit in it.

When you refuse a request you are often dealing with more than a specific request in a particular situation. The request is usually firmly attached to your readers' mental image of the world and their place in it. When readers react with surprise, embarrassment, frustration, or anger, they are reacting less to your refusal than to the threat it poses to their view of the world. When this happens, you are unlikely to convert your readers to your point of view or even to modify their position by merely stating your own position and the facts and reasoning it is based on. Your reader already has a firmly held conviction that is in conflict with your own. Facts and logic that contradict your reader's view of the situation will simply be ignored or assimilated as if they were consistent with it. When you refuse a request, you must respond not only to the specific request, but to the rationale on which it is based and to the mental image of the world that that implies.

You will be able to respond most effectively if you realize that you must:

1. Demonstrate that you thoroughly understand the request and the rationale on which it is based
2. Point out those portions of your reader's rationale that you believe to be valid
3. Encourage your reader to see that the two of you share similar values (integrity, fairness) and goals (the desire to reach a mutually satisfactory resolution of the situation)

Organizing to Say No

If you have planned carefully, then what remains is to organize and write your reply, using what you know about your subject, your goals, and your reader. Many people are tempted to use a direct organization plan, such as you used in Chapter 7, that states the decision in the beginning and then goes on to give the reasons for it. But this is incompatible with your goals and your reader's projected reaction.

If you begin by stating your decision or your own position, you are leading directly into the conflict between you and your reader, rather than taking the opportunity to show that you understand the request and the reasons for it. By doing this, you invite readers to stop reading as soon as it becomes clear that you are not responding positively. Even if you go on to give a clear presentation of your reasons, your readers may not get that far. They will be spending their time and energy constructing counter-arguments to every point that you make. Once that happens, you have given up any chance that the two of you will actually understand and come to terms with each other.

When you organize this kind of letter, keep in mind the tasks it must perform and the effects you want it to have on your reader. Rather than attempting to construct a flawless, logical presentation, you want to take your reader through an exploration of the situation, from both sides, that uses language to describe, rather than to judge. Your letter will usually consist of the following five parts.

1. Begin with a positive or neutral statement that announces your subject and attempts to establish common ground. This is a good place to begin showing your readers that you understand their position and their reasons for it. This first paragraph is usually short and is often called a *buffer*, because its purpose is to cushion the impact of your decision, which is yet to come.

2. Once you have established common ground, you are ready to work toward mutual understanding of the situation. Here you want to be sure your readers know you understand them and to encourage them to understand you. So you have two jobs in this portion of your letter. The first is to restate your reader's request as clearly as you can, in such a way that your reader will accept your version of it. Once you have demonstrated that you understand your reader, you can state your own position. As you do this, keep in mind that you are leading up to your decision. Your review of both sides of the situation is a means of setting the stage for the decision itself.

3. The next step is to state your decision, clearly and completely, but without hitting your readers over the head or trying to make them feel foolish for asking in the first place. It is always important to do this positively rather than negatively. All of this comes in the middle of the

letter and, if possible, in the middle of a paragraph. That way it will receive as little emphasis as possible.

4. Once you have stated your decision, you need to do something positive again. Your goal is to show your reader that the two of you are really similar in many ways. You share positive values (such as fair-mindedness and honesty), and you wish to reach a mutually satisfactory conclusion. Above all, you have no bad feelings about your readers and you want them to feel the same about you. You can accomplish this by stressing the positive aspects of yourself, your organization, and your product or idea; by presenting an alternative or compromise to the original request; or by looking positively toward the future and your continued goodwill toward each other.
5. Conclude as positively and confidently as you can. Try not to hedge on your decision and certainly don't repeat it. Perhaps ask your readers to approve the alternative you have offered by sending you instructions, or simply wish them well.

The diagram in Figure 8-1 is meant to help you visualize the overall organization of this kind of letter, so you can see how the various parts fit together and form a unit.

Putting the Principles to Work

Now that you have been through the planning stages and have a skeleton organization to work with, it's time to turn to writing the letter itself. In this section we will work through each of the five sections of the letter in detail.

Writing buffers. As you begin, remember that you want your reader to *read* your letter, so it's important to get off to a positive start. The goals of your first paragraph are:

1. To announce the subject of your letter
2. To establish common ground as a basis for the discussion that will follow
3. To set a positive tone

From the very beginning, you want your readers to see that you understand their requests and their reasoning. Suppose that you are a Customer Service

Figure 8-1 Organization of a Letter That Says No

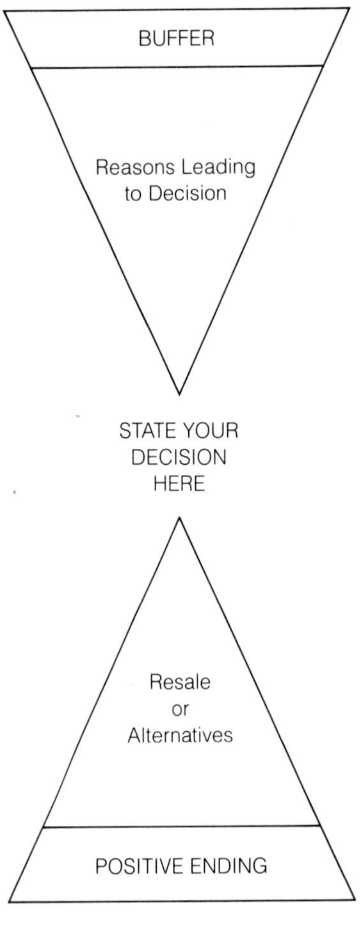

Begin with a positive or neutral statement that establishes common ground.

Restate your reader's request or position in such a way that he or she will agree with your version of it. Concentrate on those points in your reader's position that you believe are valid.

State your own position in such a way that you can lead up to your decision. Again, be positive. Talk about what you can and will do, rather than what you can't or won't do.

State your decision here, in the middle of your letter, where it will receive least emphasis. Use positive language.

Use resale or offer an alternative as a way of reestablishing your reader's confidence in you, your product, and your organization.

Emphasize the common values (goodwill, ethical practices) that you and your reader share. Show that you both aspire to a mutually satisfactory conclusion.

Be positive and enthusiastic.

Close on a positive note that will help you maintain the common ground you have worked to establish.

Representative for the Sunny Days Electric Company and that you have received the following letter from a customer.

> Dear Ms. Roberts:
>
> I am 72 years old and live on a fixed retirement income. For several months now I have had trouble with your company about the size of my monthly bill.
>
> My house is small, and I don't have electric heat or hot water, but still my bills are too high. Last month it was $55, and the month before it was $60. I remember when bills were only $20 in months when I had to run the air conditioner, and I was on a fixed income then, too.

I called your office and they came out to check my meter. The man said my meter is OK, and that there's nothing I can do but pay the bill.

I still think there's something wrong, and I want you to do something about it. Pretty soon you'll have to turn the electricity off for all of us retired people because we won't be able to pay our bills.

Please help us.

Sincerely,

John A. Jacobs, Sr.

There really isn't much you can do for Mr. Jacobs, but he deserves an answer. Your job is to help him understand the situation from both sides: his and yours. Begin by sympathetically restating his point. Some people might do it this way:

Dear Mr. Jacobs:

We're sorry your electric bills are too high.

But wait a minute. What are you actually saying there? In effect, you are granting his whole point: his electric bills *are* too high. Saying that you are sorry might even make you look cynical, for it suggests a sympathy that you really don't feel (at least the corporation you work for doesn't feel it). Since the rates utilities may charge are closely regulated and must be justified before they are approved, you must assume the rates are a fair reflection of what it costs to provide electricity, with some left over for profit. So let's revise that first opening:

Dear Mr. Jacobs:

We're sorry to hear that you feel your electric bills are too high.

Is that better? The *sorry* is still there, trying to extend a sympathetic ear to your reader's opinion, but you are no longer agreeing that he is right. Instead, by saying that he "feels" they're too high you are shifting the burden onto your reader, implying that *he* might feel that way, but you don't.

Let's try again. Think about the situation. Electric bills *are* high, or at least higher than they have ever been. Are there reasons for that? Are utilities simply increasing their profits, or have their costs increased too? Can you use this information to establish common ground with your reader without giving up your own position at the same time? Try this:

Dear Mr. Jacobs:

You have a point. Electric rates are high these days. They are higher than they have ever been. We know that, because we're customers too. We have to buy the electricity that we don't generate ourselves.

You can agree to that because it's true. What does this kind of beginning accomplish for you? By pointing out the validity of something your reader has said, you restate his position in a way that he can agree with. You also begin to lay the groundwork for stating your own position. The electric company must also buy electricity, so it is like your reader in that it must contend with rising bills. And even the electricity the company generates costs something; you don't make it out of the air. Those costs have risen, too.

In addition to a carefully stated partial agreement, there are other ways of beginning your letter. A compliment, for example, can help you establish common ground without committing you to accepting your reader's position. If your reader has suggested a new product that you might make, but you really have no plans to expand in that direction, you could offer congratulations for coming up with such a good idea.

> Dear Mrs. Smith:
>
> Your idea for modifying the intake valve on the Widget Model 40 fuel pump is a good one. Our engineering staff says it will work, and it could achieve at least the 10% fuel savings you project.

The compliment will lead naturally to a restatement of your reader's desire to find a manufacturer and the difficulties of doing that. But you have not committed yourself to the idea.

Sometimes your readers' requests will be so unreasonable that there is little you can say about them that will be positive. These are called "salvage jobs," for you want to retain your reader's goodwill at least. Even in this situation, though, it costs you nothing to say "thank you" and to attempt to restate your reader's position. What if Mr. Jacobs had written to tell you that he thinks you are nothing but "a bunch of capitalist moneygrubbers out to fleece an innocent public"? You won't want to agree with that, even if it's true. So what can you say? Instead of being angry and abusive in return, try thanking him for letting you know how he feels.

> Dear Mr. Jacobs:
>
> Thank you very much for writing to us about your recent experiences with your electric bills.

From here, you can go on to state his position, in a somewhat toned-down form, and your own, much as you saw in the earlier version of this opening paragraph.

Explaining the situation. Once you have written an introduction that attempts to establish common ground, your next job is to describe the situation in a way that shows that you understand both sides. Of course you understand your own position. You need to work to show your readers that you understand theirs, too.

Begin this section of your letter by continuing what you started in the first paragraph. Mr. Jacobs, who wrote to you about his electric bills, will be more willing to consider and understand your side of the situation if he thinks you understand his side. Try not to dwell on the obvious by telling him what his life is like; only he knows that. What you want to do is demonstrate your understanding. Try this:

> It's difficult to live on a fixed income. When the costs of living go up, there is no way to increase your monthly check at the same time. Sometimes even the modest Social Security increases come too late to do much good. By the time you get them, you're so far behind you can't really catch up. It's especially tough when it seems you're not getting any more for what you pay, and it's hard to give up some of the things that make life more pleasant so you can pay an electric bill.

The more you know about your readers, the more effectively you will be able to empathize with them and show that you really understand the way they live. Rather than try to say everything, this brief paragraph attempts to select those details that will be effective in showing understanding. The key is to focus on those points in your reader's position that you believe are valid, rather than the ones you disagree with or think are wrong.

If you were writing to Mrs. Smith about her modification to the intake valve on your Model 40 fuel pump, you might develop the following points:

> Her invention is well-designed.
>
> It looks as if it will save at least 10 percent on fuel.
>
> It is easily adaptable to any fuel pump.
>
> It seems marketable.
>
> She has obviously put a lot of effort into her invention.

So you might say this to her after your first paragraph:

> Your intake valve is well-designed and certainly represents considerable mechanical knowledge and hard work. It should be easy to market, since the concept is easily adaptable to any fuel pump presently on the market.
>
> Since our engineers produce a number of such inventions each year, we are well aware of the difficulties of marketing a new idea. It must be especially hard when you are working independently and do not have the resources of an auto parts manufacturer to support your efforts.

Just as in the response to Mr. Jacobs, you have taken the time to look at the world from Mrs. Smith's point of view and have attempted to express how that must feel. It is worth your effort. By attempting to show your understanding of your readers, you encourage them to reciprocate. You call on their sense of fair play to do for you what you have done for them.

Once you have restated your reader's position, you can state your own. Concentrate on the reasons for your decision, rather than simply citing "company policy." Policies, after all, come from somewhere. If they have been thoughtfully developed and are based on sound business practices, then you should be able to explain the reasons for them, rather than simply citing the policies themselves. Use these reasons to describe your side of the situation, rather than merely stating your position. If you were writing to Mr. Jacobs about his electric bills, you might say something like this:

> Since 1973, when the price of oil began to rise, the price of electricity has also gone up. Many people don't realize that oil is used to run the generators that make the electricity that they use. We use a great deal of oil each year, and its price has more than quadrupled since 1973. At the same time, the costs of the other materials that we use to generate your electricity and maintain our lines and equipment have also risen.
>
> And we know exactly what it means to live on a fixed income. All of our rates must be approved by the State Public Utilities Commission. This sometimes takes as long as a year, or more, and by that time we've often had to borrow money so that we can continue to provide service to the people like you who depend on us. When rate increases are approved, we must use part of them to pay the interest on what we have borrowed.
>
> I've enclosed a copy of our most recent annual report to our stockholders. On page six there is a chart that shows our financial condition over the past ten years. While our costs and rates have increased considerably during that period, our profits and the dividends we pay to stockholders have increased only one percent since 1974.

Stating your position in this way makes it less of a pronouncement and more of an even-handed description of both sides of the issue. A similar description to Mrs. Smith, who invented the fuel pump intake valve, might go this way:

> A number of manufacturers have been working to produce devices that will provide greater fuel economy. Your invention certainly fits into this effort. But the general economic conditions in the auto-related industries have made it difficult for all but a few companies to survive in what has become a highly competitive market. Here at Auto-Tech, we have decided to leave the general auto components market to companies that are leading the industry. We want to place our

> limited financial assets into the development of technological breakthroughs that will insure that we are still doing business twenty years from now, regardless of what the petroleum and automotive industries are doing at that time.

Again, this is a description rather than a pronouncement. Both of these descriptions attempt to explain the present state of affairs without judging them as bad or good. Also, as they move from a description of the reader's position to a description of the writer's, they avoid beginning with "However," or its equivalent, which would signal a rejection and perhaps encourage the reader to stop reading.

Stating your decision. When you are satisfied that you have described both sides of the situation accurately and fairly, you can move on to state your decision.

It is important that you state your decision as positively as you can, even though it is a refusal of your reader's request. Concentrate on what you *will* do, rather than on what you will not do. Use words that have positive meanings, and phrase your decision in a way that will exclude your reader's requested action from the group of actions that you say you *will* take.

In your letter about Mr. Jacobs' electric bill, positive statements will help you a great deal. You are not going to reduce his rates, and his meter has been checked and judged accurate. What you can do is assure him that you are conscious of costs and their effect on him.

> Sunny Days Electric Company is keenly aware of the rising costs of electricity and will continue to do everything possible to control costs without curtailing essential services. Our work force has been reduced three percent during the past year, and recently we announced an eight percent reduction in all budget lines for the next fiscal year.

Rather than saying bluntly that there is nothing you can do for him and thus risking his anger or disbelief (he clearly thinks you *can* do something, since you keep raising his bills), you have shown that you are doing something and trying to remain in business. The same principle will work with Mrs. Smith and her intake valve.

> From now until 1989 Auto-Tech will be slowly entering the field of Alternative Energy and phasing out its line of automobile components. By doing this we hope to become less dependent on the overall financial condition of the auto industry. At the same time, we think we will be able to make significant contributions to the technology of affordable alternative energy. In the next few months we'll be changing our name to Energetics, to illustrate this new emphasis.

Instead of telling Mrs. Smith that you're sorry, but she'll have to look elsewhere, you have explained the shift in your manufacturing emphasis and thus in the kinds of new products you will need.

Building to a positive ending. Try to end your letter so that your reader finishes it with a positive impression of you and your organization, in spite of the decision you have made. You can accomplish this in several ways. If possible, offer an alternative to your reader's request, something that you believe you will both find satisfactory. This can be a partial approval of the request. Or you can describe some positive action that you *will* take or that your reader can take to achieve a goal. For example, if your reader has not received a much-wanted promotion, you might explain what will increase the chances of success in the future. The idea is to focus your reader's attention on positive actions or attitudes.

For example, we have not been able to do much for Mr. Jacobs so far except to show that we understand his situation and point out that we are doing all we can to keep costs under control. Is there anything else that we can suggest, short of telling him to convert to a coal furnace and whale oil lamps? There is nothing we can do to reduce what he pays for electricity, but we can suggest ways in which he can reduce the amount of electricity he uses. Try it this way:

> Your meter has been checked twice, and both times the service department reported that it is working properly. It is possible, though, that you can modify your house, or the way you use electricity, so that you would use fewer kilowatt hours each month and thus reduce your bill.
>
> Many consumers could use all forms of energy more efficiently than they do. Our recently established group of Energy Efficiency Consultants will be glad to assist you by doing a complete survey of your energy use and suggesting ways you can save money. The average cost for this service is between $35 and $50. Many people who have taken advantage of the service have experienced an average eight to fifteen percent reduction in their monthly electric bills.

You can take a similar approach with Mrs. Smith's intake valve, perhaps suggesting other companies that might be willing to manufacture and market her invention. In addition, you can use a second method for building to a positive ending. This is usually called *resale.* This involves pointing out the advantages of using your products, now and in the future, and attempts to create a favorable image of your organization.

> Your modification of the intake valve for the Auto-Tech Model 40 fuel pump is a very marketable idea, especially

> since it can be adapted to many of the other fuel pumps on the market. I suggest that you write to the companies on the enclosed list to see if they are willing to do the manufacturing and marketing. When you write, let them know that you've heard from us. We'll be glad to furnish our engineering report to anyone you would like to see it. Auto components is a highly competitive industry, and I feel certain that one of these companies will be interested in your invention.
>
> I am also enclosing the most recent catalog of current Auto-Tech products. For the next thirty days you will be able to order from this catalog and receive a 30% discount simply by using the voucher stapled in at page 41. And, Mrs. Smith, watch for new Energetics products that will soon be available. We have worked to make them affordable to the average homeowner, and we think you'll like the energy-saving potential that they represent.

Resale is especially important if you have had to refuse a request for an adjustment for a damaged product, or if you are offering a substitute for a product that is no longer available. It is essential to re-establish your reader's confidence in you, your organization, and your product. While it is neither rational nor fair to judge a company and its products on the basis of one example, we do it all the time. If you think your reader has suffered a loss of confidence in your company or product, do some resale. Remember to stress the positive aspects of the product or the company. In the letter to Mr. Jacobs, this was done by emphasizing service.

Writing a positive ending. As you end your letter, try to maintain the positive tone that you have established from the beginning, so that your reader will finish with a favorable impression. Remember, because this comes last it will receive almost as much emphasis as your first paragraph, so it deserves some care and attention. Sometimes it can be effective to return to an idea or theme that you used earlier in the letter. If you do this, resist the temptation to return to your decision. All too often writers lose faith in what they have written and refuse to believe that their readers will really get the point. When this happens, they try to make the point again, saying something like "So, Mr. Jacobs, once again I am sorry that there is really nothing we can do about your electric bills"; or "We're really sorry, Mrs. Smith, that we can't do anything to help you." The first effect of this is to place your decision at the end of the letter, where it can only call attention to itself. More importantly, it casts doubt on all you have said so far. In both of these cases the writer *has* done something, though it is not quite what was asked for. To revert to the decision at the end of your letter is really to throw the whole thing away. You might just as well send out preprinted postcards that say "Forget It!"

Also try to avoid words and phrases that suggest a condescending attitude or imply that you are not entirely convinced that what you have said is adequate. When you say, "I trust you will understand our position," you are really suggesting that your readers won't understand, but that they have no choice. Similarly, to say "I hope I have explained this to your satisfaction" is to imply that you think you really haven't, but that you hope they will accept your explanation anyway because it's the best you can do. Another way to be sure your letter will self-destruct is to apologize at the end. You have worked hard to show that you understand your readers and to encourage them to understand you. To apologize is to throw all of that effort away and suggest that you *could* do something but choose not to.

There are several ways of writing a positive ending. Begin by looking back through what you have written to see if there is an idea somewhere in the letter that you can echo at the end. This will help you tie the whole letter together. Perhaps you have asked your reader to take a specific action or to provide you with information. The ending is an ideal place to re-emphasize this request, with complete instructions. In our letter to Mr. Jacobs we said that he'd be receiving a call about an energy survey of his home. Mention this again in the last paragraph. And it never hurts to express your willingness to be of help in the future.

> The energy use survey takes less than an hour, and it could pay off in substantial savings. You can call 833–2000 to schedule the survey for the day and time that will be most convenient for you. At any time that you have further questions about your electric service, please write, or call 877–9908. We're here to help you.

In your letter to Mrs. Smith, you might close this way:

> Please be sure to contact the people on the enclosed list. You have a product that I'm sure they will be interested in. And, on behalf of Auto-Tech, I want to thank you for thinking of us.

Conclusion

After you have worked your way through each stage of your letter, put all of the pieces together and review the whole thing to see if you think it will accomplish your goal. If you follow the process one step at a time and work carefully to plan and write your letter, you will discover that saying no successfully is not magic. It is mostly hard work.

But will it pay off? Will you actually be successful in retaining goodwill and modifying your reader's position? That remains an open question. Sometimes it works like magic, and occasionally readers will even thank you for the "nice" letter you sent them. But not always. There are times when the perfectly written letter that follows all the rules will cause a reaction that will make you wish you'd been rude in the first place. When that happens, don't take it personally. Allow your reader to ventilate such feelings, reply if you need to, and move on. Maybe tomorrow will be a better day.

In the long run, the thoughtful, courteous refusal will pay off in goodwill, and your readers will come to respect you for your honest attempts to understand what they want and how they feel.

Examples

Figures 8-2 through 8-9 are examples of how a number of business writers have written about information or decisions that they believed would be bad news for their readers. Are these letters successful? Review them carefully, using the principles explained in this chapter, and decide how the examples could be more effective. You can use the examples for individual practice by revising them or as the basis for in-class exercises and discussions.

■

Exercises: Chapter Eight

1. You are the Assistant Sales Manager for Top Tech, a small but growing East Coast firm that sells electronics components to manufacturers. In recent weeks you have noticed that John Howser, your Field Representative for New Jersey and southern New York, has reported three sales in Connecticut, which is Arlene Smith's territory. You are glad to have the orders, but you would prefer that Howser stay in his own territory and develop contacts with the companies that are there. You know that three firms, Fastronics, Switchboard, and ARI, are expanding rapidly and that they should be a ready market for your standard and specialty products. But Top Tech has never made a sale to these firms.

   Write Howser a letter that tells him that he will get credit toward his annual quota for the Connecticut sales, but that you want him to begin working his own territory.

2. You work for the Vice President—Manufacturing of Hydro-Valve, Inc.,

Figure 8-2 Letter Declining an Offer

YORK CONTAINER COMPANY

YORK, PENNSYLVANIA 17402

CHARLES S. WOLF
President

June 28, 198_

Mr. John B. Wyatt
2 Cromwell Dr.
Morristown, NJ 07960

Dear John:

Since we've been so close over the years, it occurs that you might be interested in the fact that York Container is now 25 years old. When we incorporated in June 1954 I recall we had some discussions with you. I suppose the Superior-St. Regis merger and the Hinde & Dauch merger with West Virginia Pulp & Paper Co. were among the very first. Then we went through that exciting decade of many paper mills getting into the box business and vice-versa.

John, we have chosen to remain independent through these years even though we've occasionally had some rather enticing offers to sell out. Our current status is that the Willmans own half the company and our family the other half, and we think this is a good structure for the future. Fortunately, there is an exciting younger generation of Rube's two sons and our one son. We're all in the business and are making a positive impact.

One of the joys to me of the box business has been the association with good people over the years. We continue to count you as a good friend, John. We would be pleased if you could visit us some time.

All best wishes,

Charles S. Wolf

CSW:mrg

Figure 8-3 Notice of Foreclosure

717/843-8651

CERTIFIED MAIL
RETURN RECEIPT REQUESTED

(Date)

NOTICE OF INTENTION TO FORECLOSE RESIDENTIAL REAL PROPERTY
NO. (Number)

(Name)
(Address)
(City, State, Zip Code)

Dear (Title and Last Name):

This is a notice of default and our intent to forclose on your Demand Note referenced above.

We hold a Demand Note dated (Date) and signed by (Name), in the original amount of $(Amount). We also hold a judgment on your real estate at (Location) to secure the obligation.

Your loan is now in default because you have failed to pay the amount of $(Amount) as demanded in our letter to you (Date).

You may cure the default by paying the principal balance of $(Amount) plus interest of $(Amount) as of this date, plus additional interest beyond this date at the rate of $(Amount)per day.

If the default is not cured within 30 days after the date of this notice, we may without further notice to you do one or more of the following:

(1) We may begin legal proceedings to execute on the judgment we hold which could result in the sale of your real estate at Sheriff's Sale.

(2) We may sue you personally for the unpaid balance and all other sums that would be due.

THE YORK BANK & TRUST COMPANY • P.O. BOX 869 • YORK, PENNSYLVANIA 17405

(figure continues on next page)

Figure 8-3 Continued

(Name)
(Date)
Page 2

If we schedule your property for sale you or anyone on your behalf have the right to cure the default by paying in cash or certified funds the amount due until one hour before the Sheriff has scheduled your real estate to be sold. Additionally, the default can be cured by any one of the following:

(1) Refinancing your loan with another lender and paying us in full all amounts owed.

(2) Selling your real estate and paying in full all amounts owed.

(3) Any other means that would pay all amounts owed.

The earliest date on which your real estate could be sold at Sheriff's Sale is (Date).

The amounts indicated as needed to cure the default are subject to change, and it is suggested you contact the writer at 843-8651 to get the correct amount owed if payment is to be made after 30 days from the date of this letter. If payment is made after 30 days, some of the additional expenses that might be added to the amount owed are title search, attorneys fees, advertising, court costs, etc.

Sincerely yours,

(Author)
Assistant Vice President

wp

Figure 8-4 Refusal of a Request

YORK MACHINERY & SUPPLY CO.
20 NORTH PENN ST., P.O. BOX 1272, YORK, PA 17405-1272 (717) 854-9531

INDUSTRIAL SUPPLIES

ABRASIVES
MAINTENANCE
CUTTING TOOLS
PRECISION TOOLS
SHOP EQUIPMENT
MATERIAL HANDLING
POWER TRANSMISSION
PERSONAL SAFETY EQUIP.

Campbell Chain Division
McGraw-Edison Company
3990 East Market Street
P.O. Box 3056
York, Pennsylvania 17402

Attention: Mr. Daniel E. Jennings

Dear Mr. Jennings:

This letter is in reply to your recent request for a price reduction from our company due to the current cost-price squeeze.

Unfortunately, like most distributors in the U.S.A. today, we are feeling the pressure of rising costs of labor and interest rates, as well as declining sales. The profit picture today with industrial distributors like our company is fragile at best and in many cases a loss situation.

We have contacted all our suppliers regarding a price reduction that we could pass along to you. So far we have not been able to obtain from them any price lower than those you are presently paying.

What can we do to help?

There are opportunities where we can help you improve productivity and lower costs through advanced products and improved application techniques. Our experience shows that the savings achieved through this approach can frequently be many times more valuable than a price reduction.

May we have the opportunity to review your requirements for industrial products to show you how these savings might be achieved. Our representative will be in touch with your company to make specific recommendations.

We hope you will understand our reasoning here and I am sorry to tell you that we cannot extend any additional discount.

Sincerely yours,

YORK MACHINERY & SUPPLY CO.

G. A. Snodgrass
Vice President-Sales

GAS:ns

Figure 8-5 Letter Acknowledging Receipt of a Request

INDUSTRIAL SUPPLIES
ABRASIVES
MAINTENANCE
CUTTING TOOLS
PRECISION TOOLS
SHOP EQUIPMENT
MATERIAL HANDLING
POWER TRANSMISSION
PERSONAL SAFETY EQUIP.

March 1, 1982

Keystone Seneca Wire Cloth Co.
Factory St., P.O. Box 521
Hanover, Pennsylvania 17331-0521

Attention: Mr. Charles R. Hastings, Vice President

Dear Mr. Hastings:

We have received your letter in reference to the step the auto industry has taken to stimulate the car sales market, which is severely depressed.

We are not in a position to give you a positive or negative answer to your request of 2% price reduction at this particular time.

Your request has been forwarded to our suppliers and we have asked them for an urgent reply. We will be in contact with your company as soon as we have additional information.

Sincerely yours,

YORK MACHINERY & SUPPLY CO.

G. A. Snodgrass
Vice President - Sales

GAS:ns

Figure 8-6 Refusal of a Loan Application

T & J LOAN COMPANY

March 15, 1983

Mrs. Alice Baker
467 First Street
Miller, TX 78000

Dear Mrs. Baker

Enclosed is a "Notice of Adverse Action" stating the principal reasons why we are unable to approve your loan application.

We value you as our customer. Although we are unable to help you with this request, we welcome the opportunity to consider your future loan needs.

Sincerely,

Albert I. Johnson
Manager

Figure 8-7 Letter Requesting Payment

717/843-8651

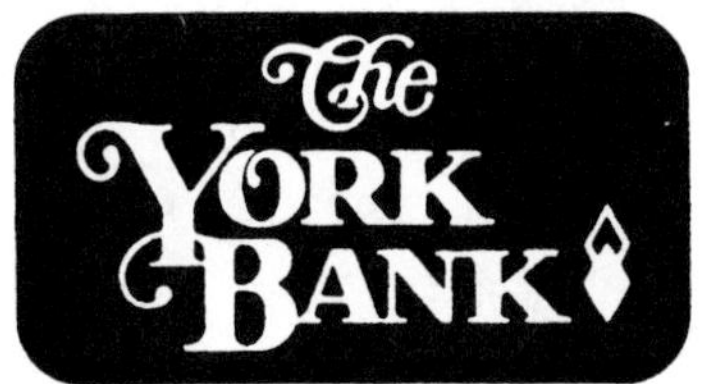

(Date)

(Name)
(Address)
(City, State, Zip Code)

Dear (Title and Last Name):

Your rental on safe deposit box number (Number) located at (Branch) has not been received. It was due on (Date) in the amount of $(Amount).

Prompt payment of the rental fee will release restrictions on access to the box. Should you no longer desire to maintain your safe deposit box, stop in at our office to sign a release and return your safe deposit box keys.

Please contact me at (Number) with any questions you may have concerning this matter.

Sincerely,

(Author)
(Title)
(Branch Location)

wp

THE YORK BANK & TRUST COMPANY • P.O. BOX 869 • YORK, PENNSYLVANIA 17405

Figure 8-8 Letter Requesting Additional Action

July 6, 1982

Mr. William J. Hartlaub
3325 Anderson Rd.
Laurinburg, NC 29880

Dear Mr. Hartlaub:

Thank you for returning your Proxy for the Annual Meeting to be held on September 28. Upon examination we discovered that we will not be able to use your Proxy because the Proxy is not signed. Therefore, we are returning your Proxy so that you may comply with requirements.

A stamped envelope has been included for your convenience in returning your Proxy to us.

Thank you for your cooperation in this matter.

Very truly yours,

T. R. Morgan
Senior Vice President
and Secretary

Enclosures (2)

Figure 8-9 Letter Describing a Service

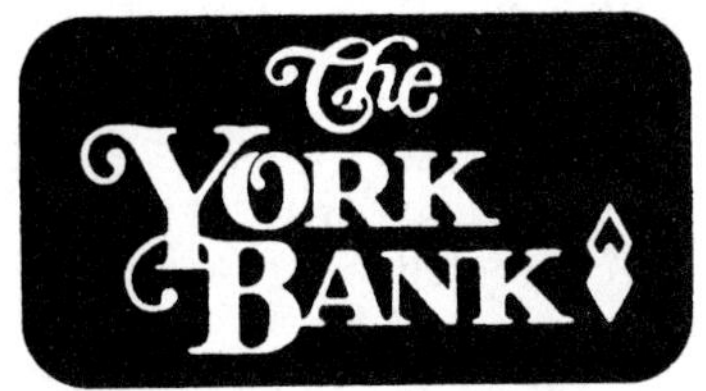

717/843-8651

(Date)

(Name)
(Address)
(City, State, Zip Code)

Dear (Title and Last Name):

Thank you for your deposit which we received through the night depository. Your receipt is enclosed.

Are you aware that this transaction can also be handled through our QuickBank? By doing so, you receive a deposit receipt immediately. If you deposited a check, a cash withdrawal could be made for a portion of the amount deposited at the same time.

QuickBank offers many other convenient services and features. I've enclosed a brochure that describes them and an application you can complete and return to receive your card.

Should you be interested in seeing QuickBank operate, stop by and we'll be glad to give you a demonstration.

Yours truly,

(Author)
(Title)
(Branch Location)

wp

Enclosures

THE YORK BANK & TRUST COMPANY • P.O. BOX 869 • YORK, PENNSYLVANIA 17405

which has just received a government contract with a very tight deadline. You normally allow six weeks for retooling for such a contract, but this time it must be done in three weeks.

Write a memo to all shop employees, in which you announce that all vacations for the next three months have been postponed. No one will lose vacation time, but all will have to reschedule after this contract is well under way. First, the line must be retooled and many operators must be retrained. The contract is worth $12 million and must be completed within six months. If the company meets this deadline, everyone will receive a substantial bonus, up to 10 percent of annual pay. During the six-month period of the contract, and especially during the retooling period, there will be plenty of overtime. All shifts will work ten hours, and volunteers (up to 20 percent of each shift) will be accepted for up to four hours of overtime on each of four out of every five days. In addition, the plant will not have its mandatory two-week shutdown in January for which employees are usually not paid.

3. You work in the Customer Relations department of Everkold, which manufactures refrigerators and dishwashers. Mr. Arnold Bates, 110 Karl St., Chillicothe, Ohio 45000, has written to ask you to replace his dishwasher with a new one. It is two years old, and he originally purchased it at a local store for $450. Since he bought it the tub has rusted in several places. Your dealer has repaired the rust spots each time that Mr. Bates asked him to and once replaced the entire tub. But the rust is getting worse, and Bates has written to you after the dealer refused to replace the machine.

Write to Mr. Bates to inform him that you will authorize another repair or you will allow the dealer to purchase the dishwasher from him for $75.00, but you will not replace it. Feel free to assume any other details that you need.

4. Kathleen Sommers is a former sales representative for Widget Manufacturing, where you are Assistant Sales Manager. This morning you received a letter from her, asking for a letter of reference. She has been working as a field sales representative for one of your competitors and is now being considered for the position of Sales Manager with a company in another part of the country. You remember Sommers. She was nice but a lousy sales rep. She missed her quota for two years (the only person to do so) and was constantly involved with some sort of disagreement with someone else in the company. She took customers from other sales reps more than once, and her paperwork was never up-to-date. In fact, on several occasions she fouled up major orders because of her lax attitude toward paperwork, and you lost customers to competitors. After two years she was told to look for another job. Write to Sommers and tell her that you cannot write the letter.

5. You are the Executive Vice President—Personnel, for Lock Tron, which makes locks and electronic security devices. On your desk this morning is a request from Bob Watson, who wants a lateral transfer from Boston, where he is District Manager, to Atlanta, where there is an opening for a District Manager in your new office. The usual company policy is that managers are transferred only when they are promoted. A review of Watson's file shows that he is an excellent District Manager but is not yet ready for a promotion. He has been a District Manager for only two years, and the usual time in this job is five years before promotion to Regional Manager—if there is a vacancy. Watson has made it clear that he thinks he is ready for a regional appointment, and he wants to use the Atlanta job, which he would have to build from scratch, to prove it. You believe the additional experience in Boston will make him a better Regional Manager, and you happen to know that he will be considered for promotion early, perhaps next year. Write to him to explain that he will not be going to Atlanta, but be sure you do not destroy his commitment to the company or his motivation. If you mention the prospect of early promotion, you will have to do it carefully.

6. Lorraine Anderson has applied for a position as a Management Trainee with your company. She recently graduated from a large midwestern university with a bachelor's degree in management and a minor in accounting. Normally you would consider her a strong candidate and perhaps interview her. But this year you have been swamped with highly qualified applicants, many of whom have one to three years of experience in financial management and accounting. You have narrowed the field to three candidates (Anderson is not among them), and you hope to make a decision within the next week. Write to Anderson to tell her that you will not be considering her for the position.

7. As Chief Loan Officer for the Second State Bank of Seattle you must approve all loan applications. Todd Detwiler, who recently opened an auto agency and repair service in the city, has applied for a mortgage of $104,000 to buy a house. He has an account with your bank, which at the moment has a balance of $5000. A credit check shows that he has no other accounts and that he recently declared bankruptcy in Minneapolis. He presently owes $16,000 on his car and furniture. The auto agency is in his father's name, so you cannot count it among his assets. Write to Detwiler and tell him that you will approve a mortgage of $55,000 and that he must provide security in the form of property or a cosigner for the note.

8. As Assistant Purchasing Manager for OMR Corporation, one of your jobs is to correct errors that your suppliers make when they ship your orders. This morning you learned that an order for 15,000 ¼-

inch stove bolts arrived as 10,000 1/2-inch lag screws. They have already been repacked and returned, but you need to write the supplier to notify him of the error, be sure the correct order is shipped, and get reimbursement for the return shipping costs. In addition, you need these stove bolts within five working days, or you will have to delay shipment on an important order of your own. The stove bolts are needed to assemble the product you are making. Each day's delay will probably cost you about $5000 in contract penalties.

9. John Bowers has been a foreman with your company for ten years. During that time he has had an exemplary work record, and last year he received an Associate Degree in Engineering Management. He has just applied for the job of Production Supervisor and is well-qualified. However, the Plant Manager has decided to upgrade the position so that it requires at least a bachelor's degree. Bowers has been considered because of his experience with the company, and he was the second of three candidates for the job. The top applicant, who has accepted the position, has a degree in mechanical engineering and an M.B.A. You now have to write Bowers a letter, with a copy to his personnel folder, which explains that he did not get the job but that his future is secure. Also, you might try to show that future promotions are not out of the question. He is a good worker, and you do not want to destroy his motivation.

10. Your company operates an aggressive employee suggestion program that pays $100.00, or 10 percent of any savings, for each suggestion. At present, about one in every ten suggestions is accepted. Write a form letter that you can send to those whose suggestions are not adopted. You want to show that the program is administered impartially, and you certainly want people to continue submitting their ideas.

■

9

Writing to Persuade

At one time or another we all need to persuade someone to do something. But few of us understand persuasion as well as we could or should. Mention persuasion in almost any group of people, and many will assume that you are talking about television commercials and direct mail sales. Most of us, in fact, encounter persuasion through sales in our role as consumers. If our jobs do not involve sales, we may believe that we have little use for persuasion. But persuasion has a larger and more important role in business and management than these strictly sales-oriented uses.

Even if you never have to sell a product, run for public office, raise money for a project, or become involved in social action, you will have almost daily uses for persuasion in your job. Any time you must work with other people as part of an organization you will use persuasion as a means of establishing policy, making decisions, and resolving conflicts. Ultimately, persuasion is one of the ways that groups have of creating the uniformity of attitudes and behaviors that allows them to function as units. Persuasion will be a part of your continuing interaction with coworkers, supervisors, and subordinates, and of your negotiations with labor and management, clients, and suppliers.

You will use it in discussions, letters, memos, reports, and oral presentations.

The goal of this chapter is to help you learn to write persuasively by showing you how to:

Establish goals for persuasion
Select appeals that motivate change
Organize persuasive messages
Write and revise a persuasive letter

Setting Goals for Persuasion

What do you want to accomplish with a persuasive message? Begin by stating the ideal, because you can always revise it later. It is probably best to begin planning for what you want, rather than for what you think you can get. If you plan for less, rather than more, you will probably get less. If you work for the Bright Smile Toothpaste Company, your ideal goal might be that everyone would buy your toothpaste. Later in the planning process you may discover that 12 percent of the market would be a respectable showing. But what if you had settled for a 2 percent market share at the beginning and planned for that?

Begin setting your goal by asking what you want your readers to think or do after they read your presentation. Then consider how much your readers will have to change if they move from where they are now to where you want them to be in the future. Will your goal require your readers to change a great deal, moderately, or only slightly? Of course, slight changes are usually easier to achieve than drastic ones. The more you know about your readers, the more accurately you will be able to identify the ways in which you can influence their attitudes and behaviors.

Once you have considered how much you are asking your readers to change, try to decide whether the attitudes you must influence are central or peripheral. Deeply held attitudes that people regard as central to their sense of themselves are going to be difficult to change. In fact, it is often easier to accomplish a significant change in a peripheral attitude than to achieve only a slight change in a centrally held attitude. That is, a person's choice of toothpaste is a matter of personal taste, but it is not likely to be based on a deeply held attitude. Influencing someone to switch from one toothpaste to another may be relatively easy. But other changes can be more difficult to achieve, especially if they represent a challenge to a central core of firmly held convictions. People have gone to jail rather than to war because they believe it is wrong to take a human life or to assist others in doing so. And they have done this in spite of intense social pressure to do otherwise. Some attitudes are extremely difficult to change, in spite of what may appear to be compelling reasons to change.

When you set goals for persuasion, remember that we are not all alike. On any given issue an audience or a particular member of an audience may hold views that range from open hostility to a high level of positive commitment. Thus, there is every reason for persuaders to choose from a correspondingly wide range of goals. Rather than assume that complete success is the only alternative available to you, try to set your goal according to your readers' position on a scale ranging from openly hostile to actively committed.

Reducing Hostility

Some of your readers will be actively hostile, either to you or to the proposal you are offering. Or they may hold views that prevent them from listening to you at all, let alone seriously considering your position. For example, a person who is deeply committed to strong government regulation of business may be either unwilling or unable to listen to a rationale for deregulation. An appropriate goal for persuasive messages directed to such people is to attempt to reduce their hostile actions or attitudes, rather than to attempt to convert them to an opposing point of view. At best, you may be able to create doubt or indecision about the views that they presently hold.

One approach that is sometimes effective with hostile readers is to appeal to their sense of fair play and suggest that everyone deserves a fair hearing. We'll discuss such appeals in more detail later on in this chapter.

Converting the Undecided

Your readers may be willing to pay attention to you, but they may also be apathetic, uninformed, skeptical, or undecided about what you have to say. If you can identify the reasons for their lack of commitment, you may be able to bring them closer to your own position. Your goal will be to inform them, reduce their skepticism, or motivate them out of their apathy. Depending on what your readers need in this situation, you may try any of several approaches. For example, the uninformed reader, who resists you because of a lack of information, may be reached by a solid presentation of evidence. An apathetic reader, who seems not to care, may be aroused by emotional appeals.

Maintaining Commitment

Some readers will already agree with you. But this does not mean that there is no need for persuasion. There are constant pressures on all of us to adopt competing points of view or to return to earlier states of apathy or skepticism. Thus, we need to work to reinforce and maintain attitudes that are favorable to our own points of view. Sometimes we will want to intensify the attitudes of those who agree with us or even convert them into action. For example, many organizations survive only because a few members work actively for the common good. It is often necessary to persuade people to move from mere membership to active participation.

Once people have decided to commit themselves to a particular cause or point of view, they need reassurance that they have done the right thing. They need new and updated information, so that they can stay informed. And they need to know that there are reasons for maintaining their commitment, evidence that the issue remains active and important.

Maintaining commitment through persuasion deserves more attention than it often receives. We tend to forget about people once they agree with us. But continued attention to them is a primary means of building a long-term relationship with a group of active supporters. Politicians know that they must continue to work with constituents after an election. Businesses know that they must advertise for those who are already their customers, not only for new ones.

Motivating Change: Using Appeals

Motivating change in others involves more than simply assembling evidence that supports your goal and then making your case. Of course, evidence is important, but it is not always sufficient in itself. If your readers are well-educated, well-informed, intelligent, and inclined to evaluate and analyze issues carefully and completely, then simply presenting your evidence may work. But such readers are rare, and even the most rational reader will also expect you to provide an argument that is emotionally satisfying as well as logically consistent.

You can often provide your readers with emotional satisfaction by using what are commonly called *motivational appeals.* You are familiar with these, because you experience them every day. When people tell you to stop smoking because you might develop lung cancer or to use a particular toothpaste because it will lead to success in romantic relationships, they are using motivational appeals. These appeals may not be logical or even factual, but they often have the appearance of logical propositions. Such appeals often go beyond the available facts, and they offer not proof, but probability.

For instance, while it is clear that using a toothpaste may whiten your teeth and help prevent tooth decay, it is less clear that the same toothpaste will make you irresistibly attractive to the opposite sex. At least it is not clear that it will do so beyond ensuring that your teeth have a pleasant appearance and your breath has an inoffensive odor.

Similarly, when someone attempts to sell you a life insurance policy, the facts of the situation concern whether insurance is a sound investment, how much it costs, and how much it will pay your beneficiaries in case of your death. But few insurance companies use this approach alone. The problem, of course, is that you are setting aside money for someone else, money that you will never see again. A motive appeal can provide a way around this problem by pointing out that you have a responsibility to your family, which depends on you for food, clothing, and shelter. This appeal is at least more logical that the one usually attached to toothpaste. You probably do have a family that depends on you, and life might be very difficult for them if you were not there. It makes sense, then, to provide for them. And that is the requirement for appeals. However logical or illogical they may be, they must in some way make sense to your readers.

Do motive appeals work? It is obvious that people continue to smoke, and not everyone is using the same brand of toothpaste. So, no, they don't always work. Success depends, in part, on whether the appeals are appropriate to the subject, the situation, and your readers. But success also depends on how you define it. No one has developed a persuasive technique that will always work with all readers. In fact, many users of direct mail advertising are delighted with a success rate of 2 to 5 percent of their initial mailing.

Types of Motive Appeals

There are four basic types of motive appeals.

Emotional appeals are attempts to arouse strong positive or negative feelings. This is most easily done with the words we use to describe something or by associating a person, object, or situation with something else that already arouses strong positive or negative responses. For example, it makes a difference whether you say that a company is "placing processed industrial by-products in Mill Lake" or "polluting Mill Lake with toxic industrial wastes." Likewise, a small, struggling firm that supplies parts for military vehicles can be associated with the "military industrial complex," presumably in a negative way, or characterized as a "defense contractor," which is perhaps a more exalted position than it actually holds.

Reward appeals are just what their name suggests: They offer your readers a reward for agreeing to your request. A reward might be a discount on one product for buying another at full price, or a free gift for opening a new bank account. When companies negotiate with unions for lower wages, fewer vacation days and benefits, and less mandatory overtime, the reward is often that these concessions will allow employees to keep their jobs. Without the concessions, the company may say, it will be forced to go out of business, close a particular plant, or lay off workers in large numbers.

Some rewards may be long-term rather than immediate. For instance, insurance companies have attempted to show that by exposing false claims and settling others out of court, they can reduce their costs significantly and pass the savings along to their customers in the form of lower rates. No one will write you a check next week, but the reward does exist.

Some rewards are intangible. For example, antismoking campaigns do not promise that you will not get lung cancer. Rather, they offer a reduced probability that you will get lung cancer. Probability, of course, is intangible.

Fear appeals offer intangible benefits, but they can be very effective. Their basic approach is to arouse a reader's fears about something and then to offer release from that fear. People who are learning to drive or who have been convicted of traffic violations are often shown films of especially grisly auto accidents. They can avoid these accidents, they are told, by driving safely. Contractors may show photographs of what can happen to a building if its roof leaks or it is not otherwise carefully maintained. Since a house or office building represents a considerable investment, its owner will not want to lose it through negligence. They can escape this fear, of course, by asking the contractor to fix the roof and inspect the building for other signs of neglect and decay.

Fear appeals work best when readers believe the event they fear will actually happen. For example, when negotiating with a union for concessions, a company may combine the reward appeal of everyone's remaining employed with the fear appeal that the company will actually close down. If the fear appeal is to work, the union members must believe that the company will follow through with its actual or implied threat.

Learned motive appeals depend on culturally acquired attitudes and may involve such intangibles as fair play, responsibility, power, status, prestige, patriotism, hard work, cooperation, and, of course, sex. There are many others, and you can probably make your own list of several dozen without too much effort. Appeals to these learned attitudes imply that readers can fulfill their needs for these intangibles by complying with your request. An advertisement may suggest that people can have friends if they purchase a certain kind of car, or status if they buy a particular brand of clothing. Contributions to charity may be linked to readers' needs to believe that they are responsible citizens and their belief that everyone deserves a "fair shake" in life.

The difficulty of appealing to learned motives is that you cannot always be certain that you have selected the ones most appropriate to your audience and the situation. People who believe that status is unimportant are not likely to respond to appeals based on it. Patriotism will not motivate those who believe it is little more than nationalistic humbug. And, an appeal's effectiveness can depend on a reader's circumstances. People may believe that civic responsibility is important. But if they are in difficult financial circumstances themselves they may decide that their own needs are more important than the feeling of satisfaction they would receive from contributing to a worthy cause.

Motive Appeals: A Summary

You need to give considerable attention to selecting the appeals you will use for persuasion. There are many possibilities, and they will not all be equally effective with all readers. The more you know about your readers, the more likely it is that you will be able to select a successful appeal. Time spent analyzing your audience is probably the best investment you can make in any persuasive effort.

Organizing for Persuasion: The Motivated Sequence

You can organize a persuasive presentation in many different ways. There are no rules, and no one has found an organization that is always effective. There is, however, a popular and widely used organizing scheme that deserves your attention, known as the *motivated sequence.* Many people believe that it allows you to achieve maximum logical and psychological impact on your readers. The motivated sequence divides all persuasive messages into five parts, each with a specific task:

1. Getting attention
2. Demonstrating a need
3. Satisfying that need
4. Visualizing the future
5. Asking for action

As you become more experienced with persuasion you may find ways of modifying this sequence to fit your own goals and individual readers and situations. Remember that it is only a framework, a set of guidelines. Try not to approach the motivated sequence too rigidly.

Getting Attention

If you are to influence your readers you must first have their attention. That is, you need to make your message stand out against the competition. How many times have you tuned someone out or stopped reading because the first few words or sentences of a presentation did not seem interesting or rewarding enough to justify paying attention?

Demonstrating a Need

Remember that you are attempting to influence your readers to change in some way. Thus, you must show that there is some reason for the change you want. What is that reason? In short, you must show that the present situation is unsatisfactory in some way. Needs, of course, are related to the motive appeals we discussed earlier, and this is a good place to begin introducing the ones you have selected.

Satisfying the Need

Once you have identified a need and demonstrated that it exists, show how your proposal will satisfy it. At the same time, you will want to show your readers that your proposal is different from other proposals and that it satisfies the need on the best possible terms. This will involve developing the appeals you have introduced and providing a detailed description of the product, idea, or action you are proposing.

Visualizing the Future

When you identified and described a need, you were helping your readers visualize things as they are now. Next you presented a means of satisfying that need. Now you must show your readers the benefits of doing what you ask. Exactly what will life be like after your reader accepts and acts on your proposal? Showing this may require some rather detailed, precise descriptions.

Asking for Action

What action do you want your readers to take? How can they achieve the future that you have visualized for them? You will need to state the decision you want your readers to make or describe what you want them to do. And you may also need to tell them how to do what you are asking.

The action you request must be consistent with the goal you established earlier. If your goal is to reduce overt hostility toward you or your proposal, you can scarcely expect your readers to take an action that would be more appropriate to a high level of commitment.

Writing Persuasively: A Working Example

The following example will take you step by step through the process of writing a persuasive letter. As you read, try to remember that your job is to be aware of the general principles that will help you write any persuasive message, not just this one.

The Situation

Rumplemeyer's is a store that carries high-quality, expensive clothing for men and women. The owner would like to increase the number of people who take advantage of the annual end-of-summer sale. Note that this is not an attempt to get *new* customers, but to appeal to people who already know the store and its merchandise thoroughly. So the goal is to maintain these readers' interest and commitment and to offer them bargains at the same time. We will try to accomplish this through a letter to all regular customers.

The possible appeals are to savings, quality, fashion, and excellent selection. Since the store caters to people who like to dress well and don't mind paying for it, status may also be an appeal. Any one of these will work as a central appeal, but savings is a prime candidate here because the event is a sale, and prices will be reduced 20 to 40 percent. In addition, savings can be linked to quality or fashion.

The letter will probably be only one page long (single-spaced). This will help control printing costs, which must be subtracted from the proceeds of the sale. Also, the readers are already satisfied customers, so we are not asking them to do something new. Rather, we want their *continued* patronage. This should take less time and space than a request for a completely new decision.

Before you read on, stop for a minute and try to decide how you would write this letter. List the five parts of the motivated sequence and make some preliminary notes about what you might say in each part. How would you get your readers' attention? What can you offer them that they do not already have? What need will you establish, and how will you fulfill it? What information do you need about the store and its merchandise? When you visualize the future, what situation will you want your readers to see themselves in? And what action will you ask them to take?

Getting Attention

The letter should begin by getting its readers' attention and establishing common ground. The first paragraph should:

1. Provide motivation to read the letter
2. Orient readers to your subject
3. Introduce a central theme or appeal
4. Prepare for step two, establishing the need

Be positive, reader-centered, and realistic. Your offer, whatever it is, probably is not the deal of a lifetime, and your readers will probably resent your thinking them stupid or gullible enough to believe that it is. Years of "hype" have made people skeptical and wary, so try to scale your attention-getting lead to your goals and to what you know about your readers.

Not surprisingly, it takes more words to describe what you should do than to simply do it. The letter might begin this way (on letterhead stationery):

> Dear Good Friend:
> Do we ever have a deal for you! You won't believe the prices.

Well, it *might* begin that way, but it probably shouldn't. The tone does not exactly fit an exclusive store or its clientele. Try to tone it down a bit.

> Dear Friend:
> We would like to offer you the chance to purchase your favorite clothes at ridiculously low prices.

That is somewhat better, but it begins with *we,* which focuses on the writer instead of the reader. And the prices are probably something short of *ridiculously low.* Try again:

> Dear Loyal Customer:
> You have been very good to us this year. We would like to return the favor by offering you the chance to add to your wardrobe at prices you are not likely to see again.

This version does several things better than the earlier ones. It begins by focusing on the customers, both by calling them that and by beginning with *you. Clothes,* in the second version, has become *wardrobe,* and *ridiculously low prices* has become *prices you are not likely to see again.* The tone suits the reader much better, as it sounds less like a medicine show or carnival barker. This brief paragraph may change later, when the entire letter is finished. But let it stand for now.

Establishing a Need

Most people, believe it or not, prefer to keep things the way they are. We may not actually *like* the world the way it is, but we like change a good deal less. Whatever the reason, readers seldom want to solve a problem or satisfy a need that they are unaware of. Persuasive writing must clearly describe the shortcomings and disadvantages of the existing situation and show the desirability of change.

Establishing the need is both a further development of your opening and a preview of what will follow. The points you make to show that a problem or need exists are the ones that you must follow-up later when you show how you can satisfy the need. Try to avoid exaggerated claims and concentrate on problems you can solve or needs you can actually fulfill. This section of our letter might be done this way:

> The price of quality apparel has continued to increase during the past several years. And we know from our recent

> buying trips to New York that there will be substantial increases again this fall, in some cases as much as 30 percent. When you need to look your best, on the tennis court, for a casual evening out, or at the office, it's important to save money whenever you can. But at the same time you want to continue to receive the quality and value that you have come to expect from Rumplemeyer's.

That paragraph begins to get at the central appeal of quality at attractive prices. But there are some problems with it. The first sentence seems to repeat the earlier paragraph (or at least to dwell on the obvious). The sentence that begins "When you need to look your best" is not really very logical, if you read it carefully. It implies a cause-and-effect relationship between looking one's best and saving money. Finally, is it possible that in discussing price this way the writer is suggesting, or admitting, that the usual prices are too high, or even unreasonable? Let's try again.

> You may be thinking about a new sportcoat or suit to get you through those warm weather days of early fall, or a new skirt to complete a coordinated outfit. But you've been put off by the steadily increasing prices of fine apparel. At the same time you don't want to sacrifice quality or appearance by purchasing something that won't last as long or look as good as what you're used to. You know that would be false economy. Fortunately, you can get the quality you want at a price you won't mind paying.

That's better. It may need to be revised later, but for now it establishes a need and introduces the central appeal of value and quality. It still risks saying that regular prices are too high, so we'll have to work on that.

Satisfying the Need

Once you have established that a need or problem exists, the next step is to show your reader what to do about it. That, after all, is the whole point of writing. Remember that what you write will not, by itself, satisfy any need or solve any problem. Rather, your job is to point out that the need can be satisfied, the problem can be solved, and there are advantages to doing it in the way you suggest.

Now is the time to introduce your product, idea, or suggestion and describe it *in detail,* giving evidence to show how it will satisfy the need you have established. How will your product or idea alleviate or change the existing situation, which, as you have pointed out, is beset by problems? And be sure that you continue to refer to your central appeal and show how your proposal is related to it.

> At Rumplemeyer's annual end-of-summer sale, you can buy quality clothing for 20–30% less than the regular retail price. A lightweight, all-wool sportcoat or blazer can cost as little as \$70. At that price you can buy two coordinating shirts and still have enough change to refresh yourself with a tall, cool sundae across the street. That's less than you'd pay for an "economy" blazer elsewhere, and you will be getting a jacket that looks better and lasts longer.
>
> Even at these sale prices alterations are still free. In fact, we insist; you won't leave looking anything but your very best. And you can take advantage of our ninety-day, no-interest charge plan.
>
> You know that Rumplemeyer's offers only the very best; that's why you've kept coming back for years. Every item in the store will be on sale, and there is an excellent selection, including swimsuits, sport clothes, suits, skirts, and dresses.

This section may be a bit long for a one-page letter, but first drafts are always an experiment to see what will fit. It is easier to take something out later than to try to fill up the page. This portion of the letter has the advantage of giving specific details, including the example in the first paragraph. And the whole passage is consistently reader-oriented. We will save it and revise later.

Visualizing the Future

You might be tempted to think you have done enough if you have shown how your product, service, or policy will satisfy the need that you identified. Most readers seem smart enough to make a few connections on their own. Surely they will see how much easier or different life will be once they have done what you are going to ask. But why rely on your readers to do something that is so crucial to achieving *your* goal? They might get it wrong. You want your readers to see the future the way *you* see it: your product purchased or your solution adopted, working full-steam on their behalf.

You began your letter by describing the situation as it exists now, with needs or problems unrecognized and unsatisfied. Now is the time to show the situation *as it will be* once your readers have taken the action you will recommend. Review the section in which you established the need and be sure that you follow up on each point that you made there. Tie up all of the loose ends, so your reader will have no chance to say, "Yes, but what about . . . ?" or "You said that. . . ."

Sales letters, like television commercials, can afford a bit of dramatic fiction at this point, if that's the direction you want to go. Policy recommendations, however, must visualize the future by staying with the facts and inferences that the evidence will support. Keep in mind that we have all grown more skeptical and are not likely to take exaggerated claims seriously.

Our letter might visualize the future this way:

> You won't have to wait until next year to wear the great buys you'll find at our end-of-summer sale. There is plenty of warm weather left this year. You'll find plenty of occasions for "summer clothes" through Labor Day and right into football season. And, when it's winter here it isn't winter everywhere. When the snow is flying here, the sun is still warm in Palm Beach and Nassau. You'll also appreciate a summer wardrobe for those business trips to Houston, Atlanta, and Los Angeles.

This continues to point out the central appeal of value, and it does that by showing readers that they will be able to enjoy an immediate, short-term benefit from their purchase. This brief paragraph also places readers in situations they are likely to encounter: winter trips to resorts, business trips to major cities in the South and West, and a long, warm fall season.

Asking for Action

At the end of your letter you need to tell your readers what they need to do to achieve the future that you have just described. Be specific; don't settle for "buy one today" or "stop in some time." Be sure you tell your readers *how* to take the action that you want, and make it easy for them to do it. Provide a means of replying to your letter, and perhaps even a small incentive. It also helps to refer specifically to a reply card or other enclosure, so that at the end of your letter your reader's attention shifts smoothly to it.

Our letter about Rumplemeyer's end-of-summer sale might request action in this way:

> Visit us during the week of July 25 to August 2. We'll be open from 9 to 9 each day, and you'll find exceptional values, a wide selection, and our customary 90-day, no-interest credit terms. Bring this letter with you, and you'll receive an extra 5% price reduction on any single item you buy.

This takes advantage of the emphasis the final paragraph receives by including specific details about dates, times, and credit terms. It also adds an incentive that will allow you to test the letter's effectiveness. You can count the number of letters that people return and match them against your list of people who usually come in for the sale. That way, you will know whether it was worth doing the letter.

Revising Your First Draft

Now that we have written this letter, we should put it together to see what it says and try to evaluate how well it might work.

Dear Loyal Customer:

You have been very good to us this year. We'd like to return the favor by offering you the chance to add to your wardrobe at prices you're not likely to see again.

You may be thinking about a new sportcoat or suit to get you through those warm weather days of early fall, or a new skirt to complete a coordinated outfit. But you've been put off by the steadily increasing prices of fine apparel. At the same time, you don't want to sacrifice quality or appearance by purchasing something that won't last as long or look as good as what you're used to. You know that would be false economy. Fortunately, you can get the quality you want at a price you won't mind paying.

At Rumplemeyer's annual end-of-summer sale, you can buy quality clothing for 20–30% less than the regular retail price. A lightweight, all-wool sportcoat or blazer can cost as little as $70. At that price, you can buy two coordinating shirts and still have enough change to refresh yourself with a tall, cool sundae across the street. That's less than you'd pay for an "economy" blazer elsewhere, and you'll be getting a jacket that looks better and lasts longer.

Even at these sale prices alterations are still free. In fact, we insist; you won't leave looking anything but your very best. And you can take advantage of our ninety-day, no-interest charge plan.

You know that Rumplemeyer's offers only the very best. That's why you've kept coming back for years. Every item in the store will be on sale, and there is an excellent selection, including swimsuits, sport clothes, suits, skirts, and dresses.

You won't have to wait until next year to wear the great buys you'll find at our end-of-summer sale. There is plenty of warm weather left this year. You'll find plenty of occasions for "summer" clothes through Labor Day and right into football season. And when it's winter here, it isn't winter everywhere. When the snow is flying here, the sun is still warm in Palm Beach and Nassau. You'll also appreciate a summer wardrobe for those business trips to Houston, Atlanta, and Los Angeles.

Visit us during the week of July 25 to August 2. We'll be open from 9 to 9 each day, and you'll find exceptional values,

a wide selection, and our customary 90-day, no-interest credit terms. Bring this letter with you and you'll receive an extra 5% price reduction on any single item you buy.
Sincerely,

John H. Rumplemeyer III

Evaluating the Draft

Overall this letter follows the motivated sequence fairly carefully and includes all of the steps. Its tone seems appropriately low-key; in fact, it may be a bit *too* low-key, especially at the beginning and near the middle, where the pace seems to drag a bit. We will have to do something about that. Finally, the letter seems a bit long. Remember, we want it to fit on one page. So we will look for ways to make it shorter without sacrificing evidence or effectiveness.

A close review of each paragraph suggests that the following points need attention:

Paragraph 1: Seems not really an active attention-getter, but we do not want to turn it into pure hype. Customers are used to a low-pressure sales approach.

Paragraph 2: In line one, the word *may* seems a bit tentative. Also, this paragraph establishes a need (clothes). Perhaps that could be shifted to a need for quality and value, without suggesting that the usual prices are too high. It may be possible to use the other version of this paragraph and combine it with the one here.

Paragraph 3: The writer has not explained that the example of the blazer and two shirts, with money left over, is based on spending $100.

Paragraph 4: This paragraph provides necessary information, but the middle sentence, about "looking anything but your very best," is phrased somewhat negatively.

Paragraph 5: The first two sentences provide little concrete information. They can be deleted, and the rest of the paragraph can be combined with paragraph 4.

Paragraph 6: This paragraph contains repetitions of words (e.g., *plenty*) and of ideas. The writer mentions twice that it isn't winter everywhere.

Paragraph 7: This is the final paragraph, and it does ask for a specific action. It also provides an appropriate incentive. It may not need many changes.

If we revise these problem areas, the draft might read something like this:

> Dear Loyal Customer:
>
> This year, you gave us a very good year. We would like to return the favor by offering you the opportunity to add to your wardrobe at prices you are not likely to see again.
>
> The price of quality apparel has continued to increase during the past several years. And we know from our recent buying trip to New York that there will be substantial increases again this fall, in some cases as much as 30%. It is important to look your best, but it is also important to save money whenever you can. This month, at Rumplemeyer's, you can get the quality you expect at a price you won't mind paying.
>
> At our annual end-of-summer sale you will find an extensive selection of quality clothing for up to 30% off the regular retail price. A lightweight, all-wool sportcoat or blazer that usually sells for $100 can cost as little as $70. At that price, you can buy a shirt and matching tie and still pay less than you would for the blazer at its regular price.
>
> Even at these sale prices alterations are still free, and you can take advantage of our usual ninety-day, no-interest charge plan. Every item in the store will be on sale, and there is an excellent selection, including swimsuits, sport clothes, skirts, dresses, and suits for men and women.
>
> You won't have to wait until next year to wear the great buys that you find. You'll find many occasions for "summer" clothes right through Labor Day and into football season. When winter finally closes in and the snow is flying here, you will appreciate looking your best on those vacation and business trips to the sunbelt. Your "summer" wardrobe is really a year-round asset.
>
> Visit us during the week of July 25 to August 2. We will be open from 9 to 9 each day, Monday through Saturday, ready to serve you. Bring this letter with you and you will receive an extra 5% off on any item that you buy.
>
> Sincerely,
>
> John H. Rumplemeyer III

This second version seems to be an improvement over the first. Compare the two versions carefully to see exactly what changes have been made. Feel free to suggest further changes on your own, because no one is claiming that this is a final version ready for the mail.

Measuring Your Success

Once you have written a persuasive message and your readers have had a chance to react, it is important to evaluate your efforts. You need to know whether you succeeded or failed, and why. You will learn and improve only if you examine what you have done and look for ways to make it better.

There is probably no single best way to evaluate your own persuasive writing. If your reader is one person, or even a small group that you know well, you may have to rely on subjective measurements of the changes that have taken place. You might make this evaluation best by personal observation. If you have many readers, and they are not available to you for observation, perhaps their responses are direct and easily counted. Such counts will tell you how many react favorably. Of course, the complexity of your evaluation, and the time and money you invest in it, should be appropriate to the importance of what you are likely to learn.

Whatever the scope and complexity of your evaluation, you can begin it by answering the following questions.

1. What was your goal?
2. To what extent did you achieve your goal?
   a. What evidence suggests that your readers are doing what you asked them to do?
   b. What percentage of your readers accepted your proposal? And what evidence do you have for this?
   c. What degree of change of acceptance did you achieve?
3. If you achieved your goal with a segment of your audience, what do these people have in common? How do they differ, as a group, from those you did not succeed with?
4. Do the differences you discovered in question 3 suggest that other appeals or evidence might succeed with those readers who did not comply with your request?
5. Do your readers' responses suggest that your goal was too ambitious or too limited?
6. Do the responses indicate whether your directions for taking action were adequate, or were they too complex or confusing?
7. If your audience was a group, what percentage of that group had to respond favorably to make your efforts successful or cost-effective?

8. Based on the response you received, what evidence or appeals would you change if you were to try again?

Persuasion: A Summary and Checklist

Before you present any persuasive message to an audience, be sure you have:

1. Set a single, specific goal
2. Done a careful analysis of your readers and the situation in which you are attempting to persuade them
3. Selected evidence and appeals carefully
4. Worked to establish common ground by emphasizing the similarities between yourself and your readers
5. Avoided any statement that might antagonize or threaten your readers
6. Avoided challenging deeply held views
7. Achieved a careful logical and psychological organization

Examples

The persuasive letters in Figures 9-1 through 9-8 were not written by professionals as part of direct mail sales campaigns. Rather, they are by businesspeople in different kinds of companies and positions who have had to write letters to attempt to persuade others. You will have to judge for yourself whether these letters are successful at accomplishing their goals. For those that you believe are not successful, you might suggest revisions that will make them more effective.

■

Figure 9-1 Persuasive Letter Soliciting Charitable Donations

TO: All Employees

SUBJECT: United Way Campaign (1981)

The United Way Campaign for 1981 at York Division of Borg-Warner will be conducted during the period starting Tuesday, September 8 and continuing through Friday, September 11.

During the last campaign we stressed participation by payroll deduction. This year the Campaign will solicit All Employees and continue to stress Payroll Deduction and Fair Share Giving. (For salary workers this is 1% of annual income and for hourly wage earners, this is an hour's pay per month).

A movie explaining United Way will be shown to all employees and at that time you will be given the opportunity to participate. Last year's employee giving totaled $76,737 with 42.5% of our employees contributing. York Division's goal is $86,000 this year.

The way we can reach this increased goal is to encourage the remaining 57.5% of our employees to contribute at least 50¢ per week through Payroll Deduction. That's the cost of two daily newspapers, or less than one pack of cigarettes.

All Campaign contributors are eligible for a drawing of a Room Air Conditioner. If 40% or more employees contribute there will be two drawings and if 60% contribute there will be three drawings and so forth.

When you are given this opportunity to participate in the United Way for 1981, the Committee urges you to very seriously consider regular giving (whatever amount you choose) by payroll deduction. York Division of Borg-Warner employees, each giving freely, can continue to set the pace for the York Community.

UNITED WAY COMMITTEE

Thanks to you
it's working

INDUSTRIAL RELATIONS—YORK DIVISION—BORG WARNER CORP

Figure 9-2 Persuasive Letter Requesting Payment

717 843-8651

CERTIFIED MAIL
RETURN RECEIPT REQUESTED

(Date)

NOTICE OF INTENTION TO FORECLOSE RESIDENTIAL REAL PROPERTY
NO. (Number)

(Name)
(Address)
(City, State, Zip Code)

Dear (Name):

Provisions of Article IV, Section 403 and 404 of Act No. 6 of the General Assembly of the Commonwealth of Pennsylvania dated January 30, 1974, require your notification in this manner when foreclosure action is being considered.

You were granted a loan by The York Bank and Trust Company secured by a judgment against your propert(y/ies) at (Location) in the amount of $(Amount). The payments on this loan are now in default for the installments of $(Amount) due (Date(s) and accrued late charges of $(Amount).

If the total delinquent amount of $(Amount) is not paid on or before (Date), we will refer your account to our legal counsel for the action necessary to commence foreclosure proceedings without further notice to you. You are advised that if these foreclosure proceedings are pursued to conclusion, it will result in your propert(y/ies) described above being sold at Sheriff's Sale.

You may stop these legal proceedings and save your propert(y/ies) in any of the following manner:

(1) Pay the sum of $(Amount) plus accrued late charge on or before (Date), by a York Bank and Trust Company check on cleared funds, cashier's check, certified check, or cash at any office of The York Bank and Trust Company. In the event payment is made after (Date), the due date of the next payment, then the amount due is $(Amount).

THE YORK BANK & TRUST COMPANY • P.O. BOX 869 • YORK, PENNSYLVANIA 17405

Figure 9-2 Continued

(Name)
(Date)
Page 2

(2) By refinancing your loan elsewhere and paying your debt to this bank in full.

(3) The sale of your propert(y/ies)and the assumption of your loan with The York Bank and Trust Company by the buyer is not permitted. However, you may repay the loan in full by selling your propert(y/ies).

Terms, conditions and payment as described above may be made at any office of The York Bank and Trust Company during the hours of 9 a.m. to 4:30 p.m. from Monday through Thursday and Friday 9 a.m. to 6 p.m.

In the event that foreclosure action is instituted, you have the right under Section 404 of Act 6 of 1974 up to one hour prior to sale to cure the default as set forth in the foreclosure proceedings in the following manner:

(1) Pay all sums which would have been due at the regular times of payment, plus late charges and plus any other sums due to meet the requirements of the Note.

(2) Perform any other obligations which you would have been bound to perform in the absence of default or the exercise of an acceleration clause.

(3) Pay any and all reasonable fees allowed under Section 406 of the Act and the reasonable cost of proceedings to foreclosure actually incurred to the date of payment in full as described in writing by this financial institution.

Sincerely yours,

(Author)
Assistant Vice President

Figure 9-3 Persuasive Letter Soliciting Business

May 3, 1982

Asbury Graphite Mills, Inc.
Asbury, Warren County
New Jersey 08802

Attention: Mr. Tom Zak, Purchasing Agent

Dear Mr. Zak:

I have been advised of your plans to construct a new building in Sunbury, Pennsylvania.

Maynard Engle, our sales representative, lives in Selinsgrove, Pennsylvania. He currently is servicing Anthracite Ind. located in Sunbury, Pennsylvania.

Attached you will find a copy of our general catalog and a company profile to familiarize you with our company.

We would like to be a major supplier for your industrial products.

When your purchasing personnel is on site, Maynard and I invite you to visit and tour our store.

Sincerely yours,

YORK MACHINERY & SUPPLY CO.

G. A. Snodgrass
Vice President-Sales

GAS:ns
Enclosures

Figure 9-4 Persuasive Letter to a Potential Customer

717/843-8651

May 25, 1982

(Name)
(Address)
(City, State, Zip Code)

Dear (Name):

We feel that we have always provided you with our professional trouble-free service. We also know that unexpected problems can occur en route or at home. To serve you as a professional Travel Agent, we now give you 24 hours a day, 7 days a week toll-free EMERGENCY SERVICE. This toll-free service is now available for you and your employees during and after our regular business hours.

Effective June 1, 1982, The York Bank Travel Agency will join TRAVEL HELPLINE, a nationwide toll-free EMERGENCY SERVICE staffed 24 hours a day, 7 days a week, including holidays, to provide you with EMERGENCY TRAVEL assistance.

If you encounter a problem or require emergency help with airline, hotel, or car rental reservations confirmed through The York Bank Travel Agency, a simple call from anywhere in the Continental United States will connect you with TRAVEL HELPLINE. Their staff is trained to deal with your problems and get you to your destination.

We will provide each of your travelers with 800 numbers and simple instructions for using the system. We will also include a special notice with your ticket as a reminder of the TRAVEL HELPLINE 800 number.

We are happy to be able to provide this valuable service. I hope that you will see TRAVEL HELPLINE as part of our commitment toward meeting all of your travel needs.

Sincerely yours,

(Author)
Manager

wp

THE YORK BANK & TRUST COMPANY • P.O. BOX 869 • YORK, PENNSYLVANIA 17405

Figure 9-5 Persuasive Letter Advocating Membership in a Professional Association

YORK MACHINERY & SUPPLY CO.
20 NORTH PENN ST., P. O. BOX 1272, YORK, PA 17405-1272 (717) 854-9531

INDUSTRIAL SUPPLIES
ABRASIVES
MAINTENANCE
CUTTING TOOLS
PRECISION TOOLS
SHOP EQUIPMENT
MATERIAL HANDLING
POWER TRANSMISSION
PERSONAL SAFETY EQUIP.

December 9, 1977

J. Bruce Adams, President
Power Trans Distribution Division
Hugh Russel Ltd.
8 King St. E.
Toronto, Ontario
Canada M5C185

Dear Bruce,

It was a pleasure to be with you again at the Distributor Council meeting in Boston and besides the business, I think we had some fun and I enjoyed being with you very much. I am very sorry that I won't have the opportunity to be with you again at the next council meeting.

I have directed the Executive Vice President of NIDA, Bob Clifton, to send you some information concerning membership in NIDA. I know that you would find your membership to be very worthwhile and money well spent. Some of their current projects are product liability, trans net, a method of sending orders via computers to a central location and then have them relayed after editing the order to suppliers. This is a very new project and sounds extremely interesting. NIDA is also concerned about the productivity of the industrial distributor and how we can improve it. I think one of the most valuable projects of NIDA is the executive management course at Penn State University held each fall. We have had a total of about eight of our people there. They just do an excellent job and we find the seminar to be very worthwhile. Last, but not least, is the Triple Industrial Supply Convention where you get a chance to see all your suppliers and talk with other distributors across the country. The Triple next year will be held in Los Angeles on June 4 through 7. I hope you will make a positive decision and I can look forward to seeing you in Los Angeles in June.

I hope you and your family have a very Merry Christmas and a prosperous New Year.

Sincerely yours,

F. B. Shearer
President

Fbs/jr

Figure 9-6 Persuasive Letter to a Potential New Customer

717 843 8651

The York Bank

(Date)

(Name)
(Organization)
(Address)
(City, State, Zip Code)

Dear Mr. (Last Name):

Welcome to York, Pennsylvania, and the West Manchester Mall. We look forward to the October, 1981, grand opening of the mall, and we hope that your plans are progressing satisfactorily toward opening day.

Let me take a moment to tell you something about The York Bank and Trust Company. We were established here in York in 1810, and we are the largest bank headquartered in York County. Our new office opening in the West Manchester Mall is our twentieth full service office.

As the manager of our new office at the West Manchester Mall, I would like you to give consideration to making The York Bank your bank in York, Pennsylvania.

Our office will be a full service bank office supported by six tellers and an assistant manager. In addition, The York Bank Travel Agency will have an area within this office to service our travel customers. Night depository services will be available from both inside and outside the mall for your convenience. This office is also the site of our eighth QuickBank, 24-hour automated banking machine, which provides banking service 24 hours a day, seven days a week to meet the personal banking needs both for you and your employees.

The enclosed 1980 Annual Report of The York Bank and Trust Company will provide you with additional and detailed information about our bank.

I know that you wish to establish your banking connection in this area as soon as possible. Therefore, I have enclosed a signature card and two copies of a Resolution form. Please have the necessary signers sign the signature cards and indicate the number of signers required for us to process checks. Return the

THE YORK BANK & TRUST COMPANY • P.O. BOX 869 • YORK, PENNSYLVANIA 17405

Figure 9-6 Continued

(Name) **Page 2**
(Organization
(Date)

signature card and one copy of the Resolution form in the envelope I have enclosed and keep the other Resolution form for your files. I am also enclosing a listing of our commercial checking accounts fees and charges.

I hope I have been able to answer most of the questions you might have about our bank. Please contact me at The York Bank, (717) 843-8651, Ext. 393, if you have additional questions or if you would like to discuss any specific banking needs. I look forward to meeting you in the near future and working with you in the West Manchester Mall.

Sincerely yours,

(Author)
Assistant Treasurer and Manager
West Manchester Mall

wp

Enclosures

This is a form letter that can be sent through the word processing department to any potential customer.

Figure 9-7 Persuasive Letter Explaining Correct Procedures to a Client

717/843-8651

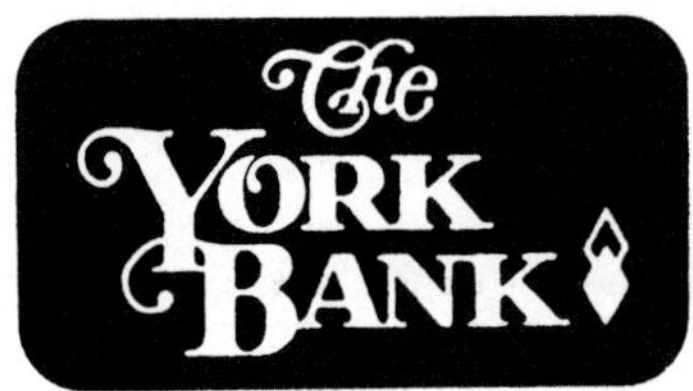

(Date)

(Name)
(Address)
(City, State, Zip Code)

Dear (Title and Last Name):

With the holiday season quickly approaching, we know that all our area merchants will experience heavy sales and, consequently, larger than normal cash deposits.

Banks, too, are extra busy during the season, and we are appealing to you to help us serve you faster and more efficiently by preparing your large cash deposits in the following manner:

1. Separate currency into denominations, face up, turned the same way.

2. Strap bills:

1's -	$ 50	Straps
5's -	250	Straps
10's -	500	Straps
20's -	1,000	Straps
50's -	1,000	Straps
100's -	1,000	Straps

3. Please use York Bank and Trust Company straps (available at any branch), as other bank straps are color-coded differently.

4. Please do not mix denominations within straps.

Your cooperation will be most appreciated. If you have any questions, please do not hesitate to call me.

Very truly yours,

(Author)
(Title)
(Branch Location)

wpo

THE YORK BANK & TRUST COMPANY • P.O. BOX 869 • YORK, PENNSYLVANIA 17405

Figure 9-8 Persuasive Letter Urging Prompt Action by a Customer

717/843-8651

(Date)

(Name)
(Address)
(City, State, Zip Code)

Dear (Name):

You are presently renting safe deposit box #(Number) at our Shrewsbury office. This box is one of a small group that we are trying to replace. Because of the age of these boxes, it is becoming increasingly difficult to maintain them.

We would like to transfer your box to a newer one of comparable size and annual rental.

Please stop by the office within the next month. Bring with you the two keys we issued for your present box, and you can transfer the contents to a new one at that time.

Perhaps this will give you an opportunity to discuss with us any other banking questions you may have. Your cooperation in this matter will be greatly appreciated.

Sincerely,

(Author)
Manager & Assistant Treasurer
Shrewsbury Office

wp

THE YORK BANK & TRUST COMPANY • P.O. BOX 869 • YORK, PENNSYLVANIA 17405

Exercises: Chapter Nine

1. As president of a campus (or civic) organization you are in charge of a fund-raising campaign to send twelve local youngsters (ages 10 to 13) to summer camp. None of them could afford to go without your organization's help. The camp is located 100 miles from the city and is operated by your organization's state headquarters. You need $1500. Write a letter to local businesses, asking for their help.

2. The Personnel Manager of your company has asked you to write a letter to all employees, encouraging them to take advantage of the provision in the company's health plan that pays the full cost of an annual physical examination. Records show that only 3 percent of the company's employees take advantage of this benefit. But 50 percent of the treated illnesses among employees could have been detected through a physical exam, and 25 percent, if treated promptly, would have resulted in less lost time and productivity. This could have saved the company as much as $250,000 last year in insurance premiums and delays. Employees would have lost one-third less time than they did. Plan and write the letter.

3. You want to apply for a scholarship that is offered each year to "the most qualified student in (your major)." No other criteria are stated, and the decision is made by "a committee of faculty members and administrators." It seems obvious to you that they will evaluate both your academic record and your extracurricular activities. Write a letter that explains why you should receive the award.

4. Safety experts have long said that commercial airliners would be safer if the seats were installed so that they faced the rear of the aircraft. Airlines have resisted this because most passengers have indicated that they would not like to fly facing the rear of an airplane. You work for South Mountain Airways, which has decided to try rear-facing seats in three of its airplanes, all Boeing 727 jets. Your job is to write a persuasive statement that can be handed to passengers on these airplanes to explain why the seats have been changed and to convince them that it is a good idea. Remember, though, that neither airlines nor passengers like to talk about safety very much at all, since that topic calls attention to the possibility that airplanes might crash.

5. You work for one of the safety experts mentioned in exercise 4. Write a letter that he can send to airlines in an attempt to get them to try moving the seats in their airplanes (or a few of their airplanes) so that they face the rear. Remember that these airline executives are probably well aware of your boss's work and know all of the advantages of turning the seats. They are resisting because passengers, they say, will not like it.

6. Your company has been hired by a nonprofit organization that is involved with a controversial issue (such as birth control, abortion, capital punishment, civil rights, or a religious belief). One of your jobs is to help this organization raise money. It makes no difference which issue you choose or which side of the issue you choose. You will be writing to people who are on a mailing list that indicates that they have contributed to this group but have given no money during the past three years. You want them to send a check. Do whatever research you believe is necessary and then write the letter.

7. You work for a magazine that has experienced declining circulation for the past two years. Your job is to write a letter to former subscribers that offers them one free issue in return for a one-year subscription. You may choose any magazine you wish, but be sure to read at least a full year's issues before you begin.

8. You believe you have an idea that will save your company money. You think it can save substantially each year by renting or leasing its vehicle fleet, rather than purchasing it. The company now buys a fleet every two years. It consists of one prestige car, four midline sedans, twelve compacts, and twenty compact pickup trucks. The company receives a discount of 15 percent off the sticker price for buying the entire fleet at once from the same dealer. Do enough research to work out the cost of such a fleet (use any make of car you wish) and the cost of renting or leasing the same fleet. (Calculate a 5 percent savings on the purchase price and include any free service.) Write a letter or memo in which you try to show the president of your company that leasing or renting would be a good idea.

9. You believe that using *flextime,* letting employees schedule their shifts more or less at their own convenience, would be a good incentive to increase productivity. Investigate this concept and write a memo in which you attempt to convince your boss to try it, at least on a partial or temporary basis.

10. Your company has recently had difficulty attracting the kinds of job applicants it wants, especially in engineering, chemistry, and physics. These people are essential to manufacturing, research, and product development in your business. In an attempt to counteract this trend, the company has decided to begin an aggressive recruiting campaign by writing to the top 5 percent of college seniors in these fields in the region. The letter will stress the benefits of working for Zomatize Industries and will invite resumes and applications. Here are some details you may need.

    Zomatize is a major developer of equipment and techniques for treating wastewater. It employs chemists and physicists as laboratory researchers and field supervisors to develop new methods of wastewater treatment and then monitor these methods as they are used. The company also manufactures the equipment and chemicals for the treatment and has proprietary patents on several processes and substances. The company recorded $75 million in sales last year and plans to double that figure in three years. The average starting salary in these fields is $23,500, and the company offers a benefits package that includes four weeks of vacation each year; one-half tuition grants for continuing education; and fully paid medical, disability, prescription, life insurance ($25,000), dental, and vision plans.

This might not be a difficult letter to write, except that wastewater treatment is not an especially glamorous career field, though it is important and interesting. You will need to stress these points, since your salaries and benefits are, in fact, about the same as these graduates could make in any other field.

■

10

Writing Memos

If you can write letters, you can write memos. There is no special trick to it. What *is* special about memos is the situation in which you write them. In this chapter we will explore that situation and the special relationship that exists between you and your readers. Among the topics we will consider are:

How memos differ from letters
What memos are good for
The ways people abuse memos
When a memo is appropriate
The politics and protocol of memos
Formats

Introduction

Memos, along with the telephone, are the workhorses of communication within any organization. They provide a fast, efficient, convenient way of exchanging information, stating policies, and asking questions.

Even though some people complain that business is about to drown in its own paper, most businesses could not survive without memos. They create an important "paper trail" that records the decisions people have made and the actions they have taken, just as financial records create a trail of information for auditors. In fact, memos are *part* of the decision-making process in any organization. They are an important means of stating and exchanging ideas, reacting to them, clarifying them, revising them, and finally agreeing about actions to be taken. Without memos, we would spend most of our time rushing from office to office looking for each other, or dialing the phone and hoping that the person we want to talk with is in. The search, rather than the work itself, would become the major focus of our day.

Some companies have attempted to do away with memos and paperwork in general, hoping to increase productivity by giving people more time to actually *do* their jobs, rather than write about them. One popular alternative is to computerize all writing and record keeping. It's simple. Just give everyone a computer terminal. Then, the Vice President for Marketing can send a message to the Sales Manager by simply typing it into the computer. The Sales Manager then displays messages on a monitor, reads them, and erases the ones there is no need to keep. Only important or permanent messages remain in the machine, available whenever they are needed. But if you think about it, these companies really haven't eliminated memos. People must still write them and read them. Only filing and retrieving have been simplified. Desks will no doubt be neater, because there will no longer be a mound of paper on top of each one. But the memos remain.

Letters vs. Memos: Some Important Differences

At first glance, memos seem quite different from letters. They are often written or typed on a special form or on "internal" stationery and begin with headings such as *TO, FROM,* and *SUBJECT,* rather than an inside address. Many have no signature, and they are often handwritten rather than typed. The memo in Figure 10-1 is reasonably typical.

These physical features may seem striking, but they concern what a memo *looks* like, rather than what it says. And matters of format are rather easy to master. If you look beyond them to the writing itself, you will see that many of the differences between letters and memos disappear. Both seem to do the same jobs and to use the same strategies and organizing principles. The real differences between letters and memos, the ones you need to know about as you write, are practically invisible in the finished product. But they exist and they are important.

Figure 10-1 Typical Memo Content and Format

```
     TO:  Marketing Planning Group        February 1, 1984
   FROM:  John Clarke, Sales Manager
SUBJECT:  Strategy Meeting for "K" Product

Copies to:  J. Haley              P. Kline
            R. Sinkowitz          S. Feldman
            L. Roudebusch         T. Antonelli
The Marketing Planning Group will meet on Wednesday
February 9 to discuss the current status of the "K"
product distributorship program.

AGENDA:
     1.  Status Report - J. Clarke
     2.  Distributor Applications - P. Kline
     3.  Geographical Distributions - L. Roudebusch
     4.  Distributorship Policies - T. Antonelli

During this meeting we will attempt to make the final
distributor selections so that the "K" product can
enter the distribution system no later than March 15.

TIME & PLACE:  9:00 a.m. in the Third Floor Conference Room

JCtr
```

Your Readers Are Different

You and your readers belong to the same organization; that is a relationship that you do not share with those outside the company. Because you both work within the same hierarchy of power, authority, and responsibility, you can affect each others' lives and careers with what you write, especially if one of you is more powerful than the other. You must both work within the expected, acceptable behaviors that the hierarchy has developed. And you are interdependent to an extent that you and your outside readers are not. You must work together for the company's continued success, and you will often depend on each other for individual success and advancement.

Personal and Professional Relationships

You will often have long-standing personal and professional relationships with your readers. You may have known many of your readers for years, and you may socialize with some of them. Your readers will expect you to show that you are aware of these relationships. In contrast, when you write letters to "outsiders" you have never met and do not expect to meet, they will expect from you only the professionalism of your position and common courtesy.

Handling Disagreements

Even though you and your readers work within the same hierarchy and share its goals, you may disagree about how to achieve these goals. That is not unusual; in fact, it may be essential to making good decisions. And your disagreements will often be the subject of memos. But you and your readers must continue to work together after the decisions have been made. Though there may occasionally be hard feelings, it is important to write so that you do not permanently damage the working relationships that are essential to your company's success and your own.

Memos Are Broadcast Messages

Letters often have one reader. Memos are a convenient way of getting the same message to several people, or even several hundred, at the same time. When you use a memo for this purpose, remember that it will have a large, heterogeneous audience that consists of people from all levels in the organization. You will have to write in such a way that *all* of your readers, with their different levels of intelligence, ability, and knowledge, will be able to understand you.

At the same time, you must write so that your message is politically acceptable to all of your readers. A production worker or shop superintendent may accept your instructions as a matter of routine. But a vice president may believe that you are overstepping your limits and making policy or intruding on territory that is not yours.

Memos Have Extended Audiences

Always expect that your audience will include more people than you thought it would. People leave memos lying around, pass them along to others, and even post them on bulletin boards. People who do not usually see you or know your work will be able to read what you write. And some of these extra readers will be above you in the hierarchy, in positions that require them to make decisions about your future. They do not know or observe you directly, but they will often base their opinions of you on what others say and on what you write.

Your audience may extend beyond your own organization as memos find their way to auditors, attorneys, and courts in the process of investigations, labor disputes, and civil or criminal trials. Difficulties arise when these people read a memo out of its original context and attempt to reconstruct your company's policies and actions. Even the most innocent memos have created legal or public relations problems for writers and companies because they have fallen into hostile hands. Of course, it is impossible to prevent all possible misinterpretations of your writing, especially willful ones. But you can review your memos to be sure they do not contain or suggest obviously detrimental statements.

Why Write Memos?

If businesses, nonprofit organizations, and government agencies are about to drown in their own paper, then why do we write memos at all? Why not just talk things over, or have meetings, or be quiet? Memos do serve some purposes that are worth the effort it takes to write and keep them. And some jobs would be much more difficult without them.

1. *Memos save time.* They really do. They can announce a policy decision or explain a procedure to many people at the same time. And those people need not be within earshot of the source. They can continue working and read the memo when they have time. There is no need to schedule a meeting. You can simply write a memo, without leaving your desk, and move on to the next job.
2. *Memos assist memory.* You can use them to restate or clarify instructions or decisions that were given orally the first time. Or you can use them to record and report what happened during a meeting or telephone conversation, and who was involved. The memo makes it difficult for anyone to say "I forgot" or "We didn't talk about that." In fact, if you write the memo and send the other parties copies of it, it becomes the official, legal version of an event unless someone adds to it or clarifies it in writing. So memos can serve as records of who was responsible for certain actions and decisions.

   Memos also help you keep track of jobs that you must do or that you have assigned to someone else. You can file a copy of a memo in a *suspense,* or *tickler,* file (a set of thirty-one files, one for each day of the month, that is rotated month by month; the entire file lets you keep track of the next year). Each day, when you check the file, you will find memos and other reminders of jobs you must do or check on.

3. *Memos provide access* to people you do not normally see or talk to. It is not always possible to have access to people who make decisions. Even when it is, they will often respond to your ideas by saying "Put it on paper so I can look it over." A well-written, carefully thought out memo is an excellent way of getting your ideas to people who must approve them. Writing the memo will force you to think through your ideas and state them carefully. If your idea is a good one, and you express it well, you will probably gain access to the decision maker.

Abusing Memos

No, not *abusive memos,* though there are plenty of those around. Nor does this section have anything to do with throwing darts at memos or tearing them to shreds, though some people would like to do that, and some memos deserve it. Memos are versatile and useful. But some people use them for the wrong reasons.

The Attention-Getter

Some people seem to spend their lives writing memos. Any subject will do, no matter how trivial, so long as it will fit on a piece of paper. These people write about the way parking spaces are assigned, the amount of trash in the wastebaskets, and the dirty windows on the fourteenth floor. Their chief goal is not so much to do a job as to convince everyone else that they are working and paying attention, even if no one else is. They often succeed in getting attention, but not the kind they want. People notice that they are always writing memos and begin to wonder when these writers have time to do their jobs. Eventually, this constant stream of memos comes to be seen as the harassment it is, rather than as a contribution, and people stop reading them and paying attention to those who write them.

Covering Your Backside

There are less elegant ways of saying that, but most of them are inappropriate here. You will learn them soon enough. You will also learn very quickly that memos can be an effective way of deflecting criticism and responsibility from yourself and dropping them neatly onto others. Some people constantly write memos that say, in effect, "It's not my fault" or "I told you so." Try to pin something on these people, even if they deserve it, and they will extract a memo from their files to prove that it was someone else's fault—probably yours—and that they warned you in advance. Eventually, of course, this becomes tiresome. Everyone becomes so preoccupied with protecting themselves or catching someone else, that very little real work gets done.

Using Memos to Avoid People

Finally, too many people use memos to avoid face-to-face interactions with others. Perhaps they are uncomfortable talking with others, or dislike the people they must talk with, or simply have an unpleasant job to do. It is especially tempting to write a memo, rather than meet face-to-face, when you must give an unfavorable performance review, or criticize a job someone has done, or refuse a request. Memos are sometimes appropriate and necessary in these situations, because you will need a permanent record. But it is often a mistake to allow a memo to substitute for a face-to-face encounter. You risk, first of all, making this a habit and conducting all of your business in writing. And you can create misunderstandings, confusion, and even hostility. You may appear to be a person who *can't* face others directly. Subordinates may decide that you think you're too good or too important to waste your time with them, or that you are not interested in their feelings, their work, or their professional development. They may be right, and that is the problem.

When Should You Use a Memo?

Memos are only one means of interacting with the other people in your organization. There are others, and sometimes one of them will be more appropriate to the situation and more effective in accomplishing your goals. Before you pick up your pen and commit a memo, think about the other means that exist and whether one of them might be more effective. Almost any medium you select will get your message across.

Practical Considerations

When you need to communicate with someone else or with a group of people in your organization, your usual choices include a memo, a phone call, a personal meeting, or a group meeting. Each has advantages and disadvantages.

The *telephone* can be fast, and it provides immediate replies, but unless you take careful notes you will have no record of whom you talked with or what you decided. And sometimes the telephone is not as fast as it seems. You may get a busy signal, or be put on hold, or find that the other person is out or in conference, and you will have to call back. You can wait for hours for people to return your calls, only to discover that they never received the message.

Telephones also encourage "impulse talking." There it is, sitting on your desk, and it's so easy to just dial and talk to someone about your new idea or your most recent problem. We all do this, sometimes without giving our ideas sufficient thought. We end up being asked to "put it on paper," and writing the memo we were trying to avoid in the first place. We may also end up with a reputation for presenting half-baked ideas that are not thoroughly developed.

Meetings, with one person or several, offer opportunities for discussion, negotiation, and other kinds of direct interaction that are not available when we phone or write. They may be the best, or one of the best, methods of group decision making, brainstorming, and consensus building. But meetings are time-consuming and sometimes difficult to arrange. You must find a time when everyone is available and then a place to have the meeting. In a busy organization these constraints may limit you to one or two times during a week if more than two or three people are involved. No matter how carefully you plan, meetings will almost always last longer than you thought they would. You need to decide whether the benefits of the meeting outweigh the time and effort to arrange and conduct it.

Before you call a meeting, plan your agenda carefully and try to decide what you want to accomplish. If you find that most of your agenda items are announcements and other "information sharing," perhaps it would be best to write a memo about these topics and confine the meeting to important matters that only a meeting can address.

Memos offer numerous practical advantages. Among the most attractive of these is that you need never leave your desk. Simply write or dictate the memo and give it to a typist. It will find its way to your reader and, with any luck, you will get the reply or the action that you want. And you are not likely to be caught unprepared, with important notes or documents back in your office, or in the files in the next room. Both of these can happen when you phone or attend meetings. Memos allow you to choose your words carefully and review them, rather than do your thinking out loud, in public, for all to see.

Memos do have disadvantages. It takes time to get them typed and through the interoffice mail to your reader. Depending on the state of your company's internal mail system, this could take several hours or several days. You give up the advantages of the give-and-take of a personal encounter, which can lead to new or better ideas. It might take you a week or more of exchanging memos to accomplish the same amount of work that you could get done in a one-hour meeting.

Interpersonal Considerations

The different media (writing, meetings, and the telephone) all send messages that are quite distinct from their content. That is, other people may believe it is significant that you wrote a memo rather than called them or walked down the hall to talk. This seems to be common knowledge among people who write letters and who will go to great effort and expense to make a form letter appear to be individually dictated and typed. They realize that their readers may regard an obvious form letter as too impersonal. And they believe that the appearance of extra effort may make a significant difference in the way a reader responds. They also realize that these differences in meaning are entirely relative, depending on the reader and the situation, rather than on anything intrinsic in the medium itself.

Remember that people do not check their human reactions at the door each day just because they work for you or with you. The person who is used to receiving memos from you will react differently if you phone or visit. Depending on the circumstances, you can use phone calls or visits to encourage or intimidate, merely because they are unusual. On the other hand, if you usually see someone frequently, a string of memos may be taken as an indication of increasing distance between you. If you deliver criticism in person, it may be taken as much more significant or even threatening than you mean it, especially if a person is not accustomed to meeting with you.

If you call a meeting about a problem or issue, you will endow it with a certain importance simply because the meeting implies that the subject is worth the time and energy of so many people gathered in the same place all at once. A brief memo or quiet talks with several people will give an issue considerably less attention, and thus less importance. You can avoid the appearance of seven people chasing a mouse.

There are really no rules for deciding which medium you should use. You will have to rely on your own knowledge of your company, the situation, and the people who are involved. But you should be aware that some people will "read" your choice of medium as carefully as they read and interpret the content of your messages. They will be more or less sensitive as they perceive themselves to be more or less involved in or affected by the issues at hand. Try to choose a medium that will be most effective in accomplishing your goal and, at the same time, send the fewest unintended messages.

Politics and Protocol

Information flows in all directions within an organization. Sometimes it moves along paths that are clearly marked by the formal lines of power, authority, and responsibility. Sometimes it disregards these lines entirely. In addition, there are all sorts of formal and informal networks: the well-known rumor mill, bulletin boards, hotlines, open-door policies, and newsletters, all designed to get information to the people who need it. Some companies have rather rigid organizations and formal, written guidelines about how people are to communicate with each other. Others observe a protocol that may be widely acknowledged but mostly unwritten. How do you function within this hierarchy?

Communication that moves upward in an organization, to those who have more authority or responsibility than you, usually follows established lines of authority, and stops at or goes through the people who are between you and your ultimate reader. A new management trainee, for example, does not write directly to the company president. Nor does a production supervisor write or call the Vice President of Marketing. The management trainee routes memos through (or to) an immediate supervisor; from there they move up through the levels of the hierarchy, perhaps being changed at each one. Likewise, the production supervisor works through those people who are responsible for the department. Sometimes this may mean that good ideas get lost or even stopped in their tracks. And sometimes the person who had the idea in the first place does not get credit for it.

But using established "channels" in this way also ensures that decisions are made at the most appropriate level of the company. And it prevents those at the upper levels of management from being swamped with paper. If company presidents took time to look at every idea that came along and read every memo, they would hardly have time to do their jobs. Perhaps the management trainee's idea has been tried before. Or it may need to be developed with the insight and perspective that can come only from years of experience.

When you send memos upward in the hierarchy, people expect you to observe the usual protocol of keeping your supervisor informed or working *through* each level above you. It is no more than common courtesy to do this, and you will earn courtesy and respect in return.

Communication that moves downward in an organization, to those who have less authority or responsibility than you, *may* follow the established lines of authority, but not always. It often depends on the purpose of the message and the situation. Company presidents may walk through the production floor or offices, greeting people by name and even stopping for brief conversations. They may even write memos or letters to employees, congratulating them for some personal success or praising their performance. In most cases these encounters will be informal and have little to do with company policy. If presidents want to give instructions about a specific product or a step in the manufacturing process, they will usually do that through the channels of responsibility that exist for that purpose. That way, everyone will know about it and people will not be working at cross-purposes.

It is generally accepted that you may communicate directly with those who are on your level of the hierarchy or with those who are under your immediate supervision. This is especially important if the subject is a matter of policy or decision making. The Vice President for Marketing may write to the Sales Manager and other vice presidents or communicate informally with a production supervisor about a product or a process. But changes in a product or a production schedule will have to go through the Vice President for Manufacturing, who has authority in such matters.

The point of this attention to protocol is not that people should not communicate with each other or that some are better than others. Many managers and corporation presidents maintain an open-door policy that allows anyone in the company to have direct access to top level decision makers. Rather, the point of following the lines of the hierarchy is to ensure that all employees have the information they need to do their jobs. For example, if company presidents make policy directly with someone on the production floor, these problems are likely to arise:

1. Those between them in the hierarchy are not likely to know about the decisions. Important details can be ignored, and people can make expensive mistakes.
2. The presidents are ignoring their own jobs to do someone else's. If they are going to do that, they might as well get rid of those hired to do the job they are usurping. But, presumably, the president has work to do too. Who is doing it?
3. It is bad for morale. Managers and supervisors begin to feel that they are being ignored, and both productivity and quality can suffer.

Communication that moves sideways in an organization, *across* lines of authority and responsibility, is by far the most frequent, and perhaps the most productive. Managers, supervisors, and workers who are at more or less equal levels in a company will frequently meet, confer by phone, and exchange memos about subjects that are of mutual interest. Most of the jobs in an organization involve the cooperation of several people who interact with each other frequently. Much of this communication, even memos and reports, takes place between people who are counterparts, equals who are involved in a product or project, without going through either one's supervisor. This is not considered "going around" anyone, but is merely an extension of the principle that decisions should be made at the lowest appropriate level in an organization. These counterparts can work out the details of a proposal or solution and then submit memos or reports through their supervisors to obtain the necessary policy decision. To consult them earlier, about each detail, might leave them no time for the rest of their jobs.

Who Gets a Copy of Your Memo?

Even if you are writing to only one person, you probably will send several copies of a memo. Remember your extended audience? Some of them need to know what you are doing or deciding, so you will want to send them copies, even though they are not your primary readers. You can divide your audience into two main groups: those who must *do* something as a result of your memo and those who simply need to know what you have said. Those who must do something are sometimes called *action addressees*, and the others *information addressees*. In fact, you can identify the different segments of your audience right on the memo, so those who receive it will know what you expect them to do.

For example, if you are working with someone in data processing to develop a new method of inventory control, the two of you might exchange memos directly as you work on the project. You will probably also send "information copies" or carbon copies of your memos to your supervisors, so that they will know what you are doing and be able to assess your progress.

The ideal is to get your message to everyone who needs to know about it or do something about it.

Format: What Do Memos Look Like?

Memos come in a variety of sizes, shapes, and colors, unlike letters, which are almost always typed according to rather strict formats. Memos may be brief, handwritten notes on scratch paper or carefully designed formal documents of several pages. You may use special stationery for memos, printed with a special logo to distinguish it from your company's letterhead. Sometimes it will have a special title, such as *internal correspondence* or *interoffice memorandum*. Some companies purchase special preprinted forms for memos. These are usually bound with carbon paper so that you can make several copies, and they contain lines or blocks for the addressees' names, the subject, date, and the message itself.

Because memos are meant for insiders, they often dispense with many of the formalities of letters and include features that will make them easy to recognize and file. Figure 10-2 is a composite memo that includes typical features. You may not need to include all of these in every memo, but it will help to know what they are.

Each major feature of the memo in Figure 10-2 is numbered, so you can follow the explanation below.

1. Typed or printed heading.
2. Date.
3. File or reference number. This lets file clerks know where

Figure 10-2 Composite Memo

INTEROFFICE MEMORANDUM

Hartley & Sons Machinery

JULY 21, 198_ FILE # MKS-83-2

TO: P. Roberts, Sales Manager

FROM: R. Coates, Customer Expediter

SUBJECT: MKS Order #83-16213-F

Thanks for calling the MKS problem to my attention this morning. I think we have it solved.

Machine shop delays this month have been due to vacations and machinery breakdowns. The MKS production run began yesterday, about eight days behind schedule. Production was unaware of the tight scheduling, so did not notify you or the customer.

The entire MKS order can be shipped on August 3. I realize this is too late, so we've arranged a partial shipment on July 29 of 10,000 rotors. The in-transit time is usually three days, so MKS should receive enough of them to begin production on the 3rd, as planned.

The remainder of the order (11,000 rotors) will be shipped on August 3, and should arrive at MKS on the 6th. I have notified Mr. Maxwell of MKS of these arrangements, and he approved.

Production (J. Trimmer) will assign two extra machine operators to this order to guarantee shipment on the 3rd. Art Baker has agreed to make two shipments and will personally supervise loading the MKS order. Our extra costs are estimated at approximately $750.

Copies to:
Production: Trimmer
Shipping: Baker
Sales: Walters

to file the memo and allows your reader to match it with previous memos and correspondence about the same subject.

4. Address block, including the reader, writer, and subject.
5. A subject line which tells your reader what the memo is about.
6. A distribution list that names everyone who is to receive a copy.

The exact arrangement of these components in the memo can vary from one company to another (and sometimes from one department to another). Some companies provide detailed instructions about what memos and correspondence should look like. If your company has such a manual, you should follow it.

One of these components, the subject line, deserves a bit of extra attention. Subject lines should provide enough information that your reader will know what the memo is about without having to dig through several paragraphs. At the same time, there is a limit to how much you can say in a subject line without turning it into a separate memo. The following subject lines are all less informative than they could be.

Your Memo of July 1

Quality Assurance

Overtime Schedules

Production Schedule Delays

Each of these needs to be more specific, because in each case the subject that is given can include dozens or even hundreds of specific situations. For example, how many memos do you suppose your reader wrote on July 1? Try to write the subject line so that your reader can identify what the memo is about quickly and clearly. These revisions should help.

New Quality Assurance Procedures for Stainless Steel Components

Overtime Schedules for Second-Shift Boring-Machine Operators

Production Schedule Delays on Printed Circuits for Model 200SD Controls

Summary and Conclusion

Memos serve some very important functions within organizations. They are an effective way of keeping records and of getting information to a large number of people at the same time. They are also an important part of the decision-making process within any company, as they provide information from those who have it to those who must use it to make decisions.

Memos are different from letters because they demand a special awareness of your continuing relationships with readers who are also your coworkers, supervisors, and subordinates. These readers will expect you to write with an awareness of them as individuals, and of their roles in the organization, that most readers outside your company will not demand.

Sometimes your knowledge of your readers or of the situation will demand that you choose another way of getting your message across. Memos are neither the only nor necessarily the best means of communicating with those who work with you.

Examples

Memos are the workhorses of internal communication in any organization. The memos on the following pages are examples of what you might find in any business. They are here for your study and review. Read them carefully and, if you have the opportunity, revise some of them so that they more closely observe the principles explained in this chapter. This will provide valuable practice for the exercises at the end of the chapter.

In Figures 10-3 through 10-7 you will find some sample memos that you can use as examples for classroom discussion or individual study. Read them carefully and critique them. But don't simply copy them. Their presence here is no guarantee that they are the best of their kind.

■

Figure 10-3 Memos Requesting and Acknowledging Services

INTER OFFICE COMMUNICATION

FROM: J. Damerst
TO: Fred Foust DATE: 1/4/8_
SUBJECT: Mall Presentation

Just a reminder to let you know that on Monday morning 1/11, I'll need somebody to haul our display from the warehouse over to West Winchester Mall and set it up. OK?

INTER-OFFICE COMMUNICATION

FROM: J. Damerst
TO: Fred Foust DATE: 1/19/8_
SUBJECT: Mall Presentation

Just a quick note of appreciation to you, Glen Walsh and George Tower for a really good job, really well done in getting the display out, up, down and back from the West Winchester Mall.

It helped us be well represented during the National Printing Week show.

Thanks.

Figure 10-4 Memo Outlining Complaint Procedure

PERSONNEL BULLETIN #1895

JUNE 30, 1982

SEXUAL HARASSMENT

FORMAL COMPLAINT PROCEDURE

1. Any employee who feels he or she has been the victim of sexual harassment should contact the Equal Employment Opportunity Manager (E.E.O. Manager) within twenty (20) days of the incident. This report can be oral or written, but a written and signed statement of the complaint must be submitted to the E.E.O. Manager at York Group by the complaining employee within seven (7) days of the initial report so an investigation can proceed into the matter.

2. Upon receipt of the written complaint, the E.E.O. Manager will contact the person who allegedly engaged in the sexual harassment and inform him or her of the basis of the complaint and the opportunity to respond. That person will then have fourteen (14) days to respond to the complaint.

3. Upon receipt of the response, the E.E.O. Manager will make a further investigation of the facts to insure that all matters have been considered and then make a written report of the findings to the Vice President of Human Resources. The findings will be reviewed and a decision issued on the allegations of the complaint. Both parties will be notified of that decision.

4. If it is determined that sexual harassment has occurred, appropriate disciplinary action up to and including discharge will be taken. The severity of the discipline will be determined by the severity and/or frequency of the offense.

5. An employee's failure to report the occurrence of sexual harassment within twenty (20) days will be deemed a waiver of any intra-company action. Failure to file a written complaint within seven (7) days of the initial report will be considered a withdrawal of that report. If the person against whom the complaint of sexual harassment is filed fails to respond to the complaint within fourteen (14) days of notification, the complaint will taken as true; and the appropriate disciplinary measure will be taken.

Figure 10-5 Memo Discussing Marketing

TO: Jim Downing 9/8/82
FROM: Bob Valentine
SUBJECT: Gravure Process

Jim, I have been thinking that the new process could have excellent market appeal if it is successful. I have been kicking some thoughts around--how about asking the field salesmen for a marketing oriented name for it? I do think the process has good advertising qualities. I do not feel that referring to it as the gravure process is a good idea at this point because it does not indicate how unique we are to adapt it to a flexo process. I am really excited about it and hope it works. When we get together in September I would like to discuss phasing it in at Filmtech, Brown and Greene as an alternate to subsurface.

Regards.

9/8/82

TO: Bob Valentine
FROM: John Downing
SUBJECT: Gravure Process-- Your memo of 9/8/82

Bob, thanks for your thoughts regarding a name for the gravure process. However, much has to be finalized before we even think of fully releasing it to our own people. Much of this has to do with the gear ratio which Tom Fields is working on.

As to introducing to Filmtech, Brown and Greene, not just yet. We do, as you know, have a trial order in for Greene, but, again, we couldn't entertain a large order at this time until Tom Fields finishes his alterations. When we next chat, I will show you why you wouldn't want it for Filmtech or Brown.

Figure 10-6 Memo to Employees about Paid Holidays

PERSONNEL BULLETIN #1894

JUNE 23, 1982

TO: A L L O U R E M P L O Y E E S

SUBJECT: J U L Y 4TH H O L I D A Y

IN ACCORDANCE WITH OUR VARIOUS LABOR AGREEMENTS, JULY 4 HOLIDAY WILL BE OBSERVED IN THE FOLLOWING MANNER:

U.A.W. MEMBERS -

THE 5TH OF JULY WILL BE OBSERVED AS THE JULY 4TH HOLIDAY. THE ADDITIONAL VACATION DAY DUE TO THE VACATION SHUTDOWN THE WEEKS OF JULY 5 AND JULY 12 WILL BE TAKEN ON FRIDAY, JULY 2ND.

SALARIED EMPLOYEES -

THE 5TH OF JULY WILL BE OBSERVED AS THE JULY 4TH HOLIDAY AND JULY 6TH HAS BEEN DESIGNATED AS A FLOATING HOLIDAY.

ANY EMPLOYEE REQUIRED TO WORK ON THESE DAYS WILL BE SO NOTIFIED BY HIS/HER SUPERVISOR.

HUMAN RESOURCES DEPARTMENT

Figure 10-7 Memo to Employees about Office Hours

PERSONNEL BULLETIN #1893

JUNE 30, 1982

TO: ALL EMPLOYEES

RE: RESTRICTED HOURS
EMPLOYEE BENEFITS DEPT.

IN AN EFFORT TO IMPROVE OUR PRODUCTIVITY, WE ARE GOING TO LIMIT THE HOURS THE EMPLOYEE BENEFITS DEPARTMENT WILL BE OPEN TO TRANSACT BUSINESS WITH OUR EMPLOYEES. EFFECTIVE MONDAY, AUGUST 2, 1982, THE BENEFITS DEPARTMENT WILL BE OPEN FROM 8:00 A.M. TO 10:00 A.M., AND FROM 3:00 P.M. TO 5:00 P.M., MONDAY THROUGH FRIDAY, FOR THE PURPOSE OF TRANSACTING BUSINESS WITH OUR EMPLOYEES.

THE ESTABLISHMENT OF THESE BUSINESS HOURS, HOPEFULLY, WILL GIVE THE BENEFITS PERSONNEL A SPAN OF TIME DURING EACH DAY TO WORK WITH A MINIMUM OF INTERRUPTIONS. IF THESE HOURS SHOULD PROVIDE INSUFFICIENT TIME TO SERVE OUR EMPLOYEES, THE BUSINESS HOURS WILL BE EXPANDED.

YOUR COOPERATION IN OBSERVING THESE HOURS, EFFECTIVE AUGUST 2, 1982, WILL BE APPRECIATED.

HUMAN RESOURCES DEPARTMENT

Exercises: Chapter Ten

1. You work for John Martin, Senior Vice President of Deltoid Corporation. This morning you found a note from him on your desk. A number of recently hired junior executives have been parking their cars in spaces that are reserved for vice presidents. Though the spaces are not marked, everyone in the company "just knows" not to park in them. They are located in the first row of the parking lot, next to the office entrance of the plant, and include the six spaces west of the president's marked parking space. The vice presidents are upset, and Martin wants a memo for his signature that will make it clear just where those below the rank of VP are to park or not to park. He wants to do this without being offensive, and he does not want to mark the spaces.

2. Two weeks from today your company will host a visit from Ms. Elizabeth Anderson, who represents the Mutual Beneficial Insurance Company of Lincoln, Nebraska. Ms. Anderson's company carries many of your company's employee benefit plans, and she will be here to explain those benefits to employees and answer their questions. She will also be conducting a preretirement workshop for anyone who plans to retire within the next year. She will be in the second floor conference room from 8:30 A.M. until 3:30 P.M. Any employee may meet with her privately during that time by making an appointment with your office and notifying his or her supervisor one day in advance.

   Ms. Quinn, your boss, wants you to write a memo for all employees to announce Ms. Anderson's visit and encourage all employees who have questions to schedule an appointment with her. By the way, she adds, the retirement orientation will be at 3:30 in the same room. She also wants a memo to all supervisors, encouraging them to release people for up to one hour to meet with Ms. Anderson (though the average meeting should last no more than fifteen minutes).

3. One of your jobs as Industrial Relations Manager for Harmony Corporation is to oversee the operation of the company cafeteria, which is run by an outside contractor. You usually pay no attention to complaints about the food because you know that complaints about institutional food are common. But today the General Manager called to say that many employees are taking up to fifteen minutes extra each day for lunch. Supervisors report that the employees say they are going out to lunch to avoid the cafeteria. Just after that, the cafeteria manager called to complain that business has dropped off 25 percent in the past two weeks because people are not eating in the cafeteria, and to assure you that the food is the same as it has always been. You eat in the cafeteria yourself, so you know that the food is not as good as it could be. Last week you visited your company's plant in Milwaukee,

which uses another food service contractor, and you thought the food was excellent.

a. Write a memo to the General Manager, explaining your experience in Milwaukee and suggesting that something has to be done about the cafeteria.

b. Write a memo to the cafeteria manager that compares the cafeteria food to the meals you had when you visited the plant in Milwaukee. Ask why your plant can't have the same menu and quality, trying not to be offensive.

c. Write a memo, for the General Manager's signature, that reminds all employees that the company allows forty-five minutes for lunch and provides a cafeteria so that employees need not go out. State your willingness to listen to legitimate, constructive criticism of the food.

5. You have just been appointed to direct your company's annual United Giving Campaign, and you need to write an appeal to all employees to contribute either a fixed amount or a percentage of their weekly pay. If each person contributes 1 percent of each weekly check, the company will once again exceed its unofficial "fair gift" contribution. The proceeds of the campaign are distributed to recognized charitable and nonprofit organizations in your city.

6. Joan Harwood is one of the new typists in the typing pool that you supervise. Today she was late for work for the third time this week. On Monday she explained that she was ten minutes late because the bus had been held up in traffic. On Tuesday she rather honestly explained that she had overslept. You were inclined to be sympathetic on Monday. You ride the bus, too, and they do get held up. Your solution has been to take an earlier bus, and you suggested that to her. Today she was an hour late and you have decided to write a memo that will be placed in her file. She will, of course, receive a copy. You do not really expect that the memo will get her to work. You merely want to document the situation in case it becomes necessary to fire her in the future.

7. A friend of yours who recently graduated from college has asked you if there is a job available where you work. There is a job, and you believe your friend is qualified for it. Write a memo to the person who will do the hiring. Recommend that your friend be considered for the position. You may, of course, choose the friend, his or her qualifications, and the job description. Be sure that you identify the job and describe your friend's qualifications fully.

8. In response to increasing awareness of the needs of retirees, and the lack of knowledge that most people seem to have about how to prepare for retirement, your company has decided to sponsor a series of retirement planning meetings for employees who are 58 or older. The meeting will be held on January 17 at 3:00 P.M. in the cafeteria. Employees will be released from their jobs and allowed to attend on company time. There will be a coffee and snack break at 5:00, and the meeting will end at 7:00 P.M. The speakers will include a financial planner, the company benefits administrator, and a local psychologist who has worked with retirees. From 6:00 to 7:00 there will be a panel discussion featuring retirees from the company.

   Write a memo that announces the meeting and encourages all eligible employees to attend.

9. The retirement planning session mentioned in exercise 8 was a success. You attended, even though you are far from being 58. One thing that you learned is that people need to begin planning for retirement in their twenties and thirties, not their fifties. Write a memo to the Executive Vice President in which you recommend and outline a series of retirement planning meetings for all employees. (Yes, you will probably have to do some research for this one.)

10. Your supervisor has recently been complaining about the way some employees come to work wearing casual slacks, boating and hiking shoes, and even sandals. He is also upset that the women in the office are not wearing suits or skirts and a jacket, but casual sweaters and, occasionally, slacks. Several men have not worn ties for several months. Your supervisor is ready to propose a dress code to the president, and he has asked your opinion. Write a memo in which you give your opinion, for or against a dress code, or suggest guidelines that can be given to employees to remind them of appropriate ways to dress in the office.

Part 3

Writing Business Reports

11

Writing Proposals

A proposal is like a suggestion. It is a way of getting your ideas to those people in your organization who make decisions.

Proposals begin as specific ideas for changes, solutions to problems, or answers to questions. Their goal is to show that a problem exists, and that the company should commit its resources to solving it. To do this, they must explain what needs to be done (or could be done), why, how it will be done, who will do it, what changes will be involved, what equipment and personnel are necessary, and how much it will cost. Finally a proposal must show that the suggested change will be an improvement over existing policies and practices.

The goal of this chapter is to explain what proposals do, how they do it, how to plan them, what information they should include, and how they can be organized.

Introduction

A proposal begins when you notice a problem that needs a solution, a question that needs an answer, or a situation that requires action.

But deciding what action to take will require that the company invest time, effort, and money to find out exactly what should be done and whether it will work. In other words, finding a solution is going to be too difficult or expensive to justify simply pursuing a whim or hunch. The job of the proposal is to convince a decision maker that the problem or situation is worth the expense and difficulty of finding a solution.

Once you have identified the problem, or a change that you believe needs to be made, the next step is to do research. To write a successful proposal you will have to know the subject thoroughly, perhaps better than anyone else. Your research will either convince you that you were right, and that the problem does in fact exist, or that you were wrong, that it isn't a problem after all. Your research will also give you the evidence you need to:

1. Convince your reader that the problem exists
2. Convince your reader that your solution will work

After you have finished your research, you will write a well-researched, thoughtful, convincing proposal which:

1. Shows that the problem actually exists
2. Explains what can be done about it
3. Shows how your solution will work
4. Recommends a specific action

Who Begins the Process?

Proposals may be solicited or unsolicited. That is, someone else may be aware of a problem and ask you to suggest what might be done about it. Or you may be the one who sees the need, so you may write a proposal to try to convince others to see it too, and to solve it in the way you suggest.

Proposals may come from inside an organization or from someone outside an organization. You may notice or be assigned to solve a problem for the organization you work for. Or you may work for a company that contracts with other organizations to solve problems.

Solicited Proposals

If you are asked to write a proposal, it's likely that your readers are already aware of the problem. The request is a first step in finding a solution or taking action. If the request comes from within your company, then it is most likely to originate with your supervisor or with someone further up in the hierarchy who has assigned it to your department. If the problem is one that a company cannot solve with its own resources, then proposals may be solicited from outside organizations that have the necessary expertise or ability. In this situation, many companies will request proposals from several competing firms, rather than simply accept the first one that comes along. When the proposals come in, executives may choose the one that costs least or offers the best results.

Unsolicited Proposals

Many times employees or outside contractors will submit proposals on their own initiative. When this happens, the decision makers in an organization may not be aware that a problem exists or that a specific situation needs attention. Such a proposal must demonstrate that a problem exists before getting down to the business of what the solution might be and how it can be implemented.

Unsolicited proposals often encounter resistance from readers. Few of us will agree to spend time, effort, or money on something that we don't believe is a problem. In fact, most of us assume that existing policies and practices are satisfactory unless someone can demonstrate that they are not. Unsolicited proposals have the special task of demonstrating compelling reasons for change.

Proposals Imply Criticism

Proposals are about the future. They show how things might be better if decision makers accept the recommended actions. And proposals attempt to portray the future in very positive ways. If they don't, they risk being disapproved. Because they are about the future, about change, proposals imply that the present is less than ideal, or worse. And this implies criticism of those who are responsible for the present situation.

Among the most compelling reasons for change is that an existing policy or procedure is not doing its job adequately. Perhaps circumstances have changed, or new technologies have made existing practices obsolete. No matter how reasonable or justified your recommendation may be, it is bound to threaten someone simply because it represents change. Remember, most of us prefer things the way they are.

Change is especially threatening to those who are responsible for the existing situation. Criticism of "the way things are" is likely to be taken as personal criticism of the people in charge. And, too often, the person whose policies or practices you want to change is also the person who must approve the change. Such readers are likely to be defensive, and defensive readers are likely to disapprove your proposal, regardless of its merits, simply to preserve their own self-esteem.

When you think this implied criticism may jeopardize your success, your best strategy is to focus on the problem, defining it carefully and describing it, rather than evaluating it. Try to avoid overt criticism. It will also help to set appropriate goals. A reader may not be ready to accept your proposed changes, so you may have to settle for making your reader aware that a problem exists. Implementing your solution may have to wait until later, when everyone can agree that something must be done.

Your Reader

One of the keys to a successful proposal is placing it with the right reader, someone who is in a position to act on your recommendation and give you the approval you need. In fact, there is little point in writing a proposal for anyone *except* those who can act on it. You may need to work through several levels of the hierarchy, but always try to work directly with the person who can give you access to the next highest level. Your ultimate objective is to reach the person who can finally say yes or no.

Almost all organizations say that they value new ideas and money-saving suggestions. But not all readers will be equally receptive to your proposals. Some will have a vested interest in keeping things the way they are. Others may need to prevent their subordinates from receiving too much attention or credit. However, many people will welcome the chance to nurture your ideas and contribute to the company's welfare and success. Find and talk with those people who can help you. Get their ideas and suggestions. Resist the temptation simply to write a proposal and drop it on your supervisor's desk. Talk it over first and try to find out how it will be received. Sometimes it will be a good idea to show your supervisor a draft of your proposal and ask for help with it. Remember that your own good ideas will reflect favorably on your supervisor and your entire department. This may help you promote your proposals and sell them to those who have the power to approve them.

Before you write a proposal, try to answer at least the following questions:

1. Is your reader in a position within a company's hierarchy to make the policy decision that you are requesting?
2. Is your reader aware of the problem you are writing about, or is your first job to create that awareness?
3. Will your reader be sympathetic, indifferent, or hostile to your proposal?
4. How much information does your reader need to make the decision you are requesting?

5. Does your reader have the technical or specialized knowledge to understand your subject, or will you have to provide that knowledge?

6. Will your reader agree with your assessment of the organization's priorities and problems?

In addition to their need for information, readers also need evidence that is intangible but has a direct bearing on your chances for success. Your reader needs to be assured of:

Your credibility as a source of information

Your qualifications to deal with the subject

Your ability to follow through on your recommendations if they are approved

Few of us are comfortable simply saying these things about ourselves. In fact, we are rarely convincing when we do. Instead, you can show your credibility and qualifications in more indirect ways:

1. By providing complete, accurate data that can be independently confirmed
2. By doing thorough research and presenting the results clearly and completely
3. By avoiding even the appearance of shading the evidence to favor your own case
4. By avoiding "doomsday" predictions about the dire consequences of ignoring your advice or recommendations
5. By avoiding extreme claims for your own solutions and recommendations

You can also provide evidence of your ability by showing that you have done similar jobs in the past or by providing recommendations and references from others. If you are submitting a proposal from outside a company, send a copy of your resume.

Planning toward Your Goal

Careful planning will help you gather the information your reader needs and test your ideas. Do each of the following steps as carefully and thoroughly as you can.

Define the Problem

Begin by writing a statement or definition of the problem or situation your proposal is about. Be sure you describe the problem's major components and provide evidence that it exists. Your main job here is to answer the question *What.*

Explain Why It Is a Problem

This step goes beyond simply showing that a problem exists. There are many problems and situations that we can safely ignore for years. They require no action, or any action we could take would be more expensive than the problem itself. Describe the situation as completely as you can and explain why it needs attention.

Explain the Consequences of Doing Nothing

What will happen if you leave things as they are? What are the tangible and intangible *costs* of allowing the situation to persist? A complete answer to this question should provide solid evidence in favor of your proposal, since the costs of doing nothing may be unacceptable. On the other hand, you may discover that the costs of inaction are less than the costs of doing what you want to do. Either way, you need to know. You will write a stronger proposal because you know, and you may avoid the embarrassment of writing a weak one.

Explain the Benefits of Acting

If there are consequences for doing nothing, then there must be benefits for doing something. What will be the result if your proposal is approved and the problem solved? Will your company save time or money? Will it have a better product, a more efficient procedure, or a better public image? The benefits of seeking a solution should outweigh the disadvantages of continuing the present policy.

Be realistic in your projections for the future. Offer only those solutions and recommendations that your evidence will support. Remember, if the proposal is approved and your recommendation adopted, someone will be watching to see if your predictions come true.

Explain What You Will Do

If your proposal is approved, what happens next? Explain exactly what you will do. What actions will you take? What research will you do?

How will you find a solution? This step is important. If you can't explain your plans to yourself, it is unlikely that you can convince someone else to spend time and money on them. Lay it all out, step by step. Think through the process, do whatever research you need, and be as specific as you can.

Explain How Your Actions Will Lead to a Solution

Now that you have explained exactly what you will do, the next step is to explain how your actions will lead to a desirable solution. Show that you have considered alternative courses of action and the solutions to which they might lead. And show how your plan will lead to the preferred solution, rather than to just any solution.

Estimate Time and Costs

How long will it take you to do what you have proposed? Remember, you will probably not be able to devote your working days entirely to this project. You still have a job to do. So try to estimate how much time the project will take and how much time you can devote to it each day or week. That way, your reader will know when to expect results, and you will have a schedule to work by.

Your time costs money, so your time will be part of the cost of doing what you recommend. You will also need to calculate the costs of the equipment, books, computer time, travel, overtime, and outside consultants you will need. It is better to know these costs in advance, so you can be precise about them, than to have your proposal disapproved because it "looks like" it will cost too much.

Estimating costs carefully may help you by showing that your proposal is so inexpensive that only a fool would disapprove it. Or, if you find the costs far in excess of what you expected, you may be spared the embarrassment of submitting the proposal to begin with. You may decide to redesign your proposal to keep costs within acceptable limits.

What Should You Include in a Proposal?

Now that you have researched your subject and planned the entire project, it's time to think about what you will say in the proposal itself. In general, some or all of the following categories should be part of any proposal. Each of these can be a section of the proposal. Or, you may need to combine them so that several appear in a single section. If your subject is a complex one you may want to subdivide these categories so that each one consists of a number of subsections. There are no hard and fast rules, so you will have to use common sense.

1. A definition of the problem or situation that shows that it is something that requires attention and does so in terms your reader will understand and accept.
2. Necessary background information that will help your reader understand how and why the problem came to your attention and where it fits within the company's priorities.
3. A description of what you plan to do. This should include the scope or limits of your research or action, and may refer specifically to what you will *not* do. That way you can be sure you are not misleading your reader.
4. A description of the benefits of taking action. This should include how your recommendation will be an improvement over existing policies or practices.
5. The consequences of inaction. What will happen if your reader does nothing at all? These consequences should be related to the benefits you have mentioned, and should show how your proposed action will help avoid those consequences.
6. Costs. Your reader needs to know exactly how much the company will be investing in your recommendation if it is approved. This is especially important when you are competing with other companies or departments, for cost may be a factor in getting approval. You may also need to state whether you are using funds that are already budgeted or requesting additional funding. If you are submitting a proposal as an outside contractor, it may be a good idea to specify the method and terms of payment.
7. Schedule. Tell your reader when your work will be finished. Also, do you need to arrange for special scheduling to use equipment or facilities? If so, you will need to be sure they are not tied up when you want to use them. List these requirements in your proposal.
8. Conclusions and recommendations. What do you want your readers to do when they finish reading your proposal? Sign a memo to implement your plan? Notify others in the company? Be specific. Your reader's approval will be your authority to proceed with your project and spend money.

You can write each of these sections separately and assemble your first draft piece by piece. In fact, if you have done a thorough job of planning and researching, much of this information can come right from your notes. Once all of the sections are complete, or nearly so, you can turn to the job of arranging them in a sequence that is appropriate to your reader and the situation.

Organizing for Success

It is important that you organize carefully to achieve the results you want. You can begin with a definition of the problem and work through each section to a recommendation and request for approval. But that is not always the best organization. It might be more effective to use a sequence which is based on the reaction you anticipate from your reader and the effect you want to create. You can choose from several organizing plans that were presented earlier in this book. We'll review them here with special emphasis on their uses in writing proposals.

Direct Organization

Direct organization is most effective when you anticipate no resistance from your reader and expect that approval will be given readily once you present your evidence. This pattern is the same as the deductive pattern you encountered in Chapters 3, 6, and 7. It begins with your main point, provides supporting information, and ends with a positive request for action. The sections of your proposal might appear in the following sequence if you use a direct presentation:

1. Recommendation
2. Definition of problem
3. Background information
4. Benefits of taking action
5. Description of what you will do
6. Costs
7. Time and work schedule
8. Request for approval

Indirect Organization

The indirect pattern proceeds inductively from the evidence to the conclusion or recommendation that it supports. You used it in Chapters 3, 6, and 8. It is most appropriate when you expect that your reader may resist your conclusion, but will listen to the evidence. It builds your case step by step and *leads* your reader to a conclusion that seems inevitable and reasonable. The indirect sequence might arrange the sections of your proposal this way:

1. Evidence of an existing problem
2. Benefits of acting
3. Problem definition
4. Background information
5. Proposed solution
6. Time and work schedule
7. Costs
8. Recommendations
9. Request for approval and action

Persuasive Organization

In some situations you may need to use the motivated sequence or some other persuasive arrangement for your proposal. Perhaps your reader is indifferent or even actively hostile. A proposal that uses the motivated sequence might be arranged like this:

1. Get your readers' attention and motivate them to read your proposal by identifying some benefit that will result if your proposal is approved.
2. Establish a need and build interest by describing the existing situation, the benefits of doing something about it, and the consequences of doing nothing.
3. Satisfy the need by describing what you propose to do and showing how it will solve the problem you have described. Include here the scope of what you will do and the methods you will use. Try to show how your proposed action will lead to a desirable solution. You can also discuss schedule and costs in this section.
4. Visualize the future by showing your reader how your proposal will change the existing situation in a positive way. How will the future be better than the present?

5. Request action by urging your reader to approve your proposal and authorize you to proceed.

As you can see from these suggested organizations, you can arrange the sections of your proposal in almost any sequence that is appropriate to your goals, the situation, and your reader. Remember that you are always free to adapt what you see here to fit your own needs.

Formats

Proposals can use any format that is appropriate. You can set them up as letters, memos, reports, or any combination of these. Some companies, foundations, and government agencies have rather specific guidelines that they expect people to follow when submitting proposals, grant applications, and bids. For this reason it is always advisable to check to see if this is the case, and then to follow instructions quite closely. Many readers will take your ability to follow their instructions as a measure of your ability to do the job you are proposing. If you are submitting a proposal within your own company, check the files and ask experienced coworkers whether there is a preferred format.

Short proposals (of one to three pages) can often stand on their own as memos or letters. Longer, more complex proposals may need some additional features to help them along. You might need to include a letter or memo of transmittal that introduces the subject to the reader and provides highlights. You may also need to provide a table of contents, visual aids, appendices, or other attachments that contain original data.

Make It Easy for Readers to Act

Remember that you are asking your reader to approve your request and authorize you to take action. In some cases you can include a memo, prepared for your reader's signature, indicating that you have the authority to proceed. It is unlikely that your reader will take the time to write a memo that says exactly what you think it should say. And in many cases your reader should not have to do this. After all, you are the one who knows about the project, so you should know what needs to be said. If you are reluctant to draft a final version of a memo for your reader to sign, you might include a "suggested draft" that is subject to revision. That way, readers can dictate a reply, probably using most of what you have said, without feeling that you have put words into their mouths.

Summary

Proposals may be among the most interesting writing assignments you do, because they give you the opportunity to identify problems, solve them, and present your solutions to people who make decisions. So proposals may have effects on company policies and procedures that are far more extensive than you might normally expect to achieve unless you are in charge yourself.

Remember that writing proposals is much like writing anything else. You begin with thorough planning, identify your goal or the problem you wish to solve, and then present your conclusions in a way that will be acceptable to your reader. This may require a direct, indirect, or persuasive approach. It is essential that you know your reader's attitude toward your subject and that you answer any potential questions before your reader asks them. When you write a proposal you are the expert, even though you may not have the authority to make the final decision.

■

Exercises: Chapter Eleven

1. Select a problem you are aware of at home, at school, or at work. Research it carefully, select a reader, and write a proposal that seeks authority to investigate the problem and propose a change or solution.

2. Your company (or school) is about to begin planning a major renovation and remodeling of one of its buildings. You believe this would be an ideal opportunity to investigate solar heating applications and see if they will save money. Do the necessary research and then write a proposal that recommends that the company (school) investigate using solar energy in its remodeling plans.

3. A number of employees in your company would like to exercise during their lunch hour, but they would have to travel too far to make it worthwhile. You think it would be a good idea if your company would convert an unused warehouse to a gymnasium and possibly install courts for tennis and racquetball. At the very least you would like to see basketball and volleyball courts, and separate weight rooms for men and women. Write a proposal that suggests this idea and seeks permission to study the costs and benefits of such a facility.

4. Assume that your proposal in exercise 3 has been approved. Now you

need to gather information about the costs of construction and equipment, as well as to survey employees to find out what they want. Write a proposal that outlines what you will do and asks permission to proceed.

5. The president of your company is concerned about recent declines in productivity and what she perceives as corresponding declines in employee morale. You recall from reading *Theory Z* by William Ouchi that interpersonal skills are an important part of anyone's management skills. Do the necessary research and propose a series of seminars on interpersonal communication for all managers and supervisors. Be sure that you provide all of the details, including an outline for each session.

6. Employees have been complaining lately that it is taking them longer and longer to get out of the parking lot after work. Some have reported that they sit in their cars for as much as half an hour each day while they wait for the lines of cars to clear. The problem seems to be increased traffic on the street where the plant exit is located. There is nowhere else to locate the exit, and the local authorities will not permit you to station a security guard in the street to direct traffic. Write a proposal that shows how you can alleviate the problem by releasing departments at different times, rather than all at once. (About 3000 people work at the plant.) Be sure you include all details and answer all potential questions.

7. In recent months the Customer Service Department has become increasingly concerned about customers' reactions to badly written, even offensive, letters that they have received from executives and managers in your company. This week the situation reached crisis proportions when a long-time customer wrote the president to complain about a letter he had received. You think the solution is a centralized word-processing department. All managers and executives would dictate their letters to a centralized recording facility, where they would be typed on word-processing equipment, screened, and approved before being mailed. In this system, unacceptable correspondence could be returned for revision, rather than mailed to customers. The dictation could be done over the telephone system, which could be adapted to the recording facility. Write a proposal that suggests this solution to the problem, explains how it would work, and gives the details of operation and cost.

■

12

Preparing to Write Reports

When you write a report you will do the same planning, organizing, writing, and revising that you would do for any other writing job. The process remains the same, even though the length and appearance of your final product may change. Reports deserve special attention because they are often the result of a research process. You need to solve a problem or learn about a subject before you can write about it for someone else. And you will often be gathering information on a much larger scale than you would for a typical letter or memo.

For these reasons, you will need skills in:

Getting access to research tools, and learning how to use them

Keeping track of information as it accumulates

Redefining your research problem as a writing problem, so you can tell readers what they need to know, rather than what you did

It is these skills that this chapter will help you build.

Purposes, Problems, and Readers

Before you begin your research you need to know something about what you are doing, where you are going, who will read it, and why. Careful answers to these questions will help you plan your project, including the questions you will ask and the answers you expect to find, before you actually begin working. In the long run, you will save time and effort by answering these questions now, rather than having it to do later. And you will improve the quality of your report if you deal with these questions thoroughly and honestly, rather than avoid them.

Establishing Purpose

Reports may be assigned to you, or you may have thought of the subject yourself and submitted a proposal. Either way, one of your first questions should be "What am I trying to accomplish here?" or "Why is my organization interested in this subject?" Will your report lead to a decision or action, or will it help solve a problem for you, or someone else, or the whole organization? Will it provide routine or special information that someone needs? What will your reader do with the information you furnish?

Suppose you are assigned to survey the different methods that your competitors use to compensate salespersons. Unless you stop to ask why your company is interested in this subject, your report may be little more than a catalog or list of the different combinations of salary, commission, and perquisites (such as a company-provided car) that your competitors offer. Though this information may be valuable by itself, there is no hint here of how it will be useful to your own company, or why it is worth the time and expense required to gather it.

Your research and subsequent report need a point of focus. That might come from knowing that your company has been losing valuable salespeople to its competitors and needs to know whether compensation is one of the reasons for this expensive drain. Once you know this, you are aware that you must *compare* your own compensation plan with the others and perhaps recommend changes.

Stating the Problem

Once you know why you are researching a question and writing about it, you are in a position to state the problem. Try to do this in writing, and as specifically as you can. A well-stated problem will guide your research and help you find a solution. In the previous example you can state the problem in several ways, and each one will lead you to a different inquiry and a different final report. If you say that the problem is to,

> "compare our sales compensation system with those of competitors,"

you will probably emerge with just such a comparison, but little else. And the comparison, by itself, may be of little value to those who must use it to make decisions.

On the other hand, you could say that the problem is to,

> "find out why our salespeople are leaving us to work for our competitors."

This would result in a far-reaching inquiry in which compensation is only one factor among many. So your research and report will lose their original focus on compensation. You may also be framing a problem that has no solution, since there may be as many reasons for leaving your company as there are people who have left. You need to work toward a problem statement that is somewhere between the simple comparison of the first and the global nature of the second. It might be something like this:

> To study our competitors' sales compensation packages, compare them with our own, and try to determine whether compensation is a major reason for losing our trained salespeople to our competitors

This statement has several advantages over the earlier ones. First, it gives your project a sharp focus on the relationship between compensation and losing salespeople. It is neither too specific nor too global. Of all the reasons that salespeople might leave your company to work for competitors, it tells you that you will focus on one: compensation. This problem statement also tells you what you need to do to conduct your research project. You will need to gather information about how your competitors compensate salespeople, compare the various methods with your own, and find out whether, and to what extent, compensation influenced people to change employers. The problem statement has given some point to the gathering and comparing of information by directing these tasks toward solving a specific problem.

Your Readers

Problems and subjects are important because someone in your organization needs the solution to a problem, or information on which to base a decision. And these solutions and decisions will in some way affect the company's welfare or success. This is what justifies the time and expense that are required to do research and write reports. So keep in mind that someone in your organization will *use* your work, and that one of your primary jobs is to meet that person's needs. If you are to do that, you will have to find out what those needs are. Your knowledge of your company will help with this, but you should never hesitate to ask the person who assigned the report, or the person who will read it, just exactly what your report is to do.

You will rarely have just one reader. Because you work in an organization, you are more likely to have several readers, on different levels of the company's hierarchy. They will have different needs, and they will read your reports for different reasons. To some extent you will have to satisfy all of them.

Your first reader will probably be the person who assigned the report or approved your proposal. This person will often be your immediate supervisor, who may or may not be the one to make a decision or take an action on the basis of what you say. But your supervisor will almost always be the one to approve your report for distribution to others in the company. For this reason, your supervisor will be interested in the *quality* of your research and your report, because they reflect directly on the quality of the work that goes on in that department. Supervisors who approve incomplete or inadequate work will quickly discover that it can affect their own careers, even though they did not write it. For these reasons, your first reader may also be your most difficult reader to please.

Your primary readers, the ones who should receive most of your attention, are those who will use your report as the basis for decisions and actions. They may be anywhere in the company's hierarchy, and you can be sure that they will bring to your report a wide variety of knowledge and ability. Some will grasp your point immediately, and others not at all. Some will read and study your report with excruciating care, and others will hardly look at it. Because these are the people who must understand and accept what you write, you must work to find out who they are and learn as much about them as you can.

Finally, there is your extended audience, in which there are several kinds of readers. First, there are those who will be affected by your report and the decisions people make because of it. In the earlier example about compensating sales representatives, those who will be most directly affected, the salespeople themselves, will have little to do with your research or with decisions about changing how they are compensated. Yet, they will have to live with those decisions, and they will be intensely interested in what you say in your report. You must take them into account as part of your audience. If they have evidence to counter your recommendations, your report could be rejected. Others, though they are not part of the sales force, will also be affected. If the method of compensating one group is changed, with the result that their pay increases, then the economic pecking order of the company will change. This can affect both morale and productivity.

Other readers may not know you, but they will regard the report as an example of the quality of your work. And they may make decisions about your future on the basis of what they read. You will need to keep these people in mind too.

Doing the Research

Almost every report you write will be the result of a research project or a process of inquiry. In this section, we will look at ways of doing research and of finding the information you need. We will not get into the specialized research techniques of the different academic disciplines or professions, such as marketing surveys, financial reports, and sampling techniques. These are more competently and completely taught in the specialized courses that you have taken or will take in your major field of study. Here, we will examine the research methods and tools that you will find useful in any inquiry.

Planning

Begin doing research by trying to plan your inquiry. Try to figure out in advance the kinds of information you will need and how and where you will obtain it. In our example about sales compensation, you know from the beginning that you will need information about:

1. How your own sales force is compensated
2. How competitors compensate salespeople
3. Whether compensation is a factor in attracting your sales representatives to competitors

Learning about the first subject should be easy, since you have been authorized to do the project. The second may be more difficult, because this kind of information is often closely guarded. You can try to ask the companies, but you may have to turn to published materials or more informal sources. Finally, to answer the third question, you will need to find some of your former salespeople and ask them. Later in this section we will deal with various methods of getting these kinds of information.

The object of doing a research plan is to focus your search, so that you will spend valuable time looking for what you need, rather than attempting to find everything that is available. It might help you to review Chapter 2 and use the brainstorming, questioning, and systematic inquiry techniques that are explained there, in order to find out what you already know about your subject. Then you can fill in the gaps through research.

An important part of your research plan is a schedule. Find out when your finished report is due, and then try to estimate the amount of time you will need for each stage of the project. Try to schedule at least 20 percent of the time available for actually writing the report. Then schedule time for research, including preparing questionnaires, reading published materials, and performing laboratory and field tests if they are necessary. Such scheduling is difficult, even with experience, because each project is different. And it may be even more difficult to stick with the schedule once you have made it out. But try. The alternative is working nights and weekends just before the report is due so that you will be sure to finish it on time. That is unpleasant, and in most cases unnecessary.

Above all, be sure you allow adequate time for editing and proofreading your final draft, typing it, proofreading the typed copy, duplicating it, and distributing it. It will do you no good to finish *your* draft at midnight on the day before the report is due. From that point it may take several days or even a week to get even a simple report into a form that is acceptable for distribution. Printers and typists are only human, too, and their priorities are not necessarily the same as yours.

With your purpose, problem statement, research plan, and schedule in hand, you are ready to begin.

Step 1: What Do We Already Know?

You can begin almost any research project by assuming that someone, somewhere has already done research, written and published something, compiled some of the information you need, or kept records that you can use. Very few problems in this world are actually new ones. Whether you are looking for general background information or material that you will actually use in your report, the difficulty is almost never that the information doesn't exist. Rather, the difficulty is in finding it.

You can approach this situation in one of two ways. The first is a random and sometimes frantic search through every source that *might* be helpful. Along the way you will pile up information in the form of notes, copies of articles, and other materials and sort it out "later," which is when most of us like to do things anyway. This method is fairly common, but it is also inefficient and terribly expensive. It exacts a price in time, effort, money, and frayed nerves that is rarely justified by the results.

It will be more efficient and more productive if you approach your research job systematically, in a way that allows you to uncover a great deal of information very quickly, and then focus on that which is most useful to you. Then, if readily available sources do not provide what you need, you can move on to sources that are more specialized and, sometimes, more difficult to obtain.

Figure 12-1 shows the general outline of just such a structured plan. It suggests that you begin with materials that are either readily available or most likely to help you find the information that you need. Then it takes you to less accessible technical and business sources.

As you work your way through the sequence outlined in Figure 12-1, here are some of the specific resources you will want to consult in each category.

Figure 12-1 Research Plan Outline

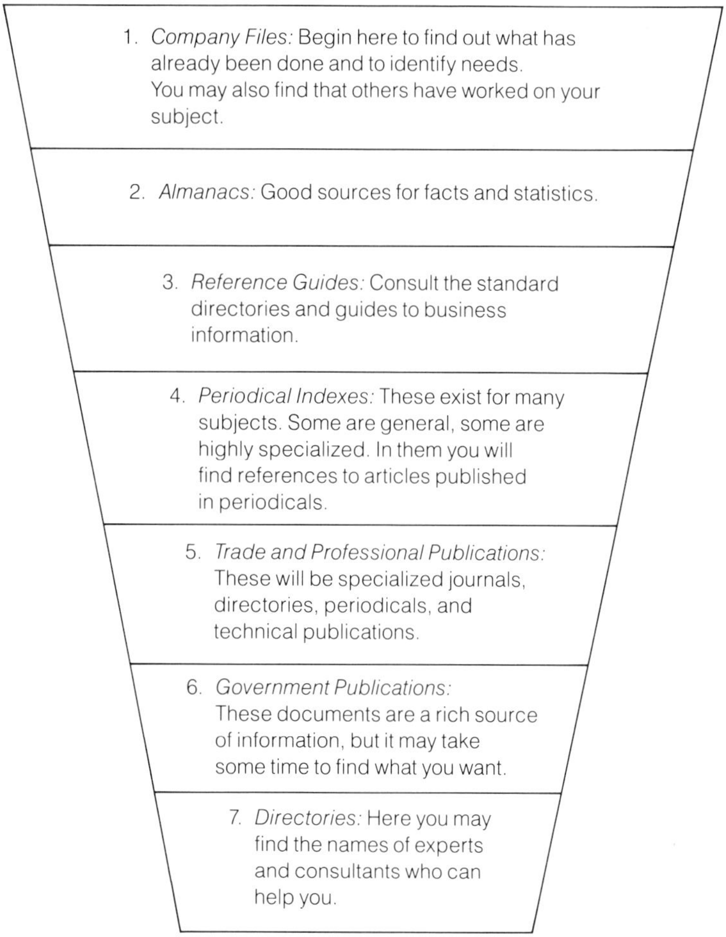

1. *Company Files:* Begin here to find out what has already been done and to identify needs. You may also find that others have worked on your subject.
2. *Almanacs:* Good sources for facts and statistics.
3. *Reference Guides:* Consult the standard directories and guides to business information.
4. *Periodical Indexes:* These exist for many subjects. Some are general, some are highly specialized. In them you will find references to articles published in periodicals.
5. *Trade and Professional Publications:* These will be specialized journals, directories, periodicals, and technical publications.
6. *Government Publications:* These documents are a rich source of information, but it may take some time to find what you want.
7. *Directories:* Here you may find the names of experts and consultants who can help you.

1. **C**ompany files. Always start with the files. You will probably learn something about the background of the problem or subject you are working on. Once in a while you will actually find what you need. On rare occasions you will strike gold and find that some benevolent packrat has saved an earlier version of the report you're writing.

Remember that all files are not kept in the same office. Ask around. Try to think of who would know, or who would be interested, then go there.

Some companies keep archives, have their own libraries, and store information in a central, computerized data base. These can be valuable sources of information.

2. **A**lmanacs. If you need facts and statistics (just how small *is* Rhode Island?), almanacs are the places to go for fast answers. Most are inexpensive and worth having in the office if you use them frequently.

The World Almanac (annual)

Economic Almanac, National Industrial Conference Board (annual)

Statistical Abstract of the United States, U.S. Bureau of Census (annual)

3. **P**eriodical indexes. Periodical indexes will help you find out if anything has been published about your subject in magazines and newspapers. That, by the way, is where you will often find the most up-to-date information. There are many specialized indexes, and a librarian can help you find them. But start with these, since they are likely to be the most valuable.

The Readers' Guide to Periodical Literature, New York, The H. W. Wilson Co. (semimonthly, accumulated annually)

Business Periodicals Index, New York, The H. W. Wilson Co. (monthly, accumulated annually)

The New York Times Index

Wall Street Journal Index

4. **C**omputerized indexes. In recent years research has become easier and less time-consuming because companies have created computerized data bases. The number of indexes available for computer search increases each year, and you can literally do two weeks work in a matter of minutes. Two of the best known services are the DIALOG Information Retrieval System and System Development Corporation's ORBIT. You will need

special training or the help of a trained operator to use either of these, but they are worth the effort if you are frequently involved in research.

Calls to local colleges or universities, hospitals, or research institutions/companies may help you locate a local DIALOG or ORBIT customer who is willing to let you use the terminal. And you will have to be prepared to pay the going rate for on-line computer time.

5. **R**eference guides. Reference guides will make your whole day. They are full of places to turn for whatever you need to know about business. Like periodical indexes, they are usually found only in libraries. It may be worth trying to convince your boss to buy the ones you use most often. (It may be cheaper than all of those trips to the library.)

Brownstone, David M., and Gordon Carruth, *Where to Find Business Information: A Worldwide Guide for Everyone Who Needs the Answers to Business Questions,* New York, John Wiley & Sons, 1979.

Daniells, Lorna M. (ed.), *Business Information Sources,* Berkeley, University of California Press, 1976.

Jablonski, Donna M. (ed.), *How to Find Information About Companies,* Washington, D.C., The Washington Researchers, 1979.

Wasserman, Paul (ed.), *Encyclopedia of Business Information Sources,* 3d ed., Detroit, Gale Research Company, 1976.

Weckesser, Timothy C., Joseph R. Whaley and Miriam Whaley (eds.), *Business Services and Information: The Guide to the Federal Government,* New York, John Wiley & Sons, 1978.

6. **T**rade and professional publications. Almost every sector of business and industry has a professional or trade association that issues special publications, and they can often provide research assistance. To find the one that might be able to help you, consult:

Denise S. Akey, (ed.) *Encyclopedia of Associations,* Detroit, Gale Research Co., 1984.

7. **U.S.** government publications. The federal government may be the biggest publisher in the United States. Few people know that, because most government publications are difficult to find. To buy one you'll probably have to order it by mail from the Government Printing Office in Washington, D.C. It might be easier to try to locate a library that is a regional depository

for government documents and see if you can get what you need there. Failing that, you might find a library that has these catalogs:

Monthly Catalog of U.S. Government Publications

Selected List of U.S. Government Publications

Or, the Government Printing Office can furnish you with a *Subject Bibliography Index,* which is a list of bibliographies of the subject areas of government publications. Using this, you can order the subject bibliographies that you are interested in. If you have detected that all of this takes time, you're right. Don't count on using government publications if your report is due next week.

Many states and cities also have publications programs, but these may be more difficult to uncover than federal publications. It might be simpler to call your state Department of Commerce or another agency that might be concerned with your subject to find out whether there are resources that will help you.

8. **D**irectories. If you have come this far in your research, and you still have not found what you need, then it is safe to say that you are into an unusual or difficult subject. Directories may help you find someone who can help or uncover a resource that you have not found yet.

Dun and Bradstreet, *Million Dollar Directory*

Klein, Bernard, *Guide to American Directories*

Standard Periodical Directory

Standard & Poors *Register of Corporations, Directors and Executives*

Thomas' Register of American Corporations

You will save time if you organize your research according to where the sources are located. Try to identify the materials that are available at the office and use them first. This will give you some idea of what you still need, and you will be able to prepare yourself carefully for a trip to a library. Make a list of the sources you wish to consult and the subjects you want to look for. This will help you avoid repeat trips, which do little but consume time and energy. If you plan to consult just a few, selected sources, it may help to call ahead to be sure the library owns the materials you need, and that they will be available.

In fact, if your request is one that will not take much time, you may discover that some librarians are willing to answer your questions over the phone. Be reasonable about this, and try not to ask for something that will take several days. Always be sure to show your appreciation. Figure 12-2 shows a generalized chart of where you are likely to find certain kinds of sources. If you do research often, you may wish to annotate it or make your own version with specific information about your local situation.

Step 2: Learning from Others

At some point in your research you may discover that other people have the information you need, but that they have not written about it or published it anywhere. Once you find out who they are, ask these people to tell you what they know. If there are just a few of them, or if you need different information from each one, you can interview each one. If you need the same kind of information from a large number of people, you may want to design a questionnaire that you can send to each one. When (and if) they are returned, you can compile the results.

Interviews will be more successful; that is, you will get more of the information you need, if you take the time to learn something about both your subject and the person you are interviewing. (You selected that person for *some* reason.) Your knowledge will help you think of questions and understand the answers. If you succeed in finding expert sources of information, only to ask them to "tell me everything you know about" the subject, you have wasted their time and yours.

Questions are the heart of your interview. Plan them in advance, even to the extent of writing them down. You will save time and avoid the embarrassment of seeming unprepared. Preparation will also help make the interview productive. Almost everyone is willing to talk with people who show an interest in them and their work. Avoid asking simple questions whose answers are readily available to anyone who looks for them. If people are going to give you their time, you need to use it as wisely as you can.

The way you ask a question will influence the quality of the answer and the amount of information it contains. Questions that can be answered "yes"

Figure 12-2 Locations of Research Materials

In the Office	By Phone or Letter	In the Library
Company files	Associations	Periodical indexes
Almanacs	Research services	Reference books
Trade publications	Other companies	Government documents
Directories	Government agencies	Vertical file
Specialized reference materials	Experts	Interlibrary loan
	Some libraries	Books
		Magazines
		Journals

or "no" tend to elicit the most uninformative answers. Apparently the temptation to simply say "yes" or "no" is irresistible. Try to ask open-ended questions that invite your respondent to talk, and then be sure that you listen. If your questions are very complex or will require your respondent to spend a considerable amount of time or research, you may need to submit them in writing, in advance, and ask for written answers. You may also need to offer a consultant's fee.

Phrasing interview questions requires some practice, as you will no doubt discover the first time you interview someone. Even open-ended questions need to be precise and to the point. For example, if you ask, "What do you think of the new banking regulations proposed by the president?" you may get an answer like this: "Well, I don't think they're a very good idea." Or you may get fifteen minutes of talk that says essentially the same thing. Try to phrase your questions so that they probe for *information,* like this:

> "Do you believe the proposed banking regulations will make it more difficult for small businesses to borrow money?"

or

> "How will this new law affect the way we report corporate income and taxes?"

If you can, prepare follow-up questions in advance. Sometimes you will have to do this on the spot. Listen carefully and pursue information and ideas as your respondent presents them to you. This will be easier to do if you know something about the subject; otherwise, you may not recognize a statement that requires a follow-up question to clarify or expand it.

Finally, once you have prepared your questions, try to organize them, much as you would a spoken or written presentation. Group questions about the same or similar subjects together, so that you and your respondent will be able to discuss them at the same time. It may confuse you both to jump around from one part of your subject to another. And never be afraid to say that you don't understand something or to ask for clarification. After all, you are there to learn, not to impress the expert with what you already know.

Questionnaires are another way of getting information. Their main advantage is that you can ask a large number of people the same questions and receive uniform, quantifiable results. You can ask your respondents for facts, opinions, or observations. And you can select your respondents by using one of several sampling techniques so that the data you receive from a small group are representative of what you would receive from a much larger group. For example, it is impossible to ask every potential customer about a product you are developing. But you can ask a carefully selected sample of that group and then use the responses to predict the behavior of the whole group. Sampling techniques are a subject all to themselves and should not be attempted by amateurs. There are too many ways to make mistakes and thus emerge with incomplete or worthless results.

It is important that you design questions carefully if you are to obtain information that you can use. As with interview questions, try to avoid those that can be answered with only "yes" or "no." They force respondents into an either/or situation that may not reflect their true opinions. On the other hand, if you ask open-ended questions, you will take forever to tabulate and quantify the results.

Many questionnaires offer respondents multiple-choice questions, with the opportunity to respond with "other" and give an answer that the writer did not anticipate. Or you may ask respondents to choose a point along a scale that ranges from total agreement to total disagreement, or any other opposites which you may choose. Like this:

> 15. I purchased this product because of its performance record.
>   1 2 3 4 5 6

In this example, a response of 1 might indicate total agreement with the statement, and a 6, total disagreement. Note that the even number of responses prevents a respondent from choosing the safe, neutral meaninglessness of the middle.

Try to organize your questionnaire so that the key questions do not come right at the start. Let your respondents get used to the questionnaire before you spring the big ones on them. Keep your questionnaires as simple as you can, and always include complete instructions. Respondents usually have no vested interest in returning the questionnaire, and a complex, difficult-to-read document simply asks to be thrown away.

Before you embark on any major efforts involving questionnaires, do some research and even consult someone who has had experience with them. If your project is a large or expensive one, you might consider doing a pilot study, with only part of your sample. This option will allow you to identify problems and correct them without jeopardizing the entire project.

Keeping Track of Where You've Been

You need a way of keeping track of the information you gather. Presumably you want to use it, and you will not be able to do that unless you can find it. The system you devise for keeping records should also allow you to retrieve information as quickly as possible. This suggests that you should adopt a system and stay with it through an entire project. That way, everything will be consistent, even to the extent that all of your notes and records are the same size and easily stored together. As you gain experience and experiment with different systems, you will find one that works for you.

Systems You Can Try

Most people who do research take notes by hand. Too many of them simply grab the nearest notebook or stray sheet of paper and take notes as they read and listen. When they are ready to write a report they discover that they have an unmanageable mess of papers, cards, notebooks and scraps. That simply makes the job more difficult.

Begin by choosing a size and format for your notes, and then use one system for the whole project. Select a notebook, file folders, slips of paper cut to a uniform size (5 × 8 or 4 × 6 are convenient sizes), or index cards.

As you work through references, make a separate card for each source of information that you want to look at. 3 × 5 cards are good for this; in fact, that is about all they are good for, since they are too small to be useful for taking notes. Figure 12-3 shows what a typical reference card might look like. It contains the author's name, the title of the article or book, and other publication information, such as the date, volume or issue number, and anything else that might help you find the source.

Figure 12-3 Reference Card Describing a Research Source

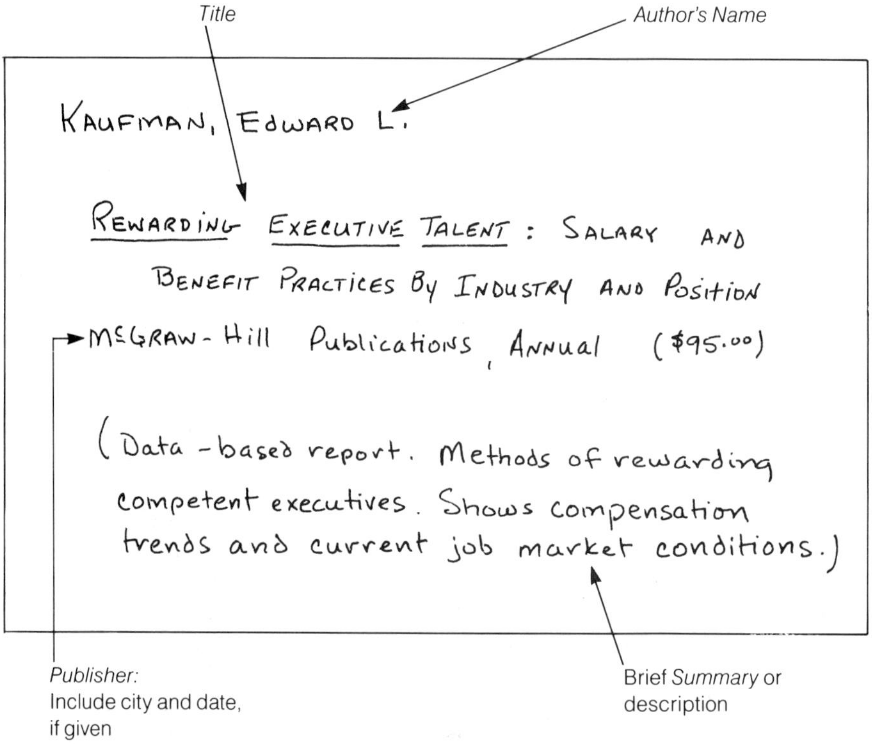

Title

Author's Name

KAUFMAN, EDWARD L.

REWARDING EXECUTIVE TALENT : SALARY AND BENEFIT PRACTICES BY INDUSTRY AND POSITION

MCGRAW-HILL PUBLICATIONS, ANNUAL ($95.00)

(Data-based report. Methods of rewarding competent executives. Shows compensation trends and current job market conditions.)

Publisher:
Include city and date, if given

Brief *Summary* or description

Later, as you read the sources you have located, you can make brief notes on these cards. These will tell you where you found a source (which library?) and whether it was valuable. You may even be able to write a brief summary on the back of the card. That way, you won't find a stray card at the end of your research and wonder if you have consulted that particular source. Your notes will tell you that you have and will give you some idea of what you found. That could save you a trip to the library to look at something you think you missed, only to discover that you looked at it weeks ago.

When you find information you want to use in your report, record it in your notes. We will get to the actual process of taking notes in a few minutes. For now, there are some general practices that will guarantee that the notes are useful.

1. Be sure you identify the source on each card or sheet of notes. That way, you will always know where you got something. Simply identify each source with a number, abbreviation of its title, author's name, or other symbol. Then be sure this appears on each note you make from the source.
2. Take all of your notes on the same size cards or sheets, and keep them together in a folder, notebook, or card file.
3. Make notes on *one side* only of each card or sheet of paper. Notes written on the backs of other notes are easy to miss later when you are trying to organize and write.
4. On each card or sheet of paper, record only one observation, idea, or set of data. Many people use the smallest handwriting they can muster and crowd as much information as possible onto one card. If you spread things out a bit, your notes will be easier to read, and they will also be valuable tools for organizing your report. That is, you can sort the cards or sheets into different categories as you organize your report, without having to write or rewrite an outline or plan. This is more difficult to do when you have used one card or sheet of paper for several notes, or for notes from several sources.

There are alternatives to writing notes. The most attractive one is to use a cassette or microcassette recorder to dictate your notes. This will eliminate the need to fool with cards, files, and other paraphernalia. When you finish a tape or return to the office, a typist can transcribe the tape in whatever format you want. (It is best to give these instructions on the tape itself.) One of the advantages of such recorders is that you can use them almost anywhere, even in libraries, because you do not really need to speak loudly for the recorder to work.

Another possibility, which will no doubt become even more popular in the future, is to store all of your research notes in a computer with word-processing capability. With the proper equipment and adequate experience, you can record your research notes, retrieve them, sort them, write a draft, revise it, and print it, all by using the computer as a word processor. If you use a cassette recorder to take notes, a typist can transcribe them directly into the computer.

Tape recorders are also effective in recording interviews. Because you do not have to take notes, break pencils, and flip through your notebook, you are free to pay attention to the questions you are asking and the answers your respondent is giving you. Recorded interviews are often more accurate than notes, because you can refer to the original conversation to check your own wording of what your source said. Microphones and tape recorders may make some people nervous, but most will get over this after a few minutes, especially if you begin the interview in a friendly and low-key way. Save the complicated and difficult questions for later in the interview.

Taking Notes

When you take notes, the goal is to record what you can use, rather than attempting to capture everything. This is where knowing your subject in advance and setting goals will really pay off. Your knowledge will allow you to discriminate the important from the unimportant, the common from the unusual. Still, you will eventually use only a small percentage of the information that you record.

Taking notes requires time, so you will want to work as efficiently as you can. This means that you will record different kinds of information in different ways.

Direct quotation. When you quote a source you copy it word-for-word and enclose what you copy in quotation marks. This takes time, and not every piece of information in every source is worth this time. Try to reserve direct quotation for information that you believe you must have in its original form. For example, if you want to use something that a well-known business executive or politician has said, then you should probably quote it, rather than rephrase it in your own words.

Paraphrase. When you want to record the essence or point of a sentence or paragraph, but not the exact words, you can paraphrase it. That is, restate it in your own words. Like this:

> We should measure executives by their ability to listen, rather than by their skills in writing and speaking.

That statement is short enough that quoting it won't take too much time, but it probably is not worth the effort. That is, there is nothing intrinsically important in the way it is phrased. So you might paraphrase it this way:

> Listening is more important to executives than writing and speaking.

The original is 18 words long, the paraphrase only 10. That might not seem like much, but in 100 or more notes the savings in time and effort will accumulate. Of course, paraphrases almost always change some of the meaning of the original. Perhaps you noticed that this one leaves out the idea of *measuring* executives. To include that, you might do the paraphrase this way:

> Evaluate executives for their listening ability, not writing and speaking.

Summaries. When you find an article or a passage that seems important, but is too long to copy, you can write a summary that records its main points but stops short of direct quotation. Like a paraphrase, this uses your own words.

Read through the entire passage first, so you will have some idea of how it is organized and of what is important. Then read through again, quickly, taking notes as you go. If the writer has done a good job, you should be able to find important points in the first paragraph, at the beginning of each section, at the end of each section, in the topic sentences of each paragraph, and in the last paragraph. Focus on these places for information that you can extract for your summary. The amount of detail you include will vary with your goal and the use you have for the information. That is one reason for reading the passage first. If you try to take notes as you read through the first time, it is easy to get caught up in details rather than main points and principles.

Which Method Should You Use?

As you are choosing among direct quotation, paraphrase, and summary, look ahead to the ways in which you will use the material from your sources when you write a draft. In most reports there is little space for direct quotations, especially long ones. Instead, you will present your research in your own words, using paraphrases and summaries when necessary. You will usually use direct quotations only when there is a specific advantage in having a source's exact wording as part of your report. Among the legitimate reasons for using direct quotations are the following:

> Accuracy and precision are extremely important. For example, if you are citing a law or regulation, paraphrasing it may in-

ject interpretations that are inaccurate. Direct quotation will help you prevent them.

An authority with greater expertise or knowledge than your own will make your point more effectively than you could in your own words.

Readers will expect you to present the exact words a source uses, so they can evaluate your use of the information.

Testimony from a source is important in making or supporting your own point or position.

Of course, you will always need to quote numbers, statistics, and other data accurately and to identify the sources where you obtained these kinds of information clearly.

A Few Words about Honesty

As you take notes, be careful to keep what you take from someone else separate from what is your own. It is simply dishonest to represent someone else's work as your own. You will be embarrassed, at the least, if you are detected doing this, and you may cast doubt on your entire report. People have been known to lose their jobs for deliberate attempts to defraud their supervisors. Before you give in to the temptation to simply copy something, ask yourself whether it is worth the consequences. It is not that much trouble to use quotation marks and give credit to your sources, either in footnotes or by mentioning their names in the text of your report.

From Research to Report

When you finish your research, you will know more about your subject than any of your readers do. You will be caught up in the details of the information you have found, and you may be excited about having a solution to a problem that has plagued the whole company. It is important at this point to shift your attention from research to writing. The purpose of research is to learn something or to solve a problem. The purpose of writing is to tell someone else what you have learned. The crucial difference is that research really has no audience, but writing does.

Before you can turn your research into a report, you will need to go through the steps of the writing process, beginning with defining your purpose. But now your purpose is the one that you hope to accomplish with your readers, not the purpose that you wanted to accomplish with your research. Focus on your readers, identify them, and ask what they need to know about your subject. What problems are you to solve for them? How much will you have to explain if they are to understand what you are saying?

■

Exercises: Chapter Twelve

1. For each of the following topics find at least five sources of information (three of them in periodicals) that are no more than two years old. Make a reference card for each one.

   Communication in management
   Employee retirement plans
   Government regulation of a specific industry
   Employee training programs
   Management by objectives
   Executive compensation

2. What kinds of information would you gather and what reference materials and other sources would you use if you were assigned one of the following reports, subjects, or topics?
   a. You work for a mining company. Your boss wants to send a letter to each employee about the importance of safety on the job.
   b. Your company wants to establish its own credit union, but no one knows the procedures or laws that apply.
   c. The Vice President for Personnel wants to know about the effectiveness of human relations seminars for employees.
   d. The advertising manager wants to know the average age for new homeowners in three cities (Dallas, Denver, and Atlanta) where your company is about to test-market a product.
   e. The Personnel Manager wants national statistics about absenteeism and information about how to fight it.
   f. The Safety Manager wants to know the average number of days lost, during the past five years, because of industrial hazards.

3. Choose one of the topics in exercise 2, develop a detailed research plan, and follow it, making reference and note cards for each source you consult.

4. Where would you find the following information:
   a. The net worth of a corporation

b. List of officers of a company
c. Information about the outlook for small business
d. Information about product safety
e. Information about liability for products

■

13

Writing a Report

You have been assigned to write a report. Your research is complete, you have selected most of the data you will use, and you have finished most of your planning. Now it is time to write, to transform the mound of data in your notes and the ideas in your head into a finished report that you can send to a reader.

This chapter is a step-by-step explanation of what you need to do, why you need to do it, and most importantly, how to do it. Writing a report will involve completing the following steps:

Organizing
Writing a first draft
Revising
Selecting an appropriate format
Preparing and distributing the final copy

Introduction

Of course, no chapter in any book can teach you everything you need to know about every report you will ever write. And this chapter is not setting out to do that. Rather, the goal here is to give you a general example of the *process* that you will follow to write most of the reports that you will be assigned. Not all of the reports that you write will be like the one you find here. Some will be simpler, and some will be more complicated. Many will have features that are not part of this report. We will discuss some of those at the end of the chapter.

Many companies have style manuals and instructions to show what reports should look like. You should find out what your company expects. One way to do that is to spend some time in the files, reading reports that others have written. Of course, it is always wise to ask someone about what is expected and what has been successful.

Reports exist because they are an effective way of getting information to the people who will use them to make decisions. Executives and managers use reports as a means of saving time. They want to deal with a limited amount of information that is highly relevant to the situation at hand. To accomplish this, they request reports from those who know most about a subject. Many executives could reach the same conclusions if they had the time and the data, but they simply do not have time, and they may not have the expertise in a specialized subject. When you write a report your job is to give your reader the benefit of your special knowledge of the subject and of your ability to gather, analyze, and organize information.

Some readers may even want you to do more. They may ask that you recommend a specific decision or course of action. This will save them even more time. They can read your recommendation and your explanation of why they should approve it and then simply say yes or no. If you are asked to do this, keep in mind that asking for recommendations is an excellent way of identifying, testing, and training talented managers. A record of successful recommendations will identify you as someone who is capable of effective analysis and decision making, and thus as someone who is likely to be an asset to the company. Your future may depend on the quality of your reports.

Organizing and Writing: A Working Example

For the rest of this chapter your job is to watch a report develop from a collection of data to a finished product. You will see the steps involved in organizing, writing, revising, selecting a format, and producing the finished copy. You will also see many of the false starts, blind alleys, and strokes of inspiration that occur when people write.

The Situation

Fred Smith is the President and principal owner of Smith Enterprises, Inc. Among its holdings are six hardware stores. They are all doing well, and Mr. Smith would like to expand. MIX Hardware, an independent store in nearby Derrydale, is for sale because the owner wants to retire. Mr. Smith wants to know if the MIX store would be a good acquisition for Smith Enterprises, so he has asked you (his General Manager) to find out and then write a report that presents all of the important information and recommends an action.

After several weeks of careful research you have decided that Smith Enterprises should buy MIX, and now you are ready to write your report. You are sure that Mr. Smith will want to see the following kinds of information about MIX in order to evaluate your recommendation:

1. Initial costs, including purchase price, real estate fees, legal fees, and taxes
2. Interest on loans
3. Fair value of the store and its inventory
4. Costs of remodeling and restocking
5. Projected operating costs
6. MIX's present financial position
7. Projected markets and profits

Organizing

Once you have gathered the data you need, the next step is to organize it. This will help you and your reader. Organized data is easier to work with as you write, and it is also easier for your reader to understand.

It is probably too early to do an outline of the data for this report, because we do not yet know the relationships of the data included. An effective way to find these relationships is to try an issue tree and then refine it until you are satisfied that it works. The first one might look like Figure 13-1, which does nothing more than divide the subject into two categories: cost and potential income. Then it subdivides these into smaller and smaller categories.

Figure 13-2 is an expanded version of the first issue tree. The additional categories come from comparing the first tree with the list of information that you thought should be included in the report. Look at the two trees carefully and see if you can identify the ways in which they are different.

In the second tree the two main categories, costs and potential income, are the same. In the left branch, under costs, inventory has been combined with the new category of operating costs to reflect the additional investment in merchandise that Smith Enterprises will have to make after it purchases the store. The category of operating costs has been added because it shows that the costs of acquiring and operating MIX will not be limited to the

Figure 13-1 Preliminary Issue Tree

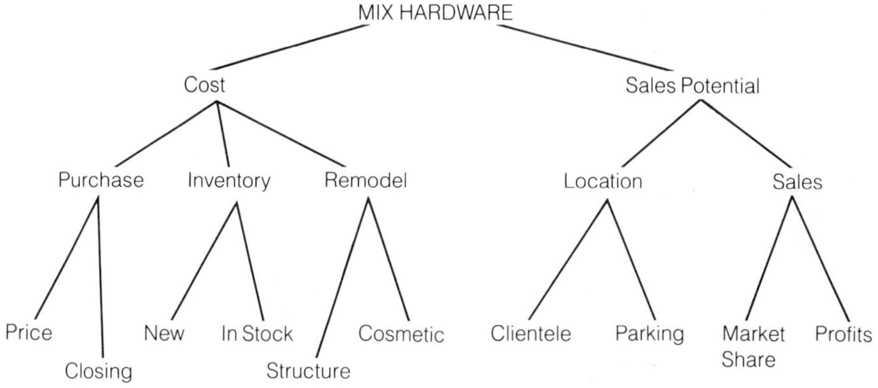

MIX HARDWARE

- Cost
  - Purchase
    - Price
    - Closing
  - Inventory
    - New
    - In Stock
  - Remodel
    - Structure
    - Cosmetic
- Sales Potential
  - Location
    - Clientele
    - Parking
  - Sales
    - Market Share
    - Profits

purchase itself, but will continue as the store demands its share of Smith's annual operating budget.

The tree's right branch has changed considerably. Now, instead of focusing on sales alone, it shows that you will need to include a survey of MIX's overall financial position. Then, instead of making location a major subcategory, it shows that location is really a point to be considered in determining MIX's overall market position. The category has been broadened to include a discussion of the MIX store's clientele and potential for growth. The second issue tree could certainly be refined, but you can work with it as it is. The most important result of doing the issue trees is that the data has been grouped to show relationships. It no longer exists merely as a "grocery list" of information that is related merely because it is about the same subject.

The issue trees are a first step in creating a plan that will allow you to manage the data and show how it bears on the question of whether Smith should purchase MIX. You have no doubt noticed that no specific dollar amounts have been given in the trees. You don't need them yet. You are working at a level of abstraction that allows you to manipulate categories of information rather than specific facts.

Is It Time to Write Yet?

It is possible to begin writing with only an issue tree as your plan and do a respectable job on the final report. As you gain experience you will probably begin working this way. But in many cases an issue tree is not an adequate foundation for a first draft. There are other considerations of organization and strategy if you want to present your information so that it serves your reader's purposes and your own. The issue tree sorts information into manageable blocks, but it is possible to do more.

Figure 13-2 Issue Tree Indicating Relationships

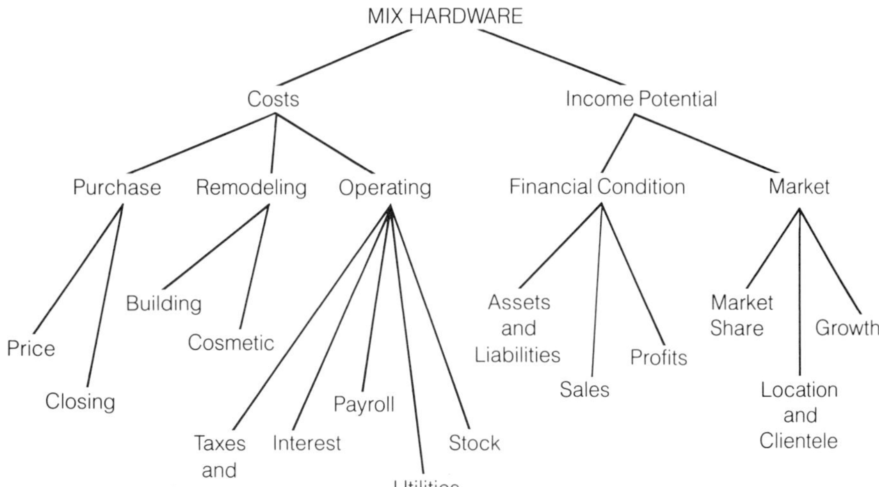

Further organizing begins with remembering what your reader has asked you to do. Mr. Smith wants a report that presents the information and a recommendation about what he should do. There are, of course, other possibilities. Readers may want any of the following:

1. Present the information but make no attempt to interpret it or to recommend a course of action. Your role here is to provide information—nothing more.
2. Present the information and interpret it, but make no recommendation. Here you are both providing and analyzing information, but you are not suggesting what action or decision might follow from your analysis.
3. Present the information, interpret it, and recommend a specific course of action. In this case you are being asked to take part in the decision-making process. Your abilities are either respected or being tested.
4. Present the information, your interpretation, and several alternative courses of action. Your reader will then choose the one that appears to offer the best solution.
5. Present conclusions and recommendations alone, with no more than a brief rationale, if that. Obviously, if you are asked to do this, your reader is showing considerable trust in your ability to find relevant data and evaluate them correctly.

Readers may not always tell you which of these options you should choose. You may need to take the initiative and find out what they want. Check the files, ask around, and talk with your reader, if you can. You will both be happier with the report if you can agree ahead of time about what it should do. Your report can meet your reader's expectations only if you know what they are.

Consider Your Reader's Attitudes

What is your reader's attitude toward the subject of your report? Have you thought about that? When you are asked for a report about the new marketing policy, are you expected to say that it is working because it is your reader's pet project? Are you expected to recommend that the new production scheduling plan be abolished because someone's rival designed it? You ignore your reader's attitudes and prejudices at your own peril. The point is not that you should always agree with your readers, but that you should take their attitudes into account when you plan and write. They will influence the reception that you and your ideas receive, and you can take advantage of them or minimize their effects.

When you and your reader agree, you can use a direct approach to organize your report. This presents your main point, or conclusions and recommendations first, then explains and supports them with the data you have collected. At the end you can provide a brief summary that wraps things up. You used this approach with good news and goodwill letters, and it adapts very easily to reports.

When you and your reader disagree, the direct approach is not likely to work. If you begin with an idea or recommendation that your readers disagree with, you can lose them right there. They may become so preoccupied with looking for reasons to prove you wrong and constructing a counter-argument, that they will pay no attention to your data and carefully reasoned arguments. To use an old phrase, "His mind's made up; don't confuse him with facts."

In this situation you need an indirect approach, like the one you used in letters that tell your readers what they don't want to hear. But reports are somewhat different from letters. Letters allow you to de-emphasize the unpopular recommendation in the middle. Many reports, however, will require you to state a specific recommendation, and your reader will want it to be prominently displayed and identified.

When you use the indirect approach you present your data first, so that it, and your reasons, lead your readers to your recommendations. Because your readers have no main point to disagree with at the beginning, they are more likely to pay attention to your facts and reasoning. Some readers will even reach your conclusions before you do, and decide that you are right. The indirect approach will not guarantee that your readers will always agree with you or follow your recommendation. It merely increases the probability that readers will pay attention to what you say and accept it as reasonable.

Once you have explored your reader's attitude toward your subject, you are able to make decisions that you could not make earlier. You did not have enough information. Using your issue tree, you can now try to decide which sequence you will use to present your information, so that you can organize according to your reader's reaction and still preserve the relationships that exist within the body of information you have gathered.

The Final Plan: Buying MIX Hardware

Before attempting a rough draft of the report, we will construct a rough topic outline which shows the sequence of the data and recommendations. Mr. Smith has asked for a report that recommends a course of action. He has let you know that he has no preconceived notions about MIX, but that he wants you to reach a sound conclusion that is supported by evidence. (He may be a rare man.) You have decided that purchasing MIX looks like a reasonable move. It won't put Smith Enterprises in the *Fortune* 500, but it will make money.

RECOMMENDATION: That Smith Enterprises should Purchase MIX Hardware.

A. Costs
   1) Purchase price, complete, of $175,275, including building, inventory and closing costs.
   2) Smith Enterprises could finance $70,000 over ten years, at an interest rate of 16%, which would cost $64,265.60.
   3) MIX's fair value (building and inventory) is $225,000.
   4) Conversion and remodeling of the store to Smith specifications would cost about $30,000.
   5) Additional inventory, to carry all standard Smith lines, would cost $50,000. Some stock could come from other Smith stores.

B. Income Potential
   1) MIX has assets of $225,000 and present liabilities of $18,000 for inventory.
   2) Annual sales for the past five years have averaged $1,000,000.
   3) Present market share: approximately 30%.
   4) Average annual profits for the past five years have been $65,000.

5) Derrydale's population of homeowners in the $30,000+ annual income range is growing at a rate of 8% each year.
6) MIX could double its sales in five years.

C. Operating Costs
1) Utilities now cost $4500 per year.
2) Taxes are $2386 per year.
3) Annual salaries and benefits for employees would cost $70,000 under Smith guidelines.
4) Building maintenance is projected to cost $3000 to $5000 per year.

D. Summary
1) After-purchase profits should be at least $100,000 per year.
2) Projected growth for this store suggests that it will be an asset to Smith Enterprises.

There: The outline is finished. It is not written in stone, and it will probably change as the report develops. But at least there is a sound plan. If you check the issue trees you will notice that something has changed already. Operating costs are no longer grouped with acquisition costs, but have been moved. This may or may not be a good idea. The reason for doing this is to show that operating costs will become a factor only after the store has been purchased.

Writing the First Draft

When you begin a draft there is no reason for you to start writing at the beginning of the report. You can begin anywhere you are comfortable. Once you have completed all of the parts, you can put them together in the sequence you used in your outline to see how it all works together. In this example we will begin at the beginning and write straight through, for the sake of convenience.

TO: Mr. Fred Smith, President
FROM: A. N. Rand, General Manager
SUBJECT: Purchase of MIX Hardware

RECOMMENDATION: That Smith Enterprises purchase the MIX Hardware store in Derrydale.

The MIX store is being offered for sale, complete with inventory, at its fair value of $225,000. The owner, Mr. Albert Michaels, has indicated that he will accept an offer of $165,000. Closing costs and legal fees will bring the purchase price to $175,275.

The Seventh State Bank will finance $70,000 for a period of

ten years at an interest rate of 16%, which will cost $64,265.60.

Remodeling to bring the building's appearance up to Smith Enterprises standards will cost an estimated $30,000. Additional inventory, so that the store will carry all Smith merchandise lines, will cost approximately $50,000. This figure could be reduced by drawing from stock which has been purchased for other stores.

MIX's financial records show liabilities of $18,000 in bills for inventory. Mr. Michaels will pay $9000 of this debt, and the other $9000 is included in the purchase price.

MIX's annual sales for the past five years have averaged $1,000,000. During the same five-year period, annual profits have averaged $65,000. The store's current market share is approximately 30%. Derrydale's population of homeowners in the $30,000+ annual income range is currently increasing at a rate of 8% per year.

Operating expenses for the MIX store are within the expected levels for its size and location. Utilities presently cost $4500 per year, and all taxes combined are $2386. Annual salaries and benefits for employees would cost Smith Enterprises approximately $70,000 under our current guidelines for a store of this size. Building maintenance is projected to cost $3000 to $5000 per year.

After-purchase profits for this store should increase to $100,000 per year, because our operating expenses will be considerably less than those of the current owner. Projected growth for this store indicates that it will be an asset to Smith Enterprises.

There it is: a first draft. Of course, not all first drafts are this neat, but as a first draft this does its job. It transforms the list of information in the outline into sentences and paragraphs. It follows the outline, though if you compare it with the outline you will see that some information has been moved. Also, a few details have been added, such as the owner's name, the arrangement for paying the $18,000 liability, and an explanation of why profits will magically increase after the purchase.

Changes like these often occur when writers move from an outline to a rough draft. Instead of following the outline blindly, they continue to think as they write, anticipating and answering readers' questions.

Revising

If you can, it will help to put your first draft away, even for an hour, and do something else. When you return to it, you will be less inclined to believe that it is as good as you thought it was and more willing to revise it. When you do return to your draft, read it carefully and try to think of questions your reader might ask. Mr. Smith will probably have a few questions as he reads this report, so let's try to figure out what they might be. We will work through the draft a paragraph at a time.

1. *Recommendation.* Many readers will wonder right away what your recommendation is based on. What kind of information will you use, and what is its source? They know you will probably explain this as you go, but they will be eager to see it. Consider adding a brief summary of your reasons to your recommendation.
2. *Paragraph 1.* Who appraised the building and inventory, and how firm is the owner's commitment to accept $165,000? Are you estimating the closing costs, taxes, and legal fees, or are they firm? Where did you get them?
3. *Paragraph 2.* Why should Smith finance $70,000 and have you talked with the bank?
4. *Paragraph 3.* Where did the remodeling and inventory estimates come from? Has a contractor looked at the building, and have our buyers looked at the stock, or are these general estimates?
5. *Paragraph 4.* Have you seen a financial statement, or did our accountants look at their books?
6. *Paragraph 5.* Where did you get the information about their current market share, and how firm are the demographic figures about the clientele? Is this growth rate "real?"
7. *Paragraph 7.* Why will profits increase so dramatically after we buy the store? We're good, but we don't print money.

Your reader might also notice that numbers are scattered throughout the report, making it difficult to compare them with each other. It might help to present them all in one place, in a table or graph that your reader could use to see the whole picture at one time.

These questions don't really come out of thin air, even though it might look as though they do. If you know your readers at all, then it is relatively easy to put yourself in their place and try to figure out what they want to know that the report has not provided. Doing this is the point of some of the techniques you learned in Chapter 1, and you might want to review them now if you have questions. The questions that we anticipate from Mr. Smith consist of nothing more than giving the documentation and evidence that any informed reader wants and deserves. Keeping these questions in mind, we will try to revise the first draft so that it answers most of them. We will also try to use informative headings for parts of the report, to break it into manageable blocks.

TO: Mr. Fred Smith, President
FROM: A. N. Rand, General Manager
SUBJECT: Purchase of MIX Hardware

RECOMMENDATION: That Smith Enterprises purchase the MIX Hardware store in Derrydale, complete with contents. This recommendation is based on a review of costs, projected sales, and market growth.

Initial Costs

The MIX Hardware building and its contents have been appraised at $225,000 by Jones and Wall, Realtors. The owner, Mr. Albert Michaels, has indicated through his attorney, Mr. John Leach, that he will accept an offer of $165,000 if he does not have to assist with financing. Our attorneys report that closing costs, taxes and legal fees will bring the purchase price to $175,275.

Comptroller Eldon Anderson reports that we will need to finance $70,000 if we want to complete the purchase during the current fiscal year. The Seventh State Bank has agreed to finance this amount for a period of ten years at an interest rate of 16%, which is below the present prime rate. Finance charges of $64,265.60 will bring the total purchase price to $239,540.60.

John Brill Associates, our usual architects, have examined the building in detail. It is in sound condition and needs no major repairs. Remodeling to bring the building's layout and appearance within Smith Enterprises' specifications will cost no more than $30,000. John Alexander, Director of Merchandising, reports that the store can be stocked with a complete inventory of the usual Smith lines for $50,000.

Our total cost to open a new store in the present MIX location would be $319,540.60 (some of which is interest to be paid over ten years).

Potential Income

Mr. Michaels has made all of his financial records available to Burg and Eich, our CPA firm. They report that the MIX store is in excellent financial condition. Its assets are currently valued at $225,000, and its only liabilities are $18,000 owed for inventory. Mr. Michaels will pay half of this, and the other half is included in our purchase price.

MIX's annual sales for the past five years have averaged

$1,000,000. Annual profits during the same period have averaged $65,000. MIX currently has a market share of approximately 30%. According to information available from the Derrydale Planning Commission, population in and around Derrydale is increasing at approximately 8% per year. Most of this growth consists of homeowners with annual family incomes of $30,000 or more.

Operating Costs

Costs of operating a new store in the MIX facility are projected at well within the acceptable levels for its size. Remodeling will reduce the annual utility costs of $4500 by up to 20%, even if energy costs continue to rise. Taxes are presently $2386, and the Derrydale Tax Assessor indicates that there are no plans to increase corporate taxes.

Annual salaries and benefits for employees will cost approximately $70,000 each year under our current guidelines for a store of this size.

Building maintenance, as projected by our Maintenance Division, will be approximately $3000 to $5000 per year.

Potential Growth

Annual profits for this store should increase to at least $100,000 during the first year. This will result from our lower operating costs, which depend on quantity purchasing, manufacturers' advertising campaigns, and efficient management. Projected population growth suggests that, with careful management, the store should quickly become a valuable asset to Smith Enterprises.

Comments about the Revision

This second draft has attempted to answer the questions that we thought Mr. Smith would ask. It has also divided the report into blocks, each with its own heading, to identify the subject of each section and make it easier for readers to keep track of where they are and where they are going. Further revisions could refine the draft even more.

But Mr. Smith needs the report. Writing and revising could go on forever, so you need to decide when you have invested enough time and effort in the project to make it good enough to do its job. In spite of what many people say, few reports are worth the time, energy, and money to make them perfect. You have other jobs to do, and this report has a deadline. At some point you need to move on to the job of putting your report into final form. The first step in that process is editing.

Editing

Editing is different from revising, because you are beyond the point of making major changes. Instead, as you edit you will take care of the details of word choice, spelling, punctuation, sentence structure, and all of the other matters that must be put in order before you turn your report over to a typist. If you can, do your editing on a typed draft. That way, you will have clean copy to work with and a typist will be able to see your changes clearly.

Mark your editorial changes with a pen or colored pencil that is a different color than any other marks on the page. Write or print legibly and be sure the typist will know where your changes and additions will go in the text. Let's look at a third draft of the MIX report, this time carefully edited. Pay attention to the changes you see and compare them with the second draft. Perhaps you can suggest further changes that will make the final report even better.

TO: Mr. Fred Smith, President
FROM: A. N. Rand, General Manager
SUBJECT: Purchase of MIX Hardware

RECOMMENDATION: That Smith Enterprises purchase the MIX Hardware store in Derrydale, complete with contents. This recommendation is based on a review of costs, projected sales, and market growth.

Initial Costs

The MIX Hardware building and its contents have been appraised at $225,000 by Jones and Wall, Realtors. The owner, Mr. Albert Michaels, has indicated through his attorney, Mr. John Leach, that he will accept an offer of $165,000 if he does not have to assist with financing. Our attorneys report that closing costs, taxes, and legal fees will bring the purchase price to $175,275.

Comptroller Eldon Anderson reports that we will need to finance $70,000 if we want to complete the purchase during the current fiscal year. The Seventh State Bank has agreed to finance this amount for a period of ten years at an interest rate of 16%, which is below the present prime rate. Finance charges of $64,540.60 will bring the total purchase price to $239,540.60.

John Brill Associates, our usual architects, have examined the building in detail. It is in sound condition and needs no major repairs. Remodeling to bring the building's layout and appearance within Smith Enterprises' specifications will cost no more than $30,000. John Alexander, Director of Merchandising, reports that the store can be stocked with a complete inventory of the usual Smith lines for $50,000.

Our total cost to open a new store in the present MIX location would be $319,540.60 (some of which is interest to be paid over ten years).

Potential Income

Mr. Michaels has made all of his financial records available to Burg and Eich, our CPA firm. They report that the MIX store is in excellent financial condition. Its assets are currently valued at $225,000, and its only liabilities are $18,000 owed for inventory. Mr. Michaels will pay half of this, and the other half is included in our purchase price.

MIX's annual sales for the past five years have averaged $1,000,000. Annual profits during the same period have averaged $65,000. MIX currently has a market share of approximately 30%. According to information available from the Derrydale Planning Commission, population in and around Derrydale is increasing at approximately 8% per year. Most of this growth consists of homeowners with annual family incomes of $30,000 or more.

Operating Costs

Costs of operating a new store in the MIX facility are projected at well within the acceptable levels for its size. Remodeling will reduce the annual utility costs of $4500 by up to 20%, even if energy costs continue to rise. Taxes are currently $2386, and the Derrydale Tax Assessor indicates that there are no plans to increase corporate taxes.

Annual salaries and benefits for employees will cost approximately $70,000 each year under our current guidelines for a store of this size.

Building maintenance, as projected by our Maintenance Division, will be approximately $3000 to $5000 per year.

Potential Growth

Annual profits for this store should increase to at least $100,000 during the first year. This will result from our lower operating costs, which depend on quantity purchasing, manufacturers' advertising campaigns, and efficient management. Projected population growth suggests that, with careful management, the store should quickly become a valuable asset to Smith Enterprises.

Comments About Editing

Most of the changes here have been made to delete information that Mr. Smith is likely to know already. For example, he knows that Brill Associates is the company's usual architect, and that 16 percent is an interest rate, not your hat size. He may or may not know what the present prime interest rate is, so that remains.

Format

Many organizations have standard guidelines for the appearance of letters, memos, and reports. But these are standard only in the sense that they apply within the company. There is no standard that all organizations use.

You need to decide whether your report should include such aids as a title page, table of contents, cover letter, abstracts, and visual aids. These decisions usually depend on your report's length and complexity, as well as your reader's expectations. For example, a one-page report needs none of this apparatus. It will, and should, stand on its own. But a longer or more complex report may need all of these features to help your reader manage it. You will find detailed suggestions and examples of report formats in Appendix B.

Attachments

Attachments are documents that accompany a report but may not be considered as part of the report itself. They can consist of additional charts, tables, analyses of data, or copies of documents that support your interpretations and conclusions. Attachments belong at the end of a report, where they will not intrude into your discussion, but where they will be available if your readers want to look at them. But the report should be able to do its job without the attachments.

The report for Mr. Smith might include any or all of the following attachments:

A copy of MIX's financial statement

A report from Smith's CPA firm

A letter from the bank

Documents from the Derrydale Planning Commission

A letter agreeing to the price of $165,000

When you select attachments, you need to achieve a balance between burying your reader under a mountain of paper and providing too little.

The Finished Report

Before you give your report to a typist you need to check it one more time. Be sure that your editing is clear and that the report says what you want it to say. Proofreading is essential at this stage, for it is the last time that corrections can be made easily. After the report is typed, you will have to spend extra time and money to have it retyped and correct errors that you find. So proofread now. Then assemble all of the attachments and visual aids and identify them. Tell the typist how many copies you will need, how they should be reproduced, and who is to receive them.

The typist should return your original and all copies to you. Proofread the original carefully and check the copies for uncorrected errors. Be sure that each copy includes everything that is supposed to be there and that it is in the proper order. Then, and only then, should you sign or initial the report and send it out.

Summary

When you write a report you use the same writing process that you would use for anything else. The major differences are that your information gathering is likely to be more extensive, and the reports themselves will usually be longer and more complex than letters and memos. Be sure to schedule adequate time for research and writing, and try to keep yourself on schedule. Otherwise, you will find yourself working late for several days before your deadline.

Be sure to find out whether your company has a manual that shows acceptable formats for reports, and look at this manual early in the process. There is no point in finishing a final draft only to discover that you must rewrite to make its format acceptable. In fact, standard formats may help you organize your report by showing you the major categories and headings you will need to use.

■

Exercises: Chapter Thirteen

1. Rewrite the report to Mr. Smith, using either an indirect or a persuasive approach.
2. Identify a procedural or policy question that you believe needs atten-

tion on your campus or at work. Do the research and planning that you believe are necessary and then write a report for the person who can make the change you believe is necessary. Remember to consider your reader's attitude carefully and organize accordingly.

3. Investigate two companies you would like to work for. Gather as much information as you can, especially about their hiring and promotion policies. Then write a report for your fellow students in which you present the advantages and disadvantages of applying for a job with these companies.

4. Using any published materials that you can find and any first-hand research you can conduct, write a report that explains the business situation within fifty miles of where you work or attend school. Your report should include an analysis of the business climate, tax situation, and employee pool, rather than simply a list of the number and types of companies.

5. Assume that you work for a consulting firm that helps companies decide where to locate offices, factories, and distribution centers. Your firm has been hired to assist the El-Jay Pizza Company (headquarters at 223 Pine St., Rochester, NY 20000) in finding a location for a new factory that will mix, cook, and freeze pizzas for delivery to retail outlets within a 300-mile radius. The company now has five factories in various locations throughout the U.S., and wants to expand into new markets. Write a report in which you explain the advantages and disadvantages of building this factory in the city where you presently live.

6. Your company is considering replacing all of its typewriters with word processors, in the belief that this will increase each typist's productivity. But no one is sure whether this assumption is true. Write a report in which you compare the cost-effectiveness and productivity of typewriters and word processors in the usual office applications of typing letters and reports.

7. Assume that the decision mentioned in exercise 6 has been made and that your company is going to convert to word processing equipment. Choose three word processors or microcomputers with word processing capability and compare them. Then write a report in which you explain the comparison and recommend that the company purchase a particular kind of machine.

8. You work for the Del-Mar Company, which sells all styles of men's and women's shoes through catalogs and other direct marketing methods. Your boss has heard about direct marketing through cable television and thinks it may be a good idea for your company. She has asked you for a report that explains this relatively new method of di-

rect marketing and shows how it might apply to your company. At this point she wants no recommendations.

9. Because you are a recent college graduate, your supervisor has approached you to help with a project. He believes that the supervisors and secretaries in your company need to write more clearly. He wants you to design a writing course for these employees. It should last eight to twelve hours and will be presented in blocks of two hours each week for four to six weeks. He has left the design of the course and the decision about who will teach it up to you. Write the report.

10. Your company has recently experienced a number of open conflicts between workers and supervisors. In some cases these have had to be resolved by the Personnel Manager, at great expense of time and effort. Others seem to have been resolved by fistfights in the parking lot. The company has no union and no grievance procedure, so each conflict is resolved as it arises, with no set standards. Some employees have complained that they are in danger, and others that they have nowhere to turn when they have a complaint. The Plant Manager has directed you to write a grievance procedure that can be followed whenever there is a dispute. You may assume any kind of organizational structure that you wish. Do whatever research you need and write the report. You may wish to consult federal and state guidelines for such procedures.

■

14

Using Visual Aids

Well-designed and intelligently used visual aids can complement your writing in almost all situations. They will not take the place of writing, but visual aids can help you express complex concepts or emphasize key ideas. And they do that with an economy and force that you may not be able to achieve with words alone. In this chapter you will learn to use the major kinds of visual aids effectively. The topics we will cover include:

What visual aids can do for you and your reader
Major kinds of visual aids and their uses
Making your own visual aids
Incorporating visual aids into your text

What Visual Aids Can Do for You and Your Reader

Too many writers believe that visual aids are little more than window dressing, certainly not as important as a whole page, or a whole report, of uninterrupted words. But visual aids have many uses as complements and supplements to your writing. They are an important way for you to present information so that your readers can understand it.

Visual aids supplement your writing by allowing you to repeat or highlight information you have discussed, thus presenting it a second time, but in a different form. Readers encounter data or concepts once in your discussion and again in related visual aids. This increases the probability that your readers will understand and remember what you have said. In fact, a well-designed visual aid will often make a point or state a conclusion more effectively than your writing.

Visual aids allow you to be concise because they take only a relatively small amount of space to display data that otherwise might occupy many pages of writing. By including a visual aid, such as a graph or table, you are free to concentrate your discussion on highlights and key points. Yet, the visual aid presents a complete set of data for readers who want to analyze it for themselves.

Visual aids can also make concise, vivid comparisons; interpret and summarize data and concepts; and simplify complicated objects, procedures, or discussions so that readers who are not specialists can understand them.

Visual aids are useful in almost any situation that requires you to write or speak. You simply need to select the proper size and medium for presentation. In reports and memos that are meant for one reader at a time, visual aids are rarely larger than a typical page. When you speak to a group you will need visual aids that everyone can see. These may be desk-top size charts or illustrations that will fit in a briefcase. Or you can use larger, free-standing visual aids that sit on an easel. For large audiences you can photograph your visual aids and project them as slides, or make transparencies for the overhead projector. These last two methods allow you to adjust the size of the projected image to the size of your audience and the room you are working in. Any blank wall makes an ideal projection surface.

Your decisions about the complexity and size of the visual aids you use will depend on:

1. *The situation.* What does your audience need? How many people must see your visual aids at one time?

2. *Technical support.* What can you do with the equipment and resources available to you? Will you have to make your own visual aids, or will you be able to rely on the help of an art department or trained illustrators?

3. *Expense.* How much time and effort will be required to make the visual aids you want to use? Is your project worth the expense, or should you scale back your plans? Are funds budgeted and available for this purpose? Is it

worth the time you will have to spend to do your own visual aids?

You are the writer, and decisions about visual aids will usually be yours to make. It will help if you try to incorporate your thinking about visual aids into your planning for your entire writing project. As you plan, organize, and search for information, identify concepts and data that will lend themselves to visual representation. Pay special attention to those concepts and data that you believe will present difficulties to your readers. As you write a rough draft, get into the habit of marking those places where you might use visual aids and perhaps even sketching them out in a preliminary way so that you can refer to them and explain them in your draft.

Major Kinds of Visual Aids and Their Uses

The visual aids that you are likely to use in your writing include various kinds of graphs, charts, tables, flow charts, illustrations, maps, and photographs. In some situations you may find that several kinds of visual aids will serve the same purpose. But some of them are capable of doing specific jobs that the others will not do. Choosing the visual aids that are most informative and appropriate to your purpose is possible only if you know what each can do.

Pie Charts

Pie charts may be the simplest kind of visual aid, both to make and to read. A *pie chart* is a circle that is divided into wedge-shaped "slices" (as in cutting a pie). Each slice represents a part of the whole, and the slices or wedges are drawn so that their size corresponds, in general, to the size of the portion that they represent. Thus, pie charts are useful when you want to show your readers an immediate visual impression of the relative sizes of the component parts of a whole. Figure 14-1 shows a pie chart that divides a company's customers into three groups according to age. In Figure 14-2 you see that the wedges in a pie chart can be given greater emphasis by various shadings that distinguish one from another.

Note that pie charts are not useful for representing absolute quantities, for showing changes in a quantity over a period of time, or for comparing units that are not part of the same whole. The pie chart's usefulness begins and ends with showing how a given whole can be or has been divided into component parts. The wedges can show the relative size of the components, but they cannot provide a detailed, accurate scale of measurement.

Figure 14-1 Pie Chart

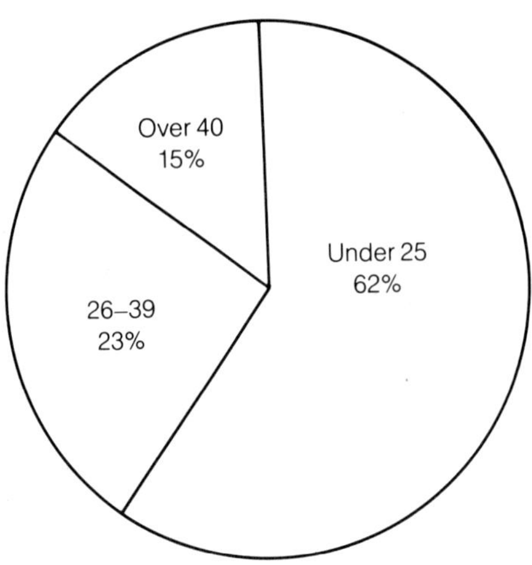

DISTRIBUTION OF CUSTOMERS
BY AGE GROUP

Figure 14-2 Pie Chart with Shaded Sections

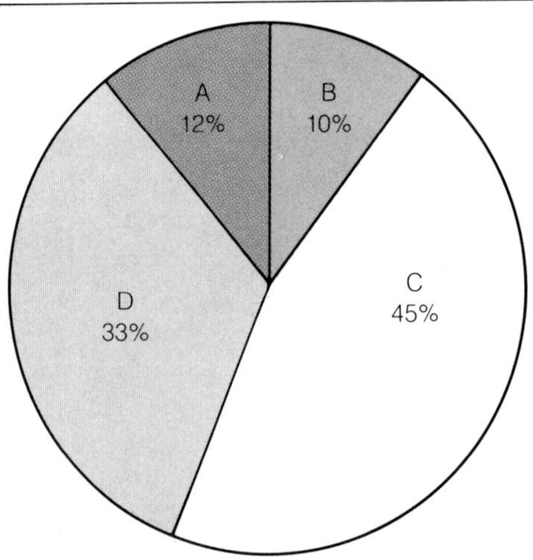

SPECIFIC PRODUCT SALES AS A
PERCENTAGE OF TOTAL SALES

Bar Graphs

Bar graphs consist of a series of horizontal or vertical bars drawn parallel to each other along a scale of measurement. Each bar can represent a different item or the same item at different times, and the scale can be either a scale of percentage or one of absolute quantities. Bar graphs are more versatile than pie charts because they can show comparisons, changes over time, and absolute quantities.

At their simplest, bar graphs do the same job as pie charts: They show the components of a whole as percentages. Thus, in Figure 14-3 you see a bar graph that shows the sales of three products as percentages of a company's total sales for 1980. Note that each bar occupies a space along the scale roughly proportional to the percentage it expresses. Thus, if you were to combine the three bars into one, they would reach the 100 percent mark of the scale. An added feature in this graph is that the exact percentages are listed at the top of each bar, because the scale itself is not graduated precisely enough for exact measurement.

Because bar graphs can use two scales of measurement, they are more versatile than pie charts. If you want to show changes over a period of time, you can use a bar graph which uses percentage or quantity as one scale, and time as the other scale, as in Figure 14-4.

Figure 14-3 Bar Graph

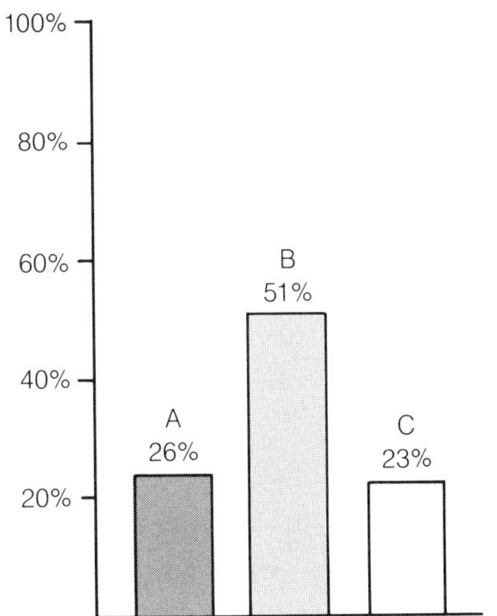

Figure 14-4 Bar Graph Showing Change Over Time

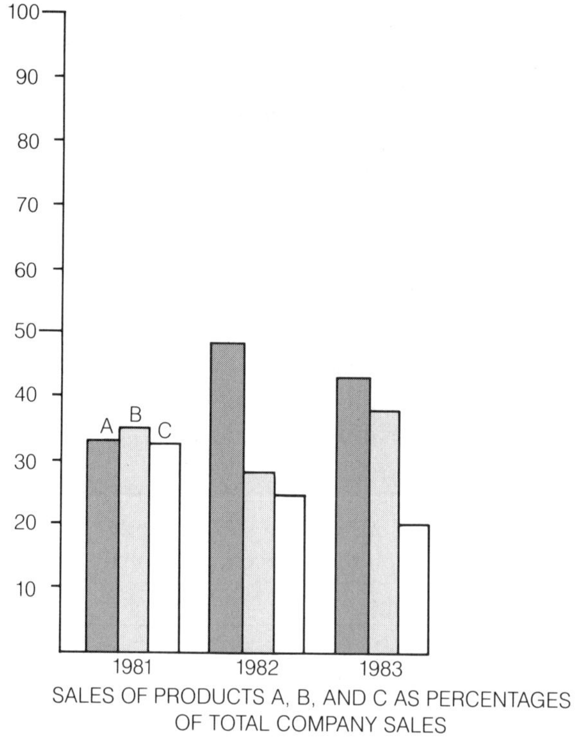

1981 1982 1983

SALES OF PRODUCTS A, B, AND C AS PERCENTAGES OF TOTAL COMPANY SALES

Figure 14-4 shows the sales of three products as percentages of a company's total sales for a period of three years. Thus, you can see changes in the sales of a product from one year to the next. But note that this bar graph does not show changes in total company sales from one year to the next. That is, sales for 1981 may have been greater or smaller than those for 1982 and 1983, but this information does not appear on the graph in Figure 14-4. To show changes in the total amount of company sales from one year to the next, you might use a bar graph such as the one in Figure 14-5.

In fact, Figure 14-5 shows more than total company sales for each of three years. It shows dollar sales for each of the company's three products for each of three years. Thus, it expresses not only the company's total sales, but the contribution of each product to the total. The person who designed this bar graph could have provided even more information by giving an exact total for each product in each year, as well as a total sales figure for each year.

Figure 14-6 shows how you can use bar graphs to help you make a point. The two bar graphs in this figure show fuel consumption and expenditures for fuel for six different years. We'll pay attention to both how they are constructed and how they help make the writer's point.

Figure 14-5 Bar Graph Showing Total Sales Over Time

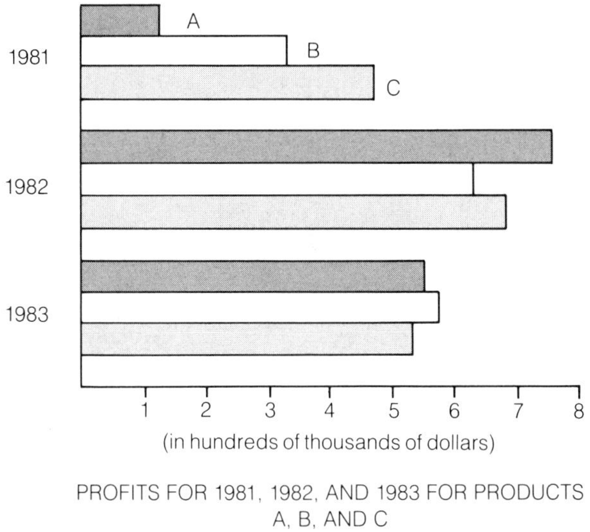

A close look at the two graphs in Figure 14-6 shows that they contain the following useful features:

> The bars are marked differently for each year, so there will be no chance that readers will confuse one year with another as they move from graph to graph.
>
> To supplement the vertical scales at the sides of each graph, exact figures are listed at the top of each bar.
>
> The horizontal scale on each graph is the time scale. In both graphs it is broken by small, vertical lines between 1967 and 1971, and again between 1971 and 1974. These breaks indicate that data for the intervening years is missing from the graph.
>
> The two graphs correspond in size, shape, and placement of the bars. This makes it easier to compare the information in one graph with that in the other.
>
> The wavy line below the bottom graph indicates that a third graph, one showing unit cost, is missing from the figure, though it is mentioned in the label.

All of these features show that some thought went into the design of this visual aid, so that it would be easy for readers to use. Because of this careful planning of the visual aid in Figure 14-6, readers can easily see the point being made: that fuel consumption has been relatively level for all of the

Figure 14-6 Bar Graph to Make a Point

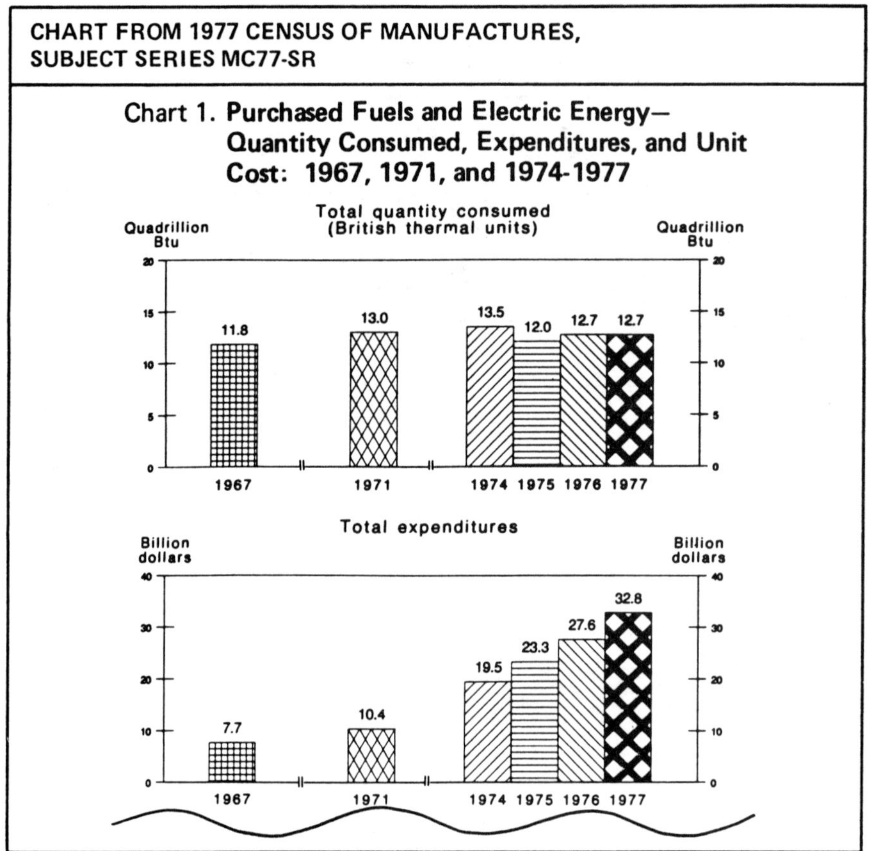

Source: *Factfinder for the Nation,* "Energy and Conservation Statistics," U.S. Bureau of the Census, CFF No. 20, Issued February 1980.

years listed, while expenditures have more than quadrupled. You could, of course, simply tell your readers that. But the graph shows it vividly.

Line Charts

Line charts display data by converting them into a line or curve that connects a series of points. These charts have two scales, one horizontal and one vertical, and each point on the line or curve represents a place where

Figure 14-7 Line Chart

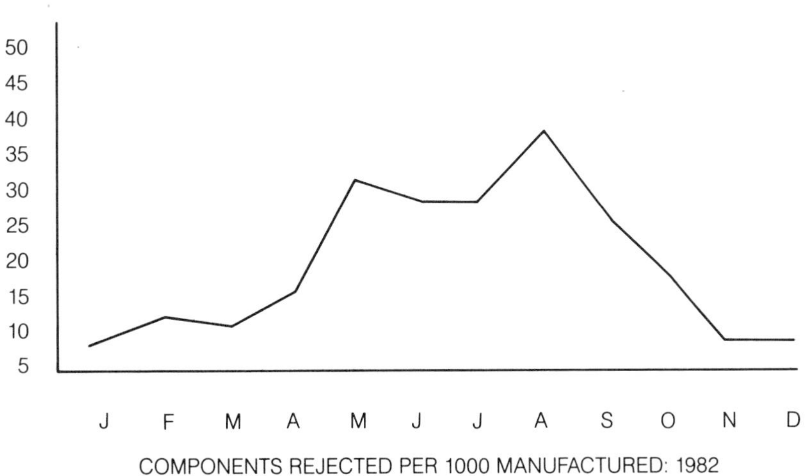

the two scales intersect. Line charts are most useful for showing changes that have taken place (or are predicted) over a period of time, as in Figure 14-7. When this is the purpose of the chart, the horizontal scale usually represents a time line, and the vertical scale represents the quantity being measured.

A line chart of the type in Figure 14-7 provides your readers with an immediate picture of general trends. Thus, this chart displays the average number of pieces that have been rejected for each one thousand that were manufactured during each month of 1982. It is true that the data in Figure 14-7 could also be shown in a bar graph, but the bars would not necessarily give the immediate, graphic impression of increases and decreases during the year. Bar graphs would also require more visual detail and thus might look more cluttered and be more difficult to read than the line chart.

Because line charts can contain several lines, they can display comparisons, so long as the different categories or items can be measured along identical scales. Figure 14-8 shows this use of multiple lines on the same chart.

Figure 14-8, which is a percentage distribution of employees by age groups over a period of 25 years, employs shading between the different lines to clearly differentiate the three categories of employees. Note that a pie chart could not display this information because a pie chart can provide percentage distributions only for a single point in time. A bar graph could show percentage distributions for specific points during the twenty-five-year period charted in Figure 14-8, but it could not show the continuous upward and downward trends.

Figure 14-8 Line Chart with Multiple Lines

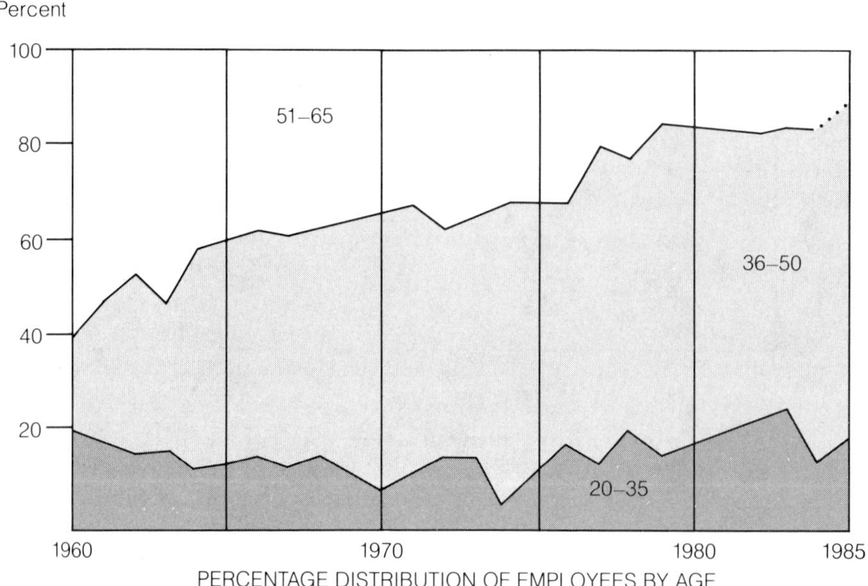

Figure 14-9 Line Chart with Lines Distinguished by Pattern

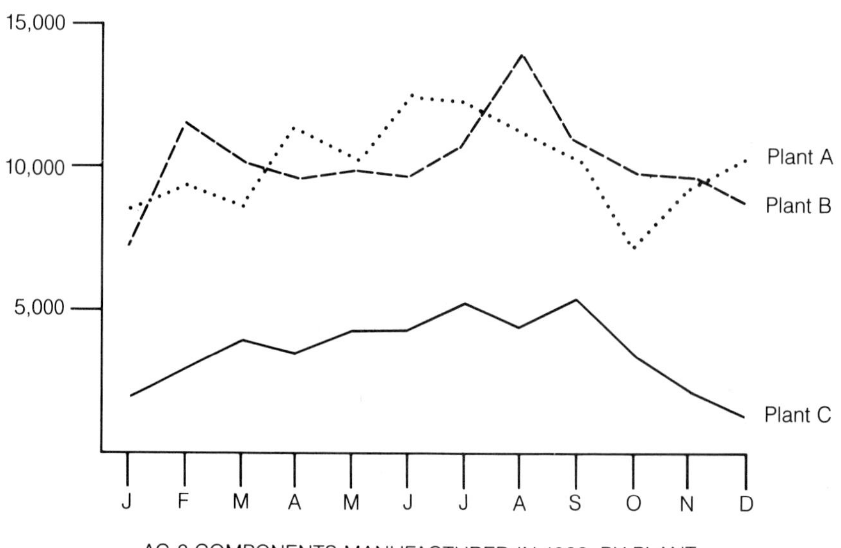

Another way to distinguish different categories when you use more than one line on a line chart is to draw each line in a different color or with a different pattern, as in Figure 14-9. This is especially important when the lines cross each other and shading between them is difficult or impossible because of the confusion that would result for your readers.

Pay Attention to Scales

When you design bar graphs or line charts there is always the danger that you can unintentionally distort or misrepresent your data unless you pay careful attention to the scales you use. That is, the visual impression that your graph or chart gives a reader will be influenced by the size of the increments on each scale. Figure 14-10 shows two line charts that display a company's profits over a five-year period.

Figure 14-10 Impressions of Modest Increase (Chart A), and Dramatic Increase (Chart B)

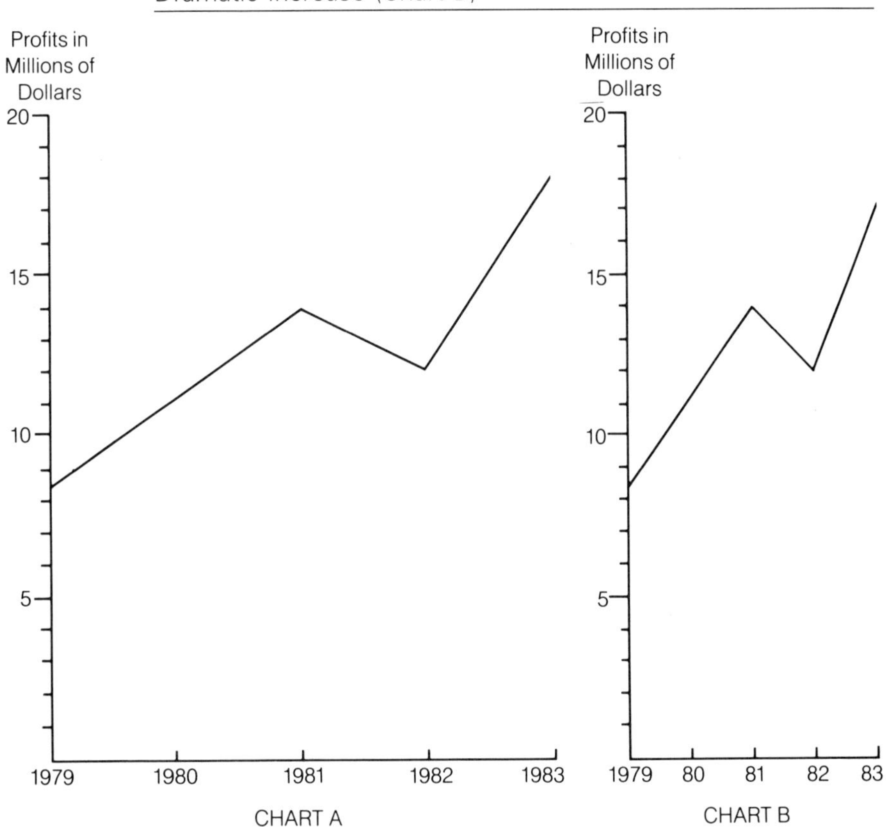

Chart A in Figure 14-10 gives the impression of rather modest increases and decreases from year to year. Chart B gives the impression of a much steeper and more dramatic growth in profits. This is the result of leaving the increments on the vertical, dollar scale the same as those in chart A but compressing the increments on the horizontal scale to half of their length in chart A. The line becomes steeper because for the same vertical increment it must travel only half the horizontal distance from year to year. Of course, it is easy to use the vertical scale and see that both charts provide the same information. But the purpose of visual aids is to create a visual impression, and these two charts create quite different visual impressions. The company has not made more or less money because the lines on the charts are steeper or flatter.

Keeping scales comparable between visual aids is especially important if you want your readers to compare one chart or graph with another, as was the case with Figure 14-6.

Tables

Strictly speaking, tables are not visual aids, but we will consider them here because they perform many of the same functions as visual aids:

1. They interrupt the written text and call attention to themselves by their different format and spacing.
2. They supplement and complement the written text by presenting data in a highly condensed form.
3. Like bar graphs and line charts, tables have horizontal and vertical scales, and data appear at the points where these scales intersect.

Figure 14-11 Table with Different, but Related, Quantitative Data: Changes in Producer and Consumer Price Indices, 1980–81

	Sept. 1980	Aug. 1981	Sept. 1981	Percent Change Aug.-Sept. 1981	Percent Change Sept. 1980-Sept. 1981
Producer Price Index (1967 = 100)	252.7	271.8	272.3	0.2	7.8
Consumer Price Index (1967 = 100)	251.7	276.5	279.3	1.0	11.0
Prime Interest Rate (Percent)	12.23	20.50	20.08	−2.0	64.2

Source: *Annual Report,* FY 81, U.S. Small Business Administration, vol. I, p. 12.

Tables arrange data in columns and rows, and readers locate the information they need by reading across a row and up or down a column. When you design tables your major concern is to provide adequate spacing between columns and rows so that your readers can find information easily. And tables must, of course, be proofread with extra care because errors are easy to miss when all data is in the same form (numbers, in most cases) and packed tightly into the format of a table.

Tables are most often used to present homogeneous data, but they can also present data that cannot easily be placed on a chart or graph because of different methods of measurement. Figure 14-11 shows such a table, which contains two quite different but related kinds of quantitative data.

In Figure 14-11 the table shows the consumer price index and the producer price index for specific months during 1980 and 1981. These indices could easily be placed on a line chart because they are both calculated from the baseline of 100 that has been established for the year 1967. But the line chart could not also show the prime interest rate for these same months, because it is a percentage and has nothing to do with the 1967 base of 100. The table accommodates these different scales of measurement and allows the writer to suggest a relationship between the price indices and the prime interest rate.

A major shortcoming of tables is that, in most cases, they simply present data rather than summarize or highlight it. To get the information they need, your readers must analyze the tables and dig the data out of the rows and columns. For this reason, and because you know that not all readers will work that hard, you need to provide the summaries and highlights yourself. You can do this by using shading or underlining on the table itself, to point to what you believe are significant figures. Or you can prepare bar graphs, pie charts, and line charts that show important data that you have extracted from a table.

Some Visual Aids Are Not Quantitative

Many times you will want to use a visual aid to provide emphasis to a point you are making or to help your reader, although the information you are working with may not be quantitative. For example, you may wish to illustrate the stages of a process, point out locations, give instructions or directions, or show relationships. You can do these jobs by using flow charts, maps, diagrams, illustrations, and photographs.

Flow Charts

Flow charts are excellent ways of illustrating the stages or steps of a process, or the pathways along which information or manufacturing

Figure 14-12 Flow Chart

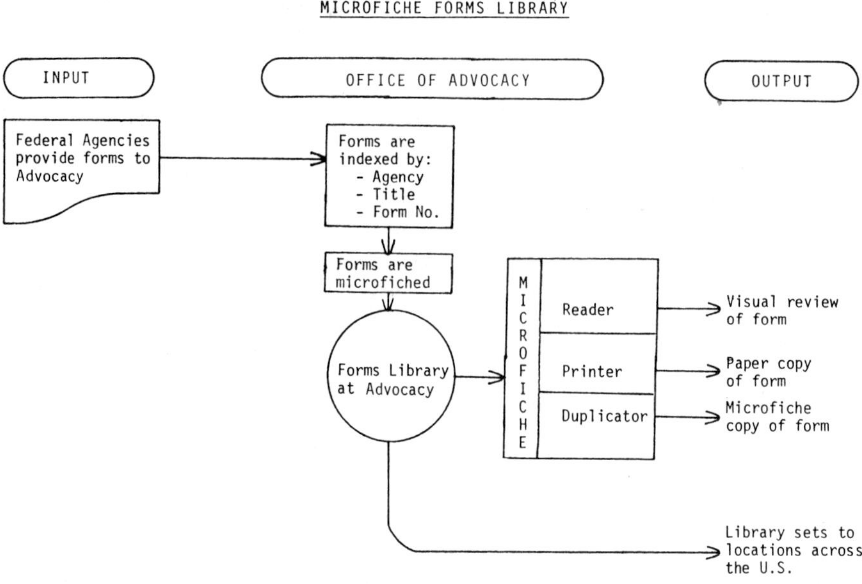

Source: *Government Paperwork and Small Business: Problems and Solutions,* U.S. Small Business Administration, Office of Chief Counsel for Advocacy, December, 1979, p. 54.

components are to travel during specific operations. Flow charts can show a series of steps that occur in sequence, or they can show a number of steps or processes that occur simultaneously. Their format ranges from a relatively complex diagram that a computer systems designer might prepare, to a simple series of pictures, each of which illustrates a separate step. The processes outlined in the flow charts in Figure 14-12 and Figure 14-13 might take several paragraphs, or several pages, to describe. Using the flow charts as visual aids will help you simplify your descriptions and provide an easy-to-use visual reference for your readers. Well-designed flow charts can help you guide your readers through complex descriptions because they present the entire process at once and thus serve as a map of where you are going and how you are getting there. Flow charts also prevent readers from attempting to visualize processes for themselves and making mistakes in the process.

Try this experiment when you wonder whether you should include a flow chart to illustrate a process or show a sequence of steps. Give your written description to half a dozen people and ask each one to draw a flow chart based on what you have written. You may be surprised to see the different versions of what you thought you had described. The solution, of course, is to anticipate your readers' creativity and do the chart yourself.

Figure 14-13 Flow Chart

SIMPLIFIED FORM OF PAPERMAKING PROCESS

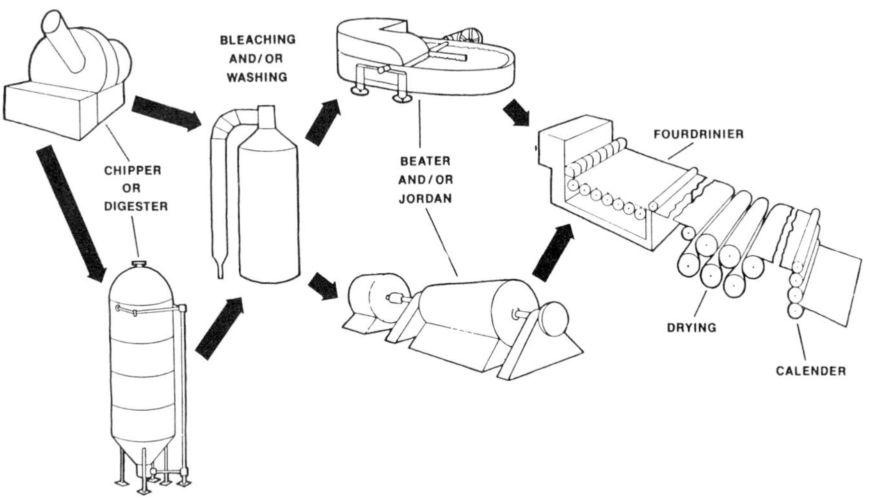

Source: USDA Forest Service, *Making Paper from Trees* (Washington, D.C.: U.S. Government Printing Office, 1981), p. 4.

Maps

We all know that maps are useful for giving directions and pinpointing locations. But they also serve as charts that show the distribution and density of populations, markets, products, and other units. The map in Figure 14-14 shows how a single visual aid can present information that might otherwise require a page or more of lists to do the same job. Without the map this writer would have to list the states that comprise each district and give the percentage change for each district. By the time readers finish the last entry in such a list, they will have forgotten the data for the first district. The map makes comparisons easy and instantaneous. In addition, in the lower-left corner the writer has given the total percentage change for the entire United States.

Maps are effective visual aids any time your data are linked to geography, whether the area you are discussing is as small as a neighborhood or as large as the entire world. When you use maps, always consider using different shadings or colors to indicate clearly the different areas or regions and to minimize the chance that your readers will become confused.

Figure 14-14 Map

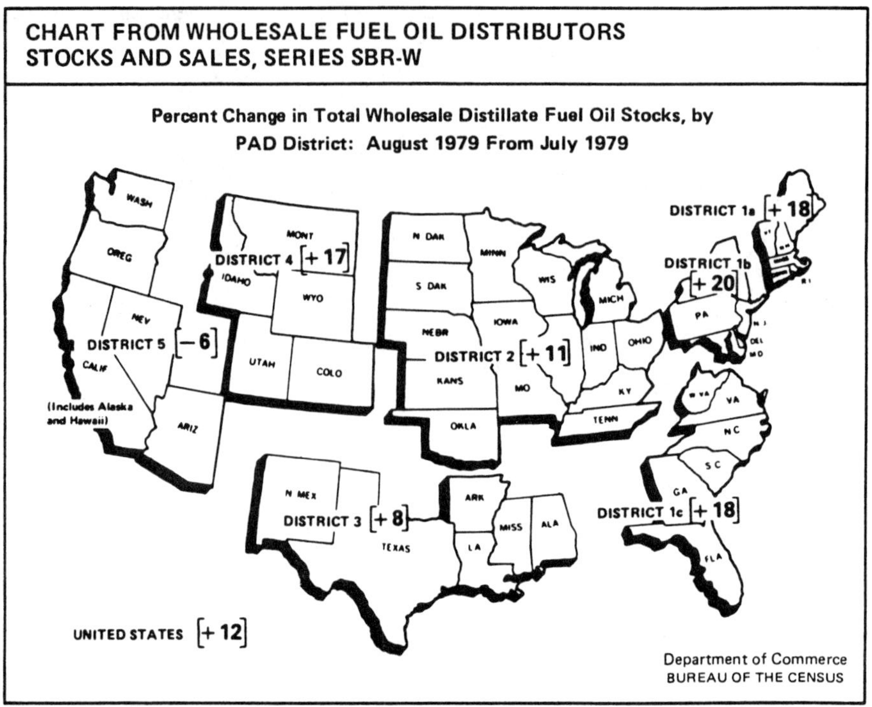

Source: *Factfinder for the Nation,* "Energy and Conservation Statistics," U.S. Bureau of the Census, CFF No. 20, Issued February 1980.

Illustrations

Illustrations serve a variety of purposes, including showing readers exactly what a piece of equipment or a product looks like, showing how to perform a procedure, giving the exact location of a component or part, and adding to the tone or atmosphere of a report. The most commonly used types of illustrations are line drawings, as in Figure 14-15, and half-tone drawings, as in Figure 14-16. In most of your writing, illustrations will appear in black and white, because using color will dramatically increase printing or duplication costs.

When you use illustrations, you must be careful that you do not violate copyright laws. Artists, companies, and publishers usually own the rights to illustrations that they have made, paid for, or published. Thus, if you want to reproduce illustrations that you find in publications you will need to secure permission from the copyright owner and perhaps pay a fee. If you have the assistance of an art department, it may be easier to have illustrations made

Figure 14-15 Illustration

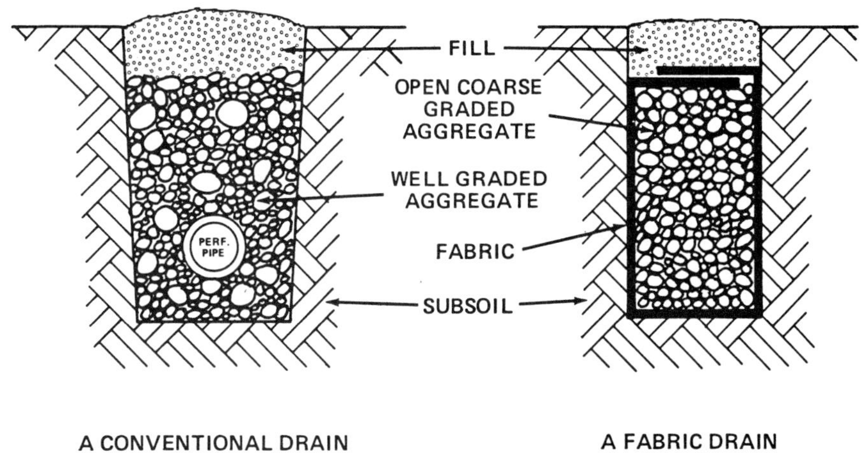

Fabrics for filtration. (Schematic.) Drainage systems with fabrics are usually more economical and more effective. Since their coarse-graded aggregate/fabric structure is more permeable than a comparable cross-sectional area of a drain with coarse- and fine-graded aggregates, fabric drains often do not need a drainage pipe.

Source: U.S. Department of Transportation, Federal Highway Administration, *Sample Specifications for Engineering Fabrics* (Washington, D.C.: U.S. Government Printing Office, 1982), p. 2.

to order for your report or publication. Or you may be able to find appropriate illustrations in publications of the U.S. government. These are in the public domain and thus require no permission or fee to reproduce. However, searching for illustrations may take more time and effort than you want to spend on a particular project.

Photographs

Sometimes the best way to show your reader what something looks like is to provide a photograph. They can be enlarged to fill an entire page, or reduced so that they will occupy only part of a page. If your report will exist in only one, or very few, copies, you can mount a photograph directly on the page without the expense of reproduction. However, if your report is to be printed you will discover that photographs are often the most expensive visual aids to reproduce in quantity.

Figure 14-16 Illustration

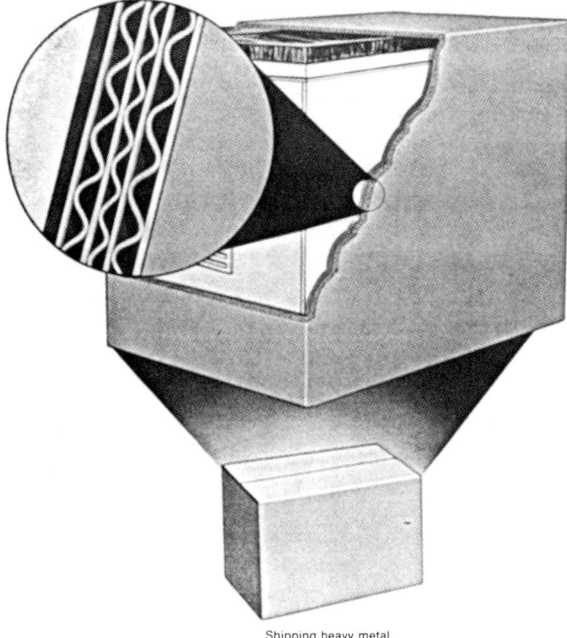

Triple wall corrugated fibreboard.
Triple wall strength and durability is remarkable. Three distinct corrugated mediums combine with four linerboard layers to offer exceptional strength in packaging. Triple wall can be the solution to difficult packaging needs.
• Manufactured in grades ranging from 700# to 1300# puncture test.
• Combined with bleached or mottled white outer liners and natural Kraft.
• Printed with the same quality and versatility as other corrugated fibreboards.
Shipping heavy metal office furniture.

Source: York Container Company.

When you use photographs, insist on the best quality you can achieve. A poor photograph, with little contrast and definition, may be worse than no photograph at all. Use black-and-white film and, especially if you are taking the photographs yourself, take several, even a dozen, with different exposures, to increase the chances that you will get at least one that you can use. Photography looks easy, but achieving prints that will reproduce well is often a job for an expert. If photographs are important to help you make your point, it may be worth hiring a professional photographer.

Making Your Own Visual Aids

Some writers can depend on artists, illustrators, photographers, and even well-staffed art departments to produce their visual aids. Others will have to make their own. But even if you can depend on artists to do the work for you, you will need to be able to show them what you want and what data should be included, and even to give them preliminary sketches of what you think the final version should look like. If you are on your own, you will have to complete both the sketches and the final copies yourself.

You *can* make your own visual aids. It requires a bit of planning, a few readily available tools, and enough artistic ability to draw a straight line along the edge of a ruler. You need to think about the data or information you want to include, the format that will best make your point, and the medium you will need to use to reach your audience. You will probably also have to do several drafts before you find a version that will work.

Begin by thinking *why* you want to use a visual aid and what you want it to accomplish. Will it help you make or support a point? Will it help you explain a difficult concept or procedure, or a complicated body of data? Will it allow you to simplify your presentation by placing relevant, related data together in a table or chart? Once you have established that a visual aid is either helpful or necessary, the next step is to analyze the data it will present so you can select a format that will help you accomplish your purpose. Sometimes you can do this only by sketching several different types of visual aids for the same data, to see which one does the best job.

You may discover that you can use either a bar graph or a line chart to present certain data. Which one will you choose? The best way to decide is to make a sketch of each one and then compare them. You should select the one that has less clutter and detail. For example, if you want to show increases and decreases in sales, profits, or some other quantity over a period of years, you can use a bar graph that shows a bar for each year. But a bar graph with many bars may be too cluttered and confusing. A much better choice would be a line chart, which contains less visual clutter and thus is likely to be both more attractive and easier to read.

At some point you will need to consider how much your readers know about your subject and how much attention they will pay to detail. Will you be able to present your data in a complex form to someone whose knowledge and expertise are equal to yours? Will you have to simplify, perhaps presenting only partial data or broad categories, in order to reach readers who are not experts? Or do your readers know more than you do about the subject and expect you to present all of the data so they can examine it and reach their own conclusions? These factors will influence both the kinds of visual aids you select and the ways you design them.

For example, readers with only a general knowledge or interest in your subject may be satisfied with a bar graph or line chart that shows selected information or trends and gives approximate figures. Expert readers may want detailed tables that provide exact data.

The final step is to design the visual aid, considering its size in your final report, the scales you will use, and such details as colors, shading, line thickness, label placement, and titles. All of these factors will influence the ease with which your readers can interpret and understand your visual aids. Once you have settled on a final design, test it by asking others to look at it and react. Then you can revise it before you prepare the final copy.

Tools

You will need very few tools to make most visual aids. For simple pie charts and most line charts and bar graphs these tools include:

Graph paper
Tracing paper
A fine-point pencil
A fine-point pen
Compasses
A 12-inch ruler scaled in inches
A small protractor for measuring angles

More ambitious projects, such as overhead transparencies and slide shows, will require:

Access to a copy machine that makes transparencies
Clear acetate sheets (8½ by 11 inches)
Marking pens for acetate
A 35mm camera with a tripod or copy stand

If you encounter a job that presents problems you can usually find help in art stores, office supply stores, and shops that sell supplies to architects and engineers. Describe what you are trying to achieve, and the salespersons will often be able to suggest a tool or a solution that will help.

Drawing

Remember, for many visual aids you need only enough artistic ability to draw a straight line along the edge of a ruler. You can draw bar graphs and line charts on graph paper, sometimes in final form. If you want a final version without the graph, some graph papers are made with fine blue lines that will not reproduce in copy machines. Or, you can trace the graph paper version on tracing paper or even on regular paper. The graph paper will help you maintain consistent scales, straight lines, and square corners without using a T square and drafting table.

Establish vertical and horizontal scales by counting squares on the graph paper, marking them off with a pencil, and then adding the bars or the points for your line. Remember to leave spaces between the bars to minimize the chance that you or your readers will become confused. For line charts, simply plot the points (you may have to interpolate between lines on the graph paper), and then connect the points with a line.

Pie charts are just as easy to make. Draw a circle with your compasses (some will accept pens as well as pencils) and draw the dividing lines for the wedges from the center to the edge. The protractor is useful for this job. Since pie charts usually show percentages, and the circles are divided into 360 degrees, 1 percent of the circumference is 3.6 degrees. But remember, pie charts are not exact. Your reader will probably not be able to distinguish 3.4 degrees from 3.8 degrees any better than you can.

Illustrations present more of a problem for most of us, because they do require some artistic ability. Most are best left to an artist or illustrator. But, in a pinch, you do have some options. One is to trace over drawings that already exist, if you can find some that are appropriate. Maps and some line drawings are especially easy to do this way. Sometimes it is possible to cut and paste existing drawings and then photocopy the composite. And some photocopy machines will also enlarge and reduce. If you decide to do your own illustrations in this way, be sure that you observe applicable copyright laws.

Labeling Your Visual Aids

All visual aids need clear, legible labels; captions; and legends that accurately describe the chart or graph and identify its parts. If you have planned well, you have left room for these labels and legends, and you know exactly where they will go. Do them with a typewriter. If you can't handle a typewriter yourself, show a typist exactly what you want by penciling the labels on your rough sketch. Many typewriters are capable of using a wide variety of typefaces, so in most cases you will be able to select one or several that will be effective. Experiment with your rough draft before you try anything on the final copy.

When you add labels to your visual aids, be sure they can all be read from the same edge of the page. It is common practice to label visual aids as follows:

1. Whenever possible, place visual aids and tables so that readers can read them from the bottom of the page. Then place labels and legends so that they too can be read from the bottom of the page.
2. If you must place visual aids so that they can be read only from an edge of the page, you should orient them so that the bottom of the visual aid is parallel to the *right* edge of the page. Then place labels and legends so that they too can be read from the right edge of the page.

Finally, be sure that your legends, labels, and captions do not obscure any of the information the visual aid presents.

Reproducing and Enlarging Visual Aids

If your visual aid is to be part of a written report you can simply insert the original in the report and keep a photocopy for your files. If the report or other document is to be distributed in multiple copies, the visual aids can be reproduced by photocopying, multilith, printing, or other standard reproduction processes. The only limitation on the method you choose will be the quality of your final draft and the ability of the reproduction method to capture its details. Always have a few samples reproduced to see what they look like before you order six dozen or six hundred copies.

Transparencies

If your visual aids are part of a spoken presentation you can easily make them into transparencies for use with an overhead projector. Some copy machines will transfer your graph, chart, table, or illustration directly to acetate. Or, you can make the visual aid directly on transparent acetate, just as you would on paper, by placing a piece of graph paper under the blank acetate and drawing with pens specially made for overhead projection. Or you can trace a prepared visual aid on acetate. The advantage of working directly on acetate with special pens is that you can use color, while most machine-made transparencies will show details only in black and white.

A major advantage of using transparencies and the overhead projector is that you can stand next to the projector as you speak and mark directly on the transparency for emphasis. Also, if you want to discuss a graph or chart in a specific sequence, you can put different parts of it on separate pieces of acetate. As you speak, you can place one transparency on top of another and thus add to the chart as you progress. Or, you can simplify and show only one variable or type of data at a time, so that your audience will not be distracted by other kinds of data.

Slides

You may prefer to use a slide projector rather than an overhead projector. It offers the advantages of remote control, easy focusing, and excellent reproduction of detail. It also reproduces your visual aids and photographs in color.

To photograph visual aids you can use a commercially made slide maker that includes a camera and stand. You simply position the material under the stand and take a picture of it. Or, you can use a 35mm camera and a copy stand or tripod to hold the camera steady. If you do this, you will need to pay attention to shutter speed, lighting, and image size. And you may need a special lens. Acceptable results may require experimentation and several rolls of film. But once you learn the technique, the results are well worth the effort.

Stand-up Charts

You can transfer your visual aids to poster board, illustration board, or large sheets of paper by projecting your final copy onto these surfaces with an opaque projector. Or if you have already made transparencies, you can also use an overhead projector. Adjust the size of the image by varying the distance between the projector and the surface you will draw on. These, by the way, should be attached to a wall or other solid, vertical surface. Once you are satisfied with the projected image, you can trace the visual aid using the lines projected from the original.

When you are making large, stand-up visual aids in this way, you will need a straightedge at least three feet long and markers with both broad and fine points. It is probably a good idea to complete your tracing in pencil first, and to use wide-tipped marking pens later when you can place the board or paper on a large, flat surface where it will be easier to work with.

Incorporating Visual Aids into Your Writing

Visual aids will be most effective if you take the time to make them an integral part of your presentation, rather than merely an added attraction. This is relatively easy to do.

Refer to Visual Aids

Even though you design visual aids so that they will stand on their own and make their points without help, you still need to refer to them as you write or speak. When you discuss the data or concept that a visual aid illustrates, refer directly to the aid so that you focus your reader's attention on it. You can do this with phrases like "see figure 1" or "as is shown in figure 2."

It will also help to interpret the visual aid in your discussion, so your readers will understand why it is there and what point it is making. This not only reinforces the point but also helps the reader "read" and interpret the visual aid itself.

For easy reference, number your visual aids consecutively throughout a report or chapter. Graphs, charts, and illustrations are usually referred to as *figures,* and tables, unsurprisingly, are called *tables.* The numbering is important, especially when a presentation is to be printed. Visual aids will not always appear right next to the related discussion in your text, and in some cases they may be several pages away. The numbers will help your readers find the figure or table you are referring to in the discussion.

Placement of Visual Aids Is Important

Pay attention to where you place visual aids in your presentation. Many times, writers group visual aids and tables together, at the end of a report. Now just imagine what it would be like if a speaker gave a talk and said at the end, "OK, folks, here are all of my visual aids." Fortunately, few of us get to experience that because most speakers know better. They project visual aids as they speak, pointing to them and explaining them as they go. But some writers seem to believe that there is no problem in asking readers to flip constantly to the end of a report to find visual aids. In fact, putting visual aids at the end is easier for writers. But the point is to make life easier for readers.

Try to put visual aids as close as you can get them to the part of your discussion that they illustrate. If you do that, you will be helping both your reader and yourself. Readers who must constantly flip to the end of a report, back to the discussion, and then again to the end soon find their patience in very short supply. They are likely to give up on your visual aids or on your whole presentation. If your visual aids are in the report for a reason, as they should be, then they belong where readers can get to them easily.

Of course, some visual aids are appropriately placed at the end of a report. Those that present extensive raw data, evidence, or other substantiating information that readers might want to analyze for themselves can be placed in an appendix. But visual aids that highlight, summarize, or otherwise directly support your discussion belong in the text, where readers can have easy access to them.

Format, Size, and Layout of Visual Aids

Visual aids need to be large enough so that readers can actually make sense of them without using a magnifying glass or risking eye strain. If your presentation is being typed, and graphs and charts will be added later, be sure you show the typist exactly where each one will go and how much space to leave for it. Allow for normal margins at all edges of the page and for adequate space around each visual aid to separate it from the rest of the text. An attractive layout on the page will encourage your readers to look at your visual aids.

Most visual aids in your reports will probably occupy pages of their own, especially if you are using the standard $8^1/_2 \times 11$-inch typewritten format. Using a full page for each visual aid will guarantee that it will be large enough to read, and that all of its labels, legends, and captions will be legible.

Orient visual aids so that readers will be able to read them from the bottom of the page, just as they read the rest of your report. If a graph or chart is too large for this, orient it so that it can be read from the *right* hand edge of the page. And remember to leave enough space along this edge so that there will be room for the title and figure number.

Reports are usually typed on only one side of a page, so a full-page chart or table may not be visible at the same time as the page on which it is discussed. You can solve this by placing the visual aid on what would normally be the *back* of a page (leaving the other side blank) and placing the visual aid to the *left* of the page on which it is discussed. When you do this, the chart or graph should be oriented so that it can be read from the bottom or right edge of the page it is on. You can include a note on the blank side of the page, indicating that a visual aid appears on the reverse.

If your presentation is being sent to a printer for publication, you will have little control over the exact placement of visual aids. But you still need to provide instructions for approximate locations. You can do this by typing a note, in square brackets and on a line by itself, to indicate where the visual aid should be placed. Like this:

[INSERT FIGURE 3 HERE.]

If you can, always arrange to see galley or page proofs of the printing job, to be sure that visual aids and the text itself are the way you want them. It is easier to make changes while a text is in proof than to wait until the job is finished and bound.

Summary

Visual aids are an important part of almost any presentation. They will help you summarize, highlight, and explain data and concepts. And they will help you achieve emphasis on data and concepts that are especially important. When you decide to use visual aids, you will need to:

Select a type of graph, chart, table, or illustration that is appropriate to your data or concept.

Arrange for the visual aid to be produced so that it is clear, legible, and neatly done.

Place the visual aid close to your discussion of the data or concept it illustrates.

Refer to your visual aids in your discussion to call your readers' attention to them.

■

Exercises: Chapter Fourteen

1. For this exercise use the following table, "Short-Term Bank Loans by Loan Size," from *Annual Report FY 1981,* U.S. Small Business Administration, vol. 1, p. 4.

a. For any month listed, construct a pie chart that shows the percentage distributions of the two types of small loans and the large loans.

b. Construct a bar graph that shows the dollar amounts of loans for any five months listed.

c. Construct a line chart that shows the dollar amounts of loans for all months shown.

Short-Term Bank Loans by Loan Size

	Total		Small Size Loans (Thousands of Dollars)		Large Size Loans (Thousands of Dollars)
			Under $50	$50 to $500	Over $500
	Dollars (Millions)	Percent	Percent	Percent	Percent
November 1978	9,534	100.0	12.9	25.8	61.3
February 1979	6,850	100.0	19.5	31.5	49.0
May 1979	8,576	100.0	18.5	23.5	58.0
August 1979	8,295	100.0	16.9	22.5	60.6
November 1979	8,107	100.0	13.1	26.6	60.3
February 1980	9,920	100.0	12.6	22.5	64.9
May 1980	11,317	100.0	12.4	24.4	62.3
August 1980	13,475	100.0	8.9	20.6	70.5
November 1980	13,101	100.0	9.8	18.2	72.1
February 1981	16,986	100.0	7.9	20.1	72.0
May 1981	16,841	100.0	8.0	17.2	74.9
August 1981	24,597	100.0	5.8	13.9	82.7

d. Construct a bar graph that shows, for any five months listed, the percentage distribution of small and large loans. (Small loans should be divided into two categories, as they are in the table.)

e. Construct a multiple-line chart that traces the percentage distribution of both categories of small loans and for large loans for all months shown.

2. Using standard business reference sources, select three companies that are engaged in the same kind of business or industry. For example, you might select three steel manufacturers, three retail chains, or three service businesses. Construct visual aids that compare these companies for the past five years in the following categories:

Number of employees
Annual sales
Average dividend per share
Earnings
Assets
Liabilities
Profits
Expansion

3. Select and copy a line chart from a magazine, book, or newspaper. Redraw the chart, using at least three different scales, so that you achieve visual impressions that are as widely different as possible.

4. Using figures that you obtain from the most recent U.S. Census Report, compare three cities (of your choice) by constructing visual aids that present the following information:

Population
Average number of people per household
Hispanics, blacks, and other minorities as a percentage of the total population
Personal disposable income per household in increments of $10,000
Males and females as percentages of total population

5. For one of the cities you used in exercise 4, compare the figures from the two most recent U.S. Census reports. Present information about two of the categories of information requested in exercise 4 by using visual aids.

6. Using Figure 14-6 (from this chapter), construct line charts that show the information displayed in the two bar graphs.

15

Speaking and Listening

Much of your communication on the job will consist of speaking and listening. They are such natural activities that we scarcely think about them at all. Nor does it often occur to us that they should *require* thought or training. After all, we've been doing both for longer than we can remember, so we have plenty of experience. But almost all of us can improve our speaking and listening skills. We will communicate more effectively, understand and be understood more often, and build more solid relationships with others.

The goal of this chapter is not to improve your speaking and listening skills. To do that will require more than the following pages can give you. And you will need to do much of the work yourself. This chapter will give you the tools you need to begin.

Preparation

Most of your speaking and listening will be spontaneous and unplanned, as you go about your daily business. You will talk with others one on one, over the phone or in person, in small groups and in casual conversations. As you approach these situations you are unlikely to think that they require any preparation, or that they are important enough to deserve it. Most of us reserve preparation for those times when we must appear before groups and give a formal presentation. Even more rarely do we consider preparing for listening, which seems to require little more than sitting quietly and at least appearing to pay attention.

But preparation is necessary for both speaking *and* listening. In school it is easy enough to sit in the rear of the room and participate or not, as you choose. At work you will be expected to participate and contribute in private conversations and in large and small groups. If you are silent too often, or for too long, others will begin to believe that you are unprepared or that you have nothing to say. Your personal success and advancement, as well as your company's success, may depend on your ability to contribute, and this in turn will depend on how thoroughly you prepare.

Preparing to Speak

You prepare for speaking and listening in much the same way that you prepare for writing: by learning about your subject, goals, purpose, and audience. If you must give a presentation of some complexity and importance, you will also need to organize and perhaps even write at least part of it. The idea is to prepare well enough that you give the appearance of being spontaneous. That should not surprise you. It is often the speaker who seems most spontaneous who has done the most extensive preparation.

Of course, not all speaking situations will require equally detailed preparation. If you are about to make a telephone call or meet with someone in the office, you may need to merely review a few notes you have made so that you will be sure to cover all of the subjects or questions that are the reason for the call or meeting. In fact, it is usually helpful to make a brief list of these subjects or questions so that you will not forget any of them.

If you are meeting with a small group, and you are responsible for part or all of the program, you will have to prepare more extensively than you would for a brief conversation. In this situation you will need to prepare an agenda of items that the meeting will cover, the materials you will give to other participants, and any visual aids you will need. Of course, you will also need a thorough knowledge of the subjects that the group will discuss and the problems it is expected to solve. Otherwise, you will not be able to provide effective leadership.

When you give a spoken presentation to a large group (or even if you are the main speaker before a small group), you will need to do your most extensive preparation of all. This might involve thorough research, writing a script (which I hope you will not actually *read* to your audience), and preparing the handouts and visual aids that will help your audience follow and understand what you say.

Preparing to Listen

You also need to prepare to be an effective listener. Perhaps you have experienced being completely mystified by a teacher's lecture, only to discover that you would have understood it quite easily if you had bothered to do the assigned reading. Many listening situations are like that.

If the group leader distributes an agenda for a meeting, read it carefully and then try to learn something about the subjects you are not familiar with. Search your own files, talk with others, and do whatever outside reading is necessary to bring yourself up to date. In this way you will have some assurance of being able to follow what others are saying. You will also be able to ask intelligent questions or at least avoid embarrassing ones. It is no fun to ask what you think is an important question only to discover that it's already been answered, or that everyone else knows the answer because they prepared in advance.

Remember: Effective speaking and listening, like effective writing, begin with thorough preparation.

Speaking

There are important differences between speaking and writing. If you want to reach your audience you will need to be aware of these differences and learn how to use them to your advantage.

Your Audience Is Present

In most cases your audience will be present when you speak. The exceptions are when you appear on television or radio. Because other people are present, they can directly affect you and the way you speak. Their postures, gestures, facial expressions, eye contact, and apparent level of attention will affect you. It is difficult to ignore people who seem to be reacting unfavorably or paying no attention. They can slow you down, discourage you, and sometimes make you quite uncomfortable. At the same time, an attentive audience that reacts favorably to you and what you say will encourage you, and this may help you turn out a better performance.

You will also directly affect your audience. Of course, that's what you have set out to do, just as when you write. But when you write your readers see only your words. They do not see *you,* in person, so they will not react to your appearance, posture, gestures, facial expression, or clothing. If you conform to what your listeners expect, there is a greater chance that they will receive your message favorably. If you think most members of your audience will wear customary business clothing, you should probably dress that way too, regardless of your preference. You should also attempt to speak without distracting gestures, such as rocking back and forth on your feet or constantly pushing your glasses up your nose.

Your voice is important, and you should learn to use it effectively. If you mumble, stutter, or speak in a noticeably nasal or whining voice, your audience may react unfavorably, no matter how important or well-prepared your message. If you must speak frequently, you might want to consult a speech instructor or therapist to help you overcome any of these problems that trouble you.

It is also important that you pay attention to the rate or speed of your speech. Most people, in normal conversation, speak at a rate of about 120 words per minute. In presentations before groups, this rate usually slows to about 100 words per minute. A rate that is too *slow* will bore listeners. They will feel that they have to wait too long to find out how your sentences will end. Also, you create other problems for yourself. One of the most important is that a slow rate gives your audience too much time to daydream and think about everything but what you are saying. Some studies indicate that most people can process words at a rate of about 400 per minute. Your listeners will already have plenty of free time. There is no need to give them more. If your rate is too fast, you may lose some listeners, or all of them may miss some of what you say. Your speech rate will probably increase if you are nervous. Adequate preparation and rehearsal may help you stay calm.

Designing and Giving an Oral Report

In the early stages, planning a speech is much the same as planning a writing project. In fact, you may want to actually write the speech and revise it, just as though your audience were going to read it. But as you approach a final version you will need to make some changes so that you will be able to reach an audience that is listening rather than reading.

First, remember that your audience will listen. This presents a special challenge to them, and to you. Most of us are accustomed to reading. We are able to stop and think, reread passages we didn't understand the first time, and stop for a break if we need one. We can even go back to a letter or report months later and review it. But listeners enjoy none of these conveniences. In most cases they must get everything the first time. And as they listen they are attempting to understand, evaluate, distinguish important from unimportant, and perhaps even make decisions, all at the same time. Listeners have a great deal of work to do, and you will be a more successful speaker if you help them. You can do this in a number of ways.

1. **O**rganize carefully. A rambling, disorganized presentation is difficult to follow. Listeners need to be constantly aware of where they have

been, where they are, and where they are going. Some can figure this out for themselves, but you can help. Be sure that your main points are easily identifiable and carefully connected with each other. Choose an overall organization plan and stay with it throughout the presentation.

2. **U**se summaries. Instead of racing through your presentation from start to finish, be sure that you take the time to summarize and emphasize your main points. Frequent summaries are an ideal way to review the point you have just made and the evidence you have presented for it, and to point to the conclusions you want your audience to draw. This will assure that your listeners hear your main points more than once.

3. **U**se obvious transitions. This will be easy if you have organized carefully. Take the time to *tell* your listeners that you are moving from one point to the next. You can also tie your transitions to restatements of your major points, so your listeners will always know where they are. For example, you might say: "The second reason for reorganizing the Sales and Marketing Division is . . ." In this sentence, *second* serves as a transition to a new idea, and the restatement of the main idea shows its relation to the coming material.

4. **R**efer to earlier statements. When you want to make a point about something you have already mentioned, restate the earlier subject. This will help your listeners follow a network of cross-references in your presentation.

5. **I**dentify examples. Don't assume that your listeners will be able to distinguish your examples and evidence from the main points. Do it for them. Identify your examples clearly.

6. **U**se visual aids. Take every opportunity to use visual aids of all kinds if they will help your listeners follow your presentation. We learn new information in numerous ways. If your listeners can *see* something that illustrates what they are hearing, then they will have encountered your ideas twice. So you double the chances that what you say will be understood, or even noticed.

You can also prepare handout sheets that contain illustrations of major points, give details about difficult concepts, and even show the outline of your presentation. All of these will make it easier for your listeners to follow you.

7. **R**ehearse. Before you actually give your presentation, try it out. You can do this for a small group, or even in front of a mirror. Many speakers have improved their presentations by rehearsing for a TV camera and watching the videotape. Rehearsal will help you control such important variables as your rate of speech, physical appearance, facial expressions, and gestures. You will be able to review what you did and then rehearse again to smooth out the rough spots. It may be disconcerting at first to watch yourself on a television screen, but you will get used to it, and it will help.

Giving the Oral Report

Especially if you are speaking in unfamiliar surroundings, plan to arrive early and check the arrangements. Be sure that all microphones are working and that you have the audio-visual materials that you need. It won't do much good to arrive with a box full of slides or transparencies if the projector is missing or broken. Adjust the microphone so you won't have to fiddle with it as you begin to speak, and be sure that whatever else you need is close at hand.

Be sure that you speak clearly (you will probably be nervous, even if you're experienced, so this deserves some special attention). And speak so that everyone can hear you. If you doubt that everyone can hear, then ask. Ask the people in the back if they can hear. Ask them to let you know if at any time they can't. And pay attention to your rate. Most of us speak *faster* when we're nervous. So watch it.

Try to maintain eye contact with your audience. Actually *look* at people, rather than above their heads. They will notice, and they will look back. You will be able to establish rapport with people you are looking at. It's almost impossible to get anything going with the wall in the back of the room or with the papers in front of you. Once again, try not to read your speech. If you *must* work from a text, be sure you look up from it frequently, and try to avoid bobbing rapidly up and down from text to audience. Rehearsal will help. The better you know your material, the less you will have to depend on your notes.

Finally, *use* your voice. Instead of speaking in a monotone, use your voice for emphasis. Your voice, body, face, hands and arms can help you emphasize your main points, indicate transitions, and set up a relationship with your audience. Obvious, deliberate increases or decreases in volume or speed, along with changes in tone or pitch, will keep your audience with you and will help them identify what you believe is important.

Getting Help

You can read thousands of books about speaking, but there is no substitute for the real thing. Seasoned speakers are seasoned because they have experience. They have given dozens or even hundreds of presentations. If you are extraordinarily nervous or believe you need help, you should probably enroll in a speech course and begin getting your experience there. If you can't do that, try to form a group at work or school and try to help each other. Speak, listen, give constructive criticism, and practice some more.

Listening

Listening may be the most important communication skill you have. Almost half of the time that we spend each day communicating with others is devoted to listening. We do most of our learning by listening to others. It is also an important way of building our communication skills, because it is a major means of observing others and monitoring our own performance. Finally, listening is one of our most important ways of building effective relationships with others. Unless we listen to people, really listen, and respond, we are unlikely to know them, or care for them. And they are unlikely to know or care for us.

But most of us take our listening skills for granted until some embarrassing or disastrous event shows us, and others, that we are not listening as effectively as we need to. Even then, many people may assume that there is little they can do to help themselves. That shouldn't surprise us, because most of us know very little about listening. Nor has it received much attention in school. Most of us received our entire instruction in listening when some teacher or parent told us to sit up straight, sit still, put both feet on the floor, and look at whoever was speaking, that is, "pay attention."

Of course, most of us also learned that no one can tell if we are *actually* listening, so long as we *appear* to be listening. The problem is that it is relatively easy to *look* attentive and then check out for parts unknown. And it's tempting to do that, because really listening to someone is hard work. If you want the full benefit of an interaction, you have to take an active part in it, even if you are "only" listening. Your job may well depend on your ability to listen to and remember complicated information, repeat it for others, and ask intelligent questions about it.

You can become a more effective listener if you recognize why most of us don't listen well, and then work at the following strategies which directly address common listening problems. Practice them. Think about them as you enter a listening situation. Remind yourself to do them.

1. **Prepare.** We usually think that preparation is the speaker's responsibility. But listening and remembering will be easier if you know something about what is going on. Preparation will give you a general framework for the information and ideas you will listen to, and you will know

where they fit within it. You will also help yourself retain what you hear, because you will be able to anticipate it before you hear it. So you will double your exposure.

Preparation will also help you critically evaluate what you hear. The less you know about a subject, the more you will have to depend on a speaker to tell you what is important and even what is true.

2. **M**otivate yourself. Speakers are responsible for making their presentations and subjects interesting. But you share that responsibility. Not every speaker or subject you encounter will be rewarding and entertaining. Some speakers can take difficult, even boring, material and make it interesting. Others can make even the most interesting subject dry, lifeless, and tedious. Some subjects are boring all by themselves, and need no help from either speakers or listeners. But it will rarely matter whether the speaker or subject is boring or interesting. You will have to listen, understand, and retain, because it is part of your job.

When speaker and subject are interesting, listening can be easy. In fact, many skilled speakers will take pains to show you the rewards of listening to what they have to say. Sometimes you will have to motivate yourself. This is part of your preparation. Search the subject to find out what you might learn from a particular presentation. Examine the situation to see how a subject might relate to your job and what information you might be able to use. In short, you will have to motivate yourself by searching for evidence of some short-term or long-term reward.

3. **C**ontrol your biases. We all have preconceived ideas, notions, tastes, likes, and dislikes. And we are likely to apply these freely to speakers, their manner of delivery, and their subjects. The result is often ineffective listening, because we are too busy disagreeing to actually pay attention to what a speaker is saying.

Common biases include objections to particular people or kinds of people (perhaps we don't like management or labor leaders), the way they speak, the language they use, and the subjects they speak about. It is difficult to listen impartially when we are personally involved with a subject.

And remember that biases need not be negative. It is just as easy to be lulled into acceptance or uncritical thinking by a subject we agree with or a speaker we like or find attractive. Just because someone agrees with us doesn't necessarily mean that either of us is right.

4. **T**ry to control distractions. Of course, you can't always control distractions. But you can try. Begin by evaluating where you are sitting. If it is too far from the speaker, or too near a window (that you might gaze through),

a noisy fan, a hallway, or a door, then move if you can. Try to place yourself in the most advantageous position and situation for listening effectively.

Most distractions are minor nuisances that take on more importance than they deserve. We end up paying more attention to them than to the speaker. You can prevent this by training yourself to ignore the distractions. Practice focusing your eyes and ears on the speaker and excluding everything else. Get involved in the presentation. Try to anticipate the next point or the conclusion. Review the points that have been made so far and see how they relate to each other. With practice you will find that you can concentrate rather easily.

5. **P**ay attention to organization. The most effective speakers are not only well organized, they let you know the kind of organization they are using so you can follow it. And most presentations are organized in some way. You can usually figure it out by looking for clues to transitions, emphasis on major points, numbered sequences, and conclusions.

Of course, being well prepared will help you figure out and follow organization. If you know the subject at all, you will have some idea of what *should* come next. Try to anticipate. Then, when the idea comes at you, you will increase your learning and understanding because you have heard it twice.

Some speakers are totally disorganized. They are difficult to listen to because they don't seem to know where they are going, let alone how their audience will get there with them. Preparation is especially helpful in this situation. And often the best you can do is to attempt to identify major concepts and the evidence and examples that support them. Then try to sort it all out later.

6. **L**isten to the whole presentation. It's surprising how quickly we decide that speakers or their ideas are silly. And we spend the rest of the time devising counterarguments or embarrassing questions. But the speech goes on. And you can miss the very statement that answers your question or objection. When that happens, you, not the speaker, will be embarrassed. Listen to the whole thing, be sure you understand it, *then* evaluate and judge what you have heard. Above all, avoid repeated interruptions. They will distract others and harass the speaker. No one will be able to evaluate the presentation, because no one will have heard enough of it to make sense of what has been said. What is even worse, your hostility may make others see you as the "bad guy," and you will generate a lot of sympathy for the speaker.

7. **P**ractice listening to difficult material. Most poor listeners are ineffective because they spend most of their time listening to material that

is too easy. When they encounter a subject or presentation that is difficult, they simply collapse. Because they collapsed once, and assume that they will collapse again, they avoid any listening experience that appears as though it might be difficult. So they never improve.

You can learn to listen effectively to difficult subjects. It takes practice and an extra effort to prepare. Good listeners are no smarter than the rest of us; they are simply better prepared and more experienced.

You can practice in almost any situation, even while watching television or listening to the radio. All you need to do is select something more difficult than the most popular soap opera or comedy. Look for documentaries, science programs, business analyses, and other programs that will be demanding. Tape record them while you watch or listen. Then try to list the program's major concepts and some of the examples and evidence that it offered in support of these concepts. If you can, try to reproduce the organization that the presentation used. Then listen to the tape and check your own reconstruction.

In the office you can practice in teams. If several people attend the same meeting, arrange ahead of time for all of them to take notes or practice listening. Meet afterwards and compare your results. See if you can reconstruct what was said, or have each person prepare a summary, and then compare your summaries. If you work at this consistently and conscientiously, you will learn from others and also improve your own ability to listen.

Listening in Small Groups

Listening in one-on-one situations, or in small groups, is somewhat different from being part of a larger audience. Participants are closer together and more visible to each other, and this proximity may require different behaviors than listening to large presentations does.

1. Try to control your nonverbal behaviors. They are much more noticeable in small groups, and they will affect the quality of the meeting. If you constantly look out the window, avoid looking directly at others, or fiddle with the papers on your desk, you will give the impression that you are not interested or that you don't care about the speaker or the subject. This can quickly destroy any presentation.

   You can encourage others to talk and explain themselves if you adopt an attentive posture, maintain eye contact, and try to give encouraging nods once in a while.
2. Ask questions that extend and clarify what someone has said, rather than attack it. Phrase your questions so that

they sound like questions rather than challenges. And wait for a reply.

3. It often helps to restate what you think someone has said before you state your own question or position. This will show the others that you understand what has been said and that you are not simply asserting your own position or objecting because of a misconception. Also, doing this will force you to plan your own statement or question carefully, so that others will understand you. If the presentation has been long or complex, restating the point you want to address will help others identify the part that you are referring to.

Summary

Speaking and listening are skills, like writing, that improve with conscientious practice. They require the same preparation, planning, organizing, and rehearsal as writing. Just as you write several drafts before you achieve a final product, you should practice an oral report several times before you must give it to others. Remember that the spoken word is ephemeral; it goes by so fast that we hardly notice it. And there are rarely second chances, for us or for our listeners. Speakers and listeners need to be aware of this if they want to be effective.

■

Exercises: Chapter Fifteen

1. While you are in class or in a meeting take some time to watch the listeners instead of the speaker. Can you identify those who are daydreaming? What are they doing? Can you always tell if people are really paying attention? Try to identify and describe those behaviors which encourage or interfere with the speaker.

2. As you attend classes or meetings pay special attention to speakers' behaviors and other features (dress, gestures, posture, and facial expression) that help or interfere with your listening. Then write a brief set of instructions which will tell speakers what to avoid and what to do when they speak.

3. Make a tape recording of a class, meeting, or television or radio program that has moderately difficult content. After the presentation write a brief summary of what you heard (no more than 500 words), and then review the recording to see how much of the presentation you were able to remember.

4. What biases or other barriers are you likely to encounter in the following situations?
   a. A teacher listening to your explanation of why you have just missed three classes in a row
   b. Members of a labor union listening to an explanation of why wage and benefit concessions are necessary
   c. A group of executives listening to a presentation about the advantages of organized labor in their businesses
   d. A group of women listening to an explanation of the reasons that their hourly wages or salaries are 20 percent lower than those for men who perform the same work

5. Your boss noticed that meetings have been dragging recently and that they have not been especially productive. You have been asked to prepare a brief talk for executives at all levels on the subject of how to run a productive meeting. Research this topic and prepare the talk.

6. Select a specialized or technical subject from your major field (or from some subject that interests you) and prepare both a five-minute oral presentation that explains this subject and a five-item quiz that you think will determine whether your listeners paid attention to you. Give the talk in a small group in class and then have each member complete the quiz.

7. Select a process or procedure that you know how to do and prepare a talk that will teach that process to other members of your class. When you are finished, allow time for your listeners to ask questions, then ask them questions to determine whether they have learned what you are teaching.

8. Assume that you are interviewing for a job as a field sales representative. Choose a product that you might have to sell in such a job and prepare a five-minute sales presentation for it. Assume that the interviewer has simply handed you the product and given you five minutes to develop your talk. The presentation is one test of your suitability for the job.

■

Part 4

Your Search for Employment

16

Planning Your Job Campaign

It is as important to know how to look for a job and what to look for in a job, as it is to know how to do the job once you are hired. The books and articles about how to find a job would fill a small library, and this chapter will not attempt to duplicate them. Rather, it will provide you with an overview of the process and a way of getting started. You will find some of the best books about job hunting listed in Appendix D. Once you know what you need to do, you can turn to them for additional help. For now, we will concentrate on:

1. Getting help from others
2. Helping yourself
3. The steps in a job campaign

Getting Help from Others

There is no need to conduct a job search alone and isolated from the rest of the world. Help is available to you at almost every step, and you should take advantage of it whenever you can. But keep in mind that much of this help is for sale.

Reading and Research

One of the best ways to begin a job search is to find out how others have done it. There are hundreds of books and articles about getting a job. Some of these are by former job seekers who were successful and want to pass on the good word. Others are by professionals whose business is showing others how to find work. Some of these are excellent resources, and others are not. At the beginning you should spend your time with the best, so start with these:

Richard N. Bolles, *What Color Is Your Parachute?* Berkeley, California, Ten Speed Press, updated each year in March.

Richard K. Irish, *Go Hire Yourself an Employer,* Garden City, New York, revised Anchor Press edition, 1978.

Richard Lathrop, *Who's Hiring Who,* Berkeley, California, Ten Speed Press, 1977.

The first of these contains extensive bibliographies. If you read everything listed there you will be busy well into the next century and never have to go to work. If you need to get on with finding a job you will have to do more than read. But the time you spend in research is usually time well-spent. Browse through Bolles's bibliographies and read anything that seems helpful.

Employment and Placement Services

Employment and placement services are another source of help and information, and they come in several varieties. If you are attending a college or university (or did at one time), there should be a career planning or placement office on campus. It could go by one of several names, so you may have to look around for it. These offices do not usually *place* you in a job. They simply provide a place for you and potential employers to meet. The best ones encourage companies to come to campus to interview qualified students.

Placement offices will also usually keep a file of your transcripts and letters of recommendation and send this file to employers when you ask them to. They may also provide counseling about vocational choices and career opportunities. It is worth a visit to find out what your placement office can do for you and to see what information is available there. Do this early in your search; it may save you time.

There are a number of government and private employment agencies and services. These range from services that simply list jobs that they know are available to sophisticated agencies which will do an excellent job of escorting you through your entire employment campaign. Use, or at least look into, as many different ones as you can. And always remember this: government employees are paid whether they place you in a job or not. Private agencies are paid for filling jobs. In either case there may be little motivation to match you carefully with a job you want and can do. And, since private agencies collect fees, you should always know who is paying. Some employers will pay the fee; when they do not, the agency will expect you to pay it, probably as soon as you take the job.

If you decide to use an employment service or agency, find out exactly which services each one offers and what it will agree to do for you. Talk to former clients and ask their opinion of the services they received. Before you sign a contract, read it very carefully.

Finding People Who Can Help

There are many people who can help you. They include others who are also looking for jobs, as well as those who are already employed. Look for these people and ask them to help you. You may be surprised at how often they will.

You probably know at least one other person who is looking for a job at the same time that you are. Perhaps there are several. Find them and ask if they are willing to pool their talents and information. You can all meet once a week while you look for a job, and such a group can be a valuable source of support and information. You will probably not compete directly with each other for the same jobs, so there is no harm in exchanging information about jobs and companies. What may be of no value to one person may be just what someone else has been looking for.

Such a group can also provide its members important emotional support during a job search. Everyone in the group will have experienced the same frustration and feelings of rejection. You can help each other deal with these feelings, and in doing so you will also help each other present a more positive, confident image to the rest of the world. There is tremendous value in knowing that someone else has been looking for a job as long as you have, and has had many of the same experiences.

Develop contacts whenever and wherever you can. These will usually be people who are already working. In fact, many of them may be in positions of authority and influence. They are valuable sources of information. Because they know people who are hiring, and may even do it themselves, they will be able to tell you what businesses are looking for. And they can help you present your skills and focus your search. Some will be able to provide leads about where to look for jobs, or about jobs that are actually available.

You might be surprised at how many contacts you have. They will include former employers, teachers, alumni of your college or university, family friends, and former classmates who are now working. Most of these people will be willing to talk with you, especially if you can show that you are interested in learning about their businesses and that you know what you are doing in your job search. When you call them, explain that you would like fifteen minutes, half an hour at the most, to talk about jobs and careers. Make it clear that you are seeking information rather than a job. Be on time for your appointment, be prepared with specific questions, and leave when your time is up.

Whenever you visit businesspeople in the office, be sure that you are well-dressed and carefully groomed. It is important to look and act like a serious job seeker. Contacts may want to refer you to someone else who can help, and you want to look like someone they won't be embarrassed to be associated with. When someone gives you time or help, always write a brief "thank you" note afterward to express your appreciation.

Helping Yourself

You can divide your job search into the following four stages:

1. Learning about yourself
2. Learning about jobs and careers
3. Learning about companies
4. Presenting yourself to employers

In each of these stages you will benefit from the help you receive from others. But the most valuable help you receive may be from yourself. Too many people approach a job search quite casually, as though it were a spectator sport. They watch classified advertisements, send out an occasional resume, and expect placement counselors and contacts to do most of the work for them. They spend much of their time "waiting for something to come along" or hoping they will "get lucky." If these people get jobs, it will probably be by accident. And the jobs they get are likely to be much like the ones they leave. These people are allowing others to make decisions about their future.

No one has as much of a stake in your future as you do. And you can control your future only if you are actively involved in making decisions about it. This means being a participant in your job search, not an observer. If you are serious about finding a job, you will do something about it every day. There is always something to do, and many of the tasks are the kind that you can fit into the odd half-hour that you don't know what else to do with.

In a well-conducted job search almost everything you do will help to prepare you for those important few minutes that you spend with a potential employer in an interview. The knowledge and skills you acquire while looking for a job will stay with you after you are hired, and they may help you do your job.

Learning about Yourself

Most of us think we know ourselves pretty well. At times, however, it is useful to stop and look at ourselves carefully to find out what we really know. This is especially important if you are about to finish school and enter your career, because for most people that is an entirely new context in which to see themselves. As you do this, you will want to find out:

1. What you want for a work situation and lifestyle
2. What you want to do
3. What you can do

What kind of life do you want? A thoughtful answer to this question will influence the kinds of jobs you look for and the companies you approach. Your job is a major part of your life and affects almost everything you do. Rather than being satisfied with a vague, all-purpose goal statement, try to answer the following questions. You may be surprised at the person you find.

1. Where do you want to live? A large city? A small town? A specific place? Why?
2. Do you want to travel as part of your job? How often? How much is too much? Talk with people who travel and ask them about the advantages and disadvantages of being on the road.
3. Do you like to work alone or as part of a team or group?
4. Do you want to be independent, or do you work best when you have support, direction, and structure?
5. Do you want to work for a big company or a small one? Talk to people to learn the advantages and disadvantages of both.
6. Do you want a job you can leave behind at 5:00 P.M., or are you willing to work evenings and weekends?

7. Do you want to work for a high-status company, or will you be more comfortable in smaller, less intense surroundings?
8. What sacrifices will you make to get what you want? Will you trade a family life for money and success? Are you willing to live with high stress and intense competition?
9. Describe what you think would be the ideal job for you.
10. What is the worst job you could have?
11. What do you see yourself doing in five or ten years? What will your life be like? What kind of job will you have?
12. Once you have answered question 11, describe in some detail how you will accomplish the goals that you stated there. That is, how will you get where you think you are going?

Of course, the answers you give to these questions now may not be the same answers you will give in five years. But they are a place to start. The idea here is to start you thinking about the future, what you want to do with it, and how you will get where you want to go. These questions are merely a way of getting you to think about yourself in a way that you may not have attempted before. If you have trouble with them, or want more, then you probably need help in the form of more reading or some employment counseling.

What do you want to do? You began to answer this question when you described your ideal job. But for now try to concentrate on what you want to *do* (all day, all week), rather than on the kind of job you think you want. Again, you can begin to learn this about yourself by answering a series of questions. There are no right answers to these questions, and there is every reason to answer them as honestly as you can. No one but you will see your answers, and the only person you will fool will be yourself.

If you could control the way you spend your days, what would you do? Go ahead, fantasize a bit. It won't hurt, and you may learn something important. What would your typical day be like? Would you sleep until noon, have a leisurely lunch, swim and play tennis, have dinner at eight, and party until four? If so, then say so. You need to begin somewhere. Then, rather than dismiss that fantasy as unreachable, try to visualize what a life like that would be like. Would you get tired of it? Could you take it as a steady diet? Would you find yourself wanting to do something else? What would that be?

As you answer the following questions, try to draw information from your whole life, not just the jobs you have had. Consider your hobbies, civic and school activities, the things you do at home, and anything else that wants to work its way into your answers. These questions may lead you to other questions that are not here. Ask and answer them as completely and honestly as you can. The goal is to get as complete a picture as you can of your preferences: What do you really enjoy and find satisfying?

1. List and describe your biggest successes. These need not be earth-shaking, but they will all be important to you.
2. List and describe the ten most enjoyable experiences you have had.
3. Of the things you have done in your life, which ones would you most like to do again?
4. Of the things you have done, which ones do you *never* want to do again? Why?
5. Of all the things that you have never done, which ones would you most like to try? Explain why.
6. Have you ever failed at something? What? Why?
7. Make a list of the things that bore you.

Where does all of this lead? It is an attempt to get you to identify what you enjoy doing and what you want to avoid. It is based on the notion that you should look for a job in which you can do what you enjoy and are successful at. But first you have to know what those things are. Later, when you look closely at what you must actually *do* in a job or career, you will be able to evaluate that job according to whether you actually want to do what is required. If you discover that you do not like to spend long hours at your desk, you might want to avoid jobs which require you to do that.

These questions can also lead you to look for jobs in unlikely places. Perhaps you have discovered that you really enjoyed working in theater while you were in school, but rejected the risks of working in professional theater. Now you are majoring in management. The two seem worlds apart, but entertainment and the arts need managers as much as the rest of the world. You could look for a job in arts management, with a theater, arts council, film company, or other kind of entertainment business. If you enjoy traveling and staying in hotels you might consider hotel management or the travel industry. There are many other ways to combine your career with what you enjoy, but first you have to find out what that is.

What can you do? Almost every employer will ask you some form of this question. Too many people answer with *tasks* which are specific to one job rather than with *skills* which they can use in any job. Right now, before you go any further, you need to find out what skills you have, the different kinds of jobs they fit into, and the skills you will need if you are to get the job you want. Once you have done that, you can compare your skills with what you want to do. Then you will either adapt what you want to do to the skills you possess, or you will set out to acquire the skills you will need to do what you want.

In either case you will need to know something about skills: What are they and which ones do you have? How can you show that the skills you have will transfer to the job you want? If you have worked in grocery stores, gas stations, and restaurants, but you want to be the marketing director for a large corporation someday, there are few tasks that will transfer from the jobs you have had to the one you want. But both jobs have skills in common, so you can show how the skills you learned in one job will apply to the other.

The U.S. Department of Labor has developed a convenient, easy-to-use method for examining your skills. You can find this in the *Dictionary of Occupational Titles,* 4th edition, 1977, on pages 1369 to 1371. It is based on the idea that jobs require you to work with data, people, or things, or some combination of the three.

Figure 16-1 Explanation of Data, People, and Things

Much of the information in this publication is based on the premise that every job requires a worker to function in some degree to Data, People and Things. These relationships are identified and explained below. They appear in the form of three listings arranged in each instance from the relatively simple to the complex in such a manner that each successive relationship includes those that are simpler and excludes the more complex. The identifications attached to these relationships are referred to as worker functions, and provide standard terminology for use in summarizing exactly what a worker does on the job.

A job's relationship to Data, People and Things can be expressed in terms of the lowest numbered function in each sequence. These functions taken together indicate the total level of complexity at which the worker performs. The fourth, fifth and sixth digits of the occupational code numbers reflect relationships to Data, People and Things, respectively. These digits express a job's relationship to Data, People and Things by identifying the highest appropriate function in each listing as reflected by the following table:

DATA (4th digit)	PEOPLE (5th digit)	THINGS (6th digit)
0 Synthesizing	0 Mentoring	0 Setting-Up
1 Coordinating	1 Negotiating	1 Precision Working
2 Analyzing	2 Instructing	2 Operating-Controlling
3 Compiling	3 Supervising	3 Driving-Operating
4 Computing	4 Diverting	4 Manipulating
5 Copying	5 Persuading	5 Tending
6 Comparing	6 Speaking-Signaling	6 Feeding—Offbearing
	7 Serving	7 Handling
	8 Taking Instructions—Helping	

Source: *Dictionary of Occupational Titles,* 4th ed. U.S. Department of Labor, Employment and Training Administration, 1977, pp. 1369–71

Figure 16-2 Characteristics of Data-oriented Professions

DATA: Information, knowledge, and conceptions, related to data, people, or things, obtained by observation, investigation, interpretation, visualization, and mental creation. Data are intangible and include numbers, words, symbols, ideas, concepts, and oral verbalization.

0 Synthesizing: Integrating analyses of data to discover facts and/or develop knowledge concepts or interpretations.

1 Coordinating: Determining time, place, and sequence of operations or action to be taken on the basis of analysis of data; executing determination and/or reporting on events.

2 Analyzing: Examining and evaluating data. Presenting alternative actions in relation to the evaluation is frequently involved.

3 Compiling: Gathering, collating, or classifying information about data, people, or things. Reporting and/or carrying out a prescribed action in relation to the information is frequently involved.

4 Computing: Performing arithmetic operations and reporting on and/or carrying out a prescribed action in relation to them. Does not include counting.

5 Copying: Transcribing, entering, or posting data.

6 Comparing: Judging the readily observable functional, structural, or compositional characteristics (whether similar to or divergent from obvious standards) of data, people, or things.

Source: *Dictionary of Occupational Titles,* 4th ed., U.S. Department of Labor, Employment and Training Administration, 1977, pp.1369–71

Figure 16-3 Characteristics of People-oriented Professions

PEOPLE: Human beings; also animals dealt with on an individual basis as if they were human.

0 Mentoring: Dealing with individuals in terms of their total personality in order to advise, counsel, and/or guide them with regard to problems that may be resolved by legal, scientific, clinical, spiritual, and/or other professional principles.

1 Negotiating: Exchanging ideas, information, and opinions with others to formulate policies and programs and/or arrive jointly at decisions, conclusions, or solutions.

2 Instructing: Teaching subject matter to others, or training others (including animals) through explanation, demonstration, and supervised practice; or making recommendations on the basis of technical disciplines.

3 Supervising: Determining or interpreting work procedures for a group of workers, assigning specific duties to them, maintaining harmonious relations among them, and promoting efficiency. A variety of responsibilities is involved in this function.

4 Diverting: Amusing others. (Usually accomplished through the medium of stage, screen, television, or radio.)

5 Persuading: Influencing others in favor of a product, service, or point of view.

6 Speaking-Signaling: Talking with and/or signaling people to convey or exchange information. Includes giving assignments and/or directions to helpers or assistants.

7 Serving: Attending to the needs or requests of people or animals or the expressed or implicit wishes of people. Immediate response is involved.

8 Taking Instructions—Helping: Helping applies to "non-learning" helpers. No variety of responsibility is involved in this function.

Source: *Dictionary of Occupational Titles,* 4th ed., U.S. Department of Labor, Employment and Training Administration, 1977, pp.1369–71

Figure 16-4 Characteristics of Thing-oriented Professions

THINGS: Inanimate objects as distinguished from human beings, substances or materials; machines, tools, equipment and products. A thing is tangible and has shape, form, and other physical characteristics.

0 Setting Up: Adjusting machines or equipment by replacing or altering tools, jigs, fixtures, and attachments to prepare them to perform their functions, change their performance, or restore their proper functioning if they break down. Workers who set up one or a number of machines for other workers or who set up and personally operate a variety of machines are included here.

1 Precision Working: Using body members and/or tools or work aids to work, move, guide, or place objects or materials in situations where ultimate responsibility for the attainment of standards occurs and selection of appropriate tools, objects, or materials, and the adjustment of the tool to the task require exercise of considerable judgment.

2 Operating-Controlling: Starting, stopping, controlling, and adjusting the progress of machines or equipment. Operating machines involves setting up and adjusting the machine or material(s) as the work progresses. Controlling involves observing gauges, dials, etc., and turning valves and other devices to regulate factors such as temperature, pressure, flow of liquids, speed of pumps, and reactions of materials.

3 Driving-Operating: Starting, stopping, and controlling the actions of machines or equipment for which a course must be steered, or which must be guided, in order to fabricate, process, and/or move things or people. Involves such activities as observing gages and dials; estimating distances and determining speed and direction of other objects; turning cranks and wheels; pushing or pulling gear lifts or levers. Includes such machines as cranes, conveyor systems, tractors, furnace charging machines, paving machines and hoisting machines. Excludes manually powered machines, such as handtrucks and dollies, and power assisted machines, such as electric wheelbarrows and handtrucks.

4 Manipulating: Using body members, tools, or special devices to work, move, guide, or place objects or materials. Involves some latitude for judgment with regard to precision attained and selecting appropriate tool, object, or material, although this is readily manifest.

5 Tending: Starting, stopping, and observing the functioning of machines and equipment. Involves adjusting materials or controls of the machine, such as changing guides, adjusting timers and temperature gauges, turning valves to allow flow of materials, and flipping switches in response to lights. Little judgment is involved in making these adjustments.

(continued)

(continued)

6 Feeding-Offbearing: Inserting, throwing, dumping, or placing materials in or removing them from machines or equipment which are automatic or tended or operated by other workers.

7 Handling: Using body members, handtools, and/or special devices to work, move or carry objects or materials. Involves little or no latitude for judgment with regard to attainment of standards or in selecting appropriate tool, object, or material.

Source: *Dictionary of Occupational Titles,* 4th ed., U.S. Department of Labor, Employment and Training Administration, 1977, pp. 1369–71

As you can see in the excerpts from the *Dictionary of Occupational Titles,* little attention is paid to specific jobs. Rather, in Figure 16-1 you see three lists of skills which are common to a great many jobs, and these skills are explained briefly in Figure 16-2, Figure16-3, and Figure 16-4. As you move from the top to the bottom of each list, the skills become less complex. You need to know less and have less experience to perform at the lower skill levels. Rather than concentrate on the *tasks* you have performed, examine your experience to find the highest skill level that you can legitimately claim in each list.

Perhaps you have worked in a supermarket where you supervised several employees, made out work schedules, kept track of inventory, and helped unload trucks and stock shelves. What skill levels were involved in these tasks? Clearly you supervised, and as part of that job you may have occasionally negotiated disagreements among those you supervised. It is also likely that you instructed, since you probably trained new employees. Making out work schedules and keeping track of inventory required you to coordinate, compare, and perhaps analyze data. Unloading and stocking required a relatively low skill level: handling and feeding.

Once you have finished a complete inventory of your skills, you should be able to talk about what you can do in a way that is not tied to the specific jobs or tasks that you have done. Remember, it is the skills, not the tasks, which you will attempt to transfer or apply to another job.

Of course, there is reason to be cautious in doing the transfer. The *Dictionary of Occupational Titles* gives each occupation a code, and part of that code is the skill level required with Data, People, and Things. If you look closely, you will discover that an auditor (code 160.162-014) and an executive chef (code 187.162-010) require almost exactly the same skill levels with data, people, and things. But this does not mean that either one can do the other's job. Thus, to your inventory of skills you must also add the training, knowledge, and experience that apply to the job you want. Together, these are the evidence that you can do that job.

Learning about Jobs and Careers

Once you get a job, just what will you do all day? Do studying, taking tests, writing papers, doing homework, and giving in-class presentations have anything to do with what you will do on the job? In many cases the answer is no. Too many people have finished degrees and even found jobs, only to discover that they have no interest in the tasks their jobs require. To prevent this from happening to you, it makes perfect sense to look closely at the kinds of jobs you are headed for.

You are looking for several kinds of information, and I am sure you can add to this list:

1. What will you do all day? What is the job like?
2. Do occupations have typical career patterns? Do accountants, for example, remain accountants, or can they move into management or something else?
3. What are the opportunities for growth and advancement within an occupation?
4. What does the future look like for the career you are considering? Is it overcrowded? Is it becoming obsolete?
5. Are there cycles of "boom and bust" in your chosen career? If so, you could be in for periods of unemployment.
6. Is your career tied to a particular industry? If so, you link your fortunes to that industry. When the U.S. space program was reduced in the 1970s many engineers were out of work.

There are numerous sources for information about jobs. You can learn a good deal by carefully combing the *Business Periodicals Index* for articles about the job or career or industry you are interested in. Teachers and contacts can give you first-hand information. Best of all, you can learn for yourself. One way to do that is to look for a part-time job in your career field while you are still in school. Or take advantage of internship programs offered by your college or university. You will work with experienced professionals and you will receive both valuable experience and some foretaste of what a job is actually like.

If you can find neither a job nor an internship, try to find people in your chosen career who will let you spend a day or a week with them. You can watch what they do, perhaps do some of it with them, and decide whether you would like that kind of job yourself. At the very least you should try to find people who will let you interview them about jobs and careers. Your contacts will come in handy here but, failing that, just get on the phone or write letters to those who seem likely to have the information you need. Make it clear that you want information (at least for now), prepare your questions in advance, and observe the prearranged time limits closely.

Learning about Salaries

Some of the information you need may be difficult to find: how much do jobs pay? Most companies and industries do not like to publish information about compensation. They regard it as private, confidential information which concerns only the person who receives the check. Many also realize that it may be detrimental to employee relations if everyone knows what everyone else makes. But you need to know about salaries because they are one of the important ways of comparing and evaluating job offers. And remember that salary alone is only half of the picture. You will also receive fringe benefits in the form of goods or services such as discounts, insurance, and retirement plans, among others. Salaries will tend to be relatively uniform and competitive within a given career field, type of job, and geographical area. Benefits may vary widely from one company to another.

You need to know the generally accepted salary range for the jobs you are applying for so that you can make an informed decision about a job offer. If a company says that it expects high-quality performance and that it recruits only among the best available candidates, you are right to be suspicious of a salary offer that is at or below the bottom of the recognized range. But you can recognize that, and negotiate, only if you know the range.

Any salary figure is related to how much it will purchase in the area where you will live if you take the job. The cost of living varies from one place to another, and this usually affects salaries. Two quite different salaries may have the same purchasing power because of the cost of living where the companies are located. Salaries in major urban areas may seem unusually high, even well above the top of the range. But the cost of living in those areas may reduce that high salary to the same purchasing power as those at the bottom of the range.

As you narrow your search to a few companies and locations it will be worth your time to investigate the cost of living in those locations and even to construct a tentative budget to estimate your expenses. Read local newspapers and call apartment managers and others to check the costs of housing, utilities, food, taxes, and the other essentials of life. As you do this, keep in mind that after taxes and deductions for your share of fringe benefits a salary of $14,000 may leave you with a cash flow of $9000 or $10,000 per year.

Evaluating Fringe Benefits

Fringe benefits present a research and evaluation problem that is quite different from the one posed by salaries. Salaries and salary ranges are reasonably uniform, and comparisons with the cost of living (which is always an average figure) can be fairly straightforward. Fringe benefits are more complex, and you may have to wait until a job interview to get the information you need. But it is worthwhile to be prepared to ask intelligent questions. Benefits are an important part of your total compensation, and they can affect your purchasing power in significant ways.

Benefits can include medical insurance, dental insurance, life insurance, a prescription drug plan, a vision care plan, disability insurance, a retirement plan, and profit sharing. Some companies may offer benefits which only they can provide. For example, airline employees receive free air travel.

The important information you need about fringe benefits includes which ones are available and whether, and how much, you must contribute to their cost. Your contributions will, of course, reduce your salary. But that is less of a problem than not having the benefits at all, especially essential ones. If medical insurance is not available, for example, you will need to provide it for yourself. Doing this will cost significantly more than you or the company would have paid through a group plan.

Do some research. Check the standard sources of business information and learn something about benefits. Ask people who are employed to explain their benefits to you. Go to an interview prepared to ask intelligent questions about benefits, and there is no need to be timid about asking for this information. Doing so will show that you are informed and motivated.

Finding Out about Companies

Once you have decided what you want to do and assessed what you can do, you will need to locate companies and organizations which might hire a person with your interests and qualifications. After you identify the companies you will apply to, you should try to learn as much as you can about each one.

Begin your search in the standard corporation reference guides, such as:

> Dun and Bradstreet, *Million Dollar Directory,* an annual publication that lists products, officers, annual sales, and the number of employees for corporations with assets of one million dollars or more
>
> Standard and Poors *Register of Corporations, Directors and Executives*

These guides will give you information about the range of companies, as well as some very specific information about each one. For more up-to-date information about which companies may be hiring and the kinds of employees they are looking for, you can consult the *College Placement Annual,* which is usually available in campus placement offices and many libraries. If you know the general business sector you want to work in, you can find out more about it, and the companies involved in it, by consulting the *Encyclopedia of Associations,* edited by Denise S. Akey and published by the Gale Research Company. This will tell you whether there is a trade association for the industry you are looking for, and you can then write or call that group to see if it can provide the information you want. You can usually get a limited amount of information from corporation annual reports. But remember that these are public relations documents for stockholders and are not always designed to inform.

More general information may be available in newspapers and periodicals, so you might consult the *Business Periodicals Index* and national or regional newspapers which have indexes. Unindexed newspapers are rarely worth the time or effort required to consult them.

What is the point of this research? Learning about individual companies can help you in a number of ways.

1. The more you know about a company, the better able you are to decide whether it is a likely employment prospect.
2. You will be able to conduct intelligent conversations and interviews with people who have information you need or jobs you want.
3. You will learn what companies do, and need, so you will be more capable of showing potential employers how your skills will adapt to their needs.
4. You will show your value as a potential employee by demonstrating that you have the ability and initiative to learn on your own.
5. When you receive job offers you will be able to evaluate them intelligently because you will know about individual companies and their competitors.

In short, your knowledge will help you conduct an effective job search and make the best possible impression on potential employers. If you can answer the following questions you will be an impressive job applicant for any company.

1. What does the company do?
2. How successful is it?
3. Who are its competitors?
4. What major problems does it have now?
5. What is it doing to solve those problems?
6. What problems may develop in the future?
7. How big is the company?
8. How vulnerable is it to economic conditions?
9. Is it expanding?
10. Are its markets or products changing?
11. Is it about to be bought or sold?
12. What is its corporate image?
13. Does it have an identifiable management style?

14. Does it promote from within?
15. How long do employees stay with it?
16. Do people like to work there?

You will surely be able to think of more questions to ask and answer, but these will get you started. Your knowledge will give you some idea of how you will fit into a company and how to convince interviewers that you will fit.

Putting Your Knowledge to Work

Once you have completed your self-assessment and research, all that remains is to present yourself and your skills to potential employers. The usual way of doing this is to send a resume and application letter in response to job advertisements or to those companies you would like to work for. The next two chapters will show you how to prepare these, so we will not dwell on them here. But remember that there are other methods of making that initial contact. If you have done a thorough research job you have no doubt developed contacts along the way. It is perfectly acceptable to get in touch with them again, in person or with an application letter, and make it clear that you are now looking for a job. They may be able to help. If you want to expand this method of information interviewing into a full-scale job search, you should read Richard Bolles's book *What Color Is Your Parachute?* You should read it anyway.

The immediate goal of your application letter and resume, or any other method of initial contact, is to secure an interview with a company that is actually hiring and considers you a strong applicant. Once you reach the interview, your prospects will stand or fall on how well you present yourself.

The Employment Interview

Interviews make people nervous when they are either inexperienced or unprepared. The worst way to approach any interview is to go in cold, not knowing what is likely to happen or how you will respond to it. All of the research you have done so far in your job search will help you in an interview, but you can give yourself an edge by doing just a little more.

Prepare ahead of time. No two interviews are alike, but thorough preparation will help you anticipate and respond to most of what can happen. It is obvious that someone will ask you questions, so why not prepare some answers? Skilled interviewers will construct their questions carefully and they will expect thoughtful answers. The following questions may not be exactly the ones you will encounter, but they are typical of the kinds of questions you may be asked.

What is your career goal?

What do you see yourself doing in five years?

Describe your most successful experience.

Describe one of your most glaring failures.

Why do you want to work for us?

What do you like best about this company?

What do you think this company should be doing right now?

Why did you major in _______________ ?

Describe your experience with this kind of work.

What makes you think you can do this job?

These questions are designed to let an interviewer see what you know, how well you think on your feet, and how well you handle yourself around other people. They require answers that go beyond yes and no. Effective interviewers will try to draw you out and give you an opportunity to present yourself as favorably as possible. Try not to disappoint them.

Unfortunately, some interviewers are not skilled. They do not plan questions carefully, and you may find that you are giving short, uninformative answers, even yes and no answers, which are doing you no good. When this happens the interview usually slows to a crawl. There are long silences and both of you seem to have lost interest. It is up to you to salvage this situation, because an unskilled interviewer will not know how to do it for you. In this situation you need to assume that the interviewer is really asking intelligent, planned questions, and give the answers you prepared for the skilled interviewer. It really is not difficult to do. Simply be careful that your answers are in some way related to the questions.

Sometimes you will be asked to respond to specific work related situations or problems, like cases you might find in textbooks. The questions take on the tone of "What would you do if . . . ?" Or you may even be asked quite specific questions about the company itself and its products or competitors. It is impossible to know in advance just what will happen. The more you know about a company, and about business and your career in general, the better you will be able to respond.

If you do prepare answers in advance, try to give them spontaneously so that you don't seem to be reciting something that you memorized. And be careful that you do not monopolize the conversation. Give a concise reply and then turn the conversation back to the interviewer. The most inconspicuous way of doing this is with a question. When you ask a question, it demands an answer. The other person must talk to you.

Fortunately, interviews are opportunities for you to ask questions. Interviewers expect you to. They will probably evaluate you as much by the quality of your questions as by the answers you give to their questions. If you have done your research carefully, you should have no difficulty planning the questions you want to ask. Try to focus on important issues that will help you get a clear idea of what the job involves, where it fits in the company, and the situation you would be working in. Ask about salary, fringe benefits, vacations, and even retirement, but try not to make these the central issues. Ideally, at the end of an interview you and the interviewer should know as much as you want and need to know about each other.

Interviews are the appropriate place to talk about salary. In fact, as a matter of honesty and courtesy the interviewer should give you a salary or a salary range without making you fish around for it. But you may have to ask, for sometimes there is a pointless game to see who will give in and mention a specific salary first. If interviewers want to play this game, there is no reason to disappoint them. But you need to be prepared. You need to know the range ahead of time. When the interviewer asks you how much money you expect, you can respond by asking how much the company is prepared to offer. If the interviewer presses you, say that you expect any salary offer would be competitive with what other companies are offering. Or, you can come right out and ask.

If you lose this game and have to name a salary, give a range. Be sure that your range is smaller than the usual range, and at its high end. If the usual range is from $13,000 to $15,000, you could say that you expect something between $14,500 and $15,000. And make it clear that you know what the competitive range is, that you are not simply pulling a figure out of the air.

When you leave an interview you will probably not know whether you will be offered the job. In fact, the interviewer may not have the authority to make that decision. But you do have every right to know when the decision will be made, so ask.

One of the most effective ways you can prepare for an interview is to practice. The best way to practice is to interview as often as you can, until you feel confident that you can handle anything that happens. Placement offices often have interviewers on campus every day, and you may find that they are not busy every hour that they are available. When you see that interviewers have open hours, you can schedule yourself even if you are not really interested in the job. Of course, you will have to be sure that the company is interested in people with your qualifications, or else the interviewer will have no reason to talk with you. If the company is looking for marketing majors and your field is medical records, the interview will end very quickly. So be reasonable when you schedule what you know will be a practice interview for you.

Even if you are not interested in the job you are interviewing for, take the interview itself seriously. Prepare in advance, dress appropriately, and give the best interview you can muster. Anything less than that is not worth your effort. Remember, the idea is to get experience under real conditions.

In time, you will begin to feel more confident and you will begin to handle yourself professionally. When you get to an interview for a job that you really want, you will be prepared for whatever might happen.

Summary

The decision to look for a job, or accept a job, is one of the most important you will ever make. Searching for a job can be time-consuming, difficult, and frustrating. In fact, it may be harder work than the job itself. In the course of your search you will learn about yourself, about jobs and careers, and about companies. All of this takes time. Begin your search early, long before you actually need a job. Get help when you need it. There is no such thing as being nobly unemployed. Above all, keep at it. Do something every day. Learn something every day. Use your lunch hours, evenings, and weekends. If you are really serious about finding the right job, the odds are in your favor.

■

Exercises: Chapter Sixteen

1. Use the *College Placement Annual* and standard business reference manuals to identify at least twenty companies and organizations that employ people who have your skills. List each one on a separate index card so you will have the start of a filing system. Be sure you include at least the following information on each card:

   The company's address and phone number
   Number and locations of branches, factories, etc.
   Number of employees
   Principal products and services
   Assets and annual sales
   Growth during the past five to ten years
   Hiring policies, if stated
   Qualifications wanted
   Salaries or salary ranges being offered

2. Using whatever sources of information you can find, try to identify the average annual starting salary and salary range for someone with your qualifications. Keep track of your sources for this information.

3. In this chapter there are several series of questions about yourself, the job you want to do, and your future. If you have not answered these questions, do so now. Write your answers and be as detailed as you can.

4. Using the questions an interviewer is likely to ask you, prepare answers which you believe will satisfy an interviewer. Then trade your answers with someone else and evaluate each others' responses.

5. Contact someone who has a job like the one you think you want. Explain who you are and why you are calling and try to arrange to spend some time with this person at work. After your visit, write an explanation of the differences between what you found and what you expected to find. What did you learn that you did not know earlier?

6. Contact a personnel manager for a local company. Explain that you are not yet looking for a job, but that you will be within the next several years. Explain that to prepare for your job search you would like to visit him in his office and interview him about what job applicants can do to increase their chances for success. Plan your interview carefully, conduct it, and then report the results to your class, either in a written report or an oral presentation.

7. Locate someone who is several years older than you and already working in his or her career. Ask if you may visit this person, preferably at work, and conduct a brief interview about searching for a job. Try to include at least the following topics in your talk:
   a. How did he or she conduct his or her job search?
   b. In retrospect, what would he or she do differently?
   c. Now that he or she is employed, has his or her opinion about what makes a successful job applicant changed?
   d. In retrospect, what would he or she do differently?
   e. How did he or she choose between job offers?
   f. Was he or she able to negotiate on the issue of salary? How is that done?

8. Use the *Dictionary of Occupational Titles* and its skills hierarchy to determine the skill levels you need for the job you want, and the skill levels you can honestly claim in the categories of data, people, and things. For each skill level that you think you have, list the specific work experience where you acquired it and a brief description of what you did.

9. Investigate the job or career you have chosen (or the one you think you are interested in). What is the outlook for this career in the future? Will there continue to be employment opportunities? What are the opportunities now? How many different kinds of jobs exist within this career field? Are there technological developments in process

which will change the nature of this career? What is the average entry-level salary in this career, compared to other entry-level salaries?

10. Select three cities where there are employment opportunities for you, or where you would like to live. From newspapers and other sources gather as much information as you can about each one. Pay particular attention to such things as the cost of living, the cost of housing, means and costs of transportation, taxes, and social and cultural atmosphere. You might also want to check such things as the quality and availability of entertainment, access by air or train, average age of the population, and average income by household. Once you have finished your research, prepare graphs and charts which compare the three places and then write a brief report in which you assess the advantages and disadvantages of living in each city.

■

17

Building Your Resume

In Chapter 16 you learned how to identify organizations that are most likely to hire people with your qualifications. Once you have done that, you need to present yourself to these potential employers and show them how your abilities and skills fit their needs. One way of doing this is to send each one a one-page resume and a cover letter. The resume gives a brief, factual summary of your qualifications. The cover letter explains and interprets your qualifications to show how you will meet a company's needs in a specific job.

After you have read this chapter and done the exercises and activities that it asks you to do, you should know:

- What employers want from the resumes they receive
- How to find the information to include
- How to select and organize this information
- How to create an attractive format
- How to edit, proofread, and reproduce your resume

Your goal in sending a resume and cover letter is to create enough interest in your qualifications that the company will interview you for a position. Once you are face to face with the people who have the authority to hire you, the application has done its job.

If you design your resume carefully you can copy it and send it to almost all of the companies that might hire you. Your goal in this chapter is to learn how to prepare an attractive, informative, one-page resume that will serve you throughout an employment search.

Planning

Many people look at a few sample resumes and then grind out a fast replica of one that looks like it will do the job. But it pays to plan first. Planning increases the probability that you will make informed decisions about what to include and how to arrange it on the page. This, in turn, increases the likelihood that your resume will actually do what you want it to do. As you plan you need to consider:

How to identify your goals and your readers' goals

How to gather useful information

How to select the information that you will use

How to organize your resume for content and appearance

Goals

It may seem that you and your readers have the same goals: you would both like to match a person with a position. You want an interesting job that fits your qualifications and pays well. Employers want qualified, hardworking people who can help them achieve corporate goals by doing a specific job. If you look at it this way, the job search seems little more than a matter of getting your resume to the right people. And if the system actually worked this way it is likely that more people would end up in the right job. And more companies would end up with the right employees. But, you guessed it, it is not that simple.

Unless there is a radical change in the way we do hiring in this country, you are not likely to reach everyone who might have a position you are qualified for. (If you have not read *What Color Is Your Parachute?*, put it on your list for this week.) The ones you do reach will probably be the same ones that everyone else reaches. Some companies report that they receive about 250,000 resumes each year, according to Richard N. Bolles. That is almost 5000 each week. It staggers the imagination. It also staggers the people who have to do something with all that paper. They have to read it, evaluate it, and find some place to put it. Sometimes they even answer it. The employer's problem is not finding well-qualified people to fill positions. It is eliminating those who are not qualified and then choosing the best from those who remain. This has profound consequences for anyone who is sending out resumes and cover letters.

Picture your reader. It's Monday morning and there are at least 150 new resumes on the desk, all for two or three possible job openings. Yes, the company is looking for the best qualified candidate, but how will it find her or him in *that* mess? Is the right resume even there? Maybe it will come in tomorrow or next week.

What will your readers do? Read them all carefully? Go over each one twice to be sure they don't miss something important? Wade through the list of fifteen hobbies and the bad spelling and typing? It's true! Too many resumes are uninformative, poorly designed, badly typed, hideously reproduced, and full of mistakes.

What would you do? Right! You'd find some way of eliminating all but the few resumes that you were really interested in, and doing it quickly. After all, you have other jobs to do today. So you would go through that stack of paper as quickly as you could, searching for key words and phrases that tell you whether an applicant is likely to be qualified for the job that is available. You would especially look for the slightest reason for eliminating a resume, since your first goal is to reduce that stack of paper to a manageable size.

You want a good candidate for the job, but the odds are in your favor. Especially if you are filling an entry-level position, you are likely to find several, or even several dozen, who will do quite nicely. Poor typing, confusing organization, and silly mistakes can quickly land a resume in the NO pile or the wastebasket. People who read resumes assume that qualified applicants who can select appropriate information about themselves and present it in a neat, well-organized way are displaying positive personality traits and work habits. These resumes deserve a closer look, so they go back on the desk to await another elimination round. They will get a closer look next time, but the standards will go up.

Does that story sound cruel? It probably is. It may also sound extreme unless you have actually faced such a stack of resumes. However cruel or extreme it may sound to you, it happens all the time. When everything you know about a person is on a piece of paper in your hand, and that piece of paper is an example of slipshod, hastily done work, you have the right—some would say the resonsibility—to reject that application without wasting more time. If people do sloppy work on their own resumes, what kind of work will they do for the company?

The point here is not to frighten you. It *is* possible to get a job. But a badly done resume is asking to be thrown away. You may get a polite reply which says your papers will be kept on file in case something comes up. But you may hear nothing at all. At $.20 per letter (and that's only the postage), it costs $50,000 a year to reply to 250,000 resumes. Few businesses are willing or able to invest that kind of money in people they don't want to hire.

Your goal is to design a "smart" resume, one that knows how to stay out of the wastebasket. To do that you must first anticipate what your reader expects and needs, and then you must work carefully to meet those needs.

Gathering Information: What Belongs on Your Resume?

Readers expect that you will provide information in at least these four categories: (1) personal details, (2) education, (3) experience, and (4) references. Later we will discuss other kinds of information you can include, but these four are basic. The first step is to assemble all of the information that you *could* include. Then you can decide how much of it you will use. You will rarely include everything, for this is neither an autobiography nor true confessions.

The rest of this section discusses each of the four basic categories of information, and some optional ones. As you read about each one take a few minutes to list all of the information about yourself that you could use in that category. Once you have listed all that you *might* include, you will be in a better position to select what you want to use. In the process you will begin to create permanent records that you can use whenever you need to write a resume in the future.

Name and address. Don't laugh. People have forgotten this. Be sure you provide a complete Post Office or street address and a ZIP code. Include your area code and phone number.

Here's a footnote about names. Women who have worked under their maiden names should identify those jobs somewhere on their resumes. Employers may write for references, and former employers may not be aware that your name has changed. They will probably report that you never worked there, and that will not help you.

Personal information. Employers like to know more about you than your education and work experience. Perhaps it helps us to visualize someone if we know he's 5 feet 10 inches tall, weighs 165 pounds, is married, has two children, and likes to ski and read. Most of us are only too happy to provide this kind of information, since we probably tend to agree that it makes us more human than a list of college degrees and jobs. But this information can do more than make you seem human. It can be used to disqualify you from a job if an employer thinks you are too young or too old or that you ought to be married rather than single.

Title VII of the U.S. Civil Rights Act, as amended in 1972, says that employers may not ask you about information that is not related to your qualifications for a job. The purpose of the law is to prevent employers from basing their hiring decisions on matters that have nothing to do with your ability to do a particular job. For example, women who have small children at home are not to be asked what arrangements they have made for child care. Women in general cannot be asked about their plans for marriage, divorce, childbearing, or relocation if their husbands are transferred. Employers must justify their need for this kind of information and their decision to use it when they consider you for a job.

Of course, certain kinds of personal information *are* related to the job you want. If you want to be an airline pilot or police officer, you will have to pass a physical examination. If you want to be a fashion model your appearance is a legitimate part of your qualifications. But being overweight or over forty has nothing to do with your ability to perform as an accountant or production supervisor.

The Civil Rights Act does not prevent you from volunteering personal information. If you decide to do so, be as positive as possible. Avoid identifying yourself as a member of a racial, ethnic, or religious group. Say that you are *single* rather than *divorced* or *separated.* Your health, if you mention it, is *excellent.* Only a physician is qualified to say otherwise. List only those hobbies that create a positive, stable image of you. Avoid the motorcycle racing and skydiving, which might suggest that you are a high risk to the company's investment in your training and the group insurance plan. If you think you are too young or too old, then omit your age. Let them figure it out if they can.

If you decide to include personal information, you want it to show that you are a healthy, well-adjusted, normal person. Some people have solved the problem by simply eliminating this category from their resumes.

Education. Your education is central to your qualifications for almost any job. The more recent your education, the more important it will be. If you are a recent college graduate you should probably list your education very near the top of your resume. Later, when you have been out of school for some time, your work experience will become more important and may deserve being listed first.

Keep complete records of your education, including copies of transcripts, diplomas, degrees, certificates, and licenses. To organize this information for your resume you can divide it into three categories:

1. *Formal education.* In this category include all of the work that you have done in high school and college. If you have a high grade point average for your college work, you may want to list it on your resume. If it is less than outstanding, you can compute your average in courses you have taken in your major and list that.

Some employers will want to see a selected list of the courses you have taken. But don't overdo it. Your resume is not a transcript. Select those courses which you believe will help set you apart from other applicants with similar qualifications.

2. *Special qualifications.* In addition to your formal education you will probably acquire special educational qualifications. Perhaps you are a certified public accountant or plan to take that examination soon. Or you may have taken special courses or passed examinations in your profession. You may be a licensed real estate agent or broker, or a member of the College of Life Underwriters if you work in the insurance industry. Many companies offer their employees special courses as part of a continuing in-service program. If you have taken any of these, especially those offered by recognized professional groups such as the American Management Associations or others, you should include them on your list.

   These special educational experiences can set you apart from the competition. They show that you have special skills or aptitudes that you can put to work for your new employer.

3. *Other education.* You may have educational qualifications that are not directly related to the jobs you are applying for. Keep track of these. Some of them can show that you are capable of mastering difficult concepts or procedures. Perhaps in the military you learned a second language (other than the one that most people learn in the military), or were trained in a difficult subject such as cryptanalysis or electronic repairs. Maybe you worked your way through school as an ambulance attendant and are a certified Emergency Medical Technician. What seems commonplace to you may seem quite interesting to an employer, so don't dismiss these "extra" qualifications as irrelevant.

When you list your education on your resume, select items from your list according to how well they will help show that you are qualified for the position you are applying for. As a minimum, include your college degree(s) and any special certificates or licenses that you hold. Once you have provided the minimum, you should list anything else that shows your special or unusual abilities in a positive light.

People often ask whether they should list their high school diploma and associate degree. That usually depends on how long ago you received them and how much they contribute to your qualifications. Employers will generally assume that you have finished high school if you have a college degree. If you have both associate and bachelor's degrees, you probably do not need to list both. Employers might suspect that you are filling up the page by listing every degree you have. The exception to this occurs when your associate degree is in a subject that is different from your bachelor's degree major. For example, if your bachelor's degree is in marketing or accounting, an associate degree in retailing or computer science would be a useful complement. You should list combinations of this sort.

Work experience. Employers want to know where you have worked and what you have done. Your past experience is a basis for predicting what you can do now and what you will be able to do in the future. This experience includes your paid jobs, of course, both full-time and part-time. You can also include volunteer work, internships, and positions of leadership and responsibility you have held on campus or in the community. If you have spent time in the military, you should also list that.

Keep complete records of your employment, including the following information for each job:

Your employer's company name, complete address, and phone number

Your immediate supervisor's name and job title

The dates of your employment

Your title and job description

Records of transfers, promotions, and special responsibilities

Your salary history

Keep samples of your work if you can. If you do window displays for a retailer, take pictures of them. Keep copies of letters and reports that you write. You may need your employer's permission to do this, but it is worth the extra effort. Over the years you will accumulate a portfolio of your work that you can show to potential employers.

Also keep complete records of your military service. When you were discharged or separated from the military you should have received a copy of Department of Defense form 214. This is an official summary of your service, including the type of discharge you received. Keep track of this form. Some employers may want to see it.

When it is time to list your experience on a resume, you may find that there is more than you have room for. You may need to be selective, listing only the most recent or most important of your positions. Readers like to see that you can account for your time since you finished college or entered your career. They will look for extended periods of unemployment or self-employment, which many regard as the same. They will also look for a progression to positions of increasing responsibility, importance, and salary.

On the other hand, if you are now entering your career you may need to list every job you have held simply to fill up the page. Don't be embarrassed about this. A steady work record, even if it consists of part-time and temporary jobs, can be an advantage. It shows that you have ambition (or need) and that you are diligent enough to find and keep a job, often while you attended school full time. That is no mean feat, and employers will respect it.

References. References are like witnesses. They testify that you are who and what you say you are. Most employers prefer that you provide the names of three references.

Select these people carefully. This is your chance to allow others to speak for you. Show your wisdom by choosing people who can speak favorably about you and your work. Be sure they have the business, professional, or academic status to command your reader's attention and respect. If you can, be sure they express themselves well. A badly written (or spoken) recommendation, even if it praises you, can do more harm than good.

People you have worked for, professors in your major field, and others who know your work and can evaluate it are valuable references. These are the people who can tell employers that you can get to work on time, get along with others, and do the job you are being hired for. Employers also appreciate assessments of your potential to grow and advance in their organizations. Choose people who can speak directly to these issues, favorably and in detail.

There are some people you should avoid as references, even though they may look perfect for the part. Your minister, family physician, dentist, mother, fifth grade teacher, and neighbor of twenty years will not do you or your reader much good. To begin with, few of these people are in a position to comment objectively about your ability or the quality of your work. Most of them can be assumed to have a vested interest in seeing you do well. For that reason, most employers will pay little attention to what they say. It is not that they think your minister will lie. Perish the thought. Close associates might simply neglect to tell the whole truth, if they know it.

Once you have decided which people you would like to list as references, you need to *ask* them. It is common courtesy to do so, and it can also help you get a more favorable letter than you might otherwise. The person you ask is more likely to be informed about you and committed to a positive response.

When you ask someone to serve as a reference, be specific about what you want. First, ask that person if he or she would be comfortable providing you with a *favorable* reference. Make it clear that you want an honest answer to that question, and be prepared for one. If someone says no, respond with a cordial thank you, and make a graceful exit. That person has just done you a favor. It is better to have hurt feelings now than a lukewarm or negative letter in your file.

If the answer is yes, you still have work to do. Explain what you will use the reference for. Is it for a graduate school application, a specific job, or an open-ended employment search? You might even explain some of the major issues you would like this person to write about, such as your performance in a particular job or at school. It will also help if you can leave each reference a preliminary copy of your resume.

Collect letters of reference while peoples' memories of you are fresh. Employers, supervisors, and teachers see many people in a year's time. They forget. The details of your excellent performance may fade into the woodwork of crowded days and minds. People change jobs, and it is frustrating to search for people who would make excellent references only to discover that they have moved on.

Optional information. So far we have considered the four categories of information that employers will expect to find on your resume. There are other categories you can include if you have the space or if they make important statements about your qualifications.

Scholarships and awards. Have your received academic scholarships or honors, or awards for campus or civic activities? Keep a complete list of these and what you did to earn them. Awards and honors show that other people think you have done something special. Employers will pay attention to them, and you should list the most important of them on your resume.

Are you willing to relocate? Employers may have offices in several places in the United States or around the world, and they may want you to work there instead of here. If you are willing to move, say so on your resume. If you are not willing to move, it is best to say nothing at all. Why eliminate yourself early in the process? You may change your mind after you have looked at the company closely. The question will almost certainly come up in an interview, and you should be ready with an answer.

College financing. If you paid for all or part of your college education, calculate your share of the total and list it on your resume. Employers will take this as evidence of your drive and ambition. It could be an advantage.

Social and civic activities. Many companies want their employees to be active in community and civic affairs. In fact, many insist on it. You can show that you will do this by listing what you have done in the past. Include the civic and service organizations you have belonged to and the other ways you have contributed to your campus and community. Pay special attention to leadership positions that you have held in these organizations. They are another way of demonstrating your management and leadership skills.

What Does Not Belong on Your Resume?

Yes, it is possible to say too much on your resume. You can even do it innocently by providing information that employers say they want and textbooks recommend that you include. Certain kinds of information can get you eliminated or cost you money.

Career objective. Many authorities recommend that you include a statement about your career goals. It is true that you should have given this some thought. And it seems harmless to let others know what you are thinking. But remember, you want to use your resume to apply for many different jobs. The career goal you write must be compatible with all of them. After all, it is a bit silly to expect an employer to consider you for a job as a management trainee if your career goal is to be a self-employed CPA. But if you write a career goal statement general enough to cover all of the jobs you might apply for, it will probably be meaningless. All in all, it is best to omit such statements unless you can afford to be very picky.

Salary. If you have ever followed the "help wanted" classifieds in a newspaper, you have no doubt seen instructions to send resume with salary history and salary requirements. Did you even wonder why they want to know that? It is not exactly an innocent request. To put it bluntly, it's a good way of eliminating applicants who are asking too much or too little money. Most employers know the range (upper and lower limits) of the salary they are willing to pay. And most want to hire you for the lowest figure you will accept.

If your salary history shows anything but a steady increase, many readers will assume you were demoted. Also, your most recent salary is often used as a base for calculating what you will be offered in a new job. If you state the salary that you require, your figure could be too high or too low. A figure that is too high can result in your elimination right then. If it is too low, you may be rejected because you may appear to have a low self-image. Or it could cost you money.

In short, if you mention salary on your resume you may be giving up the opportunity to negotiate a figure that is significantly higher than what you now earn. The appropriate place to discuss salaries is in an interview. Before that time, if anyone wants you to put a salary requirement in writing, tell them it is "negotiable."

Date. You will see many sample resumes that show the date they were prepared. This does nothing but tell your reader how long you have been looking for a job. The longer you have been looking, the more likely it is that a reader will assume something wrong, or else someone surely would have hired you by now. Or so the reasoning goes. See how easy that was? You didn't have a chance.

Photographs. It was once common to include a small head-and-shoulders photograph of yourself on your resume. Employers liked that. They could see right away whether you were a clean-cut, attractive person who would fit their corporate image. As you might guess, many applicants were rejected because they were fat, thin, plain, black, Hispanic, or obviously "different" in some way. The Civil Rights Act has changed that. Employers do not expect photographs because they automatically reveal all (or at least too much) of the information which the law says cannot be used in employment decisions. Some employers may even refuse to consider applications that contain photographs. They correctly want to avoid even the appearance of discrimination.

Presentation: Putting Yourself on Paper

Now that you have gathered all of the information you will need for your resume, it is time to begin putting it on paper. As you do this, one of your primary considerations will be what your resume will look like when you finish it. Its appearance may be *more* important than the information it contains. If *what* you say about yourself is going to help you at all, you must first get your reader to pay attention to it. That depends on making a positive first impression, and first impressions are often visual ones. If you want to be taken seriously as a candidate for a position, your resume must look like it came from someone who should be taken seriously.

Your resume must do the same job for you that your clothes would do if you were meeting a prospective employer face to face. At first glance your reader will decide whether you are neat, well-organized, successful, and qualified. Your resume is an example of your work. Its appearance indicates how seriously you take that work and, in turn, how seriously you should be taken.

Creating a positive first impression depends on producing neat, error free copy and a visually well-organized page that looks "clean" and easy to read. Another, more subtle goal is to get your reader to read your resume all the way through, from start to finish. Readers will not necessarily do that on their own. They may want to look immediately at the category they think is most important. Some readers will start reading at the end of your resume. Experience tells them that applicants are likely to try to "hide" unflattering information there.

Guidelines for Visual Design

1. **Get it all on one page.** One page is the ideal length for most resumes. This is especially true if you are just beginning your career. You might object that one page is not enough for what you want to say. You will even find plenty of sample resumes that are longer than one page, much longer. Employment agencies and textbooks will show you samples of three- and four-page resumes and encourage you to copy them. Bigger, apparently, is better.

Most resumes that are longer than one page could be more effectively designed and edited. They say more than they need to, and often provide explanations and interpretations that would be more effective in the cover letter.

2. **Use visual blocks.** Organize your resume into visual blocks. Each block will present all of the information related to one of the categories discussed earlier in this chapter (employment, education, and so on). You might think of these blocks as paragraphs, since each one presents a single, focused body of information. But they are not as dense as paragraphs. They contain less type and more white space than conventional paragraphs. This makes them look less imposing and easier to read.

All of the blocks on your resume will have the same general shape, though they will vary in length. As you move from one block to the next you will place similar kinds of information in similar relative positions in each block. This consistency will make it easy for your reader to follow you from one block to the next.

3. **Use headings.** Identify each block with a heading that tells your reader what kind of information it will contain. By using different positions and typography you can show your reader the relative importance of each block. The more important the information, the more prominent the heading will be.

4. **O**rganize carefully. Most readers will expect you to present the blocks in the traditional sequence of personal information, education, experience, and references. Optional information fits nicely just before your references. Once you have held a number of jobs you may want to list your experience first to emphasize it.

Within each block you should list qualifications so that the most recent or most important is the first entry. This is known as *reverse chronology,* and it helps focus your reader's attention on your most recent accomplishments.

5. **U**se action phrases. Write entries in phrases rather than in complete sentences or paragraphs. Verbs and verb phrases, such as "worked as" or "supervised" will work especially well. They suggest action and show you doing a job rather than simply occupying space. This will affect the appearance of your resume. Using phrases will help you keep your entries short and concise, and should help you use space more effectively.

Building with Blocks

There are two basic patterns to follow when you construct your resume. One places information horizontally, across the page. The other displays information vertically, from top to bottom, as though it were in columns.

Figure 17-1 is an example of the horizontal display, and Figure 17-2 shows the vertical display. Examine both of them carefully, for they are the basis of almost every resume you will see. Note that in both the headings begin at the left margin and the entries in each block are indented several spaces from the margin. Indenting the entries shows clearly that they are all included under the heading and not equal to it. Both resumes are designed so that the page is full but not crowded. The white space is evenly distributed throughout the page and there are no large blocks of either type or blank paper.

In the vertical pattern the entries in each block are divided into columns, and these are carried down the page so that they are in the same place in each block. This vertical alignment is an important way of creating a neat, well-organized appearance.

In the horizontal pattern there are no columns. Instead, each entry extends across the page to the right margin and may take more than one line. All entries begin the same distance from the left margin. The first line of each entry begins closer to the left margin than do the following lines. This is called hanging indentation. It shows clearly where each entry begins.

You may need to experiment to see which of these patterns will work best for you. To find out, you can simply choose one and begin working. Do your drafts directly on a typewriter if you can. Try to use a machine that

Figure 17-1 Horizontally Aligned Resume

BRIAN P. NAPARELLO

42166 Mojave Way
Los Angeles, CA 90000
(008) 658-9000

Age: 21
U.S. Citizen
Hobbies: skiing
tennis and computers

EDUCATION

Bachelor of Science in Accounting, California State College, June, 1985, minors in Computer Science and Marketing, Overall grade point average: 3.4

Associate of Science, Computer Science, Mojave Junior College, Sand Creek, California, 1983

EXPERIENCE

Night Auditor, Happy Valley Motel, 43279 Alameda Avenue, Los Angeles, California, August 1985 to present.

Computer Operator, Kwik Data Computer Services, 435 Pomona Street, Sand Creek, California, Summers of 1983 and 1984

Student Assistant, Academic Computer Center, California State College, 1983 and 1984, during school year.

Busboy, Andrew's Restaurant, 1165 Seaside Way, Los Angeles, California, part-time, 1982

CAMPUS AND CIVIC ACTIVITIES

President, Society for the Advancement of Management, California State College Chapter, 1984 - 1985

Treasurer, Circle K, California State College Chapter, 1983 - 1984

Student Senator, Mojave Junior College, 1982 - 1983

REFERENCES

Robert P. Smith, Associate Professor of Accounting, California State College, Long Beach, California

Jean H. Brownell, Manager, Happy Valley Motel, 43279 Alameda Avenue, Los Angeles, California 91000

Alan J. Cottrell, Associate Professor of Computer Science, California State College, Long Beach, California

Figure 17-2 Vertically Aligned Resume

SUSAN J. SMITH

54 E. Seventh Street Athens, Ohio 45701 (641) 876-9087 (Until June 6, 1985)	43258 Scanlon Road Shaker Heights, Ohio (756) 889-7513 (After June 6, 1985)

EDUCATION

Bachelor of Science Industrial Technology	Ohio University Athens, Ohio	June, 1985
Associate of Science	Belmont Technical College Belmont, Ohio	June, 1983

EXPERIENCE

Metals Technician Did metallurgical analyses of stock steel and finished products.	Athens Metal Products 223 Race Street Athens, Ohio 45701	August 1983 to present
Quality Assurance Inspector Magnetic particle and ultrasonic inspection of products.	Belmont Products 501 Third Street Belmont, Ohio 46780	January 1982 to June 1983
Waitress	Wilton's 2345 E. Main St. Columbus, Ohio 43200	Summer 1981

ACTIVITIES

Secretary Handled all correspondence and records.	Industrial Technology Society Ohio University	1984-1985

REFERENCES

Will be furnished upon request.

types the same number of spaces and lines per inch as the one you will use for your final copy. This is the only way you can know exactly how much information will fit on the page.

Some people can simply look at a typed page and figure out how to reproduce it. If you are not one of them (and few of us are), try the following step-by-step suggestions. It might help to begin by drawing a line one inch from each edge of the paper. These will not appear on your final copy, but they will make it easy to see wheie the margins are while you work. You can probably count on doing at least three drafts before you are happy with the result.

Title. If you want to use a title, such as *Resume, Data Sheet,* or *Vita* (which means "life" in Latin), center it along the top of the page one space above the margin line. Some people use rather fancy titles, such as "Qualifications of John P. Jobhunter for a Position in Marketing." You can do that if you like. Or you can use your name, centered above the top margin line.

Personal information. Personal information, including your name and address, will fit neatly into the upper corners of the page, as you see in Figure 17-1 and Figure 17-2. If you think you will be moving before your employment search is over, you can indicate that under your address. Simply type *Until June 1, 1986,* and employers will know that you will not be living there after that date. You will need to give a second address and its effective date. You can do this in the upper right corner.

If you like, you can use the upper right corner for personal information. Plan this entry carefully so that it will take up the same amount of space as the address in the opposite corner. Though it may seem that there is little space for you to work with, you will find that it is more than enough. Having less space than you would like may keep you from getting carried away. If you have already used this space for an address, you can put personal information right above your references, where it will be somewhat inconspicuous.

If you are using only one address and would like to omit personal information, then center the address at the top of the page, just below the margin.

Major visual blocks. Once you have finished the upper corners you can begin to construct the blocks that present your major qualifications. The blocks are set apart from each other in two ways, and you must make these decisions first. Each one begins with a heading. These will be easier to read if you type them in mixed upper and lower case letters, instead of using all capitals. You can underline them for emphasis if you like. Blocks are also separated by the spacing between them. You should try to leave more space between blocks than you leave between headings and entries, or between entries within blocks. It will add to the overall appearance of your resume if you leave the same number of blank lines before and after each block, heading, and entry.

Once you have decided on the spacing between blocks and typed a heading, you need to consider the sequence of the information in the entries. For example, in an entry about your education you will probably list your degree, your school, and the year you graduated. The first item in each entry will receive the most emphasis, so it's a good idea to put the most important information in that position. Your degree is probably the most important fact, unless you graduated from a well-known or prestigious school. Once you have established this sequence of *what* you did, *where* you did it, and *when* you did it, the sequence will remain the same throughout your resume. That is, if you put your degree first under education, then you will list your job titles first under experience, and the offices or positions you held will be first in the entries about civic activities.

Being consistent about where you put the different kinds of information in each entry will help your reader. After the first few entries, readers will *expect* to find certain kinds of information in specific places. When you fulfill this expectation and readers find what they expect to find, you enhance the impression that your resume is carefully planned.

Once you have finished the first block, doing the rest is simply a matter of completing each block so that it has the same organization and shape as the first.

Troubleshooting. You may encounter a few problems, but they are relatively easy to solve. If you are using the vertical pattern you may discover that entries and parts of entries are of uneven lengths. This can lead to a series of related problems. If part of an entry is too wide for its column, you may decide to continue on a second line. But if you do this for several lines you may find that your resume has dense, narrow columns of type on one side of the page and large areas of blank space on the other. The page will look lopsided. You can correct this by editing the entry to make it shorter. For example:

This:
After three years as a procurement officer I moved to
quality assurance where I
supervised a group of 12
inspectors. I was respon-
sible for writing reports
to explain deficiencies and
corrections.

Becomes this:
Worked in procurement; supervised 12 quality assurance inspectors. Wrote reports to explain corrections.

Another common problem is that your resume is too long or too short when you finish it. Resist the temptation to add or delete information before you have evaluated the whole resume. You might be able to adjust its length by using wider or narrower margins. You can also adjust the horizontal spacing within blocks and the vertical spacing between blocks. Be sure that you maintain consistent spacing throughout. If you add or subtract a blank line before the first block, do the same before all of the blocks. It helps to count how many lines you need to gain or lose in the page and then calculate the changes before you begin typing. You may also need to edit some entries to make them shorter or longer.

A final check. Once you have finished a clean draft, and everything on your resume is where you think you want it, check it carefully *before* you type the final copy.

Are all the headings the same distance from the left margin?

Are all of the margins approximately the same width?

Do all the headings have consistent typography and spacing?

Are *vertical* lines consistent as you look down the page?

Are all titles and abbreviations correct and consistent?

Is everything spelled correctly?

Did you use reverse chronology?

Are all of the names, dates, and addresses correct?

After you have checked the page carefully, pin it on a wall and step back five feet. How does it look? Is the overall visual impression a balanced, pleasing one? If so, you are ready to type the final copy.

Preparing the Final Copy

You may need to make 50, 100, or more copies of your resume. To be sure you get the best reproduction possible, you will need a master copy that is flawless. If you decide to have someone else type it, ask to see samples of other work this person has done. Be sure your typist uses a type face that is attractive and businesslike. Avoid fancy or unusual ones, such as script. Be sure the machine has clean keys and that they all function properly. Why go to all of this trouble just to discover that the *o*s punch holes in the paper.

You will get the best results if the master is typed on an electric typewriter with a black carbon ribbon. Use a heavy, white bond paper.

When the master copy is finished, *proofread* it carefully. If you can, have several other people proofread it too, so that you will increase your chances of finding all typing errors. Once you are satisfied with the master, shop around for an appropriate method of reproduction. You can use photocopying, multilith, or professional printing. Avoid such methods as mimeograph and spirit duplicator (the purple "ditto" sheets you get in school). Ask to see copies of finished work and insist that copies be made on sixteen- or twenty-pound rag bond paper. The copies should look almost identical with the original. In fact, if you place a copy next to your master you should have some difficulty telling which is which.

When your copies are finished, check all of them, not just the one on top, and compare them with your master. Do not accept work unless it is up to the quality of the samples you were shown earlier. Remember, it's your money, and your future.

Resumes for Special Circumstances

In some situations you will need to design a resume that is quite different from the conventional one-page document that presents your qualifications chronologically, in traditional categories of information. In particular, you may need a special resume if:

1. You have considerable experience and find that you simply cannot confine yourself to one page and still present your qualifications in the most attractive way. This is often the case with people who are changing jobs in midcareer.
2. You are changing careers, either to a related field or one that is quite different from the one you have been working in.

The Midcareer Resume

If you are in midcareer, and want or need to change jobs, you will probably want a resume that is longer than one page. It is likely that you have enough experience and special qualifications to fill at least two pages. And it will be important to show the depth and range of your qualifications. Employers, of course, will want to see that you can account for your time since you entered the work force full time, and they will be suspicious of gaps that may indicate unemployment, illness, or other circumstances that interrupted your "career progress."

In addition, midcareer job changers have several liabilities to overcome. Perhaps the most important one is age. Of course, everyone knows that it is illegal to discriminate against applicants or employees on the basis of age. But age discrimination does occur, and it is quite difficult to prove. The second liability, related to age, is the general assumption that people in middle age have been eased out of their positions with other employers because they have overstayed their usefulness. Thus, you may need to overcome the assumption that you are too old, tired, slow, mediocre, or out-of-date. Finally, there may be some suspicion about why you are leaving a perfectly good job, one that you know, and risking the uncertainty of something new. It may be that these assumptions and liabilities reflect the low self-esteem of those who will read your resume, but you are going to have to deal with these feelings anyway.

If you are in midcareer, you should probably design a resume that is longer than one page. In fact, a one-page resume may work against you, because it may suggest that you have done no more and have no more qualifications than the typical recent college graduate. You can use the same format and design principles that you used for a one-page resume, but you should also pay attention to some special considerations.

When you design a two-page resume, you should take care that the second page (or third) does not look like an afterthought or suggest that you simply ran out of room on the first page. Design your resume so that it actually takes up two full pages. You can do this by using spacing and margins to be sure that you fill each page. You can also provide more information about each position you have had. For example, you can give partial job descriptions, expanded titles, and descriptions or lists of the duties and responsibilities you had in each job. Adding details of this sort will help you create the impression that you have acquired and used skills and abilities, rather than simply occupied space, for the past twenty years. And you very much need to show new employers that you are not just someone in need of a job, but someone who is going to be an asset to their organization. Figure 17-3 shows a conventional resume expanded to two pages to present the qualifications of someone with considerable career experience.

Resumes for People Who Are Changing Careers

Changing jobs in midcareer is one thing; changing from one career to another, in midlife or at any other time, is something else again. It is usually easier to move from one sales job to another, or one management

Figure 17-3 Two-Page Resume

THOMAS P. BURKE

1144 Avalong Lane
Titusville, Florida 31311
(914) 887-9008

U. S. Citizen
Born 9-6-40
Married

EXPERIENCE

Director of Marketing, Central Florida Advertising, 349 S. Fourth Street, Titusville, Florida, 31314

Responsible for overall development of marketing plan for commercial, industrial, and trade advertising establishment with a clientele of over 3000 businesses in a twelve county area. Annual budget totalled $4 million plus.

March 1978 to Present

Director of Retail Accounts, JRB Agency, 1178 San Marcos Blvd., Jacksonville, Florida 34511

Account executive for major retail accounts in Duval County, and supervisor of junior account executives who handled retail businesses with budgets of less than $10,000 per year. Annual client expenditure: $2.5 million.

June 1974 to March 1978

Account Executive, J. W. Tillman Agency, 346 University Avenue, Gainesville, Florida 32601

Account executive in charge of industrial and trade accounts in a three-county area. Supervised research, photography, layout and design, and reproduction. Worked closely with newspaper, regional magazine, and trade publication editors.

April 1970 to June 1974

Assistant Advertising Manager, Starke Daily Press, Starke, Florida 32785

Supervised outside sales and did all inside sales for a regional daily newspaper with a circulation of 23,000. Supervised layout, design, printing, and photography.

August 1967 to April 1970

(figure continues on next page)

Figure 17-3 Continued

Advertising Salesman, WJZZ AM, Bosworth Building, Orlando, Florida 36099

Outside and telephone sales of radio advertising time to local businesses. Sales volume in last year $500,000.

June 1965 to August 1967

Lance Corporal, United States Marine Corps

Press Information Assistant at several USMC bases in the United States and the Far East. Honorable Discharge

April 1961 to May 1965

EDUCATION

Bachelor of Science, Business Administration, University of Florida, Gainesville, Florida 32601

January 1961

AWARDS

Trade Magazine Campaign of the Year, Aerospace Trade Association, 1979

Industrial Advertising Award, Florida Chamber of Commerce, 1973

Tri-County "Best of Year" campaign, Starke, Florida Jaycees, 1969

ACTIVITIES

President, Titusville Rotary, Titusville, Florida, 1982

Vice President, Jacksonville Rotary, Jacksonville, Florida 1977

Campaign Manager, Titusville United Charities, 1981

Treasurer, Gainesville Jaycees, Gainesville, Florida, 1971

REFERENCES

References will be furnished on request.

SALARY REQUIREMENT

Competitive for age and experience.

job to another, than to move from manufacturing to banking, or from production control to financial management.

Career changes can happen any time in your life. You may be 55 and find that you are burned out, or that technology has caught up with you and made your career obsolete. Or you may be 21, newly graduated, and decide that you don't want to be an engineer or an accountant after all, but would like to try something else.

Changing careers is becoming easier to do, because more and more people are doing it. But you must still convince an employer that you are able to do the job you are applying for. In fact, you must be able to do the job. But having the ability, and convincing someone that you have it, are two different things. In what follows we will assume that you actually have the qualifications you need, and we will concentrate on how to present those qualifications in your resume.

If you are changing careers you will need to do more than merely update your old resume. The resume that helped you get a job in marketing will not impress people with your potential as a financial manager or banker. Before you do anything with your resume, you will need to do a new skills inventory (see Chapter 16), concentrating on identifying the skills you acquired in your present career that will transfer to your new career.

Employers will still want to see that you can account for all of your time since you entered the work force, so you will probably not want to eliminate any of your full-time positions from your resume. However, you may want to change what you say about each position, and you will certainly want to add any information about education, experience, and special activities which show your interest and ability in your new career.

For example, let's consider Fred, who has been working in industrial marketing for twenty years. He's tired of all the traveling, long meetings, being away from home, deadlines, and stress involved in his career. For some time he has considered a change to a career in resort management. He knows that marketing would still be an important part of his job, but he would be able to live and work in one place. And, for the most part, he would be his own boss. He would also have to assume responsibility for actually operating a hotel or resort, including everything from arranging for the laundry, to supervising the kitchen, to keeping financial records. To prepare himself for a career change Fred has taken some refresher courses in accounting and personnel management. He has also taken a few courses in resort management. In addition, he has talked to hotel and resort managers during his business trips over the past five years. He has learned from them that the job is not that much different from the one he has been doing. It is simply management and marketing in a different setting, with a different product and a different clientele. In short—and this is important—Fred has not suddenly decided that he would like a new career. He has looked around, selected a new career field, and then prepared himself for it.

And Fred is still at a disadvantage. He is not young and fresh out of resort management school. He is middle-aged and deeply involved in another career. He has no practical experience that hotels and resorts will automatically identify as relevant to their needs. Fred will have to overcome these disadvantages as he conducts his job campaign. A new resume will not guarantee him a successful job search, but it will help.

Fred's new resume will help him by showing that he knows something about resort management, about the skills he will need to do the job, and about how his past experience has prepared him for a new field. He won't be able to do these things with the resume that got him his last job in industrial marketing. His old resume showed his ability to function in an industrial setting, selling highly specialized products to industries, managing his staff of twenty, devising advertising campaigns and sales presentations, and working with upper-level management.

Fred's new resume will need to show how his skills will transfer to his new situation: working with labor unions, supervising several dozen or several hundred employees, taking care of a building that is in constant need of maintenance and housekeeping, working with the public, and marketing to a new clientele in a highly competitive environment. Above all, he will have to control the costs and the quality of the service he provides.

Fred's career-changing resume will almost certainly be two pages or longer. Rather than simply presenting a chronological list of his positions, employers, and job titles, it will have to focus on his new career goal and on the skills he will bring to it. That is, his description of each job will have to concentrate not on what he did, but on the skills he acquired. Rather than simply listing the successful marketing campaigns he has conducted, it will need to stress his adaptability, ability to enter new markets, and capacity to be creative and innovative. He will also have to stress his experience and ability in working with and managing a variety of people, and in supervising the budgetary and financial aspects of his marketing division, details that probably received short shrift in his marketing resume. He will also have to search his background for evidence that he knows something about supervising a building, kitchen, restaurant, and laundry. None of these details would appear on a resume Fred would prepare for a marketing position, even though he may have the relevant experience. Fred's new resume might look much like the one in Figure 17-4. As you read it, keep in mind that he has no experience in hotel or resort management.

■

Figure 17-4 Fred's Career-Changing Resume

Frederick F. Harmon
8835 Newberry Lane
Holiday, Pennsylvania 16555
(215) 774-3727

Career Goal

A managerial position with a major hotel or resort utilizing my management and marketing experience and my abilities to work with people and solve problems.

Qualifications for Resort Management Position

Leadership Ability

Increasing responsibilities for the performance of others over the past twenty years has shown me that leadership is more than simply being in charge. Successful marketing of graphics products and processes has required that I coordinate a number of departments in a company and bringing the talents of each department and individual to bear on the problem a customer has presented. I have headed a number of such coordinating groups, frequently at the request of those involved or at the direction of company executives. In addition, I have also held elected positions in civic and service organizations. My ability to lead a variety of people in completing complex tasks will be an asset in hotel/resort management, where it is necessary to work effectively with a variety of people.

Problem Solving Ability

Throughout my career I have worked at matching customers' needs with available technology. This involved learning customers' manufacturing processes and products thoroughly, and then modifying available products and on some occasions inventing a new graphics product or process to perform the task. As a Technical Sales Supervisor, I was responsible for helping fourteen field representatives assist their customers in devising new graphics processes and achieving acceptable product quality.

Organizational Ability

Each position I have held has required me to organize carefully to complete my work and give the best possible service to customers. As a technical representative and technical sales supervisor I learned to keep track of daily responsibilities and tasks and complete them in order of priority. As a vice president I have had to organize not only my own work, but that of all departments within my division of the company. I have become skilled at balancing the needs of individual departments

(figure continues on next page)

Figure 17-4 Continued

against those of the entire company. Since I became vice president, every major marketing campaign has been completed and ready for distribution at least two weeks earlier than scheduled, without using overtime.

Communication Skills

Effective communication in speech and writing has always been one of my strongest skills. I can talk comfortably with corporation presidents, advertising managers, supervisors, machine operators, designers, and consumers. I have taken numerous courses in effective writing and speaking, as well as listening and managerial and organizational communication. Former supervisors have always complimented me on my communications skills, and several of my presentations have won trade awards.

Education

Bachelor of Science, Mechanical Engineering, University of Illinois, 1964

Presently taking coursework leading to a certificate in hotel and resort management from Adelphi University, New York, New York

Civic and Service Activities

Life member, Rotary International; past president, North Philadelphia Business Roundtable, coach, youth soccer and Little League baseball. Member and board member (1982-1984), International Association of Graphics Equipment Manufacturers.

Summary of Experience

Twenty years experience in Marketing, including positions as Vice President, Marketing Manager, Technical Sales Supervisor, and Technical Representative with graphics companies having annual sales of $50 million.

Vice President, Marketing, Holograph, Inc. 388 Parkway, Philadelphia, PA 1982 - present

Industrial Markets Manager, Holograph, Inc., 1978 - 1982

Manager, Industrial Marketing Division, Samson Graphics, 3890 Hyatt Road, Randallstown, Maryland 22331, 1974 - 1978

(figure continues on next page)

Figure 17-4 Continued

Supervisor, Technical Sales, Brown & Co., Graphics Products, 416 Charles Street, Baltimore, MD 21145, 1969 - 1974

Technical Representative, ARI Graphics, 3459 Military Highway, Indianapolis, Indiana 47655, 1966 - 1969

First Lieutenant, United States Army, Corps of Engineers, Combat Engineer, 1964 - 1966, Honorable Discharge

References

Will be furnished on request.

Exercises: Chapter Seventeen

1. Using a notebook or card file, prepare a complete personal and employment history of yourself. Include all of the places you have lived, the jobs you have had (including internships and volunteer positions), other abilities and skills, scholarships, awards, and the name, title, address, and phone number for each of your references.

2. Find out if there is a placement or career planning office on your campus. If there is, visit it and find out what services it provides and how you can take advantage of them. If you are about to begin a job search, go ahead and build a placement folder which this office can keep on file for you.

3. Following the procedures in this chapter, prepare at least two drafts of a general-purpose, one-page resume that you will be able to send to most prospective employers. Use the horizontal format for one, and the vertical format for the other. Then revise these drafts until you are satisfied that they are suitable to send out with application letters.

4. Adapt your resume so that you can send it with an application for a position that is not in your major field but is related to it. For example, if you are an accounting major, adapt your resume to apply for a position in management or marketing.

5. The resume you prepare now may be quite different from the one you use when you graduate. Project your qualifications into the future and prepare the resume that you will use then.

18

Writing Letters about Jobs

You will need to write letters at several times during your search for a job. The most important of these will be the application letter that you send along with your resume. The others include requests for references, follow-up letters when you receive no reply to an application, follow-up letters after interviews, and letters accepting or rejecting job offers.

In this chapter we will discuss all of these letters, but we will pay most attention to the application letter. It will require special effort if you want to succeed in convincing your reader to ask you in for an interview. It is one that can get you screened out of the applicant pool most quickly, or it can tip the balance in your favor. What should these letters say? How should they be organized? How do you write about that most difficult of subjects—yourself?

Writing Application Letters

Whenever you send a potential employer a copy of your resume, you should also send a personalized cover letter. The two travel together, and you should consider them inseparable, even if you are answering an advertisement that asks for only a resume.

The letter supplements your resume by providing information and interpretations that either do not belong in a resume (because they are not strictly factual) or will not fit for lack of space. This is an important point: an application letter is an elaboration and explanation of the facts you list in your resume. *If your letter does no more than repeat your resume, it is a waste of time.*

There are two important differences between letters and resumes. First, your resume is a straightforward, factual presentation of your education, work experience, skills, and other qualifications. Taken by themselves, these facts could fit any number of jobs and companies. In your letter you have a chance to interpret these facts and show how they fit the position you are applying for. So the letter goes beyond merely saying that you have certain qualifications; it shows that your qualifications are appropriate to a specific job and company. Your goal is to offer your reader several convincing reasons for wanting to talk with you in person.

The second major difference between your resume and application letter is almost as important as the first. You designed your resume so that you could reproduce it and send it to any number of potential employers, because each one needs the same basic information about you. But each application letter that you write is individually typed and personalized. That is, it contains details that make it evident that you are writing to a specific person to apply for a specific job with a particular company. Of course, you can still use the same basic letter each time you apply for a job. After all, there are only so many things we can say about ourselves. But each time you use the letter you must adapt it to the company you are writing to and the job that is available.

Most of your readers know that you are applying for other jobs and that you are probably using the same letter. Personalizing the letter will not fool anyone. It is merely a way of showing that you can be courteous and that you have done your homework.

Together, your letter and resume explain your qualifications. They are also important evidence of your ability to select appropriate information, organize it for a reader, and present it on paper. An effective presentation can easily make average qualifications sound pretty good. A poor presentation can just as easily make excellent qualifications look bad.

What Is Your Subject?

When you write an application letter you are writing about yourself. That much is obvious. You need to show your reader your qualifications and something about your personality. But much of that information should be evident from your resume. So, if you are not supposed to simply repeat your resume in the letter, what will you write about?

You really have two subjects in addition to yourself. Your qualifications and personality are significant in terms of the job you are applying for and an employer's needs. So these are part of your subject.

The job. You do not really need to tell your readers much about the job itself. They already know that. Besides, what could you say that wouldn't sound like it came right out of an introductory textbook or even the advertisement for the job? But it is important to show that you *understand* what the job involves and what it will require of you. This will show that you have given some thought to just how you will fit into the job. And if you do understand the job, you will be able to write about your qualifications in such a way that you show how they fit the job. To see just how important this is, you might try explaining how you would do a job that you have never heard of. How will you know you can do it or convince someone else, unless you know what it involves?

Employer's needs. Just what does an employer need? It is difficult to know *exactly* what an employer has in mind as the ideal applicant for a job. In fact, some employers do not know what they want beyond thinking they would like to hire someone who is qualified and personable. And they may not know exactly what they mean by "qualified."

You may not know what a particular employer wants, but common sense tells you that certain needs are common to all employers. First of all, employers like to see applicants who understand the job they are applying for and the career field they want to enter. And they need people who understand what it means to work for a company, to function as part of an organization, and to work toward a common goal. So try to provide evidence that you are willing and able to work hard, get to work on time, get along with coworkers, and take direction from supervisors. Finally, all employers need people who are willing to learn, who are not convinced that they already know everything. This is especially important if you are applying for an entry-level job.

A Few Words about Readers

Remember that the person who reads your letter is the same one who reads your resume, so everything we said about readers in Chapter

17 applies here as well. They are impatient, harried, and looking for a reason to eliminate you as an applicant.

And remember that you are not writing to idiots. The typical reader of job applications has probably seen several thousand letters and resumes. You are unlikely to say something new. Nor will most readers be swept away with enthusiasm for your qualifications (unless they are genuinely outstanding). Nor will they be fooled by the statement that General Motors' (or any company's) sales increased 20 percent while you worked there.

Readers will most appreciate a letter that explains and interprets your qualifications in light of their company and the job you are applying for. If you have unusual qualifications you should state them. This is no place for false humility. But it is a mistake to inflate your qualifications or claim those that you do not have. Your most important task is to show how you will fit the job.

What Will Your Letter Say?

Though not every letter will contain all of the information listed here, you may discover that you will use most of it.

1. **Where did you learn about the position?** Of course, you will not always *know* that there is a position. You may send some letters in the hope that something is available. Citing the source of your information can be an effective way of orienting your reader to your subject. At the same time you can identify the job you are applying for. You might mention the advertisement you saw, and where you saw it, or that you have been referred by a placement office or employment service.

If your information came from someone your reader knows and trusts, mentioning this person's name could be an important advantage for you.

If you do mention a source, be sure to identify it exactly. A company may have placed several advertisements in the same newspaper or professional publication. Try not to confuse your reader by being vague about the one you are referring to.

2. **Which job are you applying for?** Identify it by title, if you can. Remember that a company may have several jobs available at the same time. If you merely say that you are applying for "the job," you leave it to your reader to figure out which one. Some readers will not take the time to do that. They may consider your vagueness a sufficient reason to move on to the next application.

3. **Refer to your resume sometime during the letter.** Perhaps you can mention it when you are discussing your qualifications. Your reader probably skimmed through your resume first, but it will not hurt to point out that you have included one.

It won't hurt, that is, if you do it carefully, in passing, rather than implying that your reader is too stupid or blind to find another sheet of paper. Avoid statements like "I have enclosed a resume for your convenience" or "My qualifications are clearly outlined on the enclosed resume." Your reader knows that.

Instead, subordinate the reference to something else in a sentence, like this: "I am sure that my references, who are listed on the enclosed resume, will confirm what I have said about myself."

4. **Ask for an interview.** Yes, it is obvious that you want one. That's why you are writing the letter. But most readers expect you to ask anyway. So why disappoint them? We'll get to just *how* to ask later, as we go through the letter step-by-step.

5. **Explain how your experience and skills qualify you for the job.** This, of course, is the tough one, and it will occupy the bulk of your letter and consume most of the time and energy that you devote to writing. It will require special comment, and thus is the subject of the next section.

Showing Your Qualifications

Your resume lists the basic facts about your experience and skills. It shows the jobs you have had and the duties you performed, along with academic and extracurricular experiences that are related to your chosen career. You would expect any halfway intelligent reader to be able to assess your qualifications and decide whether you can do the job. So isn't that enough? In a word, no.

If you simply present the *facts* of your qualifications, you are leaving it to your reader to decide whether, and how well, you will fit the job. Your goal is to *show* your reader how you fit the job, and that will mean presenting more than simply the facts. You will have to show your reader what the facts mean by placing them in the context of the job you are applying for. It is probably best to do this now, before you get involved in writing the letter itself.

Almost everything you have done in the past has taught you something, given you some skill or insight that will help you do the job you are applying for. Some may have taught you a great deal. Some of this will be specific to that job, or even trivial. Almost all of us can learn to operate a cash register or make deliveries. Some of what you learned will be valuable and easily applied to other jobs. That is what you are looking for. For each job you have had, or each activity you have been involved in, try to think of an important skill or insight that you learned. Then write a brief paragraph which explains to potential employers how this skill or knowledge will help you do a job that they might hire you for. Later, you can adapt these paragraphs and use some of them in your letter. For now, think of it as brainstorming for ideas.

For example, let's assume that you spend part of your time as an undergraduate working as a counselor or advisor in a dormitory. What is central to this experience? Working with people, certainly. But can you be a bit more specific? Your paragraph might go something like this:

> While I worked in the dorm I was in charge of one floor, and occasionally of the entire building. I was responsible for twenty-five other students who lived on the floor. They often asked me for advice about school, and many of them came to me with their personal problems. Sometimes I was able to help them. When I couldn't help, I referred them to psychologists on campus. I often had to negotiate disputes between roommates or neighbors, and I was usually successful in doing that so the parties remained friends. If students presented discipline problems, it was my job to attempt to control them or to report them to the appropriate authorities. I never hesitated to issue official warnings to those who committed serious violations.

This example should give you the general idea. As you read it, you begin to get a picture of a person who has done things. Qualifications, up to now a list of facts, places, and job titles, have had a bit of life and action breathed into them. If you do this for every job or activity you list on your resume, you will have a rich source of details to use when your write your letter.

Organizing Your Letter

An application letter is a persuasive effort. The days are gone, if they ever existed, when you could simply announce that you were available and have employers begging you to please work for them.

Writing a persuasive application letter will mean using the motivated sequence, or some modified version of it. If you need to review, this might be a good time to go back to Chapter 9 and refresh your memory about persuasive writing. We will not review that material here. We will simply look at each of the five stages in the motivated sequence to see how it applies to applications, and attempt a few drafts of each by way of example.

Begin by looking through your notes to see what major themes your experiences have in common with each other and with the job you are applying for. You might find that the job will require you to work with many different kinds of people, so you will want to emphasize those experiences that show that you have already developed "people skills." Or the job may require you to work with a complex, technical subject, so you will select experiences that show your ability to do that, even though the subject itself may be one that you know very little about. You can always learn, and you will want to provide evidence of your ability to do *that*, too.

You can select your central appeal and the evidence to support it before you begin to write. But many ideas will come to you as you write, and you will need to take advantage of them.

Getting attention. What can you say that will set you apart from the other applicants and motivate your readers to want to know more about you? Remember, they are reading a stack of applications, and most of them will seem distressingly similar to each other. In part, that is because too many people simply copy or adapt their letters out of books like this one. That is the major reason why this chapter won't show you a completed application letter, but only parts of several letters.

As in any persuasive presentation, begin by announcing your subject and offering your reader an incentive to read on. In a sense you are telling your readers that you know what they are looking for, and that they will find it here. Try to keep your perspective, though, and stop short of claiming that you are the answer to the company's problems, or having your application delivered as a singing telegram.

Some people are shy about attracting too much attention, and their openings come out rather flat, like this:

> I am writing to apply for the position of . . . that you advertised in yesterday's *News*.

or this:

> Mr. John Williams, of your Accounting Department, suggested that I write you to apply for the job of accounting trainee which is presently available.

These announce the subject, but there is nothing compelling about them, nothing to suggest that the rest of the letter will be less boring.

Some people manage to attract the wrong kind of attention at the beginning of their letters. Like this:

> As I was reading the paper last night after supper, I came across your advertisement for a management trainee. . . .

This is a history lesson, and not a very good one. It makes your job search seem much too casual and identifies you as a person who concentrates on trivia.

Some people get positively carried away with their own enthusiasm, in the wrong direction. You might call it the "Oh boy!" response.

> The job of assistant account executive which you recently advertised is just what I've been looking for.

Well, yes, it probably is. But to say that in the first sentence identifies you as someone who rarely looks beyond self-interest.

Let's try again. Try to set up or preview the central appeal you will use. Give your reader something to look forward to. Focus on your strongest qualifications for the job, and then you will have something to develop and explain in the rest of the letter.

> As your new assistant account executive I would bring to the ABC Agency a thorough knowledge of marketing, a proven ability to work with all kinds of people, and valuable practical experience in sales.

That is quite different from the earlier ones, isn't it? It puts the strongest qualifications right out front, and it commits the writer to developing and explaining them. This letter from a recent college graduate might go on to describe an academic major in marketing, experience working with people in part-time jobs, and abilities as a retail salesperson. And note that the tone here is positive and enthusiastic. This paragraph identifies the job by projecting the applicant into it. And it uses adjectives: knowledge is *thorough,* ability *proven,* and experience *practical* and *valuable.*

Another applicant might begin the letter this way:

> With a degree in marketing and five years of experience as a machinist in a custom machine shop, I know I will be an effective sales representative for Bartlett Precision Tools.

This writer is going to stress knowledge of sales and marketing and practical experience as valuable assets in a field sales position. Note the emphasis on being an *effective* sales representative.

Practice writing opening paragraphs that will get your reader's attention and give you something to work with, a theme or central idea to develop. Write a dozen or more, until you are satisfied with the result. Then you can experiment with the best ones, developing them to see where they lead.

Establishing a need. Employers already know what they need. At least it appears that they do, since they have decided to hire someone with certain qualifications. Someone has probably written an advertisement for the position, and there may be a fairly detailed written job description. It is tempting simply to present your qualifications to see if they match what your reader wants. But to do that leaves your reader completely in charge when there are several things you can do to help yourself. After all, you control the quality and amount of information your reader receives about you and, to some extent, the impression it makes.

Consider a comparable situation from sales. You have decided to buy a new car, and you know what features it should have if it is to perform the job you want it to do. You will base your decision on a number of stated and unstated criteria, some of which you may not be explicitly aware of, such as economy, service, reliability, and image. When you visit a showroom the salesperson does not assume that you know what you want and simply present the cars that match the need that you state. Instead, the successful salesperson takes charge and attempts to show you that one model, among the dozens that are available, will satisfy your need best. To do that, the salesperson must anticipate your "hidden" or unstated criteria and use them to establish the need that the product will satisfy. You need to do the same thing when you present yourself to a potential employer. Anticipate the unstated qualifications that a successful applicant must have, and then show that you possess them.

In short, show your reader that there are compelling reasons for choosing you from among the dozens of similar applicants who can satisfy the obvious, stated qualifications. This means that you must anticipate the unstated qualifications and use them to establish a need that only you can satisfy.

How do you do that? Clearly you need to tell your readers more than they already know, more than the obvious minimum qualifications for the job. You need to show your readers that they need someone who can more than meet those minimum requirements. You have already introduced your central appeals in the first paragraph, now develop them.

Let's say you are applying for an outside sales position with a company that manufactures precision mechanical and electronic equipment for physicians and hospitals. The job calls for a bachelor's degree in a business-related field and some familiarity with biology, computers, or other medically-related technical fields. You believe you qualify because you have worked in the college computer center for two years, and you have spent your summers working in hospitals, a part of your experience that you had not thought important. Now you need to pull that body of experience together into a succinct paragraph that shows why this employer should need you rather than someone else.

What if you said something like this:

> An effective sales representative for KRW-Medical understands his product, can talk with a wide variety of people, and is capable of working independently, without supervision.

Does that create a need? Not really. It tells your readers what they already know, or should know. Look through your research notes and see what you know about this company that you can use here. And try to make your statements specific, so they will apply to you rather than to everyone else. Like this:

> KRW-Medical needs a special kind of sales representative, who can do more than simply understand your highly specialized products. He needs to be able to work comfortably with the physicians, hospital administrators, and technicians who will recommend purchases, authorize budgets, and use the equipment when it is in place. And it is not enough to simply be a good sales representative. He has to be able to discuss special needs and unusual installations. And he has to do all of this far from his supervisors and the engineers who designed the equipment.

Perfect? Not yet, but it is a start. The reader no doubt knows some of this, perhaps all of it. But it is obvious that this applicant knows it, too. Knowledge of the company, its products, and its customers is evident. The situations mentioned will provide material to develop in later paragraphs. The letter is also personalized so that it is obviously about a specific job with this company. And already the applicant is hinting that he has been in these kinds of situations, or at least is familiar with them, and can operate effectively in them.

As with beginnings, you should write several paragraphs of this sort. They will probably get better as you gain experience and practice. Keep at it until you believe you have a paragraph that shows employers that they need you and your special combination of experiences and abilities.

Satisfy the need. Earlier, when you were planning this letter, you wrote a paragraph about each important job or experience that you have listed on your resume. The idea was to show the important skills and knowledge that you used or learned in each of these positions. Now use those paragraphs to show what you have done and, by inference, what you can do in the future. Look through them and find the ones that demonstrate skills and knowledge that you will need in the job you are applying for. You will not use them as they are, because they are probably not adapted to a specific situation or reader. Use them as a basis for paragraphs which develop the central themes and appeals that you have already introduced.

Perhaps you are applying for a job that will require you to work closely with people in production and sales, as well as with customers. You will need to understand technical products and manufacturing processes, and you will also have to work with people as a liaison and negotiator. Even though you have never done a job like this one, you can show that you have the skills and knowledge you will need to perform well in it. To do this, select from your resume the jobs in which you used these skills and give them special emphasis in your letter.

An applicant for this job would certainly want to emphasize any kind of experience that involved working closely with different kinds of people, whether as a supervisor, counselor, advisor, go-between, or coworker. And it will also help to discuss any experience in a manufacturing situation, or something that resembles it. Within reason, nearly anything will do so long as you have a clear idea of what a job will require of you and adapt your experiences to it in a way that your readers will find credible. Consider such jobs as lifeguard, retail clerk, camp or dormitory counselor, salesperson, officer in a campus or civic organization, or others similar to these. They all require that you work with people, and each one can contribute something to your application for a job. Experience in a manufacturing setting may be full-time or part-time, in almost any capacity. What is important is your ability to show that you understand how a manufacturing operation functions and how you might fit into it.

For such a job, this portion of your letter might read like this:

> I worked my way through college as a machine operator on the second shift at Sawmill Tools in Bridgeton. My daily move from the classroom to the production line gave me immediate illustrations of the principles I was learning about in my classes in Management. I know what it is like to operate a lathe or grinder for eight hours, and I believe I can relate well with people in similar jobs.
>
> At Sawmill I talked with foremen and shift supervisors each night and observed them closely as they worked. I came to appreciate the difficulty of their jobs as I saw them caught between management and labor. And I learned from them how to see both sides of issues and settle disputes between people who were not always friendly with each other by the time the supervisor intervened.
>
> My year as a section leader in the milling department gave me valuable first-hand experience in supervising others and motivating them to maintain acceptable productivity rates. During four years with Sawmill I was able to see all parts of their manufacturing process, from raw materials to finished product. I believe I have a thorough understanding of what it takes to run a profitable manufacturing business. I am sure the references I have listed on my resume will confirm this and attest to my abilities as a supervisor and leader.

Like all early drafts, this can use some revision. But it does begin to capture the spirit of what the writer wants to do. This applicant is doing things, interacting with people, and learning from the experience. These paragraphs are the beginning of a credible, convincing picture of a person who can do the job.

Visualize the future. The future you visualize for your reader will certainly be one in which you are doing the job you are applying for, and doing it well. Don't settle for less. Up to this point your letter has concentrated on the past and attempted to relate it to the requirements of a new job. Now it is time to focus directly on the future.

What will the future be like? From your point of view it will be great. You will have a job, probably doing something you want to do, and you will receive a regular paycheck. Best of all, you will be able to forget about resumes and application letters for a while. But try to contain yourself and see the situation from your reader's point of view. What will your employer want the future to be like? The future that you visualize has to be consistent with the one your reader visualizes for you and the company. It has to match what your reader knows or expects is possible and reasonable.

Most readers are probably still asking basic questions at this point. They have read about what you have done, and you can almost hear them asking, "Yes, but can you actually do the job? Do you know what it involves? Do you understand the company, and that you are starting at the bottom? Will you fit in? Are you willing to learn from us and do things our way?" You need to do more than repeat those questions and answer yes to each one. You need to *show* yourself, in the job, doing these things. This is where your research into the company and your career field will pay off. You can use specific details to show that you understand. Like this:

> As a member of the Healy Company's accounting department I know that I will be a productive member of a team. I learn new concepts and procedures quickly, and my college record shows that I learn them well. I realize that there is much to learn about industrial accounting, and I am eager to begin. I adapt easily to new circumstances and people, and my references will certainly tell you that I am easy to work with.

When you write this section of your letter, do be careful that you avoid the impression that you are going to change the world, revolutionize your profession, and bring your employer kicking and screaming into the twentieth century. When you have finished your first version of this part of the letter, write several more. Keep working until you're satisfied that you can actually *see* yourself doing the job you are applying for.

Asking for action. The final stage of any persuasive message is to ask your reader to do something. In application letters this is the place to request an interview. It should be painfully obvious by this point that your goal is an interview. Why else would you have gone to all this trouble? The important point here is not *that* you ask, but *how* you ask. Can you ask tactfully and forcefully, without appearing to beg or demand?

What would happen if you said this:

> I'll call you on Wednesday the 25th to arrange a time for an interview.

Most readers might say that "if you need to know right now, the answer is no" and move quickly to the next letter. The decision to grant an interview is your reader's, and you will do well to remember that.

You might use this approach:

> I am sure that when you have reviewed all of the applications for this position, you will see that I am the best qualified for the job.

This writer has not seen all of the applications and so is claiming a kind of omniscience that few of us have experienced. Such a statement usurps the reader's right to be the judge of qualifications.

Try to be tactful but direct: ask for what you want, like this:

> I will appreciate the opportunity to talk with you in person about the position of Field Sales Representative for Dartron. I can be available for an interview at your convenience.

Or this:

> Can we schedule an interview to discuss my qualifications in more detail? With several days' notice I can arrange to travel to Denver at your convenience.

The last paragraph of your letter is also the place to state any realistic restrictions on when you will be available for an interview, or special instructions about how to reach you. If you can't travel until after midterms, you should say so. And tell your readers that you leave for work at 2:00 P.M., so they can phone you before that time. If it would be most convenient for you to travel to an interview during a school vacation, then give the dates so your readers will know how your schedule fits theirs.

Sometimes you will write to companies that are a considerable distance away, and getting there for an interview will be expensive. You don't really want to volunteer to pay for it yourself, but you may wonder if the company will concentrate on applicants who are closer and less expensive to interview. You may want to try to deal with this in your letter.

Some job applicants simply say that they will be visiting in New York, or Fargo, on certain dates, and suggest an interview at that time, if it's convenient. They may have no intention of being in those cities unless they obtain an interview. There is nothing wrong with this, but be careful about telling too many people, in too many places, that you will be nearby during the same week. It could be an expensive week for you.

It is also possible to suggest an interview in a regional office as a preliminary to one at the company's headquarters. Or you might inquire whether the company will be holding on-campus interviews and request an opportunity to talk with a representative. Remember, your goal is to overcome the disadvantage of your distance from the job, if it is a disadvantage. Try not to seem too eager to do your reader's thinking.

Review and revise. Once you have finished your letter, with perhaps several versions of each paragraph, go back through your material and try to choose the best version of each. Blend them together into one letter and then revise and edit it. Take your time and work carefully. Silly mistakes can be expensive.

Other Letters about Employment

You will have uses for letters throughout your search for employment, until you have accepted the job that you want and rejected other offers. This section will survey these letters briefly. They are all simply special applications of types of letters that you have written before.

Follow-up Letters

You will have two major occasions to use follow-up letters; once before an interview and once after. In the first, you are writing because your application letter seems to have fallen into a well. After a decent interval you might write a tactful reminder to inquire whether your first letter reached its destination. You will have to decide for yourself what a decent interval is, but in general it is probably at least a month. And try not to suggest that someone is actually ignoring your application, even though you suspect that to be the case. Remember, your goal is to be persistent and attempt to get a positive reply, not to alienate your readers by reminding them they have bad manners.

You can take a number of approaches with this letter. The simplest is a direct request which asks whether your original letter arrived. Common courtesy practically demands that your reader answer this and explain the status of your application. Or you may decide to write what is, in effect, another application letter. It should be somewhat different from your first one (you did keep a carbon copy, didn't you?), and it should acknowledge that you have written this company before. There is little harm in stating your qualifications again. Who knows, the second one might work. You might be tempted to include a postcard (self-addressed, of course) so your reader can let you know your application arrived. But to some people this would simply be an invitation to avoid writing you the personal reply your application deserves.

A much happier and more productive follow-up letter is the one you write after you have had an interview. It can serve several purposes. First, it is a way of saying thank you, which is never a wasted phrase. If someone has spent time with you, shown you around the company's factory or headquarters, taken you to lunch, and answered your questions, then thanks are surely appropriate. This letter is also an opportunity to reinforce the good impression that you made in the interview. (You did make a good impression, didn't you?)

The minute an interview is over, as you walk to your car or ride the taxi to the airport, you will think of something you should have said. Perhaps there was a question you did not answer well or that you could answer better now that you have had time to think about it. Put it into your follow-up letter.

This is also the time to deal with obvious weaknesses in your qualifications (the ones the interviewers noticed) and attempt to show that you recognize the problem and are prepared to deal with it or overcome it. If you are really sure of your ground, you might try to show that your assets outweigh your shortcomings.

Obviously, the follow-up letter must be tactful. You are being actively considered for the position, and you want to say enough to clarify or strengthen your case, but not so much that you create problems that did not exist earlier. The best approach is probably to write a factual, straightforward letter that does not pretend to be anything except what it is: an attempt to reinforce what your readers already know about you.

Rejecting a Job Offer

Believe it or not, you may need to say "no, thanks" to a company that offers you a job. Maybe you have a better offer, or the interview convinced you that you *don't* want to work for a particular company or person.

Begin by considering your readers. They have invested some time and effort in you, compared you with other applicants, and decided that you are the best person for the job. Most people in that position *expect* you to say yes. Their world will not end if you refuse the job, but they will have to do some of their work over again. So be tactful. Use the indirect approach that is outlined in Chapter 8 and try to give honest, sincere reasons for your refusal. If you have accepted another offer, say so, and explain why. Do everything you can to ensure that you and your readers part company as friends. They thought enough of you to offer you a job; the least you can do is return the compliment.

Accepting a Job Offer

You may not have to write a letter accepting an offer. Many employers may call and make verbal offers and take your acceptance in the same way. Still, it may be a good idea to write a brief note of acceptance, acknowledging the call and giving the terms of the offer as you understand them. You can often do this in the way of a thank you note, but at the same time you are confirming the offer and your acceptance.

Once you have accepted a job, it is perfectly acceptable to write brief notes to thank those who have helped you along the way. They will be pleased to see that you have found a job, and they will remember your thoughtfulness.

Summary

Remember that a job application letter is a persuasive presentation. Whenever possible, use the motivated sequence and provide concrete evidence of your skills and your ability to perform the job you are applying for. If you simply repeat your resume you are wasting everyone's time. The effective letter interprets your skills, experience, and interests in terms of the job you are applying for, and motivates your reader to offer you an interview.

Be sure you send follow-up letters to companies that ignore you, and to write informative thank you letters to those that interview you and offer you a position.

■

Exercises: Chapter Eighteen

1. For at least three jobs or other experiences that you list on your resume, write a paragraph that explains or illustrates an important skill or ability that you learned or had to use. These paragraphs should concentrate on explaining *what you have done,* rather than looking ahead to the job you will apply for.

2. Using the paragraphs in exercise 1 as a basis, write several paragraphs which show how the skills or knowledge you have acquired in the past will help you perform the job you would like to apply for.

3. Write at least a dozen opening paragraphs for a job application letter. Be sure you introduce central appeals that arise from your own skills and knowledge and that you can develop later in the letter.

4. Assume that you have selected a company you want to work for and the position you want to be hired for. Then answer this question: "Why should any employer (or this employer) hire you to do this job?" Give as many reasons as you can.

5. Assume that you have had two interviews within the past two weeks. Both jobs are attractive, the pay is nearly the same, and you could be happy with either company. But you would rather work for the first because you think you will learn more and that the chances for advancement are greater. Today you received a letter offering you a job with the second company. You would like to see what the first company will do, but not at the risk of losing the offer you now have. Write a letter in which you request a reasonable amount of time to delay your decision. You may give whatever explanation you want.

6. You have just accepted a position as a management trainee with QRX Industries. Today you received a call from MacDougal Aircraft offering you a similar position for several thousand dollars more, better fringe benefits, and what you think are better opportunities for advancement. Assume whatever facts you need about the positions and write QRX to inform them that you will not be reporting to work in six weeks.

7. Select a former professor or employer and write a letter that requests a general letter of reference for your placement file. Be sure that you provide enough information that your reader can identify you and that you say something about your career plans, so the letter will be appropriate to your needs.

8. Six weeks ago you wrote to Heat, Hartford and Winchell, CPAs, to apply for a position you found advertised in the *New York Times.* You have received no reply. Write a follow-up letter to the Personnel Manager, Ms. Rebecca Smollet, 113 Avenue of the Americas, New York, NY 10000. See if you can say something that will attract her attention and make a second effort at obtaining an interview.

9. Select a company you would like to work for and a position you would like to have within that company. Write an application letter in which you explain your qualifications and request an interview. (You should assume that you have graduated, or that you will graduate soon.)

■

Cases

The cases that follow are designed to present you with situations that require that you write memos, letters of several kinds, proposals, and reports. Many require research and decision making as well. The subjects are general, of a kind that anyone might encounter on the job. But, if you can complete these cases you will probably be able to do anything that you are assigned at work.

The Typographical Error

You are the Assistant Sales Manager for a large manufacturing company. This morning you discovered a serious mistake in a customer's order.

One of your sales representatives took an order for 10,000 stainless steel valves from a major customer who spends more than a million dollars each year with your company. The customer's specifications call for a part inside the valve (a #3682 stem flow adjuster) to be machined to an outside diameter of .376 inches. But when the shop order was sent to the production department the figure was changed to .276. No one knows where the error originated.

You have checked with the Engineering Department and learned that the part will not work. In fact, the project engineer is surprised that the part will stay seated in the valve at all. It does, though, because a call to the Production Department discloses that more than half of the valves have been assembled and are being packed for shipping. Yes, the inspector thought the part was a bit strange but double-checked the shop order and then decided to go ahead.

A quick review of the situation leads you to the following conclusions:

> The order will be late, you think, because it is scheduled to arrive at your customer's plant in ten days. The length of the delay will depend on how long it takes to remanufacture the part and how cooperative everyone is.
>
> It will probably take at least twelve days to manufacture the parts again, reassemble the valves, pack them, and ship them.
>
> Correcting the error will probably cost about $35,000, which cannot be charged to your customer. So your company's profits will shrink.
>
> All of this depends on there being enough stock steel on hand to make the new parts and on the ability of the production line to shift to the new parts immediately.
>
> No one is going to be pleased with this situation, but everyone involved must be told. The sales representative is going to be especially unhappy, since this is one of *his* major accounts.

It's your job to decide who must be notified and how that should be done. At the least, the people involved include:

> The Sales Manager (your supervisor)
>
> The Production Manager
>
> The Engineering Manager
>
> The sales representative
>
> The Shipping Department

Chief, Inventory Control (steel stock?)

The customer (who gets this job?)

Think through the situation carefully, decide what you would do, and do any writing that you believe is necessary.

The Summer Internship Program

As Personnel Director of Grant Manufacturing, you are a member of the Management Council, which also includes the Director of Engineering, Accounting Manager, and Executive Vice President. A recent topic of discussion in this group has been the quality of the college graduates from which Grant is able to recruit new employees each year. The members of the council have the impression that the company is not attracting applicants of the highest quality. Therefore, even if it hires the best that are available, the company is not really getting the so-called cream of the crop. If Grant is to keep up with its competitors, it must recruit from among the best engineering, accounting, and management graduates.

One possible course of action that has been discussed is that Grant Manufacturing might begin a summer internship program for highly qualified college students. The idea is to recruit college students during their freshman or sophomore years, hire them for summer work for two or three summers, and then offer the best of them full-time employment when they graduate from college. The question, of course, is whether this will work and, if so, how it would work. The Management Council has assigned you to research this idea, decide whether it is feasible, figure out how it will work, and prepare a report that the council can present to the President, Mr. T. R. Grant III.

Stage I

Prepare a report that you can present to the Management Council. Your research may suggest that summer internships are a good idea, or that they are not. That is up to you and the information that is available. The council expects its members to do thorough staff work, so you will have to make a strong case for either side, even though the council seems to favor the idea. As part of your research you may need to communicate with people who are not members of the council, including managers in businesses and industries which have tried or are now using the internship program. Include copies of all correspondence as attachments to your report, and provide any visual aids that you believe are necessary.

Stage II

Adapt your report so that you can present it orally to the Management Council. Prepare any outlines or visual aids you need, and present your report to your class.

Stage III

If your research favors beginning an internship program, assume that the Management Council has accepted your recommendation and assigned you to prepare materials for a presentation to Mr. Grant. They remind you that he pays attention to details and will want you to have most of them worked out. The council offers you the following suggestions about what Mr. Grant might want to know.

How much will it cost?

Has it worked elsewhere?

Has it failed elsewhere?

Why?

Will colleges and universities participate?

Which ones?

How will it improve the present situation?

How would you recruit the interns?

What qualifications will you require?

Will the company be obligated to offer jobs?

How many can we use? (The company now hires about twenty-five summer employees each year.)

Write a report that you believe the Management Council would approve of for presentation to Mr. Grant. Include as attachments copies of any documents or correspondence you write to gather information.

Stage IV

Your research may suggest that the internship program may not be a good idea. You may assume that the council agrees with you, but there is a complication. Mr. Grant has heard about this idea, and he wants a full report. This may suggest to you that he thinks the program is a good idea, so you have your work cut out for you if you are to convince him otherwise.

Write a report that presents the results of your research as convincingly as possible.

Motivating Workers

Recently your company's president, Jennifer W. Hyde, formed a Management Study Group to investigate new ways of motivating employees at all levels of the company. At the first meeting of this group she explained that her chief concerns are:

1. Product quality
2. Productivity
3. Employee loyalty and retention

She is concerned about the company's future, because during the past year it has experienced the following trends:

1. Returns from customers, because of unacceptable quality, up from 2% to 8%.
2. Productivity per worker hour down 4% from last year, which was down only 1% from the year before.
3. Twenty-one percent of the company's skilled employees, at all levels, left the company during the year. Two of these people were talented assistant vice presidents, and half were skilled craftspersons. Ten percent of those who left have not been replaced because people with the proper skills cannot be found. The cost of replacing the others exceeds 10% of the wages, salaries, and benefits they would have received if they had remained with the company.

Ms. Hyde believes the company's employees and executives are as well-paid (or better paid) as any in the industry, regardless of the size of the company. She has read enough about management and motivation to realize that money, in any form, is not always the most appropriate or most effective motivator. She wants the Study Group to explore the subject of motivation and recommend courses of action that the company can take. She is not against paying people more, but she believes that the real answer lies in other areas. Hyde suggested the following for the group's consideration but emphasized that it should not limit its study to these topics.

1. Implementing Japanese management techniques, such as those outlined by William Ouchi in *Theory Z*
2. Establishing quality circles
3. Considering instituting flextime, so that employees can work flexible shifts and tailor their work day to the other demands on them
4. Establishing health, recreation, and stress management

programs, either with the company's own facilities or through agreements with local health and athletic clubs

5. Considering company-wide use of company-owned vacation and resort facilities, hitherto provided only to assistant vice presidents and other high-level executives
6. Establishing opportunities for more social interaction among employees, through athletic leagues, interest group, and clubs
7. Initiating a thorough review and, if necessary, a revision, of the company's policies on promotion and other kinds of advancement

Ms. Hyde concluded by saying that she was sure there are other methods of motivating employees and that she would be open to any reasonable suggestion whose feasibility is supported by adequate evidence.

Step 1

Begin by writing a goal statement or problem definition for the Management Study Group, so that it will have something to guide and structure its efforts.

Step 2

Assemble in groups of four or five people and decide how you will divide the job ahead of you, which is to prepare a report on each major area that the president has outlined. You may, of course, decide to eliminate some of them or to add others to the list. You will also need to agree on a common format for your reports so that your results will be comparable. Then, as a group, agree on a goal statement or problem definition for each report. That way, everyone in the group will know exactly what each report is to accomplish. These jobs may require more than one meeting.

Step 3

Once the reports are finished and each member of the group has had a chance to read every report, meet again to select the motivation methods which you will propose to the president.

Then, design and write a proposal which:

1. Explains the methods that the group believes will be productive

2. Gives information about each one, so the president will understand what it is and how it works
3. Reviews the known record for each method, so the president will have some idea of how well it can be expected to work
4. Recommends ways of implementing them, so that there is a high probability that they will achieve the desired results
5. Includes drafts of memos, bulletins, and other materials that will introduce each program to employees, explain how it works, and give the details of eligibility

Step 4

At your instructor's option, prepare your proposal as an oral presentation for the president and Board of Directors. Then give the oral presentation to your class.

Alcoholism on the Job

Several weeks ago your company's Executive Vice President, Mr. Brian Huber, spent three days at a regional conference sponsored by the National Association of Manufacturers. While he was there he attended a session devoted to the problem of alcoholism and its effects on business and industry. He was shocked at what he heard, because until that time he had no idea that the problem was as serious or as widespread as the speakers indicated. Far from being confined to blue-collar or production employees, alcoholism is apparently a major problem, which is also widespread among executives and even boards of directors. It costs companies a great deal of money each year in absenteeism, lost time, accidents and injuries (both on and off the job), and reduced quality and productivity.

Mr. Huber returned from his meeting determined to find out whether your company is being affected by alcoholism and, if it is, to do something about it. He knows that the company is not unique, and he does not expect it to be an exception to national trends. He has directed the Industrial Relations Department, where you work, to approach this issue by working on three questions.

1. Just how serious and widespread is the problem of alcoholism in businesses nationwide? What kinds of problems does it create and how much money is it costing businesses and consumers every year?

2. Is it possible to learn the dimensions of the problem in your own company? He realizes that this could be difficult and tricky. After all, people are not usually eager to admit that they are alcoholics, and they may feel that they will endanger their jobs if their problem becomes known. Huber would like you to propose several methods for gathering this information in such a way that employees and executives will understand that the company wants to help, not cause more problems. He wants you to be especially careful about avoiding any approach which might result in someone being falsely accused of being an alcoholic or problem drinker.

3. Even if it is not possible to learn the scope of the problem within the company, Mr. Huber wants to know what kind of help is available for alcoholics locally, and what kinds of education, rehabilitation, and counseling programs the company could start or participate in. Perhaps people will take advantage of them if they are available, even if they will not admit that they have a problem.

Huber has suggested that he would like to have some idea of what other companies have done. He would also like to see drafts of memos, bulletins, and brochures that could be sent to employees as part of an education and awareness program.

You may approach these three questions separately or as part of the same project. Keep in mind that Huber is a businessman and that he is not likely to approve any program that will cost the company more than it is now losing to alcoholism, and that it may be difficult to calculate exactly what those losses are. You may assume that Huber's overriding concern is to do something that will help the company, and that he will use your report(s) to help him convince the president that the company should take an interest in this problem and try to do something about it.

The Businessperson's Image

You work for the Public Relations firm of Barley & Hamilton, in Philadelphia. One of the firm's clients, Mr. Warren Peterson, partner in a large brokerage house in New York, has contacted Mr. Barley with the following idea.

Mr. W. F. Barley
Barley & Hamilton
190 Rittenhouse St.
Philadelphia, PA 14000

Dear Bill:

During the past several months a rather disturbing situation has come to my attention. A recent study that I have read about shows that the image of the American businessman (and woman) is really suffering on television and in the press. It seems fair to say that, as a group, we are being portrayed as unethical, influence-peddling, overpaid, greedy, heartless boobs who will do anything in the name of corporate profits or personal gain.

I happen to know that this is not true. At least it is not the whole story. Many of the business people I know are really fine people who spend a great deal of their time every year doing community service, as volunteers. They give their time, and their money, so that everyone in their communities can have a better life. Corporations encourage this work, and do some of it themselves. Many companies provide free services to municipalities, and nonprofit organizations, and some even release executives for six weeks or more each year to coordinate local charitable fundraising campaigns.

The problem is that few people know about these good things that the business community does. They are apparently willing to believe anything they hear about us. And they will probably continue to do that unless they learn the facts. I'm not so naive as to believe that some of this image isn't deserved. I know that some businesses and some people are exactly as the press and TV describe us. But we are certainly not all that way.

I would like to do something about this. I am willing to pay for a series of advertisements in magazines and newspapers of national standing. These should present the good things that the business community does, perhaps through a series of profiles of individuals or companies. What I have in mind is something like the oil companies have been doing for almost ten years now, since the first big increase in oil prices. The idea is not so much to sell a product as to clean up the image. I am not convinced that the oil company ads were entirely successful. After all, it is difficult to say nice things about yourself without seeming to be self-serving. But I think they had the right idea.

Let me know what you think. If you are interested in doing this, send me a sample and a proposal for the series.

Sincerely,

Warren J. Peterson
President

Mr. Barley is interested in this campaign, and he has given it to you and asked you to follow through and prepare a presentation for Peterson. He wants to see it before you send it out. He suspects that Peterson has written to others and that Barley & Hamilton will be competing for the job.

You obviously have some research to do. Just what is the image that the media has been giving to businesses and businesspeople? You will need to know that if you are to write a campaign that will counteract it. And what have the oil companies and other industries been doing to counteract the image that they are profiteering polluters of the environment? Have these efforts been successful? Once you have done your research, your jobs are as follows:

1. A brief background report that provides some context for Peterson's letter and explains the problem in more detail. This should also include an analysis of the campaigns that Peterson mentioned in his letter, samples, and any information you can find about whether these were successful.
2. A proposal for Barley that outlines at least three different approaches that the campaign might take, including Peterson's suggestion for a series of profiles. In your covering memo to Barley you may either recommend a specific approach or analyze the various approaches and recommend one.
3. A proposal that Barley can send to Peterson. This should outline the entire campaign and include a finished sample of at least one item in the series.

Sexual Harassment on the Job

You are the Personnel Manager for a manufacturing company that employs 8000 people. In this morning's mail you received a letter from a woman who left your Accounting Department two weeks ago to take a job with a major accounting firm on the West Coast. In her letter she explains that she left her job, which she liked, because of sexual harassment. She states that she does not intend to file a formal complaint or lawsuit, and that she will not testify in any such action because she finds the whole episode distasteful and wishes to forget it. Her purpose in writing, she says, is simply to let you know that the problem exists in the company and that it affected many of the women who work there. She knows this, she says, because she has talked with them. Most of them, unlike her, are not able to leave their jobs and move to other parts of the country. "How long," she asks, "will you condone this conduct on the part of foremen, supervisors, and executives?"

You have been vaguely aware of this problem for some time, but it has not been your highest priority. Now you are going to have to act. She also sent her letter to the president of the company, and he has called you in to discuss it. In that meeting you agree that it is probably pointless to investigate the incidents in which this woman was involved, but that the company needs to make it clear to everyone that such harassment is not acceptable, and to provide a mechanism for reporting, investigating, and dealing with incidents of this sort.

The president wants you to do the following:

1. Prepare a report that defines *sexual harassment* and outlines the extent to which it has become a problem nationwide. He would also like to know what other companies have done about this problem.

2. Prepare a proposal for a company policy concerning sexual harassment. This should include:
   a. A policy statement and definition.
   b. A reporting procedure that recognizes that supervisors, foremen, and managers may be the principal offenders.
   c. A procedure for investigating allegations.
   d. Provisions for disciplinary action.
   e. Drafts of memos and notices that will be sent to employees and supervisors and posted on bulletin boards. These should state the policy and give instructions for reporting violations.

3. Prepare a proposal for an employee education program to be presented in each department and to all new employees, that explains sexual harassment and the company's attitude and policy toward it. All new employees and present employees should be aware of when they are victims of this and what they should do about it. This applies to men and women equally.

4. Prepare a proposal for an education program for supervisors, foremen, and managers which will make them aware of sexual harassment, the company's policy, and the consequences for those who engage in it. Supervisors will need to know how to detect harassment when it occurs, what constitutes harassment so that they can avoid it themselves, and the approved procedures for dealing with it.

■

Appendix A

A Guide to Careful Editing

Editing: A Necessary Job

No piece of writing is finished until you have edited and proofread it carefully. Only when you are satisfied that your letter, memo, or report observes the conventions of writing and grammar that the world expects of you are you ready to send it to a typist. Once the typist returns your work to you, you will need to proofread it once again before you sign it and send it to your reader.

Few of us like to concentrate on small details of grammar writing and format for long, and perhaps fewer of us know all of the rules that apply to writing and language. The purpose of this guide is to help you present your final draft in the best possible condition by reminding you of the rules and details you may have forgotten, and teaching you about the ones you are not aware of.

Some of the editorial decisions you make about punctuation, spelling, sentence structure, and word choice will make the difference between communicating with your readers or confusing them. Other decisions will help you conform to widely accepted writing conventions, just as you conform to expected standards of dress and behavior when you are at work or in a social situation. At times you may feel that you are struggling with nuisance rules and unimportant details for no good reason. And you may find yourself wondering whether anyone else knows the rules, or cares about them.

But the editorial decisions and corrections that you make are important, because incorrect and sloppy uses of language get in the way of your meaning. If you write the following sentence, you will at least confuse your readers. And some may even find the sentence unintelligible:

> Touring the shop yesterday with visitors from Japan, the horizontal boring machine broke down at 3:00 and effected the manufacturing schedual for the remaining day.

A sentence like this one should be revised so that your readers will not have to stop to figure out what you are trying to say, for example:

> The horizontal boring machine broke down yesterday at 3:00, during our tour with the Japanese visitors, and affected the production schedule for the rest of the day.

Readers who encounter sentences like the first one above may wonder not only what they mean, but whether the person who wrote them is capable of communicating at all. Thus, neglecting widely accepted conventions of writing and the correct use of language can undermine not only your attempt to communicate, but also your attempt to create a positive image of yourself and your company. Your readers may know what you mean, but your mistakes will keep them from taking you seriously. If you write *convience* rather than *convenience,* or use *who* when conventional usage calls for *whom,* you will probably not obscure your meaning; however, your readers may decide that you are less than careful about your work, or that you don't care, or know, enough to do things right. Such carelessness can make you appear ignorant, uninformed, or uncaring about all of your work, not just your writing. The result may be that your readers will decide to do business with someone else.

Using This Guide

This guide is organized like the hierarchy of editorial concerns, which you used in Part I. It encourages you to begin editing by looking at your entire draft for features which occur throughout it, such as correct format, headings, subheadings, page numbers, visual aids, and paragraphing. Once you have done that you will move on to considering individual sentences, and then words. Your last step will be to proofread carefully, using the method introduced in Chapter 5.

Before you begin to edit your own writing, take some time to skim through this guide and become familiar with the kinds of details that you will be looking for when you edit. The more familiar you become with the rules you should observe, the easier it will be to edit your writing, because you will then be able to recognize problems that need your attention.

This guide presents only highlights. It will not answer every question you have about grammar, usage, and writing conventions. To do so would require a book of at least several hundred pages. Rather, the purpose here is to give you enough information to get started, and to address some of the questions and problems which arise most frequently among business writers. From time to time you may need to consult one of the standard handbooks or reference books that are listed in Appendix D, or one that your teacher recommends.

Step One: Reviewing Your Entire Draft

1.1 Format

Your professor or employer may have a manual or handbook that specifies what letters, memos, and reports should look like. If not, use one of those in Appendix B. In many situations typists will automatically use the appropriate or required format, and you will not need to concern yourself with it. However, it is always a good idea to check for yourself, because you are responsible for anything you sign.

Before you send your draft to a typist, be sure you have included all of the information the typist will need. For example, have you numbered all of the pages? Have you indicated where paragraphs will begin? Have you proofread carefully so that a typist will not copy any of your own mistakes? Are all of the attachments present? Have you listed the people who should receive a copy of the finished draft? If you check these details now, you will reduce the need for later corrections and retyping.

1.2 Headings and Subheadings

You may have used several different levels of headings in your draft to indicate your organization and help your readers follow your discussion. As you edit, check these headings and subheadings for consistency. Specifically, look at

1.2.1 **Typography.** All headings at the same level should look the same. That is, each major heading should look like all other major headings. Each second-level subheading should look like all the other second-level subheadings. For example, if you decide to have major headings typed in all capital letters and underlined, then be sure that all of them use the same typography. Then use a different typography for each of the other levels of subheadings.

1.2.2 **P**osition. All headings at the same level should be in the same relative position on the page. Position, along with typography, will help signal your organization to your reader.

1.2.3 **N**umbering. If you use numerical or alphabetical identifiers for headings and subheadings, be sure that you have been consistent and that all of the numbers and/or letters are in the correct sequence.

1.2.4 **P**hrasing. Your headings and subheadings will be easier for your readers to follow if you use similar phrasing or grammatical structures at each level. For example, you might use such headings as these at one level: *Background, Development, Marketing Plan,* and *Sales Projections.* Because these are all nouns or noun phrases, they have a similar structure, and this will indicate to your reader that each of these phrases identifies the same kind of category or section. If you were to use different grammatical structures or different kinds of phrases for the same level of heading, you would weaken the impression that they introduce sections of similar importance or scope.

1.3 **V**isual Aids

If you have used visual aids in your draft, check them carefully for numbering, captions, and placement.

1.3.1 **N**umbering. Visual aids should be numbered in sequence through either your entire draft, or through each chapter or section. Be sure that all of your visual aids are present, and that they are numbered correctly and sequentially. While you are at it, check your text for references to your visual aids and be sure the numbers in the text refer to the correct visual aid. Finally, examine each visual aid for the following features:

1.3.2 **C**aptions and labels. Each visual aid should have a title or caption that identifies it. Captions should precisely describe the content of the visual aid. Place captions at the bottom of the visual aids they identify.
As you look at each of your visual aids, check to see that you have labeled

the major features and that all labels are oriented so that they can be read from the same edge of the page as the caption.

1.3.3 **Placement.** Have you indicated to the typist where each visual aid is to be placed in the final copy of your draft? If not, do that now, and be sure each one is placed correctly on the page. Whenever possible, position visual aids on the page so that your reader can read them from the bottom of the page. If this is not possible, position them so that readers can read them from the right-hand edge of the page.

1.4 Paragraphs

When you revised your draft you checked paragraphs for content and structure. Now, as you edit, scan your entire draft for paragraph length. Paragraphs of fifteen or more lines will present a dense, even intimidating, appearance on the page, especially if your final version is to be single spaced. If you find paragraphs that seem too long, read through them again to see if you can divide them into two or more paragraphs without destroying the continuity and coherence of what you have written. Paragraphs that average eight to twelve lines will present a more attractive page to your readers. And remember that this is an average. Some paragraphs will be longer than this, and some will be shorter.

Step Two: Editing Sentences

Once you have reviewed your entire draft, you can begin to work with individual sentences. This may be the most time-consuming of your editorial jobs, as it requires you to review each sentence for correctness and style. Among the features you should look for, the following are likely to be the most troublesome.

2.1 Sentence Structure

When you edit sentences, your first concern is to see that they are grammatically correct. To do that, check the following features in each sentence in your draft.

2.1.1 **Subject, verb, and object.** Most English sentences in the active voice follow the sequence of subject, verb, and object. Think of it as your sentence answering the question "Who does what?" For example,

We called the Accounting Department.

In this sentence, *We* is the subject, *called* is the verb, and *the Accounting Department* is the object.

Sometimes the object can be implied rather than stated:

John Andrews called this morning.

Mr. Andrews called someone, probably the speaker, but that person is not mentioned in the sentence. Sometimes the subject is implied:

Return the product to us for a refund.

Who is to do the returning? The person who is being addressed is the subject of the sentence, but it is not always necessary to name the subject in a sentence.

2.1.2 **S**ubject-verb agreement. In each sentence, the subject and verb must agree in person and number. In many cases this is no problem, for you would not write

We should *goes* to the meeting.

or

The president were pleased with the job you did on the Mason contract.

Some words and constructions, however, make agreement more difficult to achieve. For example, *data* can be used as either a singular or a plural. Some sources suggest that you use it as a plural, just to be safe. Thus, you would write

The data show that most people in our sample are over thirty-five.

But many people find the singular equally acceptable:

The data shows that most people in our sample are over thirty-five.

Some words make subject-verb agreement tricky because they have retained unusual plural forms from the languages in which they originated. For example,

the plural of:	is:
crisis	crises
analysis	analyses
hypothesis	hypotheses
criterion	criteria

Indefinite pronouns, such as *each, either, neither, everybody,* and *everyone* often cause problems because, though they seem to refer to more than one person, they are considered to be singular. Thus you will use them with singular verbs:

> Each member of the department *is* an experienced professional.
>
> Neither of the plans *has* an acceptable cost.
>
> Everyone *wants* to see the new product as soon as it is ready.

Compound subjects are constructions in which several words, often linked together with *and* or *or,* form a unit and serve as the subject of the same verb. Compound subjects require a plural verb, even if the individual words are singular:

> The Quality Assurance Department and the Inventory Control Department *are* asking to be represented at the meeting on Friday.

Some compound subjects combine both singular and plural words. In these cases, use a verb that agrees with the subject closest to it:

> The Vice-President and the Advertising and Marketing Departments want to know when the new sales campaign will begin.

Some subjects appear to be compound, but are not. For example, in the following sentence, the word *documents* may appear to be part of the subject, but it is not.

> The language of all company documents needs to be reviewed for compliance with the new "Plain English" law.

In this sentence it is tempting to make the verb agree with *documents,* which is the nearest noun, but the subject of the sentence is *language.* It is the *language* that must be reviewed, not the documents. *Documents* is the object of the preposition *of,* and objects of prepositions cannot be subjects of sentences.

A similar problem can arise if several words intervene between a subject and its verb. For example,

> Only *one* of the departments *submitted* its budget on time.

or

> *Understanding* the applicable government regulations *is* important.

Subjects and verbs are italicized in both of these sentences to show that verbs must agree with their subjects, rather than with the nouns that come between the two.

2.1.3 **S**entence fragments. Sentence fragments are phrases that lack either a subject or a verb. Readers can usually figure out what fragments mean, and you will often see them in advertising copy; however, they are of limited use in most of the writing that you will do in business. You might encounter the following kinds of fragments as you edit your draft:

> Responding to your memo of July 15.
>
> Considering your recent proposal.
>
> As early as possible.
>
> Whenever you can.
>
> If you are late.
>
> Because of the strike.

Fragments are usually closely related to the sentences around them, and in most cases you will be able to eliminate fragments by incorporating them into either the sentence that precedes them or the one that follows; for example:

> The committee decided to give you another week, considering the strength of your recent proposal.

or

> Because of the strike, the receiving department will be closed indefinitely.

You may occasionally decide to use a fragment for emphasis; for example, you might find the following in a sales letter:

> Buy any nationally advertised product during our Labor Day sale, and we'll give you two tickets to the State Fair. Absolutely free.

In this sentence the fragment helps draw attention to the phrase *absolutely free* by making it an independent unit. Remember, though, that using fragments in this way will be effective only if you don't overdo it.

2.1.4 **R**un-on sentences. Two independent clauses cannot be in the same sentence unless they are separated by a semicolon or a comma and a coordinating conjunction. An independent clause is one that can stand alone as a sentence because it has a subject and a finite verb (a verb that can function as a complete verb phrase). Verbals, which usually end in *-ing,* or forms of verbs with *to* are not finite verbs. There are two main types of run-on sentences:

1. Fused sentences, in which the independent clauses are not separated by punctuation
2. Comma splices, in which independent clauses are joined with a comma, but without a coordinating conjunction

To correct fused sentences, add a semicolon between the independent clauses, or use a period to divide them into two sentences.

Instead of this:

> The shipment should arrive tomorrow it was delayed by a major accident on Interstate 70.

write this:

> The shipment should arrive tomorrow; it was delayed by a major accident on Interstate 70.

or this:

> The shipment should arrive tomorrow. It was delayed by a major accident on Interstate 70.

To correct a comma splice, you can separate the clauses with a semicolon or a period, or add a coordinating conjunction after the comma.

Instead of this:

> Ms. Caldwell called today, she said the new software package should be available about the first of next month.

write this:

> Ms. Caldwell called today; she said the new software package should be available about the first of next month.

or this:

> Ms. Caldwell called today. She said the new software package should be available about the first of next month.

or this:

> Ms. Caldwell called today, and she said the new software package should be available about the first of next month.

Coordinating conjunctions include such words as

and	yet	nor
or	but	for
so		

2.1.5 **C**oordination. When you connect independent clauses that express ideas of relatively equal importance in the same sentence, you are using coordination. Coordination helps your readers see that the ideas in these clauses are related to each other. You can show coordination by connecting the clauses with a comma, followed by a coordinating conjunction. The following sentences show coordination in this way.

> The repair crew was working on the damaged telephone lines, but a second storm delayed the repairs.
>
> The audit began in June, and it ended in July.
>
> John did not tell us in advance about the delay, nor did he call to explain after the shipment was overdue.

2.1.6 **S**ubordination. Subordination allows you to place related ideas in the same sentence, while showing that they are not of equal importance. A subordinate clause or phrase usually provides additional details or clarifies a main clause, while the main clause expresses the sentence's main point or key idea. Effective subordination helps your readers identify the main idea of a sentence and recognize the details and explanations that are attached to it. In addition, subordination helps you write concisely because, with it, you can provide details within a single sentence rather than writing separate sentences to explain and clarify. The following sentences show effective use of subordination.

Instead of this:

> We will meet in the main conference room. In that room we can all sit around a table.

write this:

> We will meet in the main conference room, where we can all sit around a table.

Instead of this:

> He decided to take the job. The salary he was offered was not as much as he expected.

write this:

> He decided to take the job, though the salary was not as much as he expected to be offered.

Subordinating conjunctions include words like these:

though	because	that
when	if	although
while	who	which
since		

2.1.7 **Sentence variety.** As you review your sentences, check to see whether you have achieved a variety of lengths and kinds of sentences. If all of your sentences are the same length and have the same structure, your readers will become impatient with the monotony and they may stop paying attention. A series of direct, short sentences may seem choppy, so that your readers feel that they are constantly stopping and starting. A series of long, densely packed sentences will seem intimidating; moreover, your readers may get lost as they attempt to keep track of where you are taking them.

2.2 Using the Active and Passive Voice

The active voice uses the order "Who does what?" in a sentence; for example,

> Mr. Allison distributed the report at the annual meeting.

The passive voice reverses this word order:

> The report was distributed by Mr. Allison at the annual meeting.

In addition, when you use the passive voice the *agent*, the person who performs the action of the verb, often disappears from your sentence:

> The report was distributed at the annual meeting.

In this last sentence there is no indication of who distributed the report, and many people use the passive for just this reason: it allows them to hide or disguise the source of an unpopular decision by eliminating any mention of who made it.

Many handbooks advise you to avoid the passive entirely because it takes too many words, slows your reader down, and sometimes obscures your meaning. While these points are all true, it does not necessarily follow that they are disadvantages. Some situations may require you to obscure the point or the agent. A direct statement in the active voice may, in some situations, be too blunt, or may sound accusatory. Or the agent may be irrelevant or unknown.

In general, avoid overusing the passive. A letter composed entirely of passive sentences may become so boring that your reader may not finish it. Or you could give the impression that you are trying to hide or obscure something, when actually you are not.

But rather than avoiding the passive altogether, try to use it sparingly and appropriately. The passive may help you place emphasis where you want it in a sentence. The following sentence is active; that is, it emphasizes the agent:

> The Management Council has decided to accept the union's latest retirement plan proposal.

Perhaps you could use the passive to emphasize the proposal itself more effectively, rather than to make your readers wait until the end of the sentence to get your point:

> The latest retirement plan proposal from the union has been accepted by the Management Council.

As you edit, try to identify all the sentences in which you have used the passive voice. Then examine each one to see whether the passive is appropriate, or whether it simply adds extra words and needless obscurity.

2.3 Parallel Structure

Using parallel structure will help you focus your reader's attention on the similarities in your concepts and information. Parallel structure will be especially effective if you use it to highlight items that you place in series in sentences, and to construct lists. Your headings and subheadings will also be more effective if you use parallel structure to show that headings and subheadings are related to each other. Build parallel structures by using the same grammatical form or structure for the words, phrases, and clauses in your series and lists:

> The purpose of the study group will be *to coordinate* research and development, *to monitor* new product development, and *to recommend* funding for promising projects.

Note how each item in this series begins in the same way, with the infinitive form of the verb. You can use almost any word form or grammatical structure, but here are examples of some of the more typical ones. In each sentence the words that create the parallel structure are italicized.

Verb forms:

> The seminar will be devoted to *computing* your company's profits, *determining* its financial position, and *preparing* annual reports.
>
> Your writing will be most effective if you *plan, organize,* and *revise.*
>
> You will be a more successful manager if you *think* about

your ideas, *state* them carefully, and *listen* to others' responses.

Noun forms:

The interview will be about your *interests,* your *abilities,* and your *aspirations.*

The meeting will include *managers, buyers,* and section *supervisors.*

Your success in this project will depend on the *length* of time you devote to it, the *intensity* of your dedication, and the *level* of your skills.

Adjective forms:

Ms. Barnaby got the promotion because of her *excellent* sales record, her *long* service with the company, and her *systematic* approach to management.

Once you begin a series or list using parallel structure, your readers will expect you to continue using the same form or grammatical structure for all items in the series or list. As you edit your draft, look for sentences in which you have used parallel structure only partially, and look for other sentences in which you have not used parallel structure but could do so effectively.

2.4 Modifiers

Modifiers may be single words, or they may be phrases. They provide details which explain or qualify a specific word or concept.

Adjectives modify nouns:

Mr. Smith is a *masterful* organizer.

Adverbs modify verbs, adjectives, and other adverbs:

Please put the box on my desk *carefully.*

Prepositional phrases serve as modifiers:

The report *on my desk* is the latest one.

Verbal phrases can be modifiers:

The man *waiting in the outer office* is here to interview for the sales position.

Modifiers cause problems when they are in the wrong place in a sentence, or when they point to the wrong element of your sentence, and thus change your meaning.

2.4.1 **M**isplaced modifiers. Misplaced modifiers appear to modify the wrong words in a sentence. You can avoid this problem if you place modifiers so that they clearly point to the part of the sentence you want them to modify.

Instead of this:

> Because it was nearing five o'clock, the repair crew decided to finish the job tomorrow. (This sentence says that the repair crew was nearing five o'clock.)

write this:

> The repair crew decided that, since it was almost five o'clock, they would finish the job tomorrow.

Instead of this:

> He almost mumbled through the entire presentation. (Did he almost mumble?)

write this:

> He mumbled through almost the entire presentation.

Instead of this:

> We found a package on the loading dock that should have been shipped last Thursday with the Benson order. (Should the loading dock have been shipped?)

write this:

> This morning on the loading dock we found a package that should have been shipped last Thursday with the Benson order.

2.4.2 **D**angling modifiers. While misplaced modifiers point to a part of the sentence that you don't want them to point to, *dangling modifiers* point to a word or phrase that is not part of the sentence. Dangling modifiers often occur at the beginnings of sentences and often take the form of verbals ending in *-ing* (present participles); for example,

> Lying on the desk, he saw the report they had been looking for. (Was he lying on the desk when he saw the report?)
>
> Being the final report of the year, Mr. Jones decided to complete it with extra care. (Was Mr. Jones the final report of the year?)

Dangling modifiers also occur in other forms:

Dangling past participles:

> Confused by too many technical terms, the manual was of no use to him.

Revised:

> Confused by too many technical terms, he found that the manual was of no use to him.

Dangling infinitives:

> To get to work in the morning, avoid traveling Fifth Street.

Revised:

> To get to work in the morning, you should avoid traveling Fifth Street.

Dangling gerund phrase:

> By consolidating our shipping department, money was saved.

Revised:

> The company saved money by consolidating its shipping department.

2.4.3 **S**quinting modifiers. *Squinting modifiers* attempt to modify or point to too many parts of a sentence.

For example,

> After showing him how to do the report, he completed it successfully. (Who showed what to whom?)

Revised:

> He completed the report successfully after Ms. Smith showed him how to do it.

Instead of this:

> He reminded George frequently to check inventory levels. (Did he remind George frequently, or did he want George to check inventory levels frequently?)

write this:

> He frequently reminded George to check inventory levels.

or this:

> He reminded George to check inventory levels frequently.

2.5 **P**ronouns

Pronouns stand in the place of, or refer to, nouns. Most of us use pronouns correctly to replace nouns. We have few problems deciding whether to use *I; you; he, she, or it;* we; you; they; them; their; us; our; and words like them. We often have more difficulty when pronouns refer to nouns that have occurred earlier in a sentence, and when they must agree with that word (*antecedent*) in person and number.

2.5.1 **P**ronoun reference.

Problems of pronoun reference occur when you attempt to make a pronoun refer to more than one antecedent:

> Joyce sent the report to her supervisor because she wanted her approval. (Who wants whose approval?)

or:

> Managers like engineers because they are pragmatic and technically oriented. (Which group is pragmatic and technically oriented, managers or engineers?)

or:

> Employees have been bothering supervisors lately because they like to get their own way. (Which group likes to get its own way?)

or:

> John sent the preliminary report to her because he wanted to clear it with the Vice President for Marketing. (Who wants to clear the report, and is *she* the VP for Marketing, or is that someone else?)

All of these problems arise because pronouns can refer to more than one antecedent. The only way to eliminate this problem is to make sure that pronouns point clearly to the antecedent you intend them to modify. The first sentence above can be revised this way:

> Managers like engineers' pragmatism and technical orientation.

Whenever you use a pronoun, be sure that you place it so that it refers clearly to only a single antecedent.

Pronoun reference is also a problem when pronouns occur too far from their antecedents. For example, you may mention the antecedent once by name, and then use pronouns to refer to it in several succeeding sentences. If other possible antecedents intervene between the pronouns and the antecedent you intend them to refer to, your reader may get lost. The solution to this is to constantly check for accurate pronoun reference, and to repeat the antecedent often enough to ensure clear reference, but not so often that the repetition seems heavy-handed or obvious.

Sometimes we create problems of pronoun reference when we ask pronouns to do more work than they are capable of. Pronouns such as *this* and *which* are especially likely to produce vague reference, because we often use them to refer to entire concepts or ideas:

> The faulty parts could be due to either operator error or equipment failure. This will make it difficult to maintain our production schedule. (*This,* in the second sentence, can refer to any of three antecedents: *faulty parts, operator error,* or *equipment failure.*

You could revise the sentences this way:

> The faulty parts could be due to either operator error or equipment failure. Remanufacturing the parts will make it difficult to maintain our production schedule. (In the original sentences, the antecedent, *remanufacturing,* had disappeared.)

2.5.2 **P**ronoun agreement. Pronouns must agree with their antecedents as well as refer to them. That is, a third-person, singular antecedent that serves as the subject of a sentence requires a third-person singular pronoun that can also serve as the subject of a sentence:

> Joyce will arrive tomorrow. *She* will want to review the results of the most recent series of tests.
>
> Members of the Product research group are meeting in the large conference room, where *they* are viewing a presentation about our newest health and beauty-aid line.

When the antecedent is the object of a verb or preposition, or a pronoun stands as the object of a verb or preposition, then it must be in the objective case:

> The messenger comes around at 10:00. Give the envelope to *him.*

English subject and object pronouns are as follows:

Subject	*Object*	*Subject*	*Object*
I	me	she	her
we	us	they	them
he	him	who	whom
she	her		

Who and *whom* often present special problems, partly because the distinction they make is disappearing in the spoken language. Most speakers use *who* for both subject and object. But a number of authorities recommend that you continue to use *whom,* especially in your more formal letters and reports. Simply remember that if the pronoun or its antecedent is the subject of a sentence, use *who.* If the pronoun or its antecedent is the object of a verb or preposition, use *whom:*

> Who is the supervisor in this department?
>
> To whom were you speaking?
>
> Can you tell me whether she is the one who made the suggestion? (*Who* is correct here because it is the subject of its own clause, *who made the suggestion.*)

When you have a question about whether you should use *who* or *whom,* try to rephrase the sentence, or replace *who* or *whom* with another pronoun. If the rephrased sentence or replaced pronoun requires the objective case, then you should use *whom.*

2.5.3 **N**onsexist pronouns. In recent years there have been various attempts to circumvent the traditional English practice of using masculine pronouns to refer to antecedents of indeterminate gender. Traditional practice requires masculine pronouns in sentences like these:

> If anyone calls, tell him I'll be back at three.
> A machinist can never be too careful with his tools.

Suggested replacements for the masculine pronoun have taken several forms. Some authorities recommend using *he or she* and *him or her,* to make it clear that women are as much a part of the world as men. Other writers have decided to alternate the use of *she* and *he,* being careful to give each one equal time. Many people have decided to resolve this question by using *they* or *their,* especially in speech, whether the antecedent is singular or plural. This last solution may be the least advisable, because it suggests that you can't tell the difference between a singular or plural antecedent. A reasonable compromise is to use plural antecedents as often as you can and to use plural pronouns to refer to them. This requires some extra attention while you write or edit, but it does eliminate the problem of excluding half the world's population from the English language.

Instead of:

> If an employee requests leave, he must give his supervisor four working days' notice.

write this:

> Employees should give their supervisors four working days' notice when requesting leave.

2.5.4 Reflexive pronouns.

Reflexive pronouns are those that end in *-self* or *-selves.* They show that the object of an action is the same as the person who performs the action:

> I did it myself.
>
> We'll go to the plant and see the situation for ourselves.

Reflexive pronouns cause problems when people use them in place of the usual subjective and objective pronouns. Perhaps this is a result of confusion about whether to use *I* or *me, we* or *us:*

> Mrs. Anders and myself will be available to collect the completed forms.
>
> Members of the committee decided that inquiries can be sent to ourselves.

Both of these sentences would be better off with the usual objective or subjective forms of the personal pronouns rather than the reflexives:

> Mrs. Anders and I will be available to collect the completed forms.
>
> Members of the committee decided that inquiries should be sent to us.

2.6 Punctuation

Punctuation is an integral part of your sentences. Punctuation marks guide your readers through your writing, telling them when something has ended, when something else is beginning, and when to expect an idea or list to continue. The following sections will survey the types of punctuation you are most likely to encounter in business writing.

2.6.1 The period.

Use a period:

At the end of a sentence

After an abbreviation

2.6.2 **T**he comma. Use a comma:

To separate items in a series: "We called the President, the Vice-President, and the Marketing Director."

Between two adjectives that modify the same noun: "It was a long, stormy meeting."

Between coordinate clauses joined by a conjunction: "We looked at what was available, and we decided to purchase the largest truck."

After introductory participial phrases or dependent clauses: "Believing your action to be well-motivated, we decided not to suspend you."

To separate a nonrestrictive clause from the rest of a sentence (*nonrestrictive* clauses can stand alone as sentences but are not essential to the meaning of the sentence they are part of): "Damex, which makes the part that broke, has agreed to replace it at no cost to us."

To separate nonrestrictive appositives from the rest of a sentence: "Mrs. Smith, the company president, attended the negotiating session."

To separate a parenthetical statement from the rest of a sentence: "The meeting was, on the whole, a productive one."

Before and after a year when you give a date: "July 15, 1985, will be the first day of the new organization."

Before and after the name of a state when you also give the city: "He was in Bozeman, Montana, in July."

2.6.3 **T**he dash. Use dashes sparingly, and primarily for emphasis. Whenever possible, use a comma instead. Dashes consist of two hyphens with no space before, after, or in between. Use dashes to:

Emphasize an appositive or a parenthetical statement, or to set off a compound appositive that contains commas:

"Yesterday—before all of this became known to us—we were prepared to approve the proposal."

"On Friday—before, by the way, the contract was awarded—we considered the added expense of the new programs we had decided to add."

2.6.4 **T**he semicolon. Use a semicolon:

When items in a series contain commas: "Funds will be allocated as follows: the Marketing Department, $19,000; Quality Assurance, $14,000; and Production Control, $16,000."

When you omit a coordinating conjunction between two independent clauses: "We like the Model 1900; I think the boss will agree to buy it."

Before adverbs that join two independent clauses (for example, *however, therefore, thus*): "The campaign has not met its goal; therefore, we will continue to advertise for another month."

2.6.5 **T**he colon. Use a colon:

To introduce a list: "The following restrictions apply in the plant at all times:
1. Wear a hardhat.
2. Refrain from horseplay.
3. Refrain from smoking."

To introduce further explanation in a sentence: "We have reached this conclusion: in the future, all correspondence must be approved by a department head."

2.6.6 **T**he hyphen. Use a hyphen:

To connect the words of a compound adjective (one that functions as a single word):
"He showed us an out-of-date gate pass."
"He is wearing a blue-gray suit."

In compound words:
"brother-in-law"
"third-class mail"

To indicate that a word continues on the next line of type. Always divide words between syllables.

2.6.7 **T**he apostrophe. Use an apostrophe:

To form singular and plural possessives:
"We found it on Johnson's desk." (singular possessive)
"We looked through Ms. Jones's records." (singular possessive)
"We will have to ask our dealers' preferences." (plural possessive)
"Last year's sales were higher."

To form contractions (you may use contractions in all but the most formal writing, if your company approves): *"can't, should've, won't"*

To form plurals of numbers, letters, and other symbols: "She received all *A*'s in school." "The carton is marked with four *J*'s."

2.6.8 **E**llipsis. Use an ellipsis to indicate that you have omitted something from a sentence, usually from a quotation.

Ms. Brown indicated in her speech that "we need to . . . determine whether all products meet established safety standards."

At the end of a sentence use four spaced periods (instead of the usual three) to form an ellipsis. The first period serves as the period at the end of the sentence.

2.6.9 **B**rackets. Use square brackets:

To indicate material that you have inserted into a quotation: "The problem [Mr. Andrews said] is a serious one."

To enclose parentheses within parentheses without confusion: "All machine operators should report to building number 2 at 7:30 A.M. (the southwest door [near the gate] will be open at 7:15 A.M.)."

2.6.10 **P**arentheses. Use parentheses:

To provide explanations that are not essential to a sentence's meaning: "Our representative (from advertising) will serve on the Standards Committtee."

To enclose numbers that identify items in a list within a sentence: "The new benefits program will consist of (1) expanded medical coverage, (2) a new dental plan, and (3) additional disability insurance."

Step Three: Editing Words

3.1 Have You Used the Right Word?

We all confuse words from time to time. The cause might be that we have simply made a mistake while writing a draft. Or, in some cases, we actually choose the wrong word without knowing we have done so. For example, it is easy to write *affect* but mean *effect,* or to write *uninterested* when your sentence requires *disinterested.* Only a careful rereading of your draft will ensure that you have used the correct words and that all of the words you have used mean what you think they mean.

The list of easily confused words, printed at the end of this guide, will help you identify commonly confused words. You will also find there a list of commonly misspelled words.

3.2 Capitalization

In general, you should follow common usage when you capitalize. Normally, you will capitalize the first letter of—

Names of people, geographic places, countries, cities, towns, states, days of the week, months, and most words that are proper nouns (such as *English,* but not *computer science*).

Words in titles of essays, articles, books, television shows, magazines, works of art and musical compositions, except conjunctions, articles, and prepositions (unless one of these is the first word).
conjunctions: (*and, or, for, but*)
articles: (*a, an, the*)

Words used as proper names, such as *Mother* and *Darling.*

Titles of documents and names of historical events, such as the *U.S. Constitution* and the *Civil War.*

Titles and positions, when they precede or follow a name:
Professor Joyce Smith
Joan Alexander, Editor

Abbreviations of formal titles: *Prof., Pres., VP, Ed.,* etc.

Abbreviations of the names of academic degrees: *M.B.A., B.S., B.A., M.Ed., M.D.*

Standard abbreviations for states: *FL, PA, ME, CA, NM, MN, MI*

3.3 Abbreviations

Use abbreviations sparingly, especially in a written text, where it is always appropriate to use the full form of any word. If you have any reason to believe that your readers will not understand an abbreviation, you should use the complete form. You can use abbreviations as follows:

3.3.1 **T**itles that occur before and after names.

Andrea Wallace, C.P.A.
Dr. John Foreman
Paul Bolton, Jr.

3.3.2 **W**ell-known agencies and organizations.

FDA, FCC, FDIC, FHA, AFL-CIO, NBC, CBS

3.3.3 **C**ommonly used business expressions.

f.o.b., C.O.D., A.M. (a.m.), P.M. (p.m.)

3.3.4 **N**ames of cities and states. Abbreviate the names of cities and states, and the words *avenue, street, boulevard, lane,* and *drive,* only when you use them as part of an address on an envelope or part of the inside address on a letter.

3.3.5 **P**arts of organizational names. Abbreviate parts of organizational names only when the organization itself uses the abbreviation; for example, *BMY Corporation, ABC Company,* and *Jones & Allen, Ltd.*

Step Four: Writing Numbers

Your written work is likely to contain many numbers. The main question you will have about them is whether you should write them out, as words, or use figures. The following guidelines will help you decide, but remember that your goal, as always, is to achieve consistency and clarity for your readers.

4.1 **U**se Words to Express Numbers When—

The number is the first word of a sentence:
"Forty people attended the meeting."
"Thirty-five unregistered cars are in the parking lot."

The number is ten or less, or evenly divisible by ten:
"Ten Davis Drive"
"He scored a seventy on the most recent examination."

Using figures would be confusing:
"We need forty-five ½-inch connectors."
"We need 45 one-half-inch connectors."

You use *o'clock* to express time:
"The task force will meet at four o'clock."

4.2 Use Figures to Express Numbers When—

The number is an amount of money:
"The bill is for $471.34"
"He wrote a check for $75." (A decimal point and double zeros need not appear unless other, uneven dollar amounts appear in the same sentence or series:
"We have received checks for $55.00, $8.79, and $34.27.")

A sentence contains a single series of numbers:
"We will need 14 new dealers, 23 new outside salespeople, and 4 new regional distribution centers."

If a sentence contains two series, express one in numbers and the other in words:
"Fourteen salespeople achieved 100% of their quota, twelve achieved 95% of their quota, and only two achieved less than 50% of their quota."

You are expressing any of the following:
Dates
Street Numbers
Numerical street names less than ten
Page numbers
Chart numbers
Serial numbers
Telephone numbers
Decimals
Dimensions
Times

Step Five: Proofread

Once you have finished editing, it is time to proofread. You will need to do this twice, once before you send your draft to a typist, and once when it is returned to you. If you need a refresher, review the instructions for proofreading at the end of Chapter 5.

Words Commonly Confused

affect
effect

already
all ready

all right
alright

all together
altogether

allusion
illusion

breath
breathe

capital
capitol

cite
site

complement
compliment

counsel
council

descent
dissent

disinterested
uninterested

eminent
imminent

except
accept

formally
formerly

holy
wholly

infer
imply

its
it's

later
latter

loose
lose

moral
morale

naval
navel

passed
past

persecute
prosecute

personal
personnel

plain
plane

precede
proceed

principle
principal

quiet
quite

regardless
irregardless

respectfully
respectively

stationery
stationary

straight
strait

than
then

their
they're
there

waiver
waver

weather
whether

which
witch

whose
who's

Words Commonly Misspelled

acceptable
accessible
accommodate
accompany
acknowledge
advertise
advisable
advise
argument
arrangement
available

bargain
believe
beneficial
benefit
benefited
bulletin

cancellation
changeable
chargeable
collectible
column
commodities
competitive
concede
concession
congratulations
conscientious
consensus
controlling
convenience
convenient
convince
convincing
courteous
courtesy

decision
deductible
deficiency
deficient
deficit
depreciation
desirable
discrepancy
dissatisfied
distribute
distribution
distributor

efficient
eligible
embarrass
enclosed
evidently
exorbitant
extension

feasible
February
financial
flexible
foreign
forfeit
forty

grievance
guarantee
guidance

helpful
hindrance
hurriedly

illegible
immediately
incidentally
inconvenience
indispensable
initiative
inquiries
installation
interfered
irrelevant

jeopardize
judgment
justifiable

labeled
legible
leisure
liable
license

maintenance
manageable
manager
mediocre
miscellaneous
mortgage

necessary
noticeable

obsolete
occasion
occasionally
occurrence
omission
omitted
opportunity

pamphlet
parallel
permanent
permissible
personnel
perseverance
persistence
possibilities
precede
precedence
preceding
preferable
preference
preferred
prevalent
privilege
procedure
profited
proportionate

quantity
questionnaire

receipt
receive
receivable
recipient
recommend
reconcile
referred
regrettable
relief
repetition
reputable
requisition
retrieve
retroactive

satisfactory
scarcity
schedule
seize
serviceable
subsidiary
supersede
supplementary
systematic

tactfulness
technique
temporarily
transferred
truly

unanimous
undoubtedly
until
usually

versatile
vicinity
visible

warranted
warranty
writing

yield

Appendix B

Formats for Letters and Reports

It is important to pay attention to the format and appearance of your letters and reports. Just as clients, customers, and the general public expect your manner of dress and your place of business to conform to certain standards of appearance, they expect your correspondence and reports to use conventional, attractive formats. Your letters and reports are an extension of yourself and your company, and you want them to do their share in creating a positive, businesslike image. You should select your stationery, typewriters, and formats as carefully as you would select your clothes or the furniture in your office.

Many companies, realizing how important format and appearance can be, have produced their own instruction manuals so that correspondence, memos, and reports will be consistent throughout the organization. In most cases it will be a typist's job to produce final drafts that follow the acceptable formats. But you should be aware of what those formats are, and you should always check to see that they have been followed before you sign a letter or release a report.

Letters

A typical business letter consists of the following components. These are illustrated in the figures that follow the explanations.

Letterhead

Most businesses use a printed letterhead stationery for correspondence. The letterhead usually gives the company's name, address, and telephone number (including area code). Some letterheads will also contain a distinctive logo or symbol which identifies the company.

Date

All letters should be dated. In the block and semiblock formats, the date is typed in the upper right hand portion of the page, just below the letterhead. In the full block format the date is typed at the left margin.

File or Reference Number

Letters may include a file or reference number so that you, or your reader, may easily identify the subject of a specific letter, and the file in which it should be placed. Type this number or reference word in a place where it will be easily seen. Most often this will be in the upper right portion of the page, below the date.

Inside Address

Beginning at the left margin, and lower on the page than the date, type the complete name, title, and address of your reader. This should appear just as it will on the envelope.

Attention Line

You may include an attention line if you wish to direct your letter to a particular person or office within a company, like this: *ATTENTION: Personnel Manager.* Type the attention line two spaces below the last line of the inside address.

Salutation

The salutation names your reader, usually by stating: *Dear Mr. . . .* Place a colon at the end of the salutation. If you do not know your reader's name, or are not writing to a specific person, you may use *Gentlemen, Ladies, Ladies and Gentlemen, Dear Sir, Dear Madam,* or *Dear Sir or Madam,* depending on the tone you wish to establish. If your reader has a title, you may repeat it in the salutation: *Dear Dr. Smith,* or *Dear Congresswoman Andrews.* Corporate executives, such as presidents, vice presidents, and others, are usually addressed as *Ms., Mr., Mrs.,* or *Miss.*

Body

The body of the letter consists of the paragraphs of your text.

Complimentary Close

Two spaces below the last line of the body, you should type a complimentary close. Try to strike a businesslike tone with the complimentary close you choose. Among the more common ones are: *Sincerely, Sincerely yours, Warm(est) Regards, Best wishes,* and *Regards.* Remember that readers may react negatively to phrases that seem overdone or insincere, such as *Very truly yours* or *With my greatest esteem.* Capitalize only the first letter of the complimentary close and place a comma at the end of it.

Signature

After the complimentary close, leave four spaces for your signature.

Typed Name and Title

It is customary to type your name and title four spaces below the complimentary close. You can type the title on the same line as your name, or place a comma after your name and type the title on the next line. In the block and semiblock formats the complimentary close, signature, and typed name appear in the lower right portion of the page, sometimes aligned with the date. In the full block format these components begin, like the rest of the letter, at the left margin.

Initials

Near the bottom of the page, at the left margin, typists often type the initials of the person who dictated the letter, as well as their own initials, for identification. The writer or dictator's initials are usually typed in upper case letters, and the typist's in lower case. In the past it was customary to divide these sets of initials with a colon or a diagonal line (/), but this practice is no longer widespread. (Apparently it saves money to omit these symbols, and some companies no longer use initials at all.)

Additional Notations

Letters may also include notations about enclosures and copies. If there are enclosures with a letter, this is usually indicated by typing *ENCL.* (if there is only one), or *ENCLS.* (for more than one) at the left margin near the bottom of the page, above the typist's initials. Some people also like to identify the enclosures with a brief description or to indicate how many enclosures are present.

It is also customary to indicate who has received a copy of a letter. You can do this by typing *Copies to:* or *cc:* below the enclosure notation and then listing the names of those who have received copies.

Second and Subsequent Pages

If your letter is longer than one page, you should identify the second page of the letter so that, if the two pages become separated, they can be reunited. Second and subsequent pages can begin this way (typed at the top margin):

Mr. James Rawlings -2- October 1, 1983

or:

Page 2
Mr. Rawlings

Sample Letters

Figures B–1 through B–4 are samples of various letter formats which you can use when you type letters.

October 1, 1983

Mr. Harold P. Howard
President
Howard Productions
4235 St. Vincent Street
Harmony, New York 15678

Dear Mr. Howard:

This letter is typed using the conventional block format, and it contains the typical components of a business letter.

The most obvious feature of the block format is that all of the components except the date and signature block begin at the left margin. This presumably saves time, because typists need not indent paragraphs or set special tabulations on their typewriters.

Paragraphs are identified in block format by double spacing between them. The signature block, which appears in the lower right portion of the page, may be aligned with the date, but it is not necessary to do so.

The block format is widely accepted, and you can be confident that, if you use it, your correspondence will have a neat, businesslike appearance.

Sincerely,

Hamilton E. Jones
Vice President

ENCL
cc: Adam Hamish

HEJbr

Figure B–1 Sample Letter Format

B

Barlow Enterprises 81 Freedom Lane Portland, Oregon 97211 (503) 555-1212

October 1, 1983

Mrs. Jane Wallanciewicz
Marketing Director
WILD DUCK FASHIONS, LTD
417 Park Avenue
New York, New York 10012

Dear Mrs. Wallanciewicz:

I am pleased to answer your questions about an appropriate format for business letters.

This letter is typed using a semiblock format. The semiblock format places the date in the upper right portion of the page, and the signature block in the lower right portion of the page. The first line of each paragraph is indented, usually about five spaces. All other components of the letter begin at the left margin.

Some people prefer the semiblock format because they are used to documents in which the first line of each paragraph is indented. But you will notice that paragraphs are also separated from each other by double spacing, just as in the block format.

The semiblock format is widely accepted, and you can be assured that readers will respond favorably to your correspondence if you use it.

Sincerely,

Paul D. Barlow

PDBrb

Figure B–2 Sample Letter Format

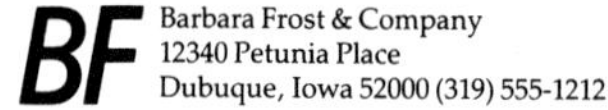
Barbara Frost & Company
12340 Petunia Place
Dubuque, Iowa 52000 (319) 555-1212

October 1, 1983

Arthur A. Banks
185 Merion Street
New Britain, Connecticut 06054

Dear Mr. Banks:

This letter is typed using a full block format.

In the full block format, all components of the letter begin at the left margin. This does have some practical advantages, because typists do not need to use special tabulation settings, or hit extra keys when they type. They can simply touch the return key at the end of each line and begin typing the next line.

Some companies believe that by reducing the number of steps a typist must take when typing a letter, they reduce the potential for mistakes, and also reduce costs. I'll leave it to the cost accountants to decide that one.

The full block format is an attractive one, and you can use it with confidence whenever you must write business correspondence.

Sincerely,

Hamilton Hampstead III
Vice President
Communications

HHmbc

Figure B–3 Sample Letter Format

Gus 'n Nate's Country Chicken Restaurants
6789 Red Mesa Court Shreveport, Louisiana 71109 (318) 555-1212

October 1, 1983

Yes . . .

. . . in some situations you can use a letter format that is quite different from the block, semiblock, or full block. This letter is an example of such a format.

As you can see, it has no inside address or salutation at the beginning. Instead, it simply begins with the body of the letter in the place where those elements would usually appear.

Your reader can begin reading the main part of your message immediately when you use this format, without being distracted by the more conventional letter components.

You should be aware, though, that some people regard this format as quite unusual, and others think it may be tactless or too blunt. It does, I think, imply some familiarity with your reader. On the other hand, it may also suggest impersonality. You are obviously not writing one letter to one reader, but a form letter to many readers.

This format may be most appropriate when you are writing sales letters, collection letters, or other types of correspondence which you intend for many different readers.

Use this format sparingly and for special purposes.

Sincerely,

Andrew Sabo
Marketing Director

Mr. M. R. Moncrief
422 Allen Street
Vacaville, CA 97863

Figure B–4 Sample Letter Format

Making a Guide Sheet

You can easily make a guide sheet to help you type letters. Such a sheet is merely a heavy piece of paper with dark lines drawn on it to represent the locations of the date, signature block, and margins of typical letter formats. If you draw the lines with a dark ink, you can place the guide sheet behind the page you are typing on and see immediately where you should place the components of a letter. Also, the guide sheet can be designed so that you can center letters of different lengths on the page. Figure B–5 is an example of such a guide sheet, with measurements included so that you can make your own.

Reports

Formats for reports are far less standardized than those for letters. One reason for this is that reports are not as well-defined as letters. There are many different kinds of reports, ranging from brief reports of one page or less, to mammoth, group-written reports that may occupy an entire shelf when they are finished. Many companies have established their own requirements for report formats, to insure consistency and uniformity within the organization. Find out whether your employer has established guidelines for reports and, if so, follow them.

Another factor that complicates report formats is that although many reports are typed and reproduced in typed format, other reports are professionally printed, so their appearance is determined by the method of printing and the decisions of the publications designer.

At the very least, you should be able to produce a finished draft of a report, ready for a typist, which is clean and businesslike in its appearance. The following instructions will help you do that.

Parts of a Report

Depending on its length and complexity, a report may contain some or all of the following elements. You will need to use common sense and company policy to decide what you will include in your report.

Letter of transmittal. In some cases you will need to write a brief letter or memo to transmit your report to a reader. This letter can be either a direct, indirect, or persuasive approach, depending on the situation. Its job is to introduce your report and perhaps present a few of the main points. This

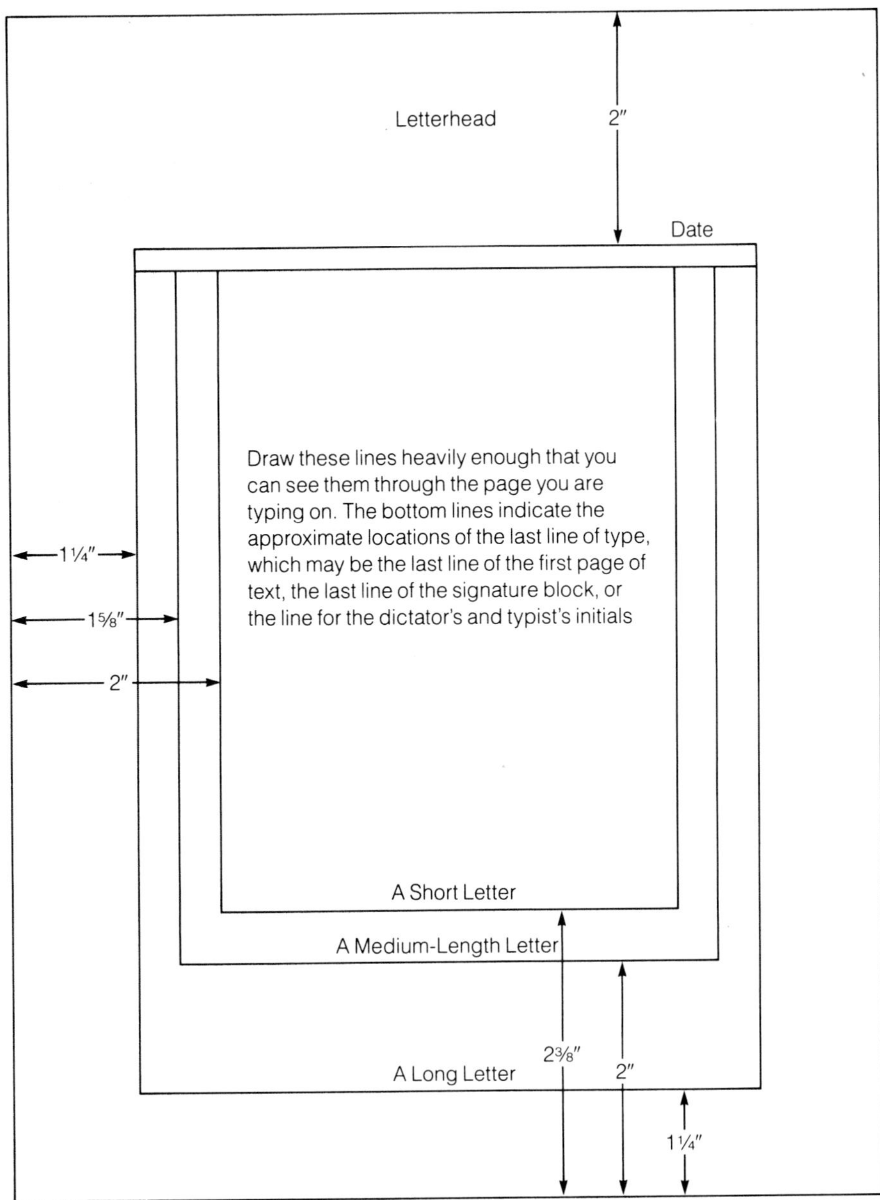
Letterhead
2″
Date
Draw these lines heavily enough that you can see them through the page you are typing on. The bottom lines indicate the approximate locations of the last line of type, which may be the last line of the first page of text, the last line of the signature block, or the line for the dictator's and typist's initials
1¼″
1⅝″
2″
A Short Letter
A Medium-Length Letter
2⅜″
A Long Letter
2″
1¼″

Figure B–5 Guide Sheet for Letters

will allow your readers to remember what the report is related to, and thus to place it in a context for understanding.

Title page. Give your report a title that describes what it is about, and place that title on a separate page. On the title page you may also include your name, the date and, if necessary, a statement that gives your authority for writing the report. Figure B–6 shows a sample title page.

Table of contents. If a report has a number of sections or chapters, or a series of appendices or documents to which readers may wish to refer frequently without searching for them, you should include a table of contents. You can write the table of contents by simply reproducing the titles of the chapters or sections, or you may want to provide a brief description of each section so that readers will be able to identify its contents. Arrange the table of contents in outline form, and be sure you give the page on which each item can be found.

Summary. If your report is longer than a few pages, you may need to write a brief summary so that readers can get an overview without having to read or skim the entire report. This does not mean that they will not read your report. Rather, the summary will allow them to identify items which must receive immediate attention and those which can be read later.

Write your summary by listing the main point of each chapter or section, and then building these subjects into a paragraph or two that describe the entire report. Some summaries even list recommendations and conclusions when they are appropriate.

Body. The body of your report is the text itself, including your data, analysis, conclusions, and recommendations.

Appendices. You may wish to include tables of raw data, calculations, background documents, questionnaires, or other materials which do not belong in the body of the report. The proper place for these materials is in appendices at the end of the report. Readers will be able to consult them if they want to, but will not have to work through them in order to understand your report. You may want to refer to appendices in the body of your report, so that readers will know they are there. It is also helpful to make appendices easy to find by using dividers or tabs to show where the appendices are located. These tabs extend beyond the edge of the page (on the right) and make it easy

OVERTIME COSTS FOR 1982

ALLEN-HAMILTON CORPORATION

Prepared By

T. A. Parker

Accounting Department

February 1, 1983

Figure B–6 Title Page for Report

for readers to turn to appendices without flipping through several dozen or several hundred pages.

Index. An index, arranged alphabetically by topic, will allow your readers easy, pinpoint access to the information in your report. While it would be silly to do an index for a five or ten page report, a report of fifty or a hundred pages is practically useless without an index.

Bibliography or list of references. If you use research materials in your report, you will need to include a list of them at the end. You should present your sources in alphabetical order and in normal bibliographic format. Almost any standard research manual will show you the proper format.

The Body of Your Report

Reports should be visually attractive and easy to read. One way of making them so is to pay attention to layout. The major elements of layout that you will need to attend to are spacing, including margins and white space, and headings.

Spacing

Modern office typewriters usually give you the option of having your report single spaced or double spaced. In addition, many typewriters offer a space-and-a-half feature. The advantage of single-spaced text is that you can include a great deal of information in just a few pages. With long reports this can result in a considerable saving in paper costs, especially if the report is reproduced or printed on both sides of each sheet.

However, single-spaced text is often difficult to read because writers produce long blocks of text that are unbroken by white space. Readers may find such a text imposing, and consequently they may only skim what they should read in detail. If you select a single-spaced format you should be doubly sure that your paragraphs are of short or moderate length, and that you triple space between paragraphs to give your readers some visual relief.

Margins

Use standard margins when you have a report typed. Usual margins for typewritten material are one inch at the top, right, and bottom edges of the page, and one-and-one-half inches at the left edge. The extra half-inch at the left allows space for the report to be bound without losing part of the text in the binding.

The first page of your report, or the first page of a new section, should begin at least two inches below the top edge of the page, and each new section should carry a descriptive title.

You can make a guide sheet for typing reports, just as you made one for letters. The example in Figure B–7 provides the measurements for such a sheet. If you draw the lines heavily enough, you will be able to insert the guide sheet in the typewriter behind the page you are typing on, and see the lines through it. This will help eliminate some of the difficulties of setting margins incorrectly and beginning or ending too far up or down the page.

Headings

Headings and subheadings are an important part of your report, because they provide guideposts to your readers and show both the location and relative importance of the information you are providing.

Most writers make the mistakes of using too few headings and writing headings that do not actually describe the content of the section they introduce. Your report will be easier to read if you use headings to identify the major sections or chapters of your reports, the major subsections of each section or chapter, and the component parts of each subsection.

If your headings actually describe the sections they introduce, you will be giving your readers a valuable preview of the information they are about to encounter. This helps them place it in a context and make a mental transition from what they have been reading to what they are about to read. Headings also help you create spaces in the text, and thus give your readers valuable visual relief. The examples in Figure B–8 will show you how to place headings of different degrees to indicate their relative importance in your report.

Citing Sources of Information

When you use information from published sources, unpublished documents, questionnaires, interviews, telephone conversations, or other sources that someone else assembled, you need to give credit for the information that you use. You do this, first of all, as a matter of honesty: to acknowledge that the material is not your own. But you also cite sources as a convenience for your readers, who may wish to consult them for themselves.

The conventional method of citing your sources is to provide footnotes with publication information. But there are other methods which are just as

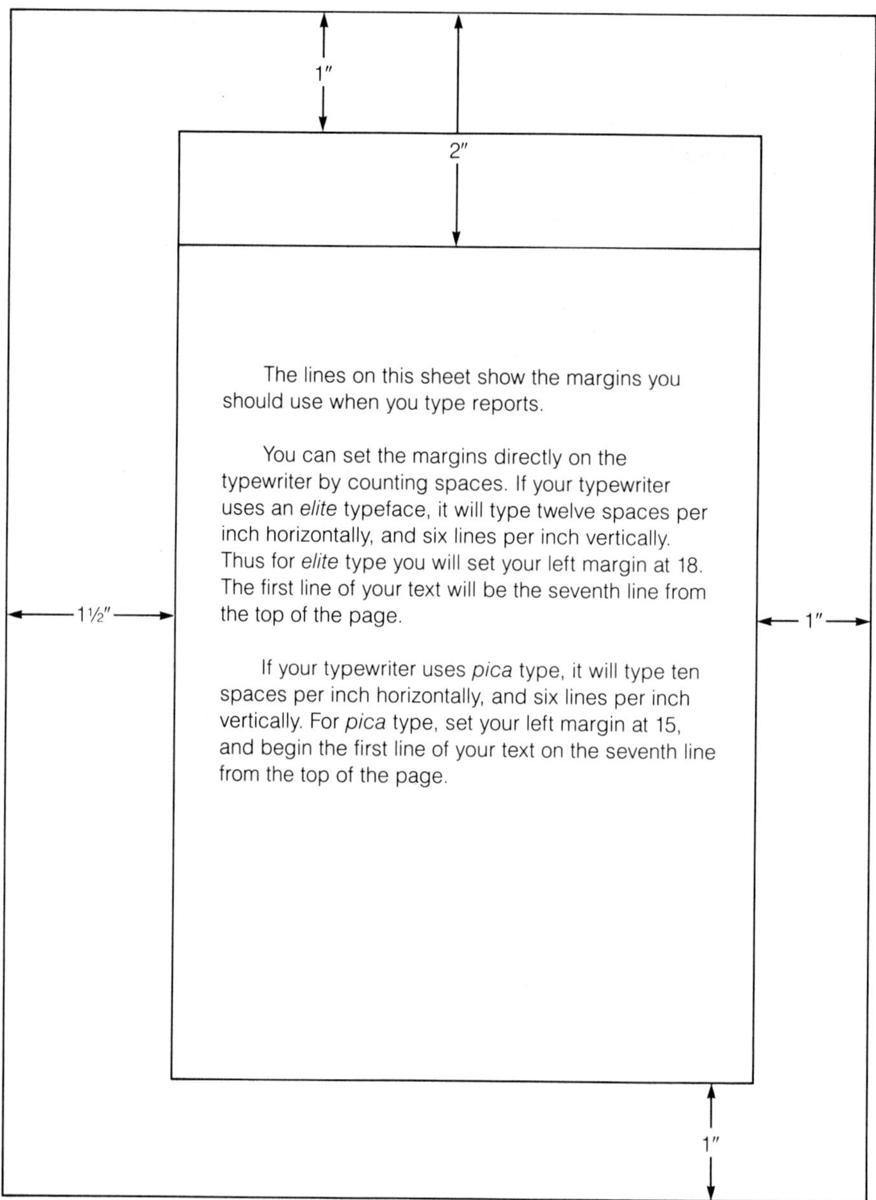

1″
2″
The lines on this sheet show the margins you should use when you type reports.
You can set the margins directly on the typewriter by counting spaces. If your typewriter uses an *elite* typeface, it will type twelve spaces per inch horizontally, and six lines per inch vertically. Thus for *elite* type you will set your left margin at 18. The first line of your text will be the seventh line from the top of the page.
1½″
1″
If your typewriter uses *pica* type, it will type ten spaces per inch horizontally, and six lines per inch vertically. For *pica* type, set your left margin at 15, and begin the first line of your text on the seventh line from the top of the page.
1″

Figure B–7 Guide Sheet Measurements for Reports

FIRST DEGREE HEADINGS

These should begin at the left margin, or be centered on the page. They are often typed in all capital letters, and underscored for emphasis.

Second Degree Headings

Second degree headings indicate major subcategories under first degree headings. They are distinguished from first degree headings by indenting them (usually at least five spaces) from the left margin, and typing them in mixed upper case and lower case letters. These headings can also be underscored for emphasis.

Third Degree Headings. These are for subcategories that fall within the sections identified by second degree headings. They are usually indented, though that is not necessary. What distinguishes them from second degree headings is that they are typed on the same line as the first line of the paragraph or section that they introduce. They are typed in mixed upper case and lower case letters, and they can also be underlined for emphasis. It may also be useful to place a period or colon at the end of the heading.

Figure B–8 Placement of Headings in Reports

effective and, in addition, can eliminate the need for most footnotes. This may be important to you because footnotes require a separate, time-consuming typing operation; they affect the layout of your report; and they are often thought to be inappropriate in business reports.

Footnotes

There is nothing mysterious or difficult about constructing footnotes. When you quote or paraphrase a source in your text, place a *superscript number* (raised above the line of type) at the end of the information that you have taken from a source. This number should correspond to the number of the footnote, whether it is at the bottom of the same page, or at the end of your report.

The note itself consists of the following elements:

1. Author's name
2. Title
3. Publisher (if a book or document)
4. Publication in which it appeared (if it is a journal or magazine article, or appeared as part of a collection)
5. Date
6. Volume and number (if it appeared in a periodical)
7. Page number on which the information you are using can be found.

If you follow this general sequence, you can construct a note for almost any source.

Entire books have been compiled to illustrate the various footnote forms that you can use. Some of these books are listed in Appendix D, and you should consult them if you need to see examples. You should also be aware that many professional groups have developed their own standards for manuscript and footnote form. If your field is one of these, you should follow the formats prescribed by the recognized association. This is especially true if you want to submit manuscripts for publication in professional journals.

However, for most purposes, a generalized footnote form will be sufficient to acknowledge the sources of the information you use in your reports. The following examples will show you what various kinds of notes look like.

For a book. [1]John R. Hayes, *The Complete Problem Solver* (Philadelphia: Franklin Institute Press, 1981), p. 3.

For a journal or magazine article. [15]David Wojick, "Planning for Discourse," *Water Spectrum,* Winter, 1975–1976, p. 32.

For an interview. [7]Andrew Denton, Personal Interview, June 5, 1983.

For a telephone conversation. [5]John Thomas, Telephone conversation with the author, August 1, 1982.

Other Uses for Footnotes

You can use footnotes for purposes other than acknowledging the sources of information you have used. Footnotes are often used to provide further explanations of ideas or data contained in the text. The footnote allows you to provide an explanation, especially of a minor point, without interrupting the flow of the report itself.

Explanatory notes are easier to construct than reference notes, because you need not worry about a special format. Simply place a superscript number in the text at the point that you wish to refer to the explanation. Then, in a note with a corresponding number, simply give your explanation, like this:[1]

> [1]This questionnaire was developed by the Marketing Department of JRB Consulting Corporation. A copy of the questionnaire, and an analysis of the pilot study, are included in this report as Appendix A.

That's all there is to it.

Placing Footnotes in Your Text

You should give some thought to where footnotes will occur in your text. The term *footnote* suggests that notes will be at the bottom of the page to which they refer. This is the most convenient placement for your readers, because they must merely glance to the bottom of the page to see the note. However, placing notes at the bottom of the page is sometimes a difficult typing job, since typists must estimate how much space to leave.

Notes are often placed at the end of a report, or at the end of a chapter or section. This makes for easy typing, because the notes may be typed on separate sheets and there is no need to estimate how much space to leave at the bottom of each page. However, *endnotes,* as they are called, may create problems for readers. Picture your readers seeing a note, thinking it may refer to valuable information, and taking the time to flip to the end of your report, only to find an author's name and page number. You have interrupted your reader's progress for no discernibly worthwhile purpose. Endnotes will certainly create this problem if you are using both reference and explanatory notes, because readers will never know whether the footnote contains a further comment, or merely the citation of a source.

One solution is to use numbered endnotes to cite sources, and to use footnotes, at the bottom of the page, for explanations. If you do this you will not number your explanatory notes, but indicate them by special symbols, such as asterisks.

Citing Sources without Using Notes

You can cite your sources without using footnotes or endnotes. The methods for doing this are often easier to type, and easier for readers to use, than conventional footnotes or endnotes. Consequently, they are becoming increasingly popular.

One such method is to include all information about your sources in the text of your report. Thus, if you have quoted a book or article, you might cite it this way:

> According to John K. Allen, in *Management Training Programs* (Wiley, 1981, p. 13), "the failure to adequately train managers at all levels is the single most important source of personnel turnover at the managerial level."

Providing complete publication information in this way does interrupt the flow of the text somewhat, and you may wish to consider something that is less obtrusive.

There are two ways of citing your sources inconspicuously in the text of a report. Both require that you prepare and include a bibliography or list of references which you place at the end of the report. Then all of your citations can refer directly to the bibliography. One way of doing this is to place an author's name, date of publication, and page number in parentheses after a quotation or other information that you have taken from a source, like this: (Baird, 1981, p. 20). If you want a method that is even simpler than this one, you can number each of the items in your list of references, and then simply citing the number of that source in the text, like this: (3, p. 14). This entry refers your readers to item number three, page 14.

When you use in-text references like this, enclosed in parentheses, you will punctuate them somewhat differently than when you use footnotes. When you use superscript numbers, end punctuation consists of a period (or comma), quotation marks (when necessary), and the superscript number. When you place reference names or numbers inside parentheses, you will place the end punctuation, a period, comma, or other mark, at the end of the parentheses, rather than inside the quotation marks. Of course, if you use in-text citations you will not need superscript numbers, which you can reserve for explanatory notes, if you wish.

Appendix C

Business Writing and the Law

Business is complicated enough without having to worry about the law. But laws regulate what you may write or say, just as they regulate the financial, manufacturing, and other aspects of business. Because of this, almost anything you write can become either the focus of a legal or quasi-legal proceeding, or it can be used as evidence. No one will enjoy the resulting loss of time and money, or the embarrassment of being accused of an illegal action.

The problem is not that you will consciously set out to break the law, though we all know that people do that. Rather, it is the seemingly innocent situation or motive that is most likely to cause you problems. The less you know about the legal implications of what you write, the more likely it is that you will make an inadvertent but expensive mistake. Ignorance is a powerful force in the world, but the law and the courts seldom recognize it as a justification for our actions. The purpose of this Appendix is to help you avoid inadvertent mistakes. It is no substitute for a thorough knowledge of the laws that regulate your own industry and your job. Somewhere along the line you should probably take a good course in business law. Whenever you have questions about the legality of something you are writing, ask for advice. Your supervisor, or someone in your company, has probably encountered the situation before. If doubts still remain, consult an attorney.

What Is Your Own Legal Status?

When you write or speak in your official business capacity you are usually assumed to be acting as an *agent* of your employer. That is, it is assumed that your employer is aware of and approves of what you are saying or doing. In more practical terms, this means that your employer has legal liability for what you write, say, and do. Thus, should legal action result from something you write, a court is likely to assume that the company is legally responsible for the consequences.

Of course, your employer is not likely to defend you happily if you have done something irresponsible or clearly illegal. Being an agent of your employer is not so much a shield for you to hide behind as a responsibility for you to fulfill. Whenever there is a legal question involving something you are writing, it is essential that you consult your supervisors and, if necessary, legal counsel, before you send a letter or submit a report.

It is also wise to confine your use of company stationery to matters that are related to your job. This may make it more difficult to claim that you take your responsibilities as an agent lightly, and it may prevent an employer from disclaiming responsibility for what you have written. To say the least, it would be embarrassing if an attorney were to introduce in court a group of private letters you had written on company stationery.

What Kinds of Trouble Can You Get into?

Ignorance of the law, or inattention to your words, can have a variety of consequences, all of them unpleasant. You and your company could become defendants in a criminal prosecution, a civil lawsuit, or state or federal administrative hearings. Even if you win, such proceedings require a great deal of time, money, and effort that could have been spent more productively elsewhere. The best defense always begins with being aware of potential problems and avoiding them whenever you can. The following situations deserve your attention.

Defamation

Defamation involves making a false or derogatory statement that injures someone's character or reputation. It can be oral or written. Oral defamation is usually called *slander,* and written defamation is called *libel.* Both can result in a civil lawsuit, and damages can be awarded to the person who is injured.

It is easy to avoid such obviously defamatory statements as calling someone a *con artist* or *crook.* But defamation is more complicated than simply avoiding the obviously derogatory remark. For example, what if someone *is* dishonest, and you can prove it? Saying so may still be defamation, depending on your motive. In court, an attorney might admit that a client is dishonest but claim that your saying so was done maliciously, solely to harm the person's reputation or business. If a judge or jury should agree, you and your employer might have to pay damages, even though you were right. So remember that truth is not always a defense in a defamation case. Also, the law often recognizes as true only those facts that have been proved in court, not those which everyone knows to be true.

One key element in defamation is that a libel or slander must be *published* before it can cause harm. In most cases, publication occurs whenever a third party (someone other than you and the person you are referring to) becomes aware of your statement. The third person can be a mailroom clerk, a secretary, or anyone else. For example, if you leave a letter or memo on your desk, and someone reads it, then it has been published in the sense required for defamation.

You can avoid defamation by avoiding words that have obvious negative or derogatory meanings or connotations. Among these are the following:

deadbeat	incompetent
crook	misconduct
dishonest	profiteer
disreputable	swindler
fraud	thief
forger	worthless
corrupt	

There are many other such words, but this brief list should give you the general idea. If you want more detailed guidance, you can consult Philip Wittenberg's *Dangerous Words—A Guide to the Law of Libel* (New York: Columbia University Press, 1947). In specific cases you should always consult an attorney if you believe you are in danger of defaming someone.

Unfortunately, defamation is also a problem with much of the writing that you will do routinely as part of your job. Almost everyone must write evaluations or performance reviews of present employees and letters of reference for former employees. Both of these situations can lead to charges of defamation unless you write very carefully and limit your statements to:

Facts that you can prove

Characteristics that are directly related to qualifications for the job a person holds or is applying for

Precise descriptions of events and behavior instead of all-purpose adjectives

For example, let's say an employee has frequently been late to work. How will you describe that in a performance evaluation or letter of reference? You might be tempted to say that this person is "chronically late to work," but will that do? Probably not. It will help if you have records and can show that a person has been late once a year or once a week. Then you should cite your records: "Smith has been late for work on twenty-five of the past one hundred working days." A statement like this begins to define what you mean by *frequently* or *chronically*. But you can do more. Just how late has Mr. Smith been? Two minutes? Two hours? It makes a difference, and you should try to give a precise number, or an average. That way, you are not stuck with "very late," or just "late." Precise descriptions, based on your records, will allow you to defend yourself against charges of defamation.

Let's assume further that you think you know why an employee is often late to work. Perhaps you know of, or suspect, a recurring health problem, a difficult domestic situation, or simply an active social life. Can you mention any of these? Not unless they are directly related to a person's qualifications for the job. In this case, it would be difficult to imagine any court agreeing that someone's domestic situation or social life is a job qualification. Nor are most managers and executives qualified to discuss a person's health. In fact, those who are qualified, physicians, are not permitted to do so without a signed release from their patients.

Invasion of Privacy

Most of the laws about privacy are intended to protect private citizens against the misuse of information about them. These laws are aimed specifically at the federal government and its computerized data banks. The Freedom of Information Act of 1966 allows you to find out what information the federal government has collected about you. In addition, the Privacy Act (1974) allows you to correct inaccurate information that may be in federal files.

The Freedom of Information Act is of interest to the private sector mainly because it may allow disclosure of information that companies have furnished to the federal government to satisfy other laws and regulations. If you submit confidential or sensitive information to the government, you may discover that consumers or your competitors may obtain it by invoking the Freedom of Information Act.

If you work in the private sector, your chief concern with rights to privacy is that you should not pry into or make use of the details of someone else's life. This restriction extends, in most cases, to property, photographs, addresses, phone numbers, and names. For example, you cannot use someone's picture as part of a promotion without a signed release giving you permission. Nor are you allowed to conduct an investigation or surveillance of someone.

Harassment

Harassment is most likely to occur when a company or individual becomes overzealous about collecting money from debtors or when a company is fighting an effort to unionize its employees.

For example, if you are trying to collect from someone who owes you or your company money, you are not allowed to contact that person's employer about the debt or communicate to others about the debt in a way that could be embarrassing to the debtor. Nor can you threaten to do these things.

When a union is attempting to organize a company's employees, it is natural for the company to want to express its opinions about unions and their effects on productivity and profits. And it is legal for the company to do so, but it must avoid any statement or action that would be considered as harassment. Company representatives should obtain legal advice before making any statements to employees about unions and collective bargaining. Labor laws are quite specific about what companies may and may not do. In general, you should avoid any statement that makes or implies a threat to employees who support or vote for union representation. And you should also avoid any statement or action that makes or implies a reward to employees who resist or oppose unions.

Fraud

Fraud is an intentional misrepresentation of fact which causes harm to another party. The harm may be financial, physical, or psychological. For example, you might misrepresent a product by claiming that it will do something you know it will not do. Or, you could misrepresent yourself by claiming qualifications you do not have. A key element in fraud is that the injured party would not have purchased the product or contracted for a service if the truth had been known.

Fraud is distinct from the sometimes exaggerated claims companies often make in advertising their products or services. Thus, if a company advertises that its toothpaste will improve your social life, or its automobile will make you a member of the proper in-group, these claims are not fraud. In fact, in recent years a number of consumer groups have been involved in hearings with the Federal Trade Commission, attempting to prove that a variety of advertising claims are false or fraudulent. These cases have often resulted in the companies making public disclaimers or retractions of their earlier claims. Or, a company may sign a *consent decree,* a legally binding agreement in which the company promises not to commit a specific offense or action, but does not admit ever having done so in the past.

Occasionally, as part of routine correspondence, you may have to describe a product to a customer or potential customer. You should be aware that the Fair Packaging and Labeling Act regulates what you may say about your products and services. Your descriptions must be precise and accurate. If they are not, you or your company may be subject to prosecution and fines.

Fraud is a criminal offense, but it is not always easy to prove. You can avoid prosecution or expensive lawsuits if you simply avoid intentional misrepresentations in what you write.

Extortion

Extortion is the use of threats or physical force to get someone else to do something. It is a criminal offense. The potential for extortion is most likely to exist when two parties are in conflict and one threatens or actually commits a harmful act against the other. The harm can be to a person's body, property, family, or livelihood. For example, if someone owes you money you might be tempted to threaten to go to his employer, or make the debt public, in order to induce him to pay. This is obviously a violation of federal credit laws, but depending on local and state laws it may also be extortion. Similarly, if a business will not make what you consider a satisfactory adjustment for inadequate performance of a product or service, you cannot threaten to "expose" it to its other customers or throw the product through the company's front window.

You avoid extortion by avoiding threats or actions that will do harm. Then, use the established means of settling your dispute. If you are attempting to collect a past-due account, you can turn it over to a collection agency, take the debtor to small claims court, or file a lawsuit. Some industries have arbitration procedures to resolve disputes over adjustments. When a conflict arises, find out what the legal means of resolving it are, and then use them.

Contracts

Contracts need not be complicated documents full of legal language. Almost anything you write can be a legally binding agreement between you or your company and a third party. A contract is nothing more than an agreement that two or more parties will engage in a specific legal activity. The activity must be legal, because courts cannot force anyone to commit an illegal act in order to comply with a contract.

In general, a contract exists if one party agrees or promises to do something, and the other party accepts that agreement or promise. Thus, you can make a contract with a letter, memo, brochure, or pamphlet. For example, a number of courts have held college catalogs to be legally binding contracts. The same reasoning extends to employee handbooks, descriptions of retirement and benefit plans, and other documents that businesses might prepare and distribute to employees, customers, and potential customers.

It is important to know that you can *inadvertently* write a contract if the language of what you write makes a promise, offer, or agreement and a court decides that the language is legally binding. Thus, you could become committed to do something that you do not want to do. If you are in doubt about whether your language could become legally binding, you should consult an attorney.

Warranties

A warranty is an explicit or implicit promise that a product or service will perform in a certain way. Warranties, like contracts, are legally binding. Explicit, formal warranties which accompany your company's products or services should rarely cause you problems. They are usually the product of careful writing and thorough legal advice. As with contracts, it is the inadvertent warranty which you need to be concerned about. A casual comment in a letter to a customer could be taken as a warranty, and a court could find that it is legally binding. For example, if in an excess of customer relations zeal, you say, "Of course, Mr. Smith, Framex Corporation always guarantees its products unconditionally," you have probably offered a legally binding warranty, and your customer can probably collect. You would be better off to say that "Framex always honors the warranties on its products." That way you are agreeing to no more than the company has already promised in its standard warranty.

Just what a warranty covers, or what "honoring a warranty" means, is often a matter of debate, and the debate may ultimately be conducted in court. Your company will probably have policies and procedures which govern what you should do when a customer requests a refund, adjustment, or replacement of a faulty product. The best course of action is to follow the established procedures. If the customer is not satisfied, allow higher management, or the courts, to resolve the issue.

Writing about Current and Former Employees

You will often have to write about your company's employees. If they are currently employed, you will write to them, or about them, concerning promotions, transfers, periodic evaluations, and other conditions of employment. When you write about former employees you will usually be writing letters of reference or recommendation to assist in their search for another job. In both cases you need to be aware of legal limitations to what you may say.

Of course, you are aware that you may not discriminate against anyone on the basis of sex, age, race, religion, or national origin. But even if you do not set out to discriminate intentionally, what you write may provide evidence of discrimination. That is, an innocent or inadvertent comment in a conversation, or in a letter, memo, or report, may be used as evidence of discrimination. Thus, whenever you write about employment or personnel decisions you should avoid any reference to age, sex, religion, race, or national origin, and any suggestion that the decision was even partly based on one of these factors.

Performance reviews. Court decisions and federal and state laws have made employee evaluation much more formal than it used to be. In fact, there was a time when promotions and salary increases were awarded more or less by whim, with no written evaluations or records to show that rewards went to those who most deserved them. For the most part this has changed. To protect themselves against charges of discrimination or defamation, many employers now require written employee evaluations which employees must read and sign. This creates a record of an employee's performance and protects the employer against charges that a promotion was denied, or someone was fired, without sufficient warning of inadequate performance.

If you must write performance reviews your company will probably provide a standard form for you to use. The form will probably give a list of characteristics and then ask you to evaluate a person's performance in that category along a numeric or descriptive scale. For example, you might need to rate a person on a scale ranging from 1 to 5, or from "excellent" to "inadequate." You should always be able to provide concrete evidence and reasons for your ratings. The form may also provide space for you to write comments or a descriptive summary. It is here that there is potential for trouble.

When you must write comments on a performance review, you should use precise descriptions of events and behavior rather than evaluative or judgmental statements. Instead of writing that someone did a "poor job" with a particular project, describe exactly what the person did and how it fell short of or exceeded your expectations. Whenever you can, compare actual performance to job descriptions or other performance standards which your company has established. For example, you might say that "Performance Standard 112 requires metal lathe operators in Division 3 to produce 65 pieces per hour. Mr. Anderson has consistently exceeded this rate. His average production is 68 pieces per hour. On three occasions he has produced 82 per hour." This is much more specific than simply saying that an operator is a "fast worker."

Precise, factual descriptions will help you avoid charges of discrimination or favoritism in your decision making and employee evaluations. Of course, being able to write a complete description will depend on your keeping careful records throughout the evaluation period.

Many companies have established procedures for keeping records of regular performance and productivity. But you may need to do more. Evaluation periods will often be several months long, and a year is not unusual. If something happens at the beginning of the period you will need to make a record of it if you believe you will want to use it in the evaluation which you write. You can do this by writing a memo which describes the event or behavior you have observed and states that it will be taken into account in the next performance review. In the case of below average or inadequate performance, such a memo will serve as a warning to the employee that his or her performance should improve. Then, when you write the evaluation, you will have the memo as evidence for a low rating. Since you wrote the memo when the event occurred, and sent the employee a copy of it, it should stand up, even in court.

It is also a good idea to keep records of outstanding performance, rather than rely on your memory. This will help to insure that employees with excellent performance records receive appropriately high evaluations. It will also protect you from charges that you are giving only average ratings to outstanding employees, and thus discriminating against them.

Letters of recommendation. When you write letters of recommendation you face the same potential problems as you do when you write employee evaluations. That is, unless you write carefully you could risk charges of discrimination or defamation. In fact, the Family Education Rights and Privacy Act of 1974, which gives parents and students over 18 years old access to their school files, has made letters from teachers almost useless. Rather than risk charges of defamation, many people now either refuse to write letters or write only the most innocent, innocuous comments they can think of. Still, the business world asks for such letters, and you will probably have to write them. What is the safe, legal way to do that?

Begin by treating a letter of recommendation as though it were a performance review or evaluation. Try to write precise descriptions of events and behavior, and then to relate these descriptions to some known standard of conduct or performance. Instead of saying that someone's performance has been *mediocre* or *outstanding,* try to describe why you believe such evaluations to be true. Give facts and evidence, and let your reader draw conclusions. You can further protect yourself and your company by being selective about the letters you agree to write. If someone asks you for a letter, and you know you cannot write a favorable one, it may be best to tell the person that and suggest someone else.

If you do agree to write a letter, be sure that you confine your comments to job related events, qualifications, and criteria. Use performance evaluations, if you can get access to them. Avoid any statement which could be taken as evidence of defamation, discrimination, or invasion of privacy. For example, even though you know that someone has a medical problem, or severe financial problems, or a difficult domestic situation, you should not refer to these in your letter. You are not qualified to comment, you probably do not have all the facts, and the situations themselves will, in most cases, be unrelated to a person's ability to perform a job. Nor can you mention handicaps, alcoholism, or any other factor which would indicate that you are basing your statements on race, religion, national origin, sex, or age.

Remember that when you write letters of recommendation you have a third party to consider: your reader. You have been asked for a fair, honest evaluation of a person's performance on the job. If your letter is false or misleading, your reader may have cause for legal action against you. This is especially true if you do not mention some crucial fact which could reasonably be expected to have a bearing on whether a person is hired. For example, if you write about a person who has embezzled money from your company, but fail to mention that fact in a letter to a company which is considering the person for a position of financial responsibility, you may be sued for concealing essential information. On the other hand, if you do mention it, the subject of your letter could sue you for defamation. What should you do? Probably refuse to write the letter.

Summary

Whenever you write, but especially if you write about sensitive matters, you need to be aware of the laws that regulate business practices and communications, as well as the laws that regulate your own industry. You can do that only through constant reading and research. Whenever you believe you may be creating a legal issue with something you write, take the time to clear it first with both the executives in your company and an attorney. To begin your research, you should become familiar with the following legislation.

Labor–Management Relations Act (Taft-Hartley Act) 1947

Civil Rights Act, Title VII, 1964, and the Equal Employment Opportunity Act, 1972

Fair Packaging and Labeling Act, 1966

Age Discrimination in Employment Act, 1967

Consumer Credit Protection Act, 1968

Truth-in-Lending Act, 1969

Fair Credit Reporting Act, 1970

Family Education Rights and Privacy Act, 1974

Privacy Act, 1974

Fair Credit Billing Act, 1974

Equal Credit Opportunity Act, 1974

Consumer Product Warranty Act and Federal Trade Commission Improvement Act, 1975

Fair Debt Collection Practices Act, 1978

Appendix D

Some Additional Resources

1. Thinking and Planning

Adams, James L. *Conceptual Blockbusting: A Guide to Better Ideas.* San Francisco: W. H. Freeman & Co., 1974.

Gordon, William. *Synectics: The Development of Creative Capacity.* New York: Harper & Row, 1961.

Hayes, John R. *The Complete Problem Solver.* Philadelphia: The Franklin Institute Press, 1982.

MacKenzie, R. Alec. *The Time Trap.* New York: The American Management Associations, 1972.

Simon, Herbert. "The Architecture of Complexity," in *The Sciences of the Artificial.* ed. H. Simon. Cambridge, MA: MIT Press, 1969.

Wojick, David. "Planning for Discourse," *Water Spectrum.* Winter, 1975–1976.

2. Writing and Revising

Elbow, Peter. *Writing Without Teachers.* New York: Oxford University Press, 1974.

______. *Writing With Power.* New York: Oxford University Press,1981.

Flower, Linda. *Problem-Solving Strategies For Writing.* New York: Harcourt Brace Jovanovich, 1981.

Flower, Linda and John R. Hayes. "The Dynamics of Composing: Making Plans and Juggling Constraints," in Lee Gregg and E. Steinberg (eds.), *Cognitive Processes in Writing.* Hillsdale, NJ: Laurence Erlbaum & Assoc., 1980.

Gould, J. D. and S. J. Boies. "Writing, dictating and speaking letters." *Science* 201 (1978) 1145–1947.

Irwin, Theodore. "Memo on Memos." *New York Times Magazine* (November 17, 1963).

Janis, J. Harold. "A Rationale for the Use of Common Business-Letter Expressions." *Journal of Business Communication* 4 (October 1966), 3–11.

Lanham, Richard. *Revising Business Prose.* New York: Scribners, 1981.

Zinsser, William. *On Writing Well.* New York: Harper & Row, 1980.

3. Research Tools

Brownstone, David M. and Gordon Carruth. *Where to Find Business Information.* New York: John Wiley & Sons, 1979.

Business Index. Menlo Park, Calif.: Information Access Corp., monthly 1979–present on microfilm.

Daniells, Lorna M. *Business Information Sources.* Berkeley: University of California Press, 1976.

Dun & Bradstreet. *Million Dollar Directory* (annual).

Akey, Denise S. *Encyclopedia of Associations.* Detroit: Gale Research Co., 1956–present.

Kruzas, Anthony T. (ed.). *Encyclopedia of Information Systems and Services.* Detroit: Gale Research Co., 1971–present (issued every two years).

Statistical Abstract of the United States. U.S. Bureau of The Census. Washington, D.C.: Government Printing Office, 1878–present (issued annually).

Thomas Register of American Manufacturers. New York: Thomas Publishing Co., 1905–present (issued annually).

Wasserman, Paul; Charlotte Georgi; and James Woy. *Encyclopedia of Business Information Sources.* Detroit: Gale Research Co., 1980.

Weckesser, Timothy C.; Joseph R. Whaley; and Miriam Whaley (eds.). *Business Services and Information: The Guide to the Federal Government.* New York: John Wiley & Sons, 1978.

Todd, Alden. *Finding Facts Fast.* Berkeley, Calif.: Ten Speed Press, 1979.

4. Computerized Data Bases

ABI/Inform. Louisville, Ky.: Data Courier, Inc., 1971–present.

Directory of Online Databases. Santa Monica, Calif.: Cuadra Associates, Inc., 1979–present.

Management Contents. Skokie, Ill.: Management Contents, Inc., 1975–present.

Predicasts Terminal System. Cleveland, Ohio: Predicasts, Inc.

5. Reports

A Manual of Style. Chicago: The University of Chicago Press, 1969.

Campbell, William G.; Stephen Ballou; and Carole Slade. *Form and Style.* 6th ed. Boston: Houghton Mifflin, 1982.

Hill, Mary and Wendell Cochran. *Into Print.* Los Altos, Calif.: Wm. Kaufmann, Inc., 1977.

Mathes, J. C. and Dwight W. Stevenson. *Designing Technical Reports.* Indianapolis: Bobbs-Merrill Educational Publishing, 1976.

McKim, Robert H. *Thinking Visually.* Belmont, Calif.: Lifetime Learning Publications, 1980.

______. *Experiences In Visual Thinking.* 2d ed. Monterey, Calif.: Brooks/Cole Publishing Company, 1980.

Rogers, Anna C. *Graphic Charts Handbook.* Washington, D.C.: Public Affairs Press, 1961.

6. Employment

Boyer, Richard and David Savageau. *Places Rated Almanac.* Chicago: Rand-McNally, 1981.

Compensation Review. New York: American Management Associations, quarterly.

Current Compensation References. New York: American Management Associations, monthly.

Dictionary of Occupational Titles. 4th ed. U.S. Department of Labor, Employment and Training Administration. Washington, D.C.: Government Printing Office, 1977.

Executive Compensation Report. Boston: Warren, Gorham and Lamont, Inc., monthly.

Jablonski, Donna M. *How to Find Information About Companies.* Washington, D.C.: The Washington Researchers, 1979.

Kaufman, Edward L. *Rewarding Executive Talent: Salary and Benefit Practices by Industry and Position.* New York: McGraw-Hill Book Company, annual.

Money (May 1982).

Salary Survey. Berea, Ohio: American Society for Personnel Administration, biennial.

Salary Survey. Bethlehem, Pa.: College Placement Council, three reports per year.

Standard and Poor's Register of Corporations, Directors, and Executives. New York: Standard & Poor's Corp., 1928–present.

Wright, John W. *The American Almanac of Jobs and Salaries.* New York: Avon, 1981.

Appendix E

Business Writing and Word Processing

The Coming of the Computer

The day may come, sooner than you think, that managers and executives will no longer use dictaphones, stenographers, secretaries, or pencils and paper to write their letters, memos, and reports. In fact, it is already here in many offices of large and small corporations. Instead, there will be a computer terminal or microcomputer at every desk, and executives as well as secretaries (if there are still secretaries) will use these machines not only as computers, but as word processors.

Keyboarding, now quaintly known as *typing,* will be an essential skill for everyone in business, from the Chief Executive Officer to the newest management trainee. Because many managers and executives already have computers at their desks, it will be easy to add word processing software so that they can use their computers to do their writing. Adding such a capability makes computer a more versatile and effective management tool than it already is.

How Will the Computer Help You Communicate?

A computer, whether it is a microprocessor or a terminal attached to a mainframe, can do all of the communications jobs that you now do with pencil and paper, typewriter, telephone, and mail.

Electronic mail. You can use a computer to communicate with other people in your office or across the country. The only requirements are that the people in your office be connected with each other in a network, that people in other locations have a telephone and a computer compatible with yours, and that both of you have a means of connecting your computers to a telephone line. You can write a letter, memo, or report, complete with visual aids, and send it to any reader in your network, or anyone with compatible equipment, all without touching a piece of paper.

At the same time that you send your letter, you can distribute copies to other people in your office and place a copy in the files, still without creating a single piece of paper. The copies you send will be stored electronically in the computer's memory, and recipients can retrieve them at will to review the day's mail, or an entire file. Systems can be designed so that only authorized users can gain access to files, and you need not worry that someone else will read the memo you sent to the boss. When you use a computer for electronic mail, you can, with the proper program, create a letterhead and format, type your text, and send it over existing telephone lines. When your readers wish to review their mail they can read each item from the monitor, or make a copy on paper.

Making multiple, personalized copies. If you wish to send a form letter to a number of people, you can store the letter in the computer and print as many copies as you want, simply changing the inside address and salutation for each copy. When you do this, each of your readers will receive an individually typed, personalized letter.

You can also create standardized letters in which you can insert a variety of sentences or paragraphs, depending on the situation. These are also easy to do with the computer as word processor. You need only store each sentence or paragraph under a different title, and then combine the paragraphs you want to use into a single letter.

Filing. Computers can store and retrieve large bodies of information very rapidly, a capability that makes them an excellent replacement for the filing cabinets that clutter every office in the country. With the proper hardware and software you can store and retrieve anything that you write. When you want to find it again, you need only ask for it by name, rather than shuffle through an endless row of file folders in a drawer. The computer will even remember the names that you have put in the file, so you will need no separate list.

In fact, using the computer for filing can make it possible for you to scan all of your files for key words and retrieve every document that is related to a particular product, person, or situation. The secret, again, is in devising a filing system that will allow you to retrieve what you want when you want it.

Graphics. In addition to writing, you can also use computers to create visual aids for your memos and reports. You will no longer have to draw graphs and charts separately, have them re-drawn, and place them on separate pages in your reports, perhaps some distance from your discussion of the information they illustrate. Instead, with a dot matrix printer and a graphics program you will be able to produce visual aids with the computer and insert them into your text exactly where you want them.

How Does a Word Processor Work?

There are a number of types of word processors. Some are merely typing machines which will do nothing else. Others are more versatile, because they are also computers, and these are the ones that will receive our attention here. Typical word processing systems include:

1. A microcomputer consisting of a computer console, CRT or monitor, disk drive, and printer
2. A minicomputer or a larger mainframe that uses hard disk packs, a printer, and terminals

Both types of systems have all of the capabilities of a computer and can be used with word processing software as easily as with any other type of program. The chief advantage of minicomputers and larger computers is that they have large memories, and thus programs for word processing and other functions can be stored permanently and called up when you need them. With either system, you will perform basically the same operations as you write. As you type your text on a keyboard, it appears on the CRT or monitor. When you have finished writing, you can store your text on either the floppy diskette, if you are using a microcomputer, or on the hard pack disk if you are using a minicomputer or mainframe.

One advantage of using a computer, rather than a machine that is simply a word processor, is that the computers in your department or company can be networked together, so that you can send memos to others, or place documents in their files, or in central files, without leaving your desk or using paper.

What Can a Word Processor Do?

Once you have created a letter or memo you can store it, retrieve it when you want to, and revise, all without retyping or using paper. When you are satisfied with your final draft you can print it in any format the program you are using is capable of.

If a word processing program is to be adequate to the demands of business writing, it should contain at least the following features.

1. Writing and editing your text on the screen without shifting modes. That is, you should be able to type your text and go back through it and edit, changing words, letters, and sequence, without having to perform extra operations.
2. You should be able to use a variety of formats, so that you can do letters, memos, reports, and other documents that require different margins, spacing, and layout on the page. You should be able to use these various formats by giving the computer simple commands and without having to modify the program you are using.
3. You should be able to store, retrieve, and print all or part of any document you are working with, so that you will be able to combine research notes, sentences, and paragraphs into a draft. In addition, you should be able to retrieve documents and add them to the ones you are working on.
4. You will want a full range of editing functions, so that you will be able to correct and change your text without retyping. Thus, you will want the ability to delete a character, an entire word, a line, or a paragraph.
5. You will want to be able to move blocks of text around, so that you can change the order of sentences, words, lines, and paragraphs without retyping.
6. If you do repetitive writing jobs, such as sending form letters or filling out forms, you will find it convenient to have a program that allows you to change words in an entire text automatically, without having to locate and retype each one. This will make it possible to personalize

your correspondence by using readers' names, or product names, and then changing them for another reader. Or, for example, if you have completed a lengthy report about a new product, only to discover that the Marketing Department has changed the product's name, you can use a change command to change the name and then reprint the entire document without retyping it.

7. Any good word processing program should display what your finished draft will look like when you print it. This capability allows you to detect problems or mistakes and correct them before you have printed your draft, and may save you from having to print an entire document over.

8. It is especially useful to have a "smart" program that helps you avoid mistakes. That is, some programs constantly help you remember how to use them, and frequently stop to ask you if you are sure you want to perform a particular operation. For example, you may make a mistake and attempt to store a new letter or memo in such a way that you will erase another document. A good program will stop and ask whether you are sure you want to do that. The result is that you can avoid a costly mistake, especially if the document you were about to erase was a valuable or irreplaceable one.

Word Processing and the Writing Process

It is obvious that word processing has advantages to any organization, because it can make written communication faster and less expensive than it is now, especially as the costs of computer hardware and software decline, and the costs of hiring secretaries and typists increase. But word processing also has advantages for anyone who writes, because it can make almost every step of the writing process easier and faster, even if you believe that you can't type, or are limited to "hunt and peck" with two fingers. Let's take a look at how it does that.

Before your first draft. Brainstorming, freewriting, listing and other techniques are easy on the computer, and once you have made a list you will not need to type it again. Instead, you can simply begin to create the parts of your draft by expanding each item on your list into sentences and paragraphs.

Writing a draft. When you write your first draft using word processing, you need not worry about making mistakes or placing parts of your draft in the wrong order, because you can make changes and corrections without typing a new copy. Your first draft can consist of lists, blank spaces, parts of paragraphs, and isolated sentences. You can expand the items on your lists into sentences, your sentences into paragraphs, and rearrange your draft in any sequence that you want, all without putting a word on paper.

Revising. Using the word processor really pays off when you revise. We all know what a project revising can be. If a first draft is on paper, we end up writing notes and changes in the margins and between the lines. Radical revisions mean cutting the draft into pieces, pasting it on other sheets of paper, and writing new transitions. Before we achieve a final version we are likely to go through several typed copies. But the computer makes most of these steps unnecessary. You can do all editing, rearranging, and correcting right on the screen, without ever having to retype a word. You will never again need scissors and paste.

Of course, you can work on paper if you want to, or if others in your organization are working with you and need or want to see a written draft. Once you have finished a draft, you can both store it and print it. That will give you two copies, one on your disk and another on paper.

Editing and proofreading. Editing and proofreading are also easy tasks with a word processor, primarily because changes are so easy to make. As you review your draft you can simply type in your corrections, rather than having to write them on a typed draft and then send the whole thing back to the typist for yet another copy. You can also display your letter or report before you print or send it, so you will be able to see what it will look like in its final form. It is necessary to preview the appearance of what you write, even though some readers may read their mail on the computer screen and never on paper. Many readers will print their mail, or your reports and letters, and pass them around, or carry them around. So you will want to be sure that what you write uses an acceptable format.

Another way that computers make editing and proofreading easy is that, with some limitations, they can do some of the work for you. That is, there are computer programs on the market that will edit your writing for some grammatical problems, for too many passive constructions, and for too many uses of the verb *to be,* among others. And, there are dictionary programs that will check your spelling. Some of these will automatically correct your spelling, and others require that you correct it yourself, after they have identified possibly misspelled words.

But you should remember that computer programs are not skilled writers, so they cannot make editorial decisions of the same quality as your own. For example, an editorial program may indicate that you have used a passive construction in a place that you consciously decided to use a passive construction. Also, computerized dictionaries cannot really spell. Rather, they compare the words in your text with the words in the dictionary. If your word does not match a word that the computer "knows," then the computer will identify that word as a possible misspelling. You will need to decide whether it is, in fact, a misspelling, or whether the word is simply not in the dictionary. Many such programs are small, because of the limitations of computer memories. Thus, you could spend time checking words that are spelled correctly. On the other hand, the computer is likely to pass over a word that is properly spelled, but in the wrong place. If you use *their* but mean *there,* the computer will not recognize that you have made a mistake. Thus, although computers can provide excellent editorial assistance, they are not really a substitute for your own careful review of what you have written.

Summary

Word processing is here to stay, and it will become more important in the future. It offers a faster, more efficient writing process, and greater ease and versatility in the production of a final copy. And everyone, not just secretaries and typists, will need to learn how to use keyboards and word processing programs and accept them as one of the tools we need to do our jobs.

Index